D1710004

Charles Trang

TOTENKOPF

HEIMDAL

Conception: Georges Bernage

Texts: Charles Trang

Translation: J.D., Claire Habart

Realisation: S.Cazenave

Layouts: Stephan Cazenave, Laura Krispin, Christel Lebret, Valérie Louis

Photoengraving: Christian Caïra

Map: Bernard Paich

Iconography: - National Archives - Washington
                    - Museum of Modern History in Ljubljana
                    - Collection Heimdal
                    - Collection Jean-Louis Roba
                    - Collection Guglielmi
                    - Private collections.

Editions Heimdal
Château de Damigny - BP 61350 - 14406 BAYEUX Cedex
Tél. : 02.31.51.68.68 - Fax : 02.31.51.68.60 - E-mail : Editions.Heimdal@wanadoo.fr

Copyright Heimdal 2006. La loi du 11 mars 1957 n'autorisant, aux termes des alinéas 2 et 3 de l'article 4, d'une part, que
les « copies ou reproductions strictement réservées à l'usage privé du copiste et non destinées à une utilisation collective » et, d'autre part, que les analyses et les courtes citations dans un but d'exemple et d'illustration, « toute reproduc-
tion ou représentation intégrale, ou partielle, faite sans le consentement de l'auteur ou de ses ayants droit ou ayants
cause, est illicite. Cette représentation, par quelque procédé que ce soit, constituerait donc une contrefaçon sanction-
née par les articles 425 et suivants du code pénal.

ISBN 2-84048-235-5

Preface

Guards in concentration camps, violence, war crimes: these are the words that first come to mind when one thinks about the *SS "Totenkopf"* division. But reducing the perception of this particular unit to these elements would only be simplistic. True, this division was made up of *SS* soldiers: thus, they were no ordinary force, since they were political soldiers fighting not for a country but for an ideology. True, more than six thousands of them came from concentration camps guards units, and their joining the division —together with the immense influence of Theodor Eicke and his assistants from the *SS-Totenkopfverbände* disciplinary body — was the major factor setting apart the *"Totenkopf"* division from other divisions of the *Waffen-SS*. But this perception is really one-dimensional for a unit whose sheer complexity makes it ultimately puzzling. This book is the result of five years of harrowing work, aimed at giving the reader a statement as complete and unbiased as possible of the division's history.

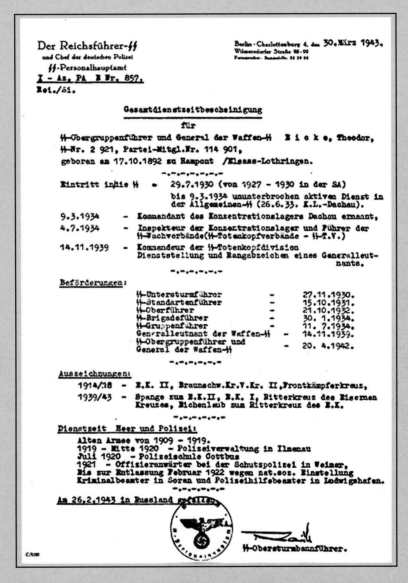

Document showing the career of Theodor Eicke symbolic creator of *Totenkopf*.

Acknowledgements

I would like to give particular thanks to Annie Fournier, Marie-Hélène Hostin, Frau Kuhl, Madame Lemercier, Madame Lempereur, Cécile et André Nguyen, André Cardon, Alain Chazette, Octave Defief, Jean-Michel Desailly, Joseph Dubost, Charles Dumont, Ekkehard Guth, Guy Hontarrède, Xavier Hourblin, Marc Josserand, Jean-Luc Leleu, M. Morreel, Bernard Rostain, Maurice Sense and Jean Vially for their precious assistance throughout the research process, Michael Cremin, Joseph Charita, Martin Mansson, Mark Riekmenspoel, Tim Willemsen and Jean-Louis Roba for the photographs they put at my disposal, Bernard Paich for the making of the maps, and Georges Bernage for the crowning achievement of long years of work.

This book is dedicated to my father: I'm sure he would have been proud of his son.

Contents

Set of papers of a soldier of the division whose route is symbolic of the first years of the unit. At first member of *10. SS Totenkopfstandarte Ostmark* in Oranienburg, he integrates *SS-Heimwehr Danzig* into which he fights, then he is moved within *Stabskp.* of *SS-Panzer-Grenadier-Regiment 3* based in Dachau. Within *Totenkopf*, he makes the campaigns of France and Russia until 1943 when he is seriously wounded. (Private collection)

Right: Coverage of Leo Heinz's notebook "Wehrstammbuch".

Above: a page from the leaflet with Heinz's career, from *III.4.SS-T. St. "Ostmark"* to Rgts. *Stab/SS-T. Pz.Gren.Rgt. 3.*

Left: Medals and decorations awarded to Leo Heinz, including one for his deeds in the battle of Danzig.

5

Creation of the division

Theodor Eicke
and the *death's head units*

On September 18, an important conference was held at Zoppot in Heinrich Himmler's private train. Apart from the *Reichführer-SS*, the commander-in-chief of the *Ordnungs-Polizei*, General Daluege, his Chief of Staff, *General* Bombard, the inspector of the SS death's head units (*SS-Totenkopfverbände*), *SS-Gruppenführer* Theodor Eicke, and Hitler were present. During the meeting, Hitler who was already thinking of the future Western campaign, ordered the formation of two divisions: one was to comprise members of the police, the other recruits from the SS death's head units.

Creation of the new division with soldiers from *SS-Totenkopfverbände (SS-TV)* was naturally assigned to Theodor Eicke. Eicke was born on October 17, 1892 and participated in the Great War as secretary in various infantry regiments. Demobilized in 1919, he settled down in Thuringe where he pursued a police career as an informer, a job perfectly suited to his character. However, he quickly lost his job due to his anti-republican activities. During the following months, he tried to join the police, first at Cottbus, then at Weimar, Sorau-Niederausitz and lastly Ludwigshafen. Although he was recruited each time, he was soon fired for participating in anti-government demonstrations or for expressing too vehemently his hatred for the Republican regime. He finally found a stable job at the factory *IG-Farben* in Ludwigshafen in January 1923. Initially employed as sales representative, he then became in charge of security. Staying politically active, he joined the ranks of the Nazi Party and the SA in December 1928. On August 20, 1930, he was transferred to the SS where there were more opportunities for rising through the ranks than in the SA. Eicke grasped these opportunities and was quickly promoted: on November 27, 1930, he became *SS-Sturmführer* and took over command of the 148th centurie SS at Ludwigshafen. Due to his exceptional organizational and recruitment skills, three months later he was promoted to *SS-Sturmbannführer* (roughly equivalent to Colonel) by Himmler who ordered him to set up a battalion for the creation of *10.SS-Standarte.* This project was so quickly completed that the *Reichsführer-SS,* impressed by his outstanding enthusiasm, offered him the command of the new regiment. He was therefore appointed *SS-Standartenführer* on November 15, 1931. However, the economic crisis cost him his job at *IG-Farben* and after being arrested for illegal possession of explosives he received a two-year prison sentence. Due to protection from Franz Gürtner, the Bavarian minister of justice (who was to hold the same position later in the Nazi government), Eicke was released after four months. After resuming his subversive activities, he came once again to the attention of the police and took refuge at Landau. On an order from Himmler, he went to Munich and then fled to Italy. He was appointed *SS-Oberführer* and commander of the SS camp that Mussolini's government had organized at Malcesine for the Ger-

man political refugees. Eicke's exile ended on January 30, 1933 when Hitler first came to power. After being given an amnesty by Gürtner, Eicke returned to Ludwigshafen. Political quarrels soon broke out between him and Josef Bürckel, *Gauleiter* of the Palatinate, who Eicke accused of having tried to take control of all the SA and SS units in his region. With the support of a few supporters, Eicke took over Bürckel's offices and locked him in the caretaker's toilets. The police quickly intervened, releasing Bürckel and arresting Eicke and his friends. Eicke was interned in a mental asylum at Würzburg and excluded from the SS. With the help of the psychiatrist, Dr Werner Heyde, Theodor Eicke was soon rehabilitated: he left the asylum on June 26 and joined the SS again with his former rank of *SS-Oberführer*. He was also remembered by Himmler, who gave him command of one of the first concentration camps, at Dachau. This camp was created on March 20, 1933 to imprison the political opponents of the Nazi regime. Eicke immediately began reforms, establishing new methods of terror for the detainees. Dachau would become the model for all future concentration camps.

Theodor Eicke was promoted to *SS-Brigadeführer* on January 30, 1934. On June 20, he was appointed *Führer im Stab* to centralize the administration of the concentration camps and reported directly to Heinrich Himmler. Although prestigious, this situation was likely to lead to jealousy, especially from Reinhard Heydrich, the all powerful head of the *Reich* security services. Having fully regained the confidence of his *Reichsführer-SS,* Eicke was even ordered to execute Ernst Röhm, which he did on July 1, 1934. This act of obedience marked a turning point in Theodor Eicke's career: four days later, he was appointed inspector of concentration camps and head of the SS guard units. On July 11, in recognition for services rendered at Dachau and for the "Röhm" affair, he was promoted to *SS-Gruppenführer*. Himmler also encouraged the development of the SS death's head units. Eicke dismissed most of the initial guards, castoffs of the Nazi regime, and had them replaced by reliable and disciplined SS soldiers. In March 1935, *SS-TV* comprised six battalions: *"Oberbayern"* for the Dachau camp, *"Ostfriedland"* for the Esterwegen camp, *"Elbe"* for the Lichtenburg camp, *"Sachsen"* for the Sachsenburg camp, *"Brandenburg"* for the Columbia Haus and the Oranienburg camps and *"Hansa"* for the Fehlsbüttel camp. Six months later, Hitler recognized *SS-TV* as Party units at the Reich's service and, consequently, ordered that their running costs should be paid for by the state. In March 1936, Eicke was even allowed to increase their numbers from 1800 to 3500 by recruiting volunteers. The volunteers signed on for four years, but from 1938 this was increased to 12 years. They had to be single, maximum age 23, at least 1.72 m tall, of German nationality, have a clean police record and prove at least a hundred years of racial purity. In spite of intensive propaganda, *SS-TV* found it difficult to recruit officers since the careers proposed were financially unrewarding. The recruits therefore joined the ranks for purely political convictions. The volunteers quickly became fanatics by almost permanent indoctrination. Those who did not display sufficient enthusiasm in their work were transferred into the police or punished by being assigned laborious tasks in the camps. Eicke also threatened anyone thinking about leaving the *SS-TV* with extremely severe punishments (reported to the *Gestapo*, no chance of finding a job in public office, social isolation). Lastly, to motivate the recruits, each battalion had an officer responsible for indoctrination. The enemies of the *Reich* were clearly pinpointed: Jews, Freemasons, Bolsheviks and the Church. Esprit de corps, similar to that of the *SS-Verfügungstruppe,* was developed through original measures: single officers, for example, left the officers' mess to go and eat with their men. Even Eicke made a habit of fraternizing with the soldiers in the canteen. Officers and ranks had to be on familiar terms and everyone could make suggestions or voice any complaints. Eicke's intention was to make himself accessible, very close to his men, and this patriarchal approach soon earned him the SS nickname, "Papa Eicke", in spite of the dread he inspired. His severity was legendary and those who had to work with him did not mince their words: he was arrogant, impulsive and devoured by ambition. His friends described him as a strict father and a jealous husband, highly satisfied with the social status he could offer his family. Although his men were paid a pittance, he himself adopted a lavish lifestyle: he lived in Berlin in a spacious, luxurious apartment which had belonged to a Jewish family and had a house built at Fronau, a very upper-class suburb of the capital. He even went as far as ordering the creation of coats of arms, inspired from those of medieval landowners. He frequently organized sumptuous receptions and behaved as the archetype of the new Third Reich bourgeois. A Reich which rewarded its heroes generously: In 1942, for example, when Eicke was awarded the Oak Leaves on his Knight's Cross, he was given a check for 50 000 RM, quite a considerable sum for the time. Eicke nevertheless possessed undeniable qualities as a leader and outstanding organizer. He was of man of great authority and his determination never doubted. He was both feared and hated.

In September 1937, after the camps were grouped into four large structures, Eicke reorganized the *SS-TV* into three regiments (*SS-Totenkopf-Standarten* "Oberbayern", "Brandenburg" and "Thüringen"). A fourth regiment ("Ostmark") was to be set up in September 1938 to guard Mauthausen camp. Development of the *SS-TV* continued with the decree of August 17, 1938 which defined their statuses and their missions, and with the order of October 15, 1938 concerning the reinforcement of the police force. A few months later therefore, in June 1939, numbers had increased to 755 officers, 5005 NCOs and 16 273 privates. In addition, to prevent the *Wehrmacht* from recruiting Theodor Eicke's men, Hitler decreed that men enrolling in the *SS-TV* would be released from any military duties. Transfer of the *SS-TV* was speeded up on September 7, 1939 when Himmler deployed the "Oberbayern", "Brandenburg" and "Thüringen" regiments in Poland under the direct command of Theodor Eicke, behind the *Wehrmacht*, operating independently for "police and security" missions. In actual fact, the three regiments were responsible for reprisals against the Polish population, especially the Jews. For example, "Brandenburg" initiated a "Judenaktion" (Jewish action) on 22 September at Wloclawek. The synagogues in the town were burnt down, shops run by Jews were destroyed and the leaders of the Jewish community were arrested then executed en masse. According to the

reports of the *Korück 581*, Paul Nostitz (*Kdr. SS-"Brandenburg"*) had apparently arrested eight hundred Jews and indicated that his intention was to kill them all. On the 24th, two "Brandenburg" battalions were sent to Bydgoszcz, where they executed about eight hundred Polish civilians whose names had been supplied by the *SD*. The civilians concerned were intellectuals and potential resistance leaders. "Oberbayern" and "Thüringen" also carried out massacres at Nisko, Rawa, Mazowiecka and Ciepielow. *SS-Heimwehr Danzig* shot 33 Polish civilians at Ksiazki and *SS-Wachsturmbann "Eimann"* perpetrated numerous crimes in the Polish corridor between Karthaus and Neustadt after September 13, 1939. After "Brandenburg" left, further massacres were committed by *12.SS-Totenkopf-Standarte*. Amongst other atrocities, it assassinated all the patients of a psychiatric hospital at Owinsk. Later, the men of this regiment were to be transferred to *SS-Totenkopf-Division* to make up for the losses it had suffered on the Eastern front.

Creation of the *SS-Totenkopf-Division*

At the start of October 1939, Theodor Eicke organized the creation of the new division. He immediately set up an *Aufstellungsstab* with officers who had served at the headquarters of the *SS-TV* inspectorate and the nucleus of an ordnance battalion whose mission was to feed the recruits expected to pour in from October 25 to Dachau, where the division was quartered. Every day, the cooks and butchers of *Totenkopf* had to scour the countryside and neighboring shops to find food, since the *Wehrmacht*, loath to see the creation of a armed unit in the SS, refused to provide any support.

The core of the division consisted of 6500 men from the *SS-TV*. They were joined by six thousand recruits from the Prettin and Breslau *SS-Totenkopf-Ergänzungs-Einheiten*, reserves of the *Allgemeine-SS* planned in the order of October 15, 1938 to reinforce the police, and members of *SS-Heimwehr Danzig*. *SS-Verfügungstruppe* also gave up some of its officers. Although empty of prisoners, who had been transferred to other concentration camps, Dachau was still too small to accommodate so many people. Some men slept on the floor inside sheds while others, less fortunate, had to sleep in the open air. The luckiest had barracks formerly occupied by the prisoners. The division was therefore created under difficult conditions, with no help from the army. Virtually all the important posts in the general staff were assigned to former members of the camp inspectorate, and very few had the experience required for their jobs. Fortunately for the division, the commander-in-chief appointed, *SS-Staf.* Freiherr Cassius von Montigny, was a competent officer. A fanatical Nazi from the *Heer* where he had commanded *IR 31* and *IR 102,* he had left the army, which he considered too reactionary, to join the *SS* on April 1, 1938 as tactical combat instructor at the Bad Tölz *SS-Junkerschule*. He mission was to transform the division into a combat unit. This was no easy task, since everything was in short supply: time, since the division had to be ready for the future western campaign that the German general staff had decided to schedule for the spring, weapons and vehicles since the *Wehrmacht* was dragging its heels to provide equipment. Theodor Eicke therefore decided to use his influence within the SS to obtain what was needed: uniforms from Buchenwald camp, drugs as well as medical and surgical equipment from the Berlin-Lichtenberg SS central medical warehouse, radio equipment and several thousand rifles from the reserve stock of the *SS-TV*, and two howitzers provided by the Bad Tölz and Braunschweig SS-Junkerschulen. A commando from the division even stole 22 trucks and 19 motorbikes at Oranienburg, infuriating Richard Glücks, Eicke's successor at the camp inspectorate. These methods, however, only procured a very small proportion of the equipment required by a motorized infantry division.

Montigny also lacked experienced officers. To give just two examples, the commander of SS-Totenkopf-Infanterie-Regiment 1 (SS-T.IR 1), SS-Staf. Max Simon, had served during WWI as a corporal in 1.Leibkürassier-Regiment. SS-Staf. Paul Nostitz, in command of SS-Totenkopf-Infanterie-Regiment 2 (SS-T.IR 2), was a former officer who had been awarded the Iron Cross 1st Class during WWI, but who had since spent most of his career until 1936 in the police force. On November 8, 1939, he was replaced by SS-Staf. Heinz Bertling, another police officer. Eicke's complaints concerning his appointment were later justified, since he proved totally incompetent in combat. Theodor Eicke therefore had to create his division with whatever means were available. The division consisted of three infantry regiments of three battalions each, an artillery regiment with three groups, an engineering battalion, a reconnaissance group, a transmission battalion, an antitank battalion and logistics support units.

SS-T.IR 1 (SS-Staf. Max Simon) was formed from 1.SS-Totenkopf-Standarte "Oberbayern" (1.SS-T.Sta.), a unit created in 1937 from the Dachau SS-Wachsturmbann I. Its three battalions were commanded by SS-Ostubaf. Becker (I.Btl.), SS-Stubaf. Deisenhofer (II.Btl.) and SS-Stubaf. Bestmann (III.Btl.).

SS-T.IR 2 (SS-Staf. Nostitz then SS-Staf. Bertling) consisted of elements of 2.SS-T.Sta. "Brandenburg" and 3.SS-T.Sta. "Thüringen". It also included recruits from the Prettin and Breslau SS-Totenkopf-Ergänzungseinheiten. The battalions were commanded by SS-Hstuf. Fortenbacher (I.Btl.), Kummer (II.Btl.) and Schulze (III.Btl.).

SS-T.IR 3 used SS-Heimwehr Danzig as its nucleus. Its commander, SS-Staf. Hans-Friedemann Götze, was a veteran of the Great War who had served for a while with the Bad Tölz SS-Junkerschule before creating III./4.SS-T.Sta. "Ostmark". This battalion formed the nucleus for the creation of SS-Heimwehr Danzig, whose first four companies formed I./SS-T.IR 3 (SS-Stubaf. Bellwidt). II./SS-T.IR 3 of SS-Stubaf. Petersen was formed from elements of 3.SS-T.Sta. "Thüringen" and reserves from the Allgemeine-SS. III./SS-T.IR 3 was created using reserves. It was first commanded by SS-Stubaf. Schulze, who was replaced by SS-Stubaf. Willi Dusenschön on November 7, 1939.

The artillery regiment, SS-Totenkopf-Artillerie-Regiment (mot.), was based at the München-Freimann barracks, its nucleus being II./SS-Artillerie-Regiment (SS-Stubaf. Priess) of the SS-Verfügungstruppe. The regimental staff came from the Oranienburg SS-Totenkopf-Ersatz-Abteilung. Command was given to SS-Staf. Allihn, a former trained staff officer from the Heer. The three regiment groups were commanded by SS-Stubaf. Brasack (I.Abt.), Priess (II.Abt.) and Sander (III.Abt.). 4., 5., 6. and 7.SS-T.Standarten supplied the remaining personnel. Theoretically, the armament consisted of thirty-six 10.5 cm howitzers shared between 9 batteries.

The reconnaissance battalion (SS-Totenkopf-Aufklärungs-Abteilung) led by SS-Stubaf. Hierthes was formed from elements of the Prag-Rusin III./SS-T.Sta. 6. Some cadres came from SS-T.Sta. "Thüringen".

The signals battalion (SS-Totenkopf-Nachrichten-Abteilung) was formed from the Unna SS-Nachrich-ten-Sturmbann. The unit was placed under the command of SS-Stubaf Sarsoni.

The division's antitank battalion (SS-Totenkopf-Panzerabwehr-Abteilung) was formed from Pz.Abw.-Kp. "Leiner" of SS-Heimwehr Danzig. It was completed by reservists. The battalion was commanded by SS-Stubaf. Leiner, a former Reichswehr officer who was in fact the son-in-law of Theodor Eicke.

The division's engineer battalion (SS-Totenkopf-Pionier-Bataillon) was sponsored by SS-Pionier-Bataillon of the SS-Verfügungstruppe. It was completed by reservists. The unit was placed under the command of SS-Stubaf. Lammerding who had served in SS-Hauptamt with the Chef des Ausbildungswesens (mit der Pionierausbildung beauftrag) before joining SS-Pionier-Sturmbann. The battalion equipment was of Czech origin.

The division's medical units (SS-Totenkopf-Sanitäts-Dienste) were formed from Sanitäts-Abteilung der SS-TV. SS-Staf. Genzken, a close friend of Theodor Eicke, was surgeon-general of the division (Div.-IV.b). He was replaced in March 1940 by SS-Staf. Dr Rothardt.

The division's supply units (Divisions-Nachschub-dienste) were directed by SS-Staf. Tschimpke, a former staff officer in the SS-Oberabschnitt "Südwest", "hired" in January 1938 by Theodor Eicke to work in the SS-TV inspectorate.

SS-Ostubaf. Anton Kaindl (Div.-IVa), another veteran of the pre-war concentration camp system, was placed in charge of the division's ordnance. Reduced to administrative tasks due to failing health and poor sight, he was responsible for similar functions at the Oranienburg SS-TV inspectorate.

The division was officially created on October 16. Still far from its theoretical size, it was then brought up to strength by elements of 4., 5. and 6.SS-Totenkopf-Standarten. From early November, weapons started to arrive in larger quantities, although still of Czech origin. To familiarize the troops with these weapons, the Heer organized several two- to three-week training courses at the Döberitz infantry school, the Jüterbog artillery school and the Halle transmission school. Nothing seemed to have been planned, however, for the motorization of the infantry regiments, the sapper battalion and the ordnance units. The medical units were only horse-drawn. Claiming that he wanted to create new units and using his contacts, Theodor Eicke nevertheless managed to motorize the entire division.

Before the French campaign

November 1939 was a month of frustrations generated by the lack of equipment and the poor quality of the supplies delivered. The bakers' company, for example, was assigned a total of 142 old bicycles and 10 Czech horse-drawn ovens dating from the First World War. Wood-fired, and each weighing nearly two and a half tons, not only were they practically impossible to use but there were no horses to pull them. When the division was transferred by rail, it proved impossible to hoist them on the flatbed cars, since no cranes were available.

November 1939 was also made difficult by numerous discipline problems and the struggle to forge an esprit de corps. The division consisted of a heterogeneous group of men, of all ages and from numerous geographical origins. The problem of discipline seemed more pronounced, however, in contrast with the traditional opinion of an SS unit. Generally, this problem was due to recruits from the Ordnungspo-lizei and the Allgemeine-SS. The men from the SS-

TV were in fact extremely motivated and well-disciplined. Serious discipline incidents were reported right from the first few weeks: for example, a second lieutenant of the division transportation unit was jailed for five days then transferred to the unit guarding the Oranienburg concentration camp for refusing to obey a superior officer. Other disciplinary difficulties were also caused by the proximity of Munich and its temptations. There were reports that men from the division visited the town brothels and caught venereal diseases. On November 20, Eicke cancelled all leave. That very night, six men from *14.Kp./SS-T.IR 2* drove out of the barracks in a stolen truck without being spotted and reached Munich to do a round of the taverns. Shortly before midnight, our six men, completely drunk, tried to return to Dachau. Their truck, an *Opel-Blitz*, crashed straight into a tram. The tram derailed under the shock and the incident soon attracted a crowd of onlookers. Quickly on the scene, the police found our six rogues fast asleep snoring heavily. This episode did not seem to amuse Theodor Eicke, who immediately decided to demote the six men, dismiss them from the SS and imprison them in the Buchenwald concentration camp. This example left a lasting impression on the men, especially the former camp guards. The threat of being interned in a concentration camp gave conclusive results and discipline improved considerably after this incident.

Training resumed. Progress was significant and the situation regarding equipment gradually improved. Numerous difficulties still remained, however. On November 19, the antitank battalion and the antitank companies of the infantry regiment were sent to Erdinger Moor, near Munich, for their first firing practice. The first infantry combat exercises were carried out at Hohenfeld camp. The next day, a section of three 10-ton type 35 Czech tanks, German name *Pzkpfw.35(t),* was created. The unit was attached to the reconnaissance battalion's "Hardieck" squadron to make up for the lack of machine guns. This was to be the very first *Panzer* unit of the *Waffen-SS*! On November 28, *General* Halder, *OKH* Chief of Staff, came to inspect the division. He reported: *"The men and equipment give an excellent impression. The officers and the level of training are mediocre."* In the meantime, the division had received orders to leave the region of Dachau: from December 1, it had to rejoin the Ludwigsburg - Heilbronn - Neckarsulm sector.

On December 3, training resumed as soon as the units had arrived. On December 20, the armored section of *SS-T.Aufkl.-Abt.* was converted into a company, becoming the *3.(schw.)Kp./SS-T.Aufkl.-Abt.*

On January 22, *Stellv. Gen.Kdo. V.AK* announced that *Totenkopf* was to move to Münsingen camp, recently vacated by *183.Infanterie-Division.* Known as "German Siberia", with its high hills, this region was unsuitable for the training of a motorized division. The intense cold (-28°C) was worsened by the shortage of winter clothing, a problem which had still not been solved in spite of Theodor Eicke's efforts to obtain supplies from the Dachau depot. Many soldiers did not even have any socks! The weather conditions (snow and fog) made the exercises difficult and dangerous. Training nevertheless continued

at an infernal rhythm. The training received by the soldiers in the combat units, both physically and in terms of discipline, was extremely tough. After several trying weeks, good news finally arrived: from March 7, *Totenkopf* was to be transferred to the Brilon - Frankenberg - Korbach - Arolsen - Niedermarsberg sector. On March 7, the departure of the Laichingen division transportation unit was delayed by elements of *SS-T.IR 3* and *I./SS-T.Art.-Rgt.* blocked between Laichingen and Feldstetten by an icy slope. Von Montigny was outraged by the division's lack of transport discipline: vehicles were grouped together on open ground, sitting ducks for enemy aircraft; the men made too much noise in the assembly sectors and there were countless breakdowns. In addition, the roadworthy vehicles became caught up in huge bottlenecks since the officers in charge of the *Marschgruppen* had chosen the wrong routes. This anger was to be followed by results: from now on, the division redoubled its efforts concerning transport discipline and excellent progress was observed.

On March 10, the units set up camp in their new sector. The division was attached to *Stellv. Gen.Kdo. IX.AK*. Training resumed the very next day. The exercises concerned night fighting, fighting in forest and town, crossing rivers, techniques on how to break off fighting and retreat, procurement of munitions during fighting, etc. Due to fuel shortages, the exercises had to be carried out as close as possible to the barracks, which sometimes led to problems. However, one exercise at regimental level and another at battalion scale had to be carried out every week with the cooperation of the artillery regiment. The transmission battalion had to participate in each exercise of the three infantry regiments in order to provide a real time, live report of their progress to the general staff.

The situation regarding the equipment continued to improve significantly. On March 22, *SS-T.Art.-Ers.-Abt.* had to set up a group of heavy howitzers for the division's artillery regiment. The *Heer* did its utmost to prevent the creation of this new group: it therefore decided that the 8th wave divisions should be equipped before delivering to *Totenkopf* the 15 cm howitzers and the eight-ton tractors required to move them.

On April 2, the commander of *2.Armee*, *General* von Weichs, came to inspect the division. Although he had expected to find a division organized and equipped like a Czech infantry division, to his great surprise he discovered a modern, motorized division. In mid-March, *SS-Ostubaf.* Geisler (*Div.-Ib*) had in fact managed to exchange the Czech armament and vehicles for their German equivalents and even increase the numbers of machine guns and mortars. The only Czech weapons still used were the excellent 10.5cm howitzers and the *ZB vz.30* machine guns which, although not as powerful as the German *MG-34*, were still suitable. In addition, following von Montigny's complaints, the unit commanders had made noticeable progress in managing their troops. Impressed by the division, Von Weichs promised to do his best to procure the 15 cm howitzers required by the heavy artillery group. They were to be delivered on May 8, 1940.

Theodor Eicke with *SS Totenkopfverbände* inspection members.
(Private collection S.)

A non identified Death's Head unit walks through a village.
(Private collection.)

On arrival the recruits are dressed and equipped. Notice the model 1916 helmets, proof that the division is not part of the priority units for the *Wehrmacht* headquarters, to the great displeasure of Himmler who considers it as a political instrument of major impact. (Private collection.)

Inside some barracks. Teaching is intense and moments of rest like this are rare. In the background a man in *Allgemeine-SS* uniform looks over. He is probably a newcomer and is waiting for a *feldgrau* uniform. (Private collection.)

View of a small dormitory. This snap from a private collection was not taken for propaganda purposes: these older men, maybe reservists from *Allgemeine-SS*, from modest backgrounds, look tired and apathetic, and the austerity of the place show a daily reality different from what official coverage would report.
(Heimdal collection.)

View of an overcrowded dormitory. The atmosphere her appears more relaxed than the previous snapshot. (Private collection.)

Assembly in a barracks courtyard before a standing at attention exercise. The guns stacks have not been strictly aligned.
(Private collection.)

Relaxation after exercises. Notice the collar tabs with death's head and numeral of the company (*Sturm*). This type of insignia ran from 1935 to May 1940. (Heimdal collection.)

Postcard showing the entry of the SS training camp at Dachau. Its construction precedes the concentration camp. (Private collection.)

Another postcard, showing this time the inside of the barracks housing *SS-Totenkopfstandardte "Oberbayern"* personnel. (Private collection.)

Located in Bavaria, the Dachau camp was in operation from 22nd March 1933. At the beginning it held 5000 political prisoners, communists and social democrats. Later, Jews, gypsies and clergy members who opposed the nazi regime would join them. In 1937, in order to humiliate the latter groups, criminals, society rejects and homosexuals were incarcerated there. (Rights reserved.)

Dachau was the first experimental concentration camp created by the nazis. On the wall of this shed, one can read: *"There is a path to freedom, its milestones are: obedience, toil, honesty, order, cleanliness, sobriety, truthfulness, spirit of sacrifice and love of the fatherland."* Note that Dachau was not an extermination camp such as Auschwitz or Treblinka, but hunger and disease, arbitrary executions and pseudo scientific experiments cost thousands of the prisoners' lives. (Rights reserved.)

Scene of torture in the Buchenwald camp. (Rights reserved.)

15

Visit of Rudolf Hess and Himmler at the *SS-Totenkopf-Standarte 1 "Oberbayern"* barracks at Dachau, probably for the opening of the gymnasium. Regiment members in sporting gear are standing at attention before the nazi dignitaries. (NA)

View of the barracks main courtyard. Big flags have been raised on the building for the visit. (NA)

Theodor Eicke's speech inside the new gymnasium before an attentive audience. The gymnasium structure is spartan, as are most the barracks buildings. (NA)

The ceremony is followed by drinks served by waiters from the officers' mess, dressed in white uniforms. (NA)

1. The Dachau camp has a fire station but it does not belong to *SS-Totenkopf-Standerte 1* but to the *Reichsführung-SS*, as the inscription indicates on the front left door. (NA)

2 and **3.** SS firemen demonstration. Notice the helmets, model 1916. These photos probably date from winter 1935-1936. (NA)

4. Excellent picture of an SS group belonging to *SS-Totenkopf-Verbände*. They belong to *3.Sturm*, except for the second man from the right who is from *20.Sturm*, as testified by the number under the death's head on his collar. (NA)

Recruits training in the Dachau area. The integration of the *SS-Totenkopverbände* into the *Waffen-SS* brings not only a problem of mental adaptation, but also mainly one of training standardisation. As *Befehlshaber der Waffen-SS "Ost"*, Karl-Maria Demelhuber complained that most of *SS-Totenkopf-Verbände* under his command did not have the faintest knowledge of army tactics. To make up for this significant gap, *Totenkopf* units then had to undergo highly intensive training programs.

First firing exercises in one of the training areas of a barracks. The instructor, who looks younger than his students, is a volunteer coming from *SS-Verfügungstruppe* or *SS-Totenkopf-Verbände*. Note that most of the students wear the rune SS collar tab, not the death's head. (Private collection.)

Firing training using a heavy machine gun. It is a Czech *ZB-53*. (Private collection.)

To illustrate a propaganda article, the *SS-KB* assigned to *"Totenkopf"* division chose a crew of three men in training uniform and firing an *MG 34* in heavy machine gun configuration on its *Lafette 34* tripod mounting. It was not an accidental choice: when *Totenkopf* was created, it received only very few *MG 34s*. Most of the machine guns issued were of Czech origin. (NA)

Zoom in on the firer and the aiming system operating like a periscope to allow firing from a trench. By removing this sight and the auxiliary trigger fitted on one of the feet of the tripod, and by replacing the *Lafette 34* by a simple bipod stand, the *MG 34* could be quickly converted into a light machine gun. (NA)

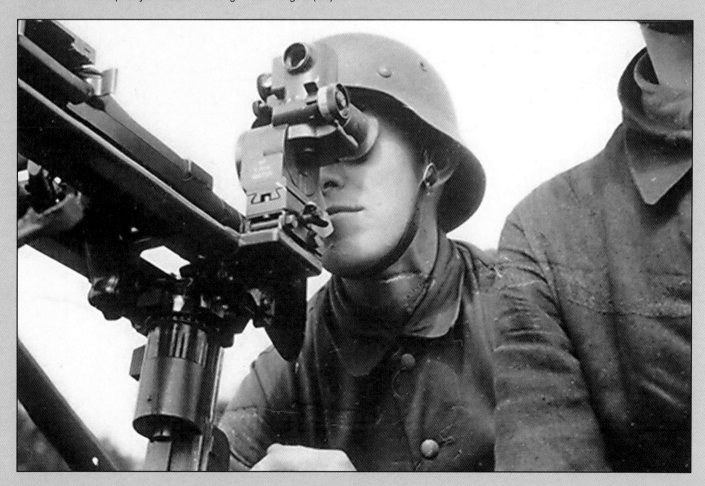

1. An NCO instructing a crew on the maintenance required to ensure correct operation of a 3.7 cm Pak 35/56 antitank gun. In 1939, it was a relatively modern weapon with its fairly long and slender tube, well-profiled shield and opening trails easy to handle. Its armor-piercing shells could penetrate 38 mm thick plating at a distance of 365 meters at an angle of incidence of 30°. This performance proved adequate during the Spanish Civil War and against the Polish armored vehicles. Note the straps over the shoulders of two soldiers: the straps were used to pull the gun which, fully equipped, weighed 440 kg. (NA)

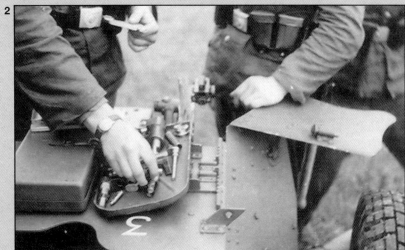

2. An extremely simple mechanism could convert the shield into a platform. A toolbox, used for maintenance of the gun, could then be placed on top. (NA)

3. Once all the checks have been carried out, the gun crew can prepare the gun for firing. Originally, it was equipped with wood-spoked wheels. After the transition from animal to mechanized traction, they were replaced by more suitable metal wheels with tires. (NA)

4

5

4. The instructor is now teaching the recruits how to handle the *MP 38* machine pistol. It was a revolutionary weapon in terms of its manufacturing since it marked the end of the tradition of armourers and their delicately finished weapons, now replaced by crudely finished stamped metal sheet and plastic parts instead of wood. Cheap and with high fire power, the *MP 38* was not without its faults: after firing, the chamber stayed open with the breach back until released by the trigger. Under a shock, the breach could come free, emptying the magazine in an uncontrolled burst of fire! (NA)

6

5. Presentation of the *Karabiner 98k* rifle to new recruits. In spite of this name, it was neither more no less than a slightly shortened version of the *Gewehr 98* rifle used by the Germans during the First World War. The gun was still very long, however (110 cm), making it difficult to use in confined spaces. (NA)

6. Radio team exercising. As we can see by looking at the photograph, most men serving in the division's transmission units were relatively old. They were mostly reserves from *Allgemeine-SS* initially intended to strengthen the police force. (NA)

Interesting photograph showing recruits from the division learning how to use an 81 mm mortar. We can see that the three men on the left are wearing the collar tabs of their former *SS-Totenkopstandarte* unit. Unfortunately, the number is illegible. (Private collection.)

Training of couriers on motorcycles. The German army always privileged this sector to maintain communications under all circumstances. (Private collection.)

Clearing the snow at Müsingen camp. As we can see, there is a considerable amount of snow. (Private collection.)

We are now in the middle of winter. The weather is cold, the men are wearing greatcoats to protect them against the cold. Note that the "standard" 1935 model helmets have finally been delivered. (Heimdal collection.)

Photograph of a barracks at Münsingen camp. (Private collection.)

The heavy artillery group was created in spring 1940 at Ippinghausen. An artillery observer is training with periscope binoculars to check the accuracy of a previous fire. Note the enormous shell case on the ground behind the soldier. (Private collection.)

Superb photograph of one of the first six *Pzkpfw.35(t)* which were used by the reconnaissance group. It was the first armored formation of the SS! (Private collection.)

Firing exercise with real bullets. The machine gun is a Czech *ZB vz.26*. The firing rate of this weapon could reach 500 rounds a minute. Its main fault was its cost, relatively high since most parts had to be machined. (Chr. Belser Verlag)

Close order is a must in order to maintain absolute discipline. (Heimdal collection.)

Exercises with stick grenades. (Heimdal collection.)

1

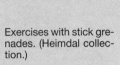

2

3

4

1. Officers supervising the exercise. (Heimdal collection.)

2. Meeting to comment on the previous exercise. (Heimdal collection.)

3. and **4.** The exercise seems to be over and these men are posing for one of their comrades. (Heimdal collection.)

This maneuvering ground is not really suitable for training a motorized division.
(Heimdal collection.)

Sporting events were organized to improve the physical condition of the soldiers. The political emphasis specific to the SS units is clearly obvious on this photograph.
(Heimdal collection.)

This outstanding photograph was taken during an *SS-Totenkopfverbände* parade in Dachau. The tall man standing on the left is *SS-Standartenführer* Max Simon, commander of *SS-Totenkopf-Standarte 1 "Oberbayern"*. The *SS-Sturmbannführer* is Hellmuth Becker, one of his battalion commanders. (Courtesy Tim Willemsen)

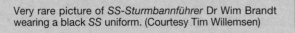

Very rare picture of *SS-Sturmbannführer* Dr Wim Brandt wearing a black *SS* uniform. (Courtesy Tim Willemsen)

Theodor Eicke is shaking hands with Hitler during a mass meeting like those the Nazi regime used to organize in the thirties. Unfortunately, his armband is hardly legible but it probably reads *"SS-Totenkopfverbände"*. (Courtesy Martin Månsson)

SS-Gruppenführer Theodor Eicke with an unidentified *SS-Obersturmführer* serving within the *SS-Inspektion der SS-Totenkopfverbände*. (Courtesy Martin Månsson)

SS-Heimwehr Danzig

Before being integrated in *SS-Totenkopf-Division*, *SS-Heimwehr Danzig* fought independently for the Hanseatic town. It was therefore its only force with military experience.

Opposite: Training within the *MG-Kp*. (*SS-Ostuf.* Urbanitz) with old water-cooled machine guns dating from the Great War. (Private collection.)

75 mm infantry gun of *IG-Kp. "Schulze"*. The countryside is typical of the Danzig region. (Private collection.)

Opposite: The unit also comprised a company equipped with infantry and *Minenwerfer* guns. Its commander was *SS-Hstuf.* Schulze. These artillery observers are training using periscope binoculars and a range-finder. (Private collection.)

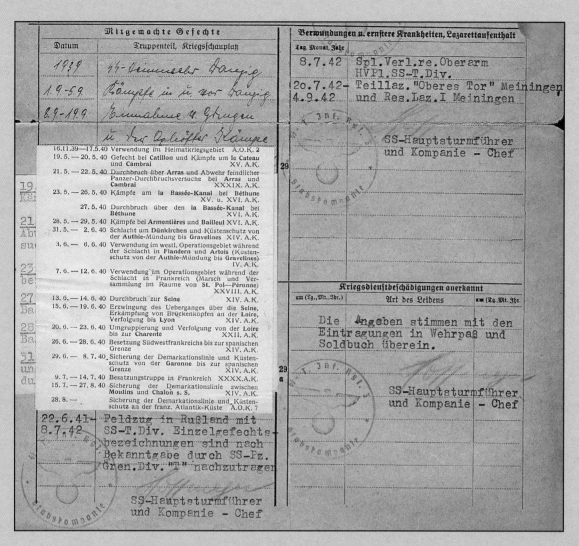

Extract from a *"Wehrstammbuch"* which belonged to Léo Heinz, a member of the Heimwehr Danzig. Thereafter he joined *Totenkopf* division, and thus took part in the French and Russian campaigns, as shown in the summary of this document. *Totenkopf* officer Hoffmeyer signed it. (Private collection.)

Men from *Heimwehr Danzig* in action during fighting for the town in September 1939. The photograph shows an *ADGZ* armored car of Austrian origin. (Rights reserved.)

1. und **2.** After the defeat of the Polish garrison, these officers from *SS-Heimwehr Danzig* inspect bunkers which were part of the town's line of defense. (Private collection.)

3. Portrait of an *SS-Untersturmführer* from the unit. It is Hans Heins (SS-Nr. 114 417), born on June 18 1913 at Zoppot. Promoted to *SS-Obersturmführer* in 1940, he was to serve in the general staff of *SS-T. IR 3* during the French campaign. In 1942, he was appointed head of *4.Kp./SS-Pz. Ers.-Abt,* then in January 1943, he took command of *4.Kp./SS-Pz.Rgt.10.* He was commander of *I.Abteilung* of the *SS-Pz. Rgt. 10* from March to April 1945. (Private collection.)

4. Hans Heins wearing a greatcoat with *SS-Heimwehr Danzig* armband stitched on.
(Private collection.)

This photograph of the same officer at the end of the war was included to show his extremely rare white tunic, even though at this time Heins was no longer serving in *Totenkopf*. (Private collection.)

SS-Ostuf. Erich Urbanitz accompanied by some of his men in September or October 1939. He was in command of *9.Kp./SS-T.IR 3* until October 1940. He was later transferred to the *Leibstandarte* where he formed the 105 mm gun battery. In July 1941, he took command of the 2nd group of *SS-Art.-Rgt. "LSSAH"*. In 1943, he was transferred to *12.SS-Pz. Div. "Hitlerjugend"* where he took command of *I. Abt./SS-Pz.Art.-Rgt.12*. He finished the war at the head of *IV.Abt./SS-Art.-Rgt.17*. (Private collection.)

2

The french campaign

Fall Gelb (Case Yellow)

On **May 10**, while *Heeresgruppen "B"* and *"A"* commanded by von Bock and von Rundstedt were attacking in the Netherlands and Belgium, Eicke was waiting for the order to march to the front. He was only worried about one thing: that *Totenkopf* would be used simply as an occupation force after all the decisive fighting was over. His fears proved to be well-founded. Although the *Wehrmacht* had only seven motorized divisions out of a total of 157 infantry divisions, the *OKH* had decided for the time being to keep *Totenkopf* in reserve. This decision was based solely on the officers' dislike of the former concentration camp guards and their contempt for Theodor Eicke, a *Feldwebel* (Sergeant) who had become a police general.

On **May 17**, the *Totenkopf* staff finally received marching orders. The division was placed at the disposal of *Heeresgruppe "B"*. The next day, the division started out towards Dinant. At 21h00, it was attached to *Gen.Kdo.XV.AK* (Hoth). On May 19, *Heeresgruppe "A"* received the mission to join the Arras sector with its mobile divisions and to resume the offensive towards the north and the west. *Totenkopf* arrived at Fraire. The journey proved difficult since the division columns had to cross roads used by the units of *Heeresgruppe "B"*, causing huge traffic jams. There were incidents at several crossroads between the SS and drivers from the *Wehrmacht*: swearing, threats, etc. By the end of the afternoon, the situation was back to normal. Theodor Eicke received the order to send a reinforced regiment to rescue *7.Panzerdivision* (*Generalmajor* Rommel) which had been stopped between Cateau and Cambrai and which was facing a fierce French counter-attack designed to restore contact with the troops fighting in the south of the Sambre. *SS-T.IR 1* was therefore attached to *7.Panzerdivision*. Max Simon set up his CP at Bazuel and immediately sent his regiment to attack Catillon. There was fighting to take every single house. The French troops, mainly formed from Moroccan soldiers, finally lost courage and gave up fighting after 22h00. 250 of their men were killed. The SS captured 55 officers and 1247 NCOs and soldiers. This first battle was a clear success for the division. In the meantime, *II./SS-T.IR 1* had taken Arbre-de-Guise. Thirteen guns and several tracked tractors were captured.

During this first day of fighting, 15 men of *Totenkopf* were killed and 48 wounded (including 3 officers). Despite its losses, the division's morale was excellent: the SS soldiers were convinced of their superiority. The next few days were to prove otherwise.

On **May 20**, *Totenkopf* received the order to reach the Sambre with two regiments. It had to reach Cambrai from two marching axes and continue to St. Pol, south of Arras. It was then placed under the orders of General Schmidt's *XXXIX.AK* . On **May 21**, *SS-T.IR 3* was sent to cover *7.Panzerdivision* south of Arras with *I./SS-T.IR 3* at Wailly, *II./SS-T.IR 3* at Mercatel and *III./SS-T.IR 3* at Neuville-Vitasse. In the morning, after hesitating for more than 24 hours, Hitler finally decided to send von Rundstedt's armored forces northward to annihilate the trapped allied units. Following this decision, at 14h00 Eicke received orders to cross the river

Scarpe in force and continue advancing north. *SS-T.IR 3* therefore started moving out at 14h30. At practically the same time, the 5th and 50th Infantry Divisions, supported by the 1st Armored Brigade, launched a counter-attack from Tilloy, Achicourt and Dainville to open a corridor southward to reach General Billotte's 1st army group. Around 15h00, on the heights of Simencourt, two English tanks burst out behind the lines of *Pz.Rgt.25* (*7.Panzerdivision*) and attacked the columns of *I./SS-T.IR 3* which were heading north. The entire battalion was disrupted. *XXXIX.AK* alerted *Totenkopf*: *"Major enemy attack south of Bapaume".* Around 15h10, six *"Mathilda"* tanks opened fire on *Pz.Jg.-Abt.42* (Mickl) whose 3.7 cm *Pak 36* guns proved incapable of penetrating the tank armor plating. Panic spread amongst the men of *7.Panzerdivision*. The British continued advancing towards the Ficheux - Mercatel road, while another unit attacked Ficheux where it surprised *5.Kp./SS-T.IR 3*. Several trucks were hit and caught fire. West of Mercatel, *III./SS-T.IR 3* was attacked by four waves of tanks. *14.(Pz.Abw.)Kp./SS-T.IR 3* was called in for support. Although the SS managed to destroy several light tanks, they were powerless to stop the heavy tanks. Panic raged amongst their ranks and they suffered heavy losses. Two *Pzkpfw.35 (t)* of the reconnaissance group were destroyed during the fighting. Further to the west, *3.Kp./SS-T.Pz.Abw.-Abt.* was also engaged in a battle against the British tanks. Its nine *Pak* guns formed a porcupine of fire around Ficheux. The SS gunners targeted the tracks and managed to knock out eight tanks. The British infantry was pushed back by *II./SS-T.IR 3*. Despite their heavy losses, the British and the French had not given up. East of Brétencourt, the English tanks advanced parallel to the road to Blairville. On reaching Hendecourt, they threatened the flank of *SS-T.IR 2* which was progressing along the Wancourt - Hénin - Boisleux road. *III./SS-T.IR 2* was hit by a new armored attack (this time by French Hotchkiss tanks) along the Croisilles - Beaumetz road. Panic spread amongst the truck drivers who tried to escape wherever they could. *III./SS-T.Art.-Rgt.*, arriving in the sector, also came under French fire. The SS tried to reorganize. All units in the sector were placed under the orders of *SS-Stubaf.* Lammerding to clean up Simencourt. Around 16h00, the armored vehicles which had opened fire on *Pz.Jg.-Abt.42* reached the west of Mercatel, where *III./SS-T.IR 3* had just arrived from Neuville-Vitasse. The SS were routed. The situation was restored when the 88 mm guns of *2.Bttr./Flak-Abt.86* came into action. Around 18h00, *Stukas* appeared in the sky, finally putting a stop to the allied counter-attack. This was a terrible day for the *Totenkopf* which had shown signs of panic, especially amongst the transportation soldiers, and which had suffered heavy losses (39 killed, 66 injured and 2 missing). The frustration generated by this first serious battle had direct repercussions on the local civilians: six men, including a Belgian refugee running to shelter holding his children by the hand, were shot down in cold blood by the SS at Mercatel, as well as five others at Simencourt, for no apparent reason. However, this violent allied counter-attacked had cooled the enthusiasm of the Germans, making them much more cautious. Theodor Eicke was forced to temporarily

SS-Sturmbannführer Hellmuth Becker was one of Theodor Eicke's favorites. Hard, uncompromising and courageous but with a tendency to drink too much. (Courtesy Marc Rikmenspoel)

A tragic end befell *General* Hoepner. In January 1942, he was leading the *4.Panzerarmee* facing Moscow when Hitler dismissed him from his duties. On the 8th of August 1944, he was hanged to a meat hook as a punishment for his taking part in the 20th of July 1944 conspiracy. (Rights reserved)

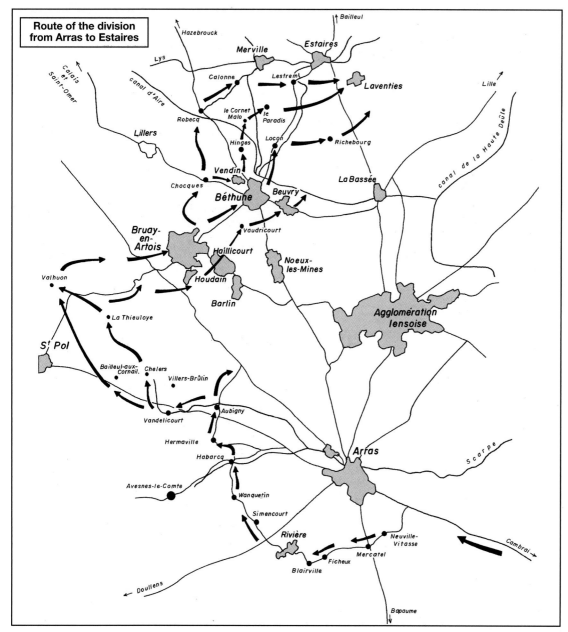

Route of the division from Arras to Estaires

postpone his attack to the north at Valhoun. The attack was launched by *I./SS-T.IR* 3 via Hermaville towards Aubigny. Its progression was marked by the murder of several civilians (5 at Habarcq and 4 at Hermaville). Around 19h00, *SS-Stubaf* Bellwidt's battalion reached Aubigny, still held by a few allied soldiers. It was rejoined by *SS-T.IR 1* during the night. *SS-T.IR 1* had received orders to finish the clean-up. The next day, Theodor Eicke set up his headquarters in the village. According to *SS-Obf.* von Montigny's diary, some allied tanks accompanied by infantry men tried to sneak away to the south through the streets of the town. The situation became chaotic. *SS-T.IR 1* appears to have suffered its first losses at this time, under the fire of French snipers, dressed as civilians. The snipers had used dum-dum bullets. These snipers were probably French soldiers over run by the German advance. In any case, this was the version given by the SS as an excuse for a war crime relatively unknown by the English-speaking public: 98 men taken hostage were shot. Not one soldier from the division was prosecuted for this war crime, probably ordered by Theodor Eicke who was present that day. On the same day, a unit of the *SS-T.IR 2* advancing along the Saint-Pol-sur-Ternoise road stopped at a hamlet, Berles-Monchel, near Vandelicourt, apparently looking for English soldiers. Furious and screaming, the SS interrogated the terrorized civilians. Suddenly, they started to throw hand grenades, which exploded amongst the unfortunate civilians trying to escape. A number of men were then executed. There were 45 victims. These two appalling massacres foreshadowed the future crimes to be perpetrated by the division.

On **May 23**, the division was attached to *XVI.AK* (Hoepner) to provide support in an offensive towards the La Bassée canal. The next day, *SS-T.IR 1* received orders to cross the La Bassée canal at Béthune and Beuvry and set up bridgeheads. *II./SS-T.Art.-Rgt.* had to support the assault. The SS gunners deployed their guns, using numerous civilians as human shields. On the north bank, the English forces had been considerably strengthened. All the bridges had been destroyed. Although crossing the canal seemed impossible, nothing seemed to stop the SS. They crossed to the other side in dinghies and opened fire on the *Queen's Own Cameron Highlanders*. A bridgehead was taken. It was at this very moment that *XVI.AK* ordered the division to stop its attack and pull back onto the southern bank. This was the result of Hitler's famous "*Halt Befehl*": he had decided to stop the Panzer units, for reasons which are still today subject to controversy.

Under the accurate fire of the British artillery, evacuating the bridgehead was not easy. The SS found out the hard way: on this day alone, the 24th, the division suffered heavy losses: 43 killed (including 4 officers, 121 wounded and 5 missing. Outraged, they exe-

Matthias Kleinheisterkamp (SS-Nr. 132 399), here with a *SS-Gruppenführer* rank, came from the *"Deutschland"* regiment, in which he served as commandant to the 3rd battalion. In July 1941, he momentarily stood in for Eicke at the head of the division; he was then a *SS-Oberführer*. In January 1942, after being promoted to *SS-Brigadeführer*, Kleinheisterkamp was given command mandment of the *"Das Reich"* division. He was given the Knight's Cross on the 31st of March 1942, and was appointed *SS-Gruppenführer* the day after. He was then moved to the command mandment of the *SS-Division "Nord"* on the Finnish front. From the 1st to the 20th of July 1944, he took the head of *IV.SS-Pz.Korps*, and later, in August, of *XI.SS-AK* formed in Slovakia. He won the Oak Leaves on the 28th of April 1945. Shortly afterwards, on the 2nd of May 1945, he died during the battle for the Halbe pocket. He was then *SS-Obergruppen führer und General der Waffen-SS* (since his promotion on the 1st of August 1944). (Rights reserved)

cuted 48 inhabitants of Beuvry. Hoepner and Eicke were to have a violent argument after these battles which cost many lives. Eicke was called a "butcher" by his superior, in front of his general staff. In the meantime, at Hinges, elements of *III./SS-T.IR 3* and *3.Kp./SS-T.Pi.-Btl.* engaged in reprisals against the population, after the death of a motorcyclist, shot near the canal: ten hostages were taken at random and executed. In the evening, *SS-Obf.* von Montigny fell sick. Suffering from a gastric hemorrhage, he had to be evacuated to Heidelberg. *SS-Ostubaf.* Geisler then acted as *Ia* and *Ib*. This was a heavy blow for the division, since von Montigny was one of the rare officers with solid military experience.

The order to resume the offensive was only given in the late afternoon on **May 26**. The attack was launched at 19h40 by *I./SS-T.IR 3* which crossed the canal at 20h30. At 23h30, Locon fell into the hands of the SS. At 22h30, *3.Kp./SS-T.IR 2* captured Riez-du-Vinage and advanced towards Le Cornet Malo. On **May 27**, *II.* and *III./SS-T.IR 2* also crossed the canal. The British put up stiff resistance and losses started to become quite heavy. After violent close combat fighting, *II./SS-T.IR 3* managed to take Le Cornet Malo. Further to the west, *SS-T.IR 2* attacked towards Bohême and Le Cornet Malo. *SS-Staf.* Bertling, however, dispersed his regiment to the north without keeping sufficient forces to protect his flanks. All contact with the rest of the division was lost and Theodor Eicke had to resort to sending *I./SS-T.IR 3* to the rescue. *I./SS-T.IR 3* launched its attack from Rue du Paradis. The enemy fire was devastating. *SS-Staf.* Götze, fighting with his men, was fatally wounded. On flat ground with no cover, the SS losses were very high. The British finally withdrew to a new line of defense along the Lawe canal. Less than 1.5 miles (2 km) further west, a hundred men from the *2nd Royal Norfolk* were barricaded in Duries farm. Encircled, they fought back until 17h15 before surrendering, coming out with their hands on their heads. The prisoners were grouped together at Creton farm where they were machine-gunned by the SS, infuriated by their heavy losses (on this day alone, May 27, *Totenkopf* casualties amounted to 155 killed, 483 wounded and 53 missing!). There were 97 victims. The survivors were finished off with bayonets. But the SS had left two English soldiers for dead: Privates Pooley and O'Callaghan. Although Pooley was seriously injured, they managed to escape and surrendered to a unit of *251.ID*. Their testimonial was to be damning evidence against Fritz Knöchlein, leader of *3.Kp./SS-T.IR 2*, who was to be hanged on January 29, 1945.

On **Tuesday May 28**, *Totenkopf* resumed its attacks against Vieille Chapelle and Pont-du-Hem. They faced greater resistance from the British at Laventie. It was eventually taken by *SS-T.IR 1*. 32 bodies were found lying in the village streets: enquiries conducted after the war were to show that at least six civilians had not been killed during the fighting but executed by the SS. In addition, an, elderly woman had been raped by a soldier from the division. This soldier, found to be drunk at the time, was to be sentenced by the *Totenkopf* tribunal and condemned to serve two years in a disciplinary company. That afternoon, further atrocities were committed against the civilian population, this time by *SS-T.IR 3*: seven men were shot at Richebourg, once again for no apparent reason. On **May 29**, *XVI.AK* received orders to break through the new allied defensive line on the river Lys. On the left flank of the corps, Totenkopf was given the mission to take Estaires. *SS-T.IR 1* captured the town in the late morning and reported that the British were pulling back northward. The SS started off in pursuit. At 16h00, Bailleul fell into the hands of *SS-T.IR 2*. In the evening, *SS-T.IR 1* managed to make contact with units of

6.Armee (*Heeresgruppe "B"*), but this success came a little too late for the Germans, since most of the *B.E.F* and the 1st French army had escaped towards the pocket of Dunkirk. Only five French divisions were encircled. The mission of the *Totenkopf* was not to clean up these forces, however: it was to be put on standby in the Boulogne region, where it was to be attached to *XIV.AK*.

In the first part of the campaign *Totenkopf* casualties amounted to 1140 killed, wounded and missing. Five hundred men were sent as reinforcements. They arrived on June 6.

On **May 31**, the division was sent to defend the coast between Gravelines and Etaples with most of the strongpoints at Calais and Boulogne. On **June 1**, *SS-Brigaf.* Knoblauch was appointed Chief of staff of the division. He was formerly inspector of the division's depot units. On June 3, *SS-Staf.* Kleinheisterkamp took over *SS-T.IR 3*, after a short period during which *SS-Staf.* Erbprinz zu Waldeck und Pyrmont had been in command.

Fall Rot (Case Red)

After the fall of the Dunkirk pocket, the Germans attacked southward. After four days of fierce fighting, *Heeresgruppe "B"* broke through the "Weygand" line between the Somme and the Oise. On **June 9**, *Heeresgruppe "A"* also launched an offensive, between the Aisne - Oise canal and the river Meuse. *Totenkopf* received orders from *XXVIII.AK* to take the Equancourt - Trescault sector. It was to be placed under authority of *6.Armee*. On **June 13** at 02h15, *Totenkopf* was to fight under *Gruppe "Kleist"*. This armored group was engaged on the right of the *9. Armee*. *Totenkopf* crossed the Marne on **June 15**. They continued advancing via Nogent-sur-Seine behind the columns of *9.Panzerdivision*. *Totenkopf* traveled 211 miles (340 km) in 36 hours. Its operational discipline had improved considerably with experience and this time there were very few incidents, in spite of roads packed by refugees trying to move in both directions. On **June 16**, *Totenkopf* was then ordered to travel via Molinons to follow *10.Panzerdivision* which had reached Clamecy. The rhythm of this headlong rush towards fuel the south was difficult to keep up, however, since petrol supplies were becoming scarce, the transportation units having been left far behind. On **June 17**, to encircle the French troops still clinging on to the Maginot line, *Panzergruppe "Guderian"* attacked from the Langres plateau towards Besançon. The aim of the *Panzergruppe "Kleist"* was to cut off the French retreat between Dijon and the Swiss border. *XVI.AK* was therefore sent to the Dole - Dijon sector. *XVI.AK* crossed the Loire at Nevers and continued its advance towards the river Saône. *Totenkopf* was still following behind *10.Panzerdivision* heading towards Lyon. In the evening of **June 18**, the day when the French government requested armistice conditions and General De Gaulle called on the French people to resist, *Totenkopf* reached Château-Chinon and Montceau-les-Mines. It continued advancing according to Hitler's orders: *"The pursuit of the defeated enemy units must be given the highest priority."*

The last battle on French soil: L'Arbresle - Lentilly

On **June 19**, around 16h30, *SS-T.Aufkl.-Abt.* entered Tarare. They met with little French resistance. The town of Arbresle then became the next objective of the SS troops. The sector was defended by the 2nd Battalion of the 25th Régiment de Tirailleurs Sénégalais. The battalion had taken up position on the Cornu, a

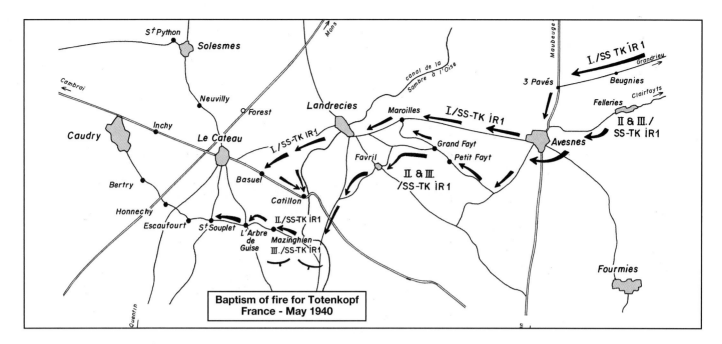

Baptism of fire for Totenkopf
France - May 1940

hill dominating the town of L'Arbresle and its access channels and which commanded the valleys of the Brévenne and the Turdine. The battle broke out at about 18h05. Pinned down by sustained fire from the Senegalese troops at Brévenne bridge, the motorcyclists were soon reinforced by *II./SS-T.IR 1*. German losses were heavy. Units arriving over the Turdine bridge were also stopped. Around 21h30, the SS prepared to launch the assault on the Cornu after first increasing the range of their artillery fire. *5.Kp. (SS-Hstuf. Häussler)* and *6.Kp./SS-T.IR 1 (SS-Hstuf. Frank)* crossed the bridge over the river Brévenne and advanced towards Eveux. Half an hour later, the Senegalese infantry started to pull back. Some continued fighting, however. They were torn to pieces. The battle of L'Arbresle had ended. In spite of the fierce fighting, the town remained intact. Five civilians were killed accidentally. According to reliable witnesses, however, several Senegalese soldiers had been massacred after being taken prisoner.

In the morning of **June 20**, *II./SS-T.IR 1* continued its advance to the south, towards Souriceux and Saint-Bel. Further over to the east *1.Kp./SS-T.IR 1 (SS-Hstuf. Kurtz)* was approaching Lentilly, where the Senegalese infantrymen were entrenched. A number of SS were killed when they came under fire about 500 yards from the town. The Germans then called in their artillery. Taking advantage of this support, the SS infiltrated along Tanneries gully. At 14h20, the French troops holding Lentilly station surrendered, their officers were taken by truck to Tarare, the NCOs and privates had to follow them on foot, guarded by motorcyclists. Stragglers were shot: according to warrant officer Icard, 28 prisoners were shot by the SS between Lentilly and Tarare. During the fighting, the SS had been merciless with the Senegalese, as demonstrated by the account of events related by *SS-Hstuf. Kurtz: "24 prisoners (white) were captured and 26 Negroes shot by the IIIrd section."* Not all of the French soldiers were captured: the units which had not heard the "cease-fire" or which did not want to surrender continued fighting. Thirteen Senegalese infantrymen were captured and taken to the main square. The Germans made them lie down on the ground with their arms out for several hours before executing them. At 22h30, a patrol captured a white Alsatian infantry soldier and three Senegalese infantrymen; *SS-Hstuf. Kurtz* then said to the mayor of Lentilly: *"These are your friends, dogs"*. The Senegalese

were shot during the night, the white soldier was sent back with the other prisoners.

Since crossing the Marne, *Totenkopf* declared that they had captured 6088 prisoners including *62 colored* (sic). The large number of prisoners caused considerable problems to the division and to the Germans in general. Units had to be withdrawn from their mission to guard the prisoners and not enough supplies had been planned to cope with these new requirements.

On **June 21**, *Totenkopf* entered Villefranche-sur-Saône where it seized a large quantity of weapons. At Saint-Sorbin, over 1300 disheartened French soldiers, were made prisoner. At the end of the day, the division received orders to stop its offensive south and head north towards Paris. It had to rejoin *XIV.AK* at Orléans. The next day, the armistice was signed at Rethondes.

On **June 23**, *Gruppe "Kleist"* was given the mission of reaching the Royan - Saintes - Angoulême - La Rochefoucauld line. It therefore had to travel right across France from east to west and then reach the Atlantic coast from the Gironde to the Pyrenees. This transfer was a feat of military acrobatics, since von Kleist troops would have to cut across the routes of the other German armies! *Totenkopf* and *SS-Verfügungsdivision* had to occupy the Landes coastline from the south of Bordeaux to the Spanish border. The first soldiers from *Marschgruppe "Simon"* reached the Tours sector via Vendôme on **June 24**, *Marschgruppe "Kleinheisterkamp"* crossed Saint-Laurent-en-Gatines to reach its new quarters.

The cease-fire was to come into force on **June 25** at 01h35. The French campaign had cost the division 339 killed (including 18 officers), 881 wounded (including 34 officers) and 32 missing. Some soldiers declared missing during the campaign, generally captured by the French, were found later, so the number of missing was lower than during the battle of Le Cornet Malo alone! Although the casualties in terms of numbers were comparatively light, considering the actual number of days fighting the losses were fairly high. The behavior under fire of the *Totenkopf* soldiers nevertheless proved to be satisfactory, even though Theodor Eicke and his officers firmly believed, before the start of the campaign, that they would outclass the adversaries. This was only rarely the case, with the units even occasionally showing signs of panic, for example south of Arras. The only really positive point was the experience gained under fire, which was to prove invaluable in the near future.

Crossing a river on a bridge of boats. Could it be the river Escaut and therefore Cambrai? (Heimdal collection.)

The division in the North

When crossing Holland and Belgium, the *Totenkopf* columns encountered no resistance since von Bock's army group had already pushed back the French and British forces more to the West.

French prisoners in front of a renaissance style building. Does one of the readers recognize where it is? (Heimdal collection.)

Improvised cemetery along a roadside. For many, the battle of France was a terrible debacle as the demoralized French soldiers were forced to retreat. We must not forget that fighting was often fierce and cost many human lives. (Heimdal collection.)

Above: Another wreck of a French *B1-bis* tank. Its name "Victorieux" does not seem to match the situation. (Heimdal collection.)

A *B1-bis* tank was destroyed or abandoned on this road in Picardy. It is inspected by a motorcyclist after a humorous sign was fastened to the back. (Heimdal collection.)

Motorcyclists looking at the wreck of a British Hurricane fighter which crashed not far from a road taken by the division. (Heimdal collection.)

Opposite: Motorcyclists have stopped to look along this antitank trench. (Chr. Belser Verlag)

Below on the right: A rather curious scene: a column of the division has stopped and an NCO is interrogating two French civilians (?) sitting down quite relaxed at the roadside. What is happening? (Private collection.)

Below: A convoy of the division is under attack by the French artillery. (Chr. Belser Verlag)

Opposite: Soldiers from the division in an unidentified town. On the right sign, you can read "Automobile Club du Nord". (Chr. Belser Verlag)

Below: Close-up of soldiers from the division. Note that the men are relatively old, probably reservists from *Allgemeine-SS* or former *SS-Totenkopfverbände* soldiers. (Private collection S.)

The battles of Arras

On 20 May, *2.Panzerdivision (XIX.AK)* reached the Channel and took Abbeville. Most of the French, Belgian and British forces were trapped between von Bock's and von Rundstedt's army groups. The next day at 2.30 p.m., the counterattack launched by the 5th and 13th Infantry Divisions clashed violently with *7.Panzerdivision* and *Totenkopf* south of Arras.

A gunner and his loader open fire with their *MG 34* machine gun. This weapon had an extremely high rate of fire (800 to 900 rounds a minute). At this rate, the belts of fifty cartridges each were quickly emptied. (NA)

A czech *MG* (*ZB-53*) on a tripod mount for antiaerial purpose. Heavily outnumbered, the French aviation forces never threatened the German progress on the battlefield. This photograph, which is not dated, certainly shows this *MG* crew on a training session. (Private collection)

A well camouflaged *Pak 35/36* on the edge of a road, preparing to open fire. Relatively efficient against light armored vehicles, this antitank gun was useless against heavy tanks such as the British *Matildas*. Its shells bounced off the armor plating of the tanks and this unexpected failure caused panic amongst the German ranks. (NA)

A destroyed *"Mathilda"* is being closely examined. *Totenkopf* lost many antitank guns during this tragic day but, more than the equipment losses, the psychological shock caused by the British tanks was a heavy blow to the SS. (Chr. Belser Verlag)

Soldiers from *Totenkopf* and the *Luftwaffe* side by side watching this 88 mm gun firing at the British tanks. (Chr. Belser Verlag)

A Czech *ZB-53* machine gun in action. (Chr. Belser Verlag)

Victorious pose around the *Renault B1 bis* "Belfort II" of the *37ᵉ BCC*, according to the writing on the back of the photograph, in the Arras region. In fact, the "Belfort II" is burned having rolled on a mine in the sector of Namur in Belgium. Note that most of the men on this photograph are wearing map pouches. (Private collection.)

Below: Numerous villages bear the dramatic scars of the fighting, extremely fierce in this area. (Heimdal collection.)

The advance towards the Aire canal at La Bassée

After being delayed for an entire day by the British counter-attack at Arras, the German general staff decided to eliminate the allied pocket and launched Hoepner's *XVI.AK* (*Totenkopf, SS-Verfügungsdivision, 3.Panzerdivision* and *4.Panzerdivision*) to the north in the morning of May 22. The objective was first to prevent the British from taking control along the Aire canal at La Bassée.

On May 22, *SS-T.IR 2* was driving towards Béthune. An SS column crossing a village where civilian refugees have abandoned many of their belongings on the footpaths. Some military equipment can be seen in the piles: a situation very similar to that found by the SS on the same day at Aubigny… (Private collection.)

The SS have reached the canal and take advantage of its high banks to shelter from firing from the other side. In the background, we can see low-flying *Do-17* bombers. (Private collection.)

A soldier belonging to one of the division infantry regiments in the canal sector. Note the helmet bearing the swastika and the SS eagle sewn on the left arm of the tunic. (Heimdal collection.)

A row of captured French artillery guns. (Heimdal collection.)

A curious scene: French prisoners spread out across this plain. Could they be surrendering, although this is unlikely considering their attitude? (Heimdal collection.)

Fighting is fierce and losses are heavy on both sides. A situation that the author of the photograph, an anonymous veteran of the division, wanted to portray. (Heimdal collection.)

In the chronological order of the photographer, we find a picture of a *Bloch MB-210* captured by men of *Totenkopf*. Was there an aerodrome in the Béthune region with a bomber unit, or was it a filing error by our veteran? (Heimdal collection.)

Motorcyclists getting their food from a truck converted into a "chuck-wagon". During the French campaign, the division reconnaissance battalion was more involved in fighting than in discovery missions. (Heimdal collection.)

British two-pounder antitank gun set up at the side of a road. It has probably been abandoned by its crew. (Heimdal collection.)

British soldiers are taken to the rear after being captured in the Cornet Malo sector. A scene which might not appear as innocent as it seems, if we remember the atrocity of the Le Paradis massacre. (Private collection.)

Opposite: Two exceptional documents: action shots taken by a soldier from the division during the battle for Le Cornet Malo. The postures of the soldiers are not necessarily flattering, but the tension of the extremely tough fighting in the sector can be felt on their faces. (Private collection.)

Opposite: The same soldier photographed the grave of two of his comrades killed in action. The division suffered terrible losses here, not only due to the stiff resistance of the British troops but also because of the officers' inexperience. The officers were not always up to the situation: according to statements from two of his subordinates, *SS-Ostuf.* Heinrich Albrecht, head of *5.Kp./SS-T.IR 2*, hid in a hole throughout the battle, leaving the attack in the hands of his section leader. Due to his cowardice, he was transferred to a non-fighting unit after the campaign. (Private collection.)

To Calais

After the terrible battle for Le Cornet Malo, Totenkopf continued its advance northwards and broke through the Franco-British defensive line, hastily set up along the Lys.

Motorcyclists from the division in a devastated town. Is it Bailleul? (Heimdal collection.)

May 29. Lull in the fighting. This infantry section grouped together in front of the café next to Bailleul church for a photograph. (Heimdal collection.)

A stout *Spiess* (company adjutant, identifiable by the white bands at the bottom of his sleeves) has found something to spice up his daily ration. (Heimdal collection.)

A group of soldiers having a good time! A 2nd class wearing a priest's hat playing the fool on a British motorbike, as his amused comrades look on. (Heimdal collection.)

A soldier from the division posing on a *Somua S-35* tank knocked out along a road strewn with military debris. (Heimdal collection.)

Another tank destroyed by numerous direct hits. This time, it is a small *Renault R-35* light tank. (Heimdal collection.)

Group of soldiers around a *"Lorraine" 37L* tank supply tractor, still in working order. The photograph shows men from the division and *Luftwaffe* soldiers, probably from a *Flak* unit. (Heimdal collection.)

A vehicle towing a *3.7 cm Pak* crosses a bridge in an unidentified town in the north of France. (Heimdal collection.)

Collection of vehicles from the division, in Bailleul. (Heimdal collection.)

The division crossing a French town. The photographer wrote on the back of the photograph that it is Tourcoing. Can one of the readers confirm? (Private collection.)

Scene of destruction in Calais. Various military vehicles and buildings damaged during the fighting. (Private collection.)

Fall Rot: Totenkopf pressing on towards the South of France

On June 14, the Germans captured Paris and Hitler ordered that the offensive should continue south of the river Marne. On June 15, _Totenkopf_ crossed the river Seine at Nogent. The next day it was ordered to head towards Lyon, to cut off the line of retreat of the French forces isolated in Alsace.

Right: A 37 mm antitank gun has been set up at the corner of a street. (Chr. Belser Verlag)

A _Mercedes_ truck on the Boulogne-sur-Mer road. According to the legend at the time, the men giving the Nazi salute on the side of the road were Dutch members of Anton Mussert's National Socialist Movement, expatriated on orders from the Den Hag government before the arrival of the Germans. (Chr. Belser Verlag)

SS-Stubaf. Sander (in the center of the photograph with motorcyclist's goggles on his cap) with members of his staff. Hans Sander (SS-Nr. 314 232) was to command the artillery regiment of the *"Frundsberg"* division from February 15 and was promoted to *SS-Standartenführer* on April 20. In July 1944, he was to replace *SS-Oberführer* Bock at the head of the *II.SS-Pz.Korps* artillery, a position which he held until October 25, 1944. In January 1945, he became *Arko* of *XIII.SS-AK* then *Arko* of *XII.SS-AK* from April 1945. (Chr. Belser Verlag)

A Ford truck crossing a river on a bridge which has just been finished by the division's sappers. (Chr. Belser Verlag)

A destroyed bridge over the river Seine. German engineers are at work. (Heimdal collection.)

SS Infantrymen take a french village by storm, somewhere in the Lyons area. (NA)

The antitank battalion advances along a road at the foot of a village high up the hillside. The air threat is virtually non-existent and the recommended distances between two vehicles are not respected. (Heimdal collection.)

During the rush of *XIV.AK* towards Lyons, *Totenkopf* used virtually the same route as *10.Panzerdivision*: SS and Heer soldiers often found themselves on the same roads. This superb photograph from the album of an SS veteran shows scouts from *Aufkl.-Abt.(mot.)90* next to their *Sd.Kfz.232* heavy armored car. (Private collection.)

The number of prisoners captured continues to increase. There is no longer any doubt as to the German victory. (Heimdal collection.)

Short break in a typical countryside setting. (Heimdal collection.)

Soldiers getting water (?) from a tanker. The end of the fighting is close and the men are relaxed. (Heimdal collection.)

Milk ration: a soldier, probably a farmer in civilian life, milking a cow for his comrades. (Heimdal collection.)

June 19, 1940, in the Lyons region. A column from *Totenkopf* has stopped on the side of the road to allow *Pzkpfw.II* from *10.Panzerdivision* to pass, which is rather strange since this division was supposed to precede Theodor Eicke's division! (Private collection.)

A *Panhard* armored car has been captured by soldiers from the division and reused immediately by the reconnaissance battalion to replace the destroyed or broken down Czech tanks. (Chr. Belser Verlag)

The division traveled hundreds of kilometers to go from the Lyons region to the Basque Country via Orléans! (Heimdal collection.)

When consulting the *SS-PK* archives, you are struck by the incredible number of photographs taken of colored prisoners, whether during the French campaign or on the Eastern front. This is due to the Nazi regime's racist policy, since these photographs would be used in propaganda against the dangers supposedly threatening Western civilization. (NA)

Native Senegalese infantrymen. They were amongst the 62 colored soldiers captured out of the 6088 prisoners taken by the division since crossing the river Marne. Speaking about the French prisoners, the head of the 3rd bureau of *Gruppe "von Kleist"* wrote in a report: *"The prisoners try to get friendly with our soldiers. They have no idea of the real situation … Most of them do not seem to understand just how serious their situation is."* (NA)

Even more surprising is the fact that soldiers themselves also took a large number of photographs of colored men for their personal albums, proof that the Nazi racist propaganda has been most efficient. (Heimdal collection.)

June 22, 1940. *Totenkopf* is going back towards the Loire where numerous bridges had been destroyed by the retreating French army. (Private collection.)

Opposite on the left and top of opposite page: June 27, 1940. Hitler ordered the division not to stop in Bordeaux: the men were forbidden to leave their vehicles, for political reasons. The provisional French government was in fact in the city. (Heimdal collection.)

The division is traveling as fat as it can to reach the Atlantic coast. The journey is exhausting men and the men are taking a short break here, along the roadside (opposite page). A look-out has been posted nearby, although the cease-fire has already been signed. (Private collection.)

Upgraded to the rank of *SS-Sturmbannführer* on the 9th of November 1941, Fritz Harjenstein did such a terrible job leading *I./SS-T.IR 3* during winter 1941-1942, that Eicke transferred him in August 1942, giving him the head of the guards detachment in the Auschwitz camp till the 10th of March 1943. After that, he became commandant of the Birkenau death camp. In May 1944, he was transferred to the concentration camp of Natzweiler, in Alsace. Captured by the French in 1945, he was sentenced to death, but died of a heart attack in Metz in 1954. (RR)

Paul-Werner Hoppe was seriously injured during the battles of spring 1942. After his convalescence, he was appointed to the head of the guards detachment in the Auschwitz camp. Upgraded *SS-Sturmbannführer* on the 1st of September 1942; at the end of the war, he was commanding the Stutthof concentration camp. Hoppe was sentenced to nine years' imprisonment and died in 1974. (Rights reserved)

Occupation of France

From June 29, *SS-T.IR 3* set up base along the Atlantic coast south of Arcachon up to Saint Julien. *SS-T.IRs 1* and *2* guarded the demarcation line. *Totenkopf* left the Landes on July 13 and after three days walking reached the region of Avallon. It was attached to *XIV.AK*. Theodor Eicke, who had gone for a few days holiday at Oranienburg, was replaced by *SS-Brigaf.* Knoblauch. Following orders from von Weichs, the SS troops of *Totenkopf* reopened the schools, public services and even some factories in the Avallon region so that life could return to normal. The division's doctors also provided medical care to the civilian population.

At this time, new recruits, drafted to make up for the losses but in particular to replace the reservists who were demobilized, arrived from Germany. From July 31 to August 6, *SS-T. Inf.Ers.-Btl. III "Breslau"* transferred 500 recruits and *SS-T.Inf.Ers.-Btl. I* another 400 men.

In August, the division took part in the harvesting, not to help the French farmers but for the benefit of the German military authorities. It was even supported by a contingent of French prisoners.

At the start of September, the division returned to the south of Bordeaux where it was under the orders of *I.AK*. A number of changes took place in the senior ranks: in *SS-T.IR 2*, *SS-Staf.* Bertling, disliked by Theodor Eicke, was replaced by *SS-Staf.* Karl Herrmann. In the artillery regiment, *SS-Staf.* Allihn was replaced by *SS-Ostubaf.* Priess, who was in turn replaced at the nead of *II./SS-T.Art.-Rgt.* by *SS-Hstuf.* Stange.

Training resumed, now with the experience gained during fighting. Not prepared to be taken for a fool again, Theodor Eicke was determined to transform his division into a shock force. To achieve this goal, he accelerated the demobilization of the oldest soldiers, replacing them by younger recruits. A large number of the former *SS-TV* troops were therefore sent back to the concentration camps where they resumed their dreadful duties. Hundreds of the oldest *Allgemeine-SS* reservists were also demobilized. On leaving the division, they had to sign a paper swearing to keep secret everything they had seen in their unit during the Western campaign, indirect proof of the atrocities inflicted against the civilian population and the prisoners of war.

Reorganization of the division

On November 1, 1940, *Totenkopf* was attached to *XXXI.AK*. Training continued and, at the same time, the division started to replace its obsolete equipment with more modern weapons: Czech machine guns, for example, were replaced by the famous *MG-34*. On December 20, *SS-Stubaf.* Heinz Lammerding became the division's new *Ia* (*1.Generalstabs-Offizier*). In May 1941, the engineer battalion was placed under the command of *SS-Stubaf.* Ullrich. In January 1941, further transfers were carried out in the senior ranks.

The start of 1941 saw a significant increase in the size of the division. On April 8, the *RF-SS* ordered the creation of a *Flak* group at Dachau. It included a battery of 8.8 cm guns, one of 3.7 cm guns and one of 2 cm guns. A machine gun company was also created for the reconnaissance group. It was equipped with *Sd.Kfz.221* and *222* and *Sd.Kfz.232* armored cars. On May 9, the heavy artillery group was renamed *IV./SS-T.Art.-Rgt.* and its batteries were renumbered from 10 to 12. The strengthening of the division was not simply restricted to equipment. Aware of the lack of skilled officers in the senior ranks, Theodor Eicke sent 86 members of the division to the Bad Tölz and Braunschweig officer training schools.

During the first three months of 1941, the following officers left the Division :

- *SS-Hstuf.* Franke-Gricksch, Benner, Hardieck (*Div.-Stab*)
- *SS-Stubaf.* Deisenhofer, *SS-Hstuf.* Stolley, Kron and Schulz (*SS-T.IR 1*)
- *SS-Ostubaf.* Lippert, *SS-Hstuf.* Spanka, Dallinger, Kaltofen and Frank (*SS-T.IR 2*)
- *SS-Stubaf.* Dusenschön, *SS-Hstuf.* Molt, Braun, Baier, Brinkmann (SS-T.IR 3)
- *SS-Stubaf.* Leiner, *SS-Ostuf.* Bildstein, *SS-Ustuf.* Unterkofler (*SS-T.Pz.Jg.-Abt.*)
- *SS-Staf.* Tschimpke (*SS-Div.-Nachschubdienste*)

They were replaced by these :
- *II./SS-T.IR 1*: *SS-Hstuf.* Wilhelm Schulze (ex *13.(IG)Kp./SS-Rgt.* "Germania")
- *II./SS-T.IR 2*: *SS-Hstuf.* Jakob Kommer (ex *SS-Division "Reich"*)
- *III./SS-T.IR 3*: *SS-Hstuf.* Otto Baum (ex *8.Kp./"LSSAH"*)
- *SS-T.Pz.Jg.-Abt.*: SS-Stubaf. Hermann Frimmersdorf (ex *SS-Pz.Jg.-Abt. "Reich"*)
- *SS-Div. Nachsch.-Dienste*: SS-Hstuf. Fritz Hartjenstein (ex *Kdt. Div.-Stabsquartier*)

Following orders from *AOK 7*, *Totenkopf* was relieved on May 17 to 21 by *212.ID* then transferred to the Parthenay - Niort - Saintes - Melle sector where it was placed under the authority of *Gen.Kdo. LIX.AK*. On May 27, still as part of the program to increase the strength of the division, a *Feldersatz-Bataillon* was created at Brno (Brünn) from *II./SS-T.IR 2* (recently dissolved, apart from *8./SS-T.IR 2*). Its commander was *SS-Stubaf.* Kommer.

On May 30, the division received orders to board rail convoys for a yet unknown destination. On June 9, after six days traveling via the Lorraine, Marburg, Frankfurt-am-Oder, Poznan and Hohensalza, the *Totenkopf* convoys reached Eastern Prussia. From June 10, the units started to set up camp south east of Marienwerder.

Above: Walter Reder took command of *3.Kp./SS-T.IR 2* on 21 July 1940 and then served as 03 (third ordnance officer) in the division's staff from 25 August 1940. On 26 April 1941, he was transferred to the staff of *SS-T.IR 1* as *Führer z.b.V.*. (Courtesy Tim Willemsen.)

Left: *SS-Sturmbannführer* Fortenbacher is leaving. He is making his farewell to Walter Reder. The officer observing the scene could be Fritz Knöchlein. (Collection Jean-Louis Roba)

This portrait of *SS-Sturmbannführer* Eduard Deisenhofer was published in *Das Schwarze Korps*. He is the *II./ SS-T.IR 1* commander since 1 November 1939. He joined the *SS* ranks as soon as October 1930 and his *SS* number is consequently very low (3642). He is to leave the division on 3 March 1941 to take the lead of the newly raised *II./SS-Freiwilligen-Regiment "Nordwest"*. (Courtesy Martin Månsson)

The bakers' company from the ordnance troops.

Logistic support units were hardly ever photographed because, however vital to a division, their daily tasks didn't bring them much glory.

On this picture, loaves of bread are being loaded into the tipper of a vehicle from the first floor of French barracks occupied by the *SS*. This ingenious though rudimentary ramp avoids needless handling. (NA)

Inside the bakery. Every day, the company had to make several thousands of loaves in ovens like these. (NA)

The supply in wood for the ovens required flawless logistics. It is worth noting that the *SS* didn't change signs on the building. (NA)

68

The division is behaving properly with the French population, as Hitler ordered. Here is a distribution of food during winter 40-41. (Heimdal collection.)

A little break on a bench, at the bottom of a big farm typical of the Landes region. These not so young reservists may be waiting for their demobilization. (Private collection.)

The division and the lessons of the French campaign.

After the French campaign, Theodor Eicke and his staff were quick to draw lessons from the battles: officers who hadn't been up to the task, either because they had proved incompetent or cowardly, were transferred to other units, and the oldest reservists were demobilized and replaced by much younger men. Thanks to the experience acquired during those fights and the granting of more modern equipment, the division became much more fearsome than it had been several months before.

1. At the end of June 1940. In the Landes region, drill starts again, but apparently in a much more relaxed way. This picture shows a shooting drill with captured French machine guns. (Private collection.)

2. A group of infantrymen in combat dress somewhere in the Landes forest during summer 1940. (Private collection.)

3. July 1940. The weather is splendid and men make the most of it by going for a dip in the rollers of the Atlantic Ocean, or taking a walk along the never-ending beaches of the Landes' coast. (Private collection.).

4. Summer 1940. The division leaves momentarily the Landes to go to the area of Auxerre, south-east of Paris. A short lunch-break on the roads leading to Burgundy. (Private collection.)

A *Ford G917T* on the roads of France. The "N" stands for *"Nachschub"*, it is thus a vehicle from the supply corps. (Private collection.)

Village of Provency (?). Three men from the division are posing for posterity. From left to right: *SS-Uscha.* Heitz, *SS-Rttf.* Meyer and *SS-Uscha.* Schulz. (Private collection.)

Provency (?). Men from a service corps column during a snack organized in summer 1940. (Private collection.)

Surveillance of Auxerre's prisoners camp. Since the task isn't really demanding, officers use this opportunity to enhance the training of their men. (Private collection.)

Autumn-winter 1940-1941. Drill resumes in the Landes, now with the benefit of the ever so precious experience acquired in combat. (Private collection.)

Two infantrymen in their drill dress, covered in sweat and mud. "Sweat spares blood" was the SS drill officers' motto. (Private collection.)

Marching follows marching. These men look really confident. Some of them, probably new recruits from the *SS-Verfügungstruppe*, still carry the SS rune on their collar, and not the death's-head characteristic of the division and the *SS-Totenkopfverbände*. (Private collection.)

Road movement drill for the crew of this *Hanomag Sturm Modell 1937/38*. (Private collection.)

Opposite: Marches and drills in close order alternate according to a specific pattern. (Heimdal collection.)

An engineers' battalion in Podensac during the ceremony of the 20th of April 1941 celebrating Hitler's birthday. On the left is *SS-Hstuf.* Erich Becker (*Btl.-Fhr.*), in the middle *SS-Hstuf.* Max Seela, and on the right *SS-Ostuf.* Hans Paetznik (*Btl.-Adj.*). (Private collection.)

Men off-duty, on a spree in Mont-de-Marsan. (Private collection.)

Soldiers on leave in Germany. They are welcomed at the station by their wives; two men are wearing a 2nd class Iron Cross. (Private collection.)

Those who didn't get the chance to go to Germany on leave find ways to pass the time between drills. This soldier, who might have been a farmer in civilian life, is trying his hand at driving a French tractor. (Private collection.)

A field officer is welcomed in the barracks yard in Mont-de-Marsan. (Private collection.)

Motorized march drill in autumn 1940. The division was far from perfect in this matter. But with the experience gathered during the French campaign, there is considerable improvement. (Private collection.)

A road accident. Men do not seem to care. (Private collection.)

A one-ton light tractor (Sd.Kfz.10) is being washed in a farmyard. (Heimdal collection.)

This model of side-car is quite rare: it is a 600 ccm motorbike of type Victoria KR 6 Bergmeister mit Seitenwagen. Production stopped in 1938. In this configuration, the vehicle can't go faster than 85 km/h, and has only a range of 250 km. (Private collection.)

1. Given the sentinel on guard in front of this large house in Burgundy, one can guess that headquarters have been set there. (Heimdal collection.)

2. Excellent photograph of an *SS-Unterscharführer* from the division who has been decorated with a 2nd class Iron Cross and the wound medal. Note the double armband for *Heimwehr Danzig* and *SS-Totenkopf-Standarte "Oberbayern"*; the latter model, with a death's-head, was introduced in September 1938. (Private collection.)

3. The division is in charge of guarding the demarcation line; here is a checkpoint. (Heimdal collection.)

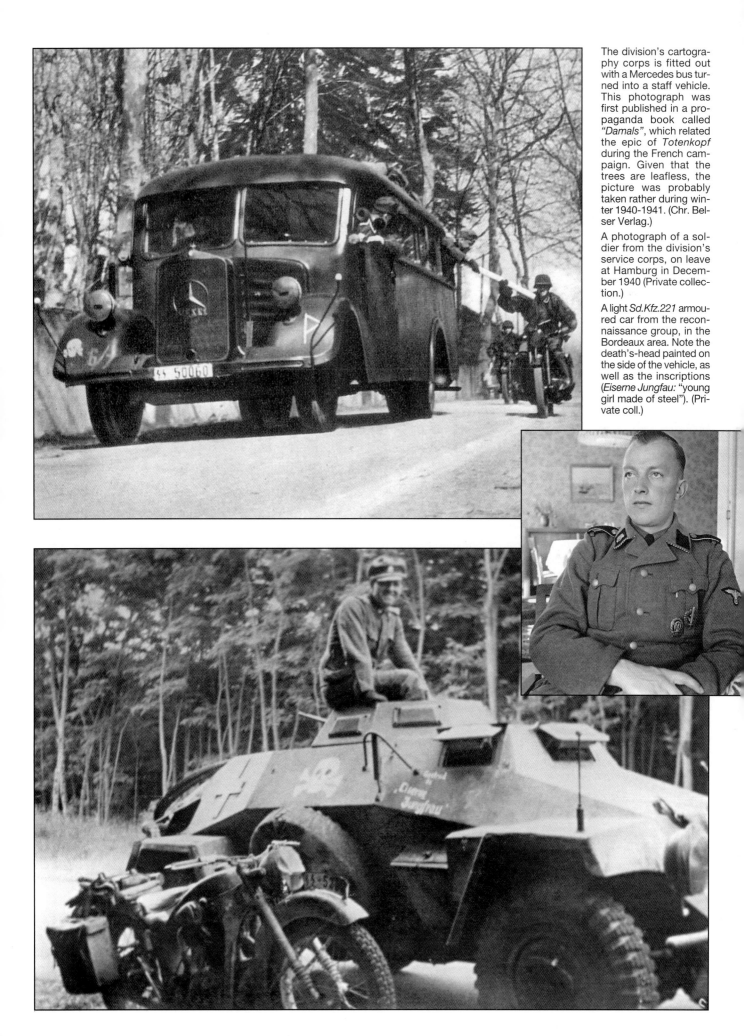

The division's cartography corps is fitted out with a Mercedes bus turned into a staff vehicle. This photograph was first published in a propaganda book called *"Damals"*, which related the epic of *Totenkopf* during the French campaign. Given that the trees are leafless, the picture was probably taken rather during winter 1940-1941. (Chr. Belser Verlag.)

A photograph of a soldier from the division's service corps, on leave at Hamburg in December 1940 (Private collection.)

A light *Sd.Kfz.221* armoured car from the reconnaissance group, in the Bordeaux area. Note the death's-head painted on the side of the vehicle, as well as the inscriptions (*Eiserne Jungfau:* "young girl made of steel"). (Private coll.)

A report on the division's Instandsetzungsstaffel, made in France at the end of winter 1941.

A truck from this repair echelon has partially fallen on the ditch along a country road in the Landes region. (Private collection.)

A *Feldgendarme* comes to secure the road and improve traffic. The damaged truck is a four-ton *Matford F917WS* driven by a 3.6 litres V8 engine. Many French vehicles like this one were put into service by the German army. (Private collection.)

1. A wheel is being changed on a car from the repair echelon. Note how both mechanics are well on in years. (Private collection.)

2. These men from the repair echelon are wearing camouflage overalls. Apparently, they've taken in a puppy on the side of the road during a stop. (Private collection.)

3. Maintenance and cleaning of vehicles, here three-ton *Opel Blitz*. (Private collection.)

4. A halt along the road, spring 1941. (Private collection.)

Invasion of the Soviet Union Operation "Barbarossa"

Beginning of operations

To invade the Soviet Union, the *OKH* split its troops into three army groups: von Rundstedt's *Heeresgruppe "Süd"*, aiming at the Donets Basin, von Bock's *Heeresgruppe "Mitte"*, aiming at Moscow, and von Leeb's *Heeresgruppe "Nord"*, aiming at Leningrad, a city eight hundred kilometres from its base. The latter was composed of twenty infantry divisions, three armoured divisions and three motorized infantry divisions, divided up into *16.Armee*, *18.Armee* and *Panzergruppe 4*. Its mission was to wipe out enemy Soviet units that were stationed at intervals down to Ostrow and Pskow (Pleskau). The first major obstacle was the Daugava (Düna in German): to cover the three hundred kilometres separating the troops from it, *Heeresgruppe "Nord"* gathered its motorized divisions inside *Panzergruppe 4*, that comprised two army corps: *XXXXI.AK* and the *LVI.AK (mot.)*, with the *1.*, *6.* and *8.Panzerdivisionen*, *3.ID (mot.)*, *269.ID* and *290.ID*. From the 9th of June 1941, *Totenkopf* was attached to *Generaloberst* Hoepner's *Panzergruppe 4*. But Hoepner kept a low opinion of *Totenkopf*, and especially of Theodor Eicke: therefore he decided to keep it as reserve, even though he had very few motorized units at his disposal.

On the evening of June 21st, men were informed that the war against the Soviet Union would break out the next day. They were ordered to execute all the political representatives of the Red Army. This measure concerned both the *Waffen-SS* and the *Wehrmacht*. The Germans took it as an excuse that the Soviets hadn't signed the Geneva Convention. Thus, they shouldn't expect the Germans to be merciful, just as the Germans didn't expect them to be. Besides, the "Barbarossa" decree from the 13th of May allowed acts of violence against enemy prisoners or the population, as long as it didn't interfere with combat discipline. Finally, a decree about "the troops' behaviour in Russia", passed at the very beginning of the invasion, ordered German units to act roughly against partisans, saboteurs and Jews.

On the **22nd of June 1941**, war against the USSR broke out. On the very first day, *Panzergruppe 4* managed to break through enemy defences. On the 24th of June, *8.Panzerdivision* (LVI.AK) seized Ukmerge (Wilkomierz). The German offensive was at its height. Meanwhile, *Totenkopf* was restless. But just before eight o'clock in the evening, it received at last the order to reach the Raseiniai area. Thus the division started out.

On the **26th**, *Totenkopf* was assigned to close the gap that inevitably formed between von Manstein's *LVI.AK (mot.)* – which made more than a two hundred kilometre headway in three days – and the infantry divisions from *16.Armee* (Busch), advancing at the pace of its infantrymen. The next day, the division's headquarters settled in Saukura. *Totenkopf*'s progress was only hampered by the state of the roads, that put drivers and mechanics to the test. To this point, the Red Army didn't show much resistance: isolated soldiers and Russian deserters gave themselves up in towns the divisions' convoys went through. On the other hand, the forests were packed with Soviet units, certainly

surpassed by the fast progression of Hoepner's troops, but nevertheless ready to fight. Hence, the division's reconnaissance battalion (*SS-Stubaf.* Bestmann) was severely challenged and lost eleven men around Ukmerge. During the day, the division arrived at Ukmerge where it was joined to *LVI.AK (mot.)*. It received the order to take over from the troops of *3.ID (mot.)* in Zarasai.

On the **28th of June**, *Totenkopf* cleaned the Stelmuze - Turmantas area, where there were still many groups of isolated Soviet soldiers. This was caused by the lightning progression of panzer divisions, who didn't bother about the subsequent threat that would hang over their flanks and back. Meanwhile, *8.Panzerdivision* and *3.ID (mot.)* devoted themselves to enlarge the Daugavpils bridgehead established the day before on the Daugava, so as to prepare the offensive against Latvia. On the **29th of June**, these units were backed up by *SS-T.IR 1*: Max Simon's regiment was to attack along the Dunskaja - Isvalta road. In the meantime, much of the division gathered to reach Daugavpils via Zarasai, except *SS-T.IR 2*, who was put at the disposal of the *LVI.AK (mot.)* in Kalkuni.

On the **30th of June**, following an order from *LVI.AK (mot.)*, the division moved to the corps' right flank and took care of the area between the Daugava and the Skeltovo - Auleja - Dagda road. After a fierce battle, *Totenkopf* reached the line Uzinavka - Izvalta - Lieltruli. In many cases, the Soviets fought to death without yielding. Izvalta, for instance, was taken after a battle during which hardly any Soviet soldier surrendered. In such conditions, men had to fight hand-to-hand for every inch of ground, for every house. *SS-T.IR 3* reported losses its officers found much too heavy.

Combats in Latvia

At the beginning of July, *Panzergruppe 4* was ordered to break through the "Stalin" line in the Ostrow – Opotschka area, before Soviet units could entrench themselves behind it. Traps and ambushes slowed down the German progress. But the awful state of the roads was what delayed *Totenkopf* most. The region was particularly wild, with dark forests, lakes and swamps. The only roads available were just narrow sandy paths many vehicles got stuck in. Men and engines suffered. *LVI.AK (mot.)* moved into the attack again on the **2nd of July**. *Totenkopf*'s mission was to protect its right flank. The attack on Kraslava was launched at three o'clock in the morning. The Soviets resisted fiercely. *III./SS-T.IR 1* was stopped right away and didn't seem to be able to go on with the fight. Its comander, *SS-Hstuf.* Kurtz, was fatally wounded and replaced by *SS-Hstuf.* Witte. Then *SS-Stubaf.* Becker's *I./SS-T.IR 1* was called to smash the Soviet bolt. At 7 pm, he seized Kraslava, regardless of the two regiments backed up by tanks and infantry defending it. This first real battle gave the Germans a foretaste of things to come. Soviet soldiers had preferred to be killed on the spot rather than recede. Such die-hard behaviour made the SS think they weren't regular soldiers but communist irregulars. So from then on, the division took the habit of not making too many prisoners.

SS-T.IR 3 seized Dagda on the **3rd of July** after a violent fight, and then Zilupe on the following day. On the **5th of July**, *Totenkopf* was told to cross the border between Latvia and Russia to reach the Dubrowka – Sebesh line. This was no easy task, since the Soviets were firmly settled on the hills east of Zilupe, but the mission was essential to the offensive of *LVI.AK (mot.)*.

The battle for the "Stalin" line

The "Stalin" line was a fortified line about eight kilometres deep, a network of concrete bunkers, machine guns nests, buried tanks, minefields and various traps. It was built along the Soviet border with Latvia and Estonia. It was a large but not insurmountable obstacle. Indeed, the Soviets hadn't had time to finish the fortification works and there were still many flaws in the defence line.

On the **6th of July**, preceded by a violent artillery barrage, the *Totenkopf* men launched an attack from Zilupe. In the afternoon, they broke through the Soviet positions. But for the SS, it was the hardest battle since the beginning of the Eastern campaign. They had to take by assault every bunker, every trench, every nest of machine guns. Losses added up to 50 killed and 160 injured! Around midnight, while going back from a conference at von Manstein's headquarters, Theodor Eicke's vehicle blew up on a mine. He was injured, and had to be hospitalized in Lauderi. The head of the division was therefore passed on to *SS-Staf.* Kleinheisterkamp, who was replaced by *SS-Ostubaf.* Becker at the head of *SS-T.IR 3*.

The following day, after vicious combats, the SS penetrated the suburbs of Opotschka at about 9.30 pm, and in fear of an enemy counter-attack, buried themselves right away. The enemy did attack at about 3 am. The Germans had difficulty stopping them. Under much pressure, they had to withdraw till the heights where Max Simon's headquarters were. Max Simon was ordered to resist till there was only one man standing, and swore to abide by it! The battle was fierce, with the SS preferring to get killed rather than to retreat. The Soviets were finally pushed back to their initial positions, but this combat inflicted heavy losses on the SS.

On the **8th of July**, battle was still harsh for the division opposite Opotschka on the fortifications of the "Stalin" line. The Soviets brought new troops for backup, and for the first time since the beginning of the campaign, the SS had to face numerous tanks, especially some *KV-2*, strongly armoured but heavy and hard to manoeuvre: they were easy targets for the *Panzerjäger* that stopped them aiming at their caterpillar tracks, and then let the sappers destroy them with magnetic mines. Sebesh finally fell at 4.45 pm. Meanwhile, *SS-T.IR 1* failed to reach Opotschka because it was attacked by the Soviet first armoured corps, and its contacts with division headquarters were repetitively cut. *SS-Staf.* Simon was injured that day, and then replaced by *SS-Ostubaf.* Becker, who left the head of *SS-T.IR 3* to *SS-Staf.* Herrmann. The next day, *SS-Kampfgruppe "Herrmann"*, composed of *SS-T.IR 2* and *SS-T.IR 3*, was to attack Opotschka from Sebesh, so as to back up *SS-Kampfgruppe "Simon"*. But around noon, crisis in Opotschka reached its peak: the head of the division found itself surrounded. Fortunately for them, thanks to reconnaissance planes, enemy batteries in Opotschka were located and destroyed. At about 10 pm, after several hours of bitter combat, elements from *SS-T.IR 3* were able at last to make contact with division staff.

On the 10th of July, *III./SS-T.IR 3* managed to skirt round the Soviet defence from the west and to besiege Opotschka from the north. At 11.15 am, the town finally fell into the hands of the *SS*. This was undeniable victory, but Pyrrhic nonetheless: Totenkopf reported 164 soldiers dead (including 10 officers), 340 injured (including 58 officers) and 34 missing from the beginning of the "Barbarossa". To compensate these heavy losses, *SS-T.IR 1* and *3* were sent soldiers from the *I.* and *III./SS-T.IR 2*, and from *SS-T.IR 2* unranked companies, units that were immediately dissolved. However, there were some positive results as well: the "Stalin" line was perforated for good, and what remained of Soviet defenders were withdrawing towards north-east.

Offensive towards the Mschaga

Once the "Stalin" line was breached, only one major obstacle remained for the Germans to clear on their way to Leningrad: the Luga. *XXXXI.AK (mot.)* had to attack between the lakes of Peipous and Ilmen to reach Leningrad, and *LVI.AK (mot.)* had to cut the road Moscow - Leningrad around Nowgorod, a city on the north bank of Lake Ilmen. *Totenkopf* was at first kept as reserve in the area of Porchow, a road and rail junction along the Shelon.

On the **18th of July**, *SS-Brigaf.* Georg Keppler took the head of the division. His arrival coincided with *Totenkopf*'s return to operation. The division's men had just made the most of the last days of rest they would know for a very long time; indeed, they were about to reach the front and fight there ceaselessly for more than a year!

On the night from the 18th to the 19th of July, *Totenkopf* replaced *8.Panzerdivision* in the area of Lemno. On the **20th**, *SS-T.IR 1* attacked towards the heights of Dubrowy. These hills overlooked the whole region, and especially the regiment's zone of approach. It was fiercely defended by the Soviets. On the following day, *SS-T.IR 1* carried on with its attack towards the railroad west of Szoltzy. On the **22nd of July**, *Totenkopf* kept on moving east and north-east on a muddy ground totally unsuitable for the deployment of a motorized division. Impassable ground considerably favoured defenders. The Soviets proved particularly brave and tenacious fighters. Tough and strong, they were way fitter for this type of territory than the Germans. Not only did they cling to their positions, but they also launched several murderous counter-attacks: for instance, on the night of the 22nd, they forced *SS-T.IR 1* to withdraw as far as the Possoschwa area. Their stubborn resistance could only come as an unpleasant surprise for the SS, who were still thoroughly imbued with Nazi propaganda portraying the Soviets as a bunch of "sub-humans".

On the **25th of July**, the division's mission was to pursue the Soviets to the Luga, via Stary Mjedwjed and Bol. Ugorody. At this point, men had been squelching through the mud and fighting continuously against a fierce opponent for six days. The muddy ground made supplying an issue, as vehicles often got bogged down and much energy was spent to have them move again. Besides, contacts between units were uneasy: couriers were often shot by snipers waiting in ambush on tree tops. It all started to affect the morale of the troops. Men were exhausted: they had to attack during the day, and then to repel counter-attacks from the Soviets at night. Losses were heavy. In three days only, the division had 91 men killed, 406 injured and 5 missing!

On the **26th of July**, *Totenkopf* made another attack up north, to drive the Soviets beyond the Mschaga between Mjedwjed and Sakibje. On the following day, in order to carry on the offensive towards Leningrad, *Heeresgruppe "Nord"* modified its plan of action: *I.AK* (*11.ID* and *21.ID*) was now depended on *16.Armee*, whose objective was Nowgorod. Between *LVI.AK (mot)* and *I.AK* came another army corps: General Wiktorin's *XXVIII. AK*, which was now in charge of the whole marshy area. *Totenkopf* was joined to it. In its sector, the front was stabilized on the Mschaga.

On the **30th of July**, *XXVIII.AK* was told to attack towards the Luga river, and to push north of it the Soviet units that could jeopardize the progress of *Panzergruppe 4* towards Leningrad. The offensive was set to happen on the 4th of August. But it was finally postponed to the 10th of August because of bad weather conditions. Such delay allowed the Soviets to build fortifications behind the Mschaga. They managed to intercept the division's phone calls and to decipher the Germans' radio messages. Furthermore, the partisans started to be active in the division's rear. Isolated posts and supply convoys got attacked. Soviet intelligence proved much more efficient than the German's, all the more so since the *Luftwaffe*, which had no petrol left and whose pilots were exhausted, had stopped reconnaissance flights over the area. On the frontline, the situation was by no means better: the Soviets had positioned new batteries east of the Mschaga and were incessantly shelling the *Totenkopf*'s positions, inflicting further losses on infantry companies. These were filled up again after the dissolve of *SS-Totenkopf-Feldersatz-Bataillon*, which counted 11 officers, 13 non-commissioned officers and 559 men. On the 8th of August, Max Simon took up again the commandment of *SS-T.IR 1*.

The battle for Sakibje

The offensive towards Sakibje started on the **10th of August**. Assault was given after considerable shelling from the artillery. *SS-T.Art.-Rgt.* shot no fewer than two thousand shells within the space of ten minutes! At 7.50 am, engineers from *16.(Pi.)Kp./SS-T.IR 3* and infantrymen from *III./SS-T.IR 3* started crossing the Mschaga on inflatable dinghies. Meanwhile, *SS-T.IR 1* crossed the Kiba under strikes from the Soviet artillery. At about 7 pm, *SS-T.IR 1* units attacked Soviet positions north-west of Sakibje. At 10 pm, the SS finally cleaned out Sakibje after rough combats. Next step was defending the bridgehead against proliferating Soviet attacks. In the meantime, a crisis burst out in the area occupied by the *16.Armee* south-east of Lake Ilmen: on the **14th of August**, the Soviets launched a dozen divisions against them, crossed the *X.AK*I's front in Ramuschewo, crossed the Lowat, the Redja, the Porussja and the Polist, went up north towards the Dno - Staraja Russa railway. Their aim was to reach Lake Peipous and thus to isolate German forces that were attacking towards Leningrad. On the **15th of August**, *Totenkopf* was given order to reach the area east and north-east of Dno. Units started off via Utorgosch, Dubrowy and Porchow towards Dno. The division reached their destination the next day.

The German counter-attack was launched on the 17th of August by *LVI.AK (mot.)*, which was formed *Totenkopf* and by *3.ID (mot.)*, against the 34th Soviet army's left flank, from Dno towards the Polist. Up north, *X.AK* was to contain Soviet attacks south and south-wet of Staraja Russa.

On the **19th**, *Totenkopf*'s assault units reached their starting positions, south-east of the Djergljetz – Wojascha line. The attack was launched at 7 am. *III./SS-T.IR 1* progressed quickly and took Ostrowo at 12.30 am. It carried on as far as the north-east part of Nikulina heights, thus cutting the withdrawal path of the Soviets. At 5.20 pm, *SS-T.IR 1* took Schilowa Gora. Meanwhile, *SS-T.IR 3* moved into the attack towards Meschuretschje and Kosnobizy. Due to the Soviet strong resistance, these targets were only reached at 7 pm. So as to prevent the Soviets from reorganizing

themselves, Manstein ordered the continuation of the offensive towards the Polist river without worrying about the situation on the flanks. Attack was launched on the **20th of August** at 5 am. *Totenkopf* made a twenty kilometres progress during the day, seizing successively Dawydowo, Tschepjentzowo and Samosche (*SS-T.IR 1*), as well as Litschino, Tschudinowo, Marinnitzy and Bory (*SS-T.IR 3*). The next day, *3.ID (mot.)* and *Totenkopf* really exploited the victories of the two previous days and annihilated the Soviet units which had been trapped on the west bank of the Polist in the Felistowo - Kassarowa sector. On top of that, *X.AK* joined the offensive and attacked from the north. The Soviets were caught on a pincer movement. Swept by *LVI.AK (mot.)*'s artillery, their losses were appalling. *Totenkopf* moved forward as if it was on parade and quickly set bridgeheads on the Polist. They reported the taking of more than a thousand prisoners that day, and the capture of huge amounts of equipment. Very few Soviet soldiers managed to escape on the west bank of the Polist. The right flank of *Heeresgruppe "Nord"* looked safe at last, but it had taken von Manstein five days to eradicate the 34th Soviet army – five days the Russians took advantage of to build up their defence before Leningrad.

On the **22nd of August**, the Redja river was crossed as well. On the following day, *Totenkopf* attacked again. Its target was now the Lowat river, the former fluvial link between Nowgorod and Kiew. Mission was accomplished at about 7.30 pm, when Kobylkino was seized.

Combats on the Lowat and the Pola

Once *Totenkopf* had reached the Lowat, it was ordered by *LVI.AK (mot.)* to settle along its banks for defence. They were joined by reinforcements: *SS-Totenkopf-Sturmgeschütz-Batterie* formed in June 1941 in Berlin, under the supervision of *SS-Hstuf.* Laackmann. From the **25th of August**, the division progressed slowly towards the Pola river, Soviet resistance was stronger than expected, and the SS had to bury themselves on captured positions. Patrols were sent towards Upolosy, Sorokopenno and Wassiljewschtschina. On these last August days, it started raining and in no time, paths turned into quagmires even vehicles with caterpillar tracks got stuck in. On the **29th**, although the Soviets were multiplying their attacks against the division's positions, von Manstein reiterated his orders for an offensive beyond the Pola. In the afternoon, Georg Keppler managed to convince him to postpone attack temporarily. Indeed, after nine weeks of continuous fighting, the *Totenkopf* was totally worn out. Exhaustion, erratic resupplying and torrential rains caused an epidemic of dysentery. Losses hadn't been compensated and vehicles were deadbeat after such long journeys on chaotic paths. On the **2nd of September**, rain was still heavy and horses started to replace vehicles to allow couriers to circulate and supplies to arrive on sledges. Worsening of conditions as regards equipment and motorization, and consequently the return to more archaic forms of war, didn't only concern *Totenkopf* but every German unit engaged on the Eastern front. The "lightning war" (*Blitzkrieg*) was just a remote memory…

On the **5th of September**, the return of milder weather allowed offensive to resume: *Totenkopf* attacked towards the Pola at 6 am. A bridgehead was established in Stepanowa regardless of fearsome barrage fire from the Russian artillery. The next day, *Totenkopf* managed to get some space and to have most of its infantry and some of its artillery crossing the Pola. The toughest part of the job was indisputably behind them. Indeed, on the **7th of September**, seeing that both *II.AK* and *X.AK* had resumed their offensive, the Soviets had to bring themselves to a general retreat. On the

8th of September, *Totenkopf* headed towards the area of Polometj. The next day, *SS-T.IR 3* led an attack on towards Demjansk. The Polometj was crossed. The SS forced themselves four kilometres into Soviet positions. However, on the **12th of September**, a revival of offensive from the Red Army forced *LVI.AK (mot.)* to adopt a more defensive approach. In the afternoon, *Totenkopf* was subordinated to *II.AK*. The latter had no reserve at its disposal, and it was thus decided that a motorcyclist battalion should be formed out of *15.(Kradsch.) Kp./SS-T.IR 1* and *3*, and the remnants of *SS-T.IR 2*. Its commander was *SS-Ostubaf.* Becker.

On the **14th of September**, the division settled down in defence on the line Krutiki - Chilkowo (*SS-T.IR 1*) - Lushno (*SS-T.IR 3*).

Defensive combats around Lushno

From mid-September, *Totenkopf* built defensive positions along the banks of the Pola. Each opponent had its own bridgeheads, so the river didn't really mark the frontline. Furthermore, terrain was made of dense forests and swamps, and thus easy to infiltrate. At about noon, the Soviets came to measure against the twenty-kilometre-long division's lines. Every company, with strength down to 70 soldiers each, had to control a kilometre of frontline. On the **17th of September**, worrying engine noises were heard beyond the frontline. It was obvious the Soviets were preparing a counter-offensive.

On the 19th, Theodor Eicke came back to the head of division. Shocked by the poor state of his troops, he immediately wrote to Karl Wolff to ask him to intercede with Hitler to give the division some rest. In vain: situation on the front required *Totenkopf* to remain on the first line.

In the morning of **September 24th**, even though it had frozen for the first time during the night, Soviet artillery and air force were very active indeed. At 11.30 am, a terrible pounding shattered SS positions on either side of the Lushno. At 12.30, the Russian suddenly came out of the forest in front of *2.Kp./SS-T.IR 3*, which was shaken and had to withdraw. *SS-Hstuf.* Thier's *II./SS-T.IR 3* was attacked by tanks coming out of the woods north of Lushno. *7.Kp./SS-T.IR 3* was hit by compact masses of infantry north-east of Lushno. At about 2 pm, the Soviets seized the town with three tanks. Then they emerged west of Lushno in compact masses. For a moment, panic seemed to seize hold of the SS ranks. Many platoons of infantrymen were seen rushing back to Hill 58 shouting *"Back! Ivan broke through our lines!"* Indeed, hundreds of Soviet soldiers had come out of the swamps and were threatening Ilowka. Troops there tried to join with the several thousands of men surrounded in the Newij Moch swamps. However, in the evening, a *Kampfgruppe* composed of three companies and backed-up by a section of assault guns managed to take Lushno back. The next day, the Soviets resumed their suicidal charges. They endured dreadful losses without showing any sign of that affecting their offensive determination. Reports from *SS-T.IR 3* claim that Russian soldiers were made drunk with Vodka before being sent to slaughter. The SS repelled all their assaults. On **the 26th**, the battle carried on before Lushno, where the Soviets launched another attack at 5.40 am with tanks and what seemed like countless infantrymen. Machine guns and mortars took down dozens of assailants. Four tanks were destroyed by the SS. Disheartened, the Soviets finally withdrew. At 1.30 pm, three regiments backed up by tanks attacked again. They were repulsed again with heavy losses. On **the 27th**, the Soviets attempted another assault with infantry troops from what

appeared like inexhaustible reserves. *3.Kp./SS-T.IR 3* had to evacuate the town before it got flattened by *Totenkopf*'s artillery. *II.AK* asked the division to counter the enemy breakthrough with every force available, especially *SS-T.IR 1*. But *SS-T.IR 1* was already struggling to control eleven kilometres of frontline against three Soviet divisions. Therefore, Theodor Eicke called men from staff companies and drivers from division trains as reinforcements. Insufficiently trained for infantry combat, they inevitably underwent excessive losses. In the morning, the Russians withdrew from Lushno, which had been turned into an inferno by the *Totenkopf*'s artillery. At 2 pm, Lushno fell again into the hands of *I./SS-T.IR 3*. At about 6 pm, the former frontline, prior to the 24th of September, was restored.

In four days of combat, *Totenkopf* had 194 men killed (including 13 officers), 629 wounded and 66 missing. *II./SS-T.IR 3* alone reported 119 men killed (including its commander, *SS-Hstuf.* Thier and his substitute, *SS-Hstuf.* Witte), 424 wounded and 63 missing! From the 22nd of June, the total of *Totenkopf*'s losses amounted to 6610 men killed, injured and missing; only 2500 men were sent to replace them. Thus, Theodor Eicke reiterated his request to have his division relieved, but he only received vague promises in return. At the beginning of October, *Totenkopf* went on with fortification works, and buried itself to face any offensive return from the Soviets. On the 10th of October, snow fell for the first time; the ground was already deep-frost.

Attack towards Ljubniza

On the **17th of October**, *Totenkopf* moved into attack north-east of Kirillowschtschina. The SS came up against a particularly dense defensive network on an undulating field covered with thick woods. Air reconnaissance revealed that these fortifications, made of trenches, minefields, barbwire networks, heavy artillery positions and buried tanks, stretched out ten kilometres in width. Against such particularly efficient defence, *Totenkopf* suffered disproportionate losses compared with seized territory. On the **19th of October**, Soviet artillery pounded *Totenkopf* with harassing fire. The SS ended up nailed to the ground by the intensive shelling of their lines. On the **21st of October**, with a sudden spell of milder weather, the whole area turned into an ocean of mud, in which men got stuck up to the knees. Only tracked vehicles could now circulate, only with the greatest difficulty. In such conditions, food and munitions resupplying became highly problematic. The attack had to stop.

For a whole week, *Totenkopf* wore itself out by cleaning countless bunkers. *X.AK*'s offensive failed. The frontline was now stabilized on the line Lushno - Ssuchaja Niwa - Plemewizy. The division controlled a 25-kilometre-wide sector, with companies of fewer and fewer strength. From then on, the Wehrmacht concentrated all its offensive priorities on Moscow.

War of position

October had been the hardest month for the German army since the onset of the war. The Soviet resistance had stiffened again and weather conditions had worn the men out, but for the Germans, the worse was yet to come.

In early November, *Totenkopf* buried itself on the north rim of the Waldaï. With the arrival of the cold weather the battle calmed down. The division started to receive some winter clothes from the general collect ordered in Germany. It was still far from enough though, considering the harsh weather conditions at the end of autumn. The ground was frost 75 centimetres deep, which made the building of shel-

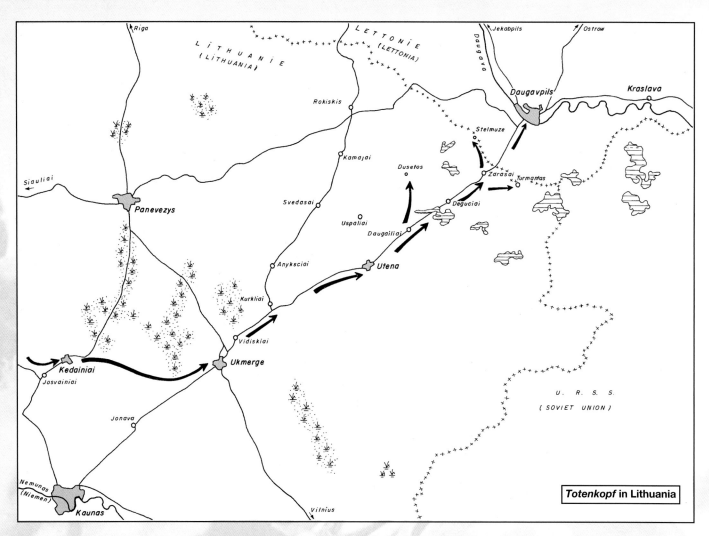

Totenkopf in Lithuania

ters very difficult. Engineers had to use explosives to dig the earth!

On the 6th of December, the division counted 450 officers, 1202 non-commissioned officers and 12660 men. Most men weren't given winter clothes, and many cases of frostbites were reported. At the beginning of December, temperatures got below -30°C (-22°F). With this cold, guns jammed, engines wouldn't start, and supplies got stopped on the way. The only unit that could still move was the ski company, recently formed under the command of *SS-Ostuf.* Weber.

Christmas and New Year's Eve went off quietly. Theodor Eicke came to visit his units. Everywhere, the same questions were fretfully asked: what will the new year bring us?

A non-commissioned officer is showing Theodor Eicke the way to the Dwina's banks. Note the death's-head on the vehicle's pennant. (NA)

Theodor Eicke in front of the Dwina, in the area of Ellern. Judging by the attitude of the people on this picture, the opposite bank has already been secured. (NA)

A machine gunner and his *MG-34*, whose support device hasn't been set on the barrel's end, which is quite odd. (NA)

Totenkopf *marches into Lithuania*

The division starts the "Barbarossa" operation only from the 25th June 1941. On the 27th, it enters deep into Lithuania and is met by a serious first opposition. Its reconnaissance group lost a machine gun and 11 are killed, among them *SS-Ostuf.* Splitt, a *"Deutschland"* regiment vet and chief of the 2nd company.

End of June 1941. The German march into Lithuania is so fast that thousands of soviet soldiers find themselves cut off behind *Panzergruppe 4*. For the time being, *Totenkopf* division advance following in the tracks of the panzer divisions and collect prisoners. (Private collection.)

Above: In the vastness of the East, the advance is interrupted by a few clashes. Firing came from a wood and some division officers are trying to locate it. (Private collection.)

On the right: Exceptional photograph of Theodor Eicke taken by one of his soldiers. His visits on the front line were frequent and partly explain his popularity with his men. (Private collection.)

1. In one of numerous villages passed through, this man found this little horse, seemingly docile and probably abandoned by the Red Army. (Private collection.)

2. and **3.** And suddenly, things get rougher. The Soviet resistance hardens and clashes increase. Reconnaissance men are sent forward, under the surveillance of officers sheltered under a shack. (Private collection.)

4. Once the village is secured, a section gathers while waiting for new instructions. (Private collection.)

5. While waiting for the engineers to build a bridge to allow the passage of vehicles, the infantrymen cross the stream on a rudimentary footbridge. (Private collection.)

An *SS-T.IR 3* column in a Lithuanian village. The couriers in the foreground ride 350cc *DKW NZ* motorbikes. They could reach 100km/hr, had a range of 350 km and were manufactured until the end of the war. (NA)

Close-up on the same bikes. Notice the death's head, the division symbol, and the number 3 identifying *SS-T.IR 3*, on the mudguard on the front right of the *Mercedes Benz Typ 340 Kfz.15*, an extremely rare vehicle, only 42 models were built! Equipped with a 3.4 litre engine with 6 cylinders, it could move its weight of 2520 kg at 118 km/hr and needed not refuelling for 700 km. (NA)

Above: An unidentified *SS-Untersturmführer* receives a message carried by a courier. This time the motorbike is a 342cc *Victoria KR 35 WH*. Made from 1938 to 1945 and stood out by having a better refuelling time than BMW and DKW. (NA)

Left: These two motorcyclists bikes are less rare. They are 350cc *BMW R35* which were produced in large quantities from 1937 to 1940 by the famous Bavarian factory. Their performance was close to that of the *DKW NZ 350*. (NA)

Below: The *SS-Untersturmführer* and an *SS-Oberscharführer* read the message. Notice the skull on both sides of the collar worn by the officer, a rather common custom among the division, despite the inconvenience that if he wore a camouflage overcoat over his jacket, it would then be impossible to determine his grade. (NA)

SS-Ostubaf. Hellmuth Becker is speaking to a non-commissioned officer belonging probably to *I./SS-T.IR 1*. Perhaps a reader could tell the author what is the mysterious object which is in the slipcover behind the driver. (NA)

Below: A *Mercedes-Benz Stuttgart 260* the belonging to the engineers batallion headquarters is squeezing through the busy streets of a village. It might be Kedainiai where the division lost precious hours due to a massive traffic jam.(NA)

Above right: In the area of Ukmerge, around the 28th June 1941. Some men from a motorbike division have stopped on the Neris river, a tributary of the Niemen, to freshen up and clean their motorbikes covered in dust. This here is a 750cc *BMW R12*. (NA).

Right: The engineer battalion builds a log bridge on a Daugava tributary, near Zarasai.(NA)

River crossings

The *Totenkopf* division has to cross several rivers during its march through Lithuania. Hence the engineers batallion is often called for. Later in September the division would have to cross other rivers, like the Lowat, the Shelon or the Pola.

Construction of a new bridge on the Daugava at Daugavpils. A surveyor checks the alignment of the beams. (NA)

Left: The construction of a bridge is supervised by an *SS-Untersturmführer*: it might be Erich Muth (*Chef Brückenkolonne*) who will be killed on the 7th February 1942 in Korowitschina. (NA)

Below: a snap of the finished bridge. (NA)

Daugavpils

The speed of the capture of Daugavpils, formerly Dünaburg and Dwinsk, provoked a fundamental question in the heart of the *OKW*: should the *Heeresgruppe "North"* continue to march towards Leningrad or should it turn to Moscow? Hitler responds that destroying the enemy is more important than to seize its capital.

Right: Daugavpils, 30th June 1941. According to witnesses, the town was totally burnt down during the fighting.This is a *Pzkpfw.35 (t)* of *8.Panzerdivision* in the city streets. (NA)

The *Totenkopf* division has installed a *2 cm Flak* gun on the outskirts of the town to shield a major road. The gun is not deployed, proof that the soviet air force hardly operates at the end of June 1941. Close-up on the *2cm-Flak 30*, an unusually complex weapon for such a small size. Its shooting range (280 rounds per minute) is deemed unsuitable for the modern aircraft speed and it is already replaced by the *2cm-Flak 38*. (NA)

Some members of the *NKVD* have been arrested, their fate is not an enviable one. (NA)

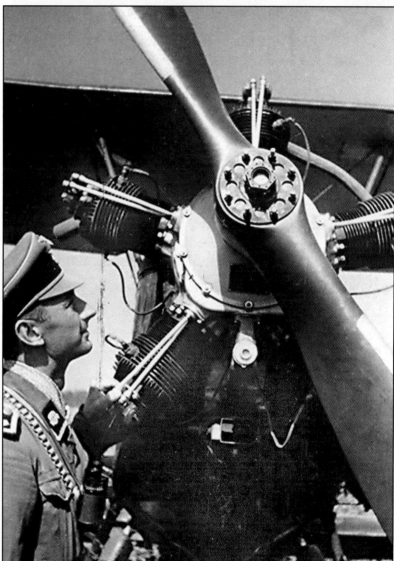

The *Totenkopf* division have captured a small aerodrome that the Soviets did not have time to completely evacuate. Officers from the division pose in front of a *Polikarpov Po-2*, a do-it-all airplane widely used by the Soviets for twenty years. (NA)

Totenkopf in Latvia (beginning July 1941)

Due to the horrendous state of Latvian roads, the division soldiers often have to get off their vehicles to walk in the heat and dust. Despite this and the increasing opposition from the Red Army, *Totenkopf* pass through Latvia in one week.

"*SS marschiert in Feindesland*": the SS march through enemy territory. This song often sung by the SS is perfectly illustrated here by these propaganda photographs. (NA)

In their dusty and ragged uniforms, these two soldiers are both carrying a *Panzerbüchse 39*, an antitank weapon which was already obsolete during the French campaign. Produced in large quantities, this weapon will later be turned into a grenade launcher (*Granatebüchse 39*). (NA)

Right: The weariness of an exhausting walk can be seen on the face of this SS. He is carrying the plate of a 50 mortar (*5cm le.Gr.W.36*). Behind him is the soldier from the photo above, carrying an ammunition box and wearing a non regulation neck scarf. They both seem relieved to be able to get back on a truck. (NA)

Below: The fighting gets harder and harder. The Soviets have numerous tanks that they launch against the flanks of the German attack. This *BT-7*, hit on its tracks, has toppled in a pond. It is being inspected by a man from the division. (Private collection.)

Above: Outstanding photograph taken by a soldier form the division: a man has been hit in the head which is being bound at his battle station by his comrades and a nurse who can be identified by his armband. The tension from the battle can be seen on their faces. (Private collection.)

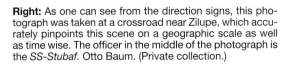

Right: As one can see from the direction signs, this photograph was taken at a crossroad near Zilupe, which accurately pinpoints this scene on a geographic scale as well as time wise. The officer in the middle of the photograph is the *SS-Stubaf.* Otto Baum. (Private collection.)

The battle for the "Stalin" line

Even though the Soviets did not have time to complete this fortified line, to break through it is a hard task for the *Totenkopf* division. For this mission the division is reinforced by *Stab Art.-Rgt.803* and *schw.Art.-Abt.506* to get a sufficient artillery backup.

The Soviets are expert at camouflaging. The hideouts of this type are sometimes turned towards their own lines in order to shoot the back of the assailants. However, when found, the hidden soldier has no way of getting out alive. (NA)

Left: The "Stalin" line is broken through and the long march toward the east carries on. A heavily laden troop is making its way along a dusty road. (Private collection.)

Right: The loss of life is increasing, as seen by this photograph of these burial places. (Private collection.)

A division's motorcyclist looking weary after weeks of fighting.

Photographs of the division is soldiers taken by the German propaganda. (Heimdal collection.)

The Totenkopf *division in front of Opotschka*

These photographs have been taken in the Opotschka sector, probably on the 10th July, when *SS-Stubaf.* Hellmuth Becker was slightly wounded, but carried on with his command.

Battle in the forest south of Opotschka. A *2cm-Flak* gun is used against ground targets, a common practice in the German army. (NA)

Left: The gun seen on the other page might have destroyed this unidentified vehicle which is burning, releasing lots of smoke. The men are not trying to shelter as they are no longer in danger. (NA)

Above: Hellmuth Becker among his soldiers. His left shoulder was wounded, but not seriously as he carries on issuing orders. In the SS the infantry battalion commanders lead their troops from the front, not from some sheltered post far behind. This aggressive method allows to react fast to events but has its downside: from June 1941 to February 1942, at least six division infantry battalion commanders were killed in action. (NA)

Right: A courier from Hellmuth Becker's headquarters. He is a rather old and could have taken part in the rejuvenation program launched by Theodor Eicke after the French campaign.

1. Picture of a division soldier during the same combat. The *SS-KB* did not choose him randomly: this man is the archetype of the SS soldier as represented by the propaganda: blond, pale eyes, harsh look, square jaw, sign of a strong character. (NA)

2. Another anti-aircraft gun has been taken to the edge of the forest to prevent any offensive from the Soviets. (NA)

3. Close-up on the gun commander. Notice that the men on the photograph wear goggles usually worn by motorcycling troops. (NA)

4. The battle round Opotschka lasts three days with heavy casualties. Here is a seriously wounded man being transferred to a sidecar. (NA)

5. A doctor from *SS-T.IR 1* has installed a makeshift medical station in this wooden house to give first aid. During wartime, the basic hygiene rules cannot always be followed and a lot of soldiers died from secondary infection to their wounds.

Soviet Counter attacks at Sebesh and Opotschka

For the first time since the eastern campaign, the *Totenkopf* division confront violent Soviet counter attacks supported by tanks. The losses on both sides are particularly heavy. They are huge on the Soviet side. Lots of experts believed then that the Red Army, after three weeks of battle, would not recover from such a slaughter.

An SS examine two destroyed 85mm anti-aircraft guns. Like the Germans, the Soviets often use their anti-aircraft weapons against tanks. (NA)

A piece of Russian artillery has been sabotaged by its crew. Notice the rough finish of the ribbed tube. (NA)

Reconnaissance men from *Totenkopf* (in 1941 only the division machine gun crew wear the panzers black uniforms) search the wreckage of a *BA-10*. On the right hand side of the photo is a *Kübelwagen Adler Typ 3Gd*. (NA)

Below: A *BT-7* tank has been destroyed by the SS near Opotschka. Derived from the American Christie tank, the *BT* has the unusual capability of moving on its tracks on all terrain, or on its wheels on roads. Very fast (73km/hr on wheels), the BTs are the most frequently encountered tanks by the Germans during the summer of 1941. (NA)

Infantrymen *Totenkopf's* pass a *T-26* abandoned by its crew. It seems indeed intact. Maybe it broke down or ran out of petrol. (NA)

Wreckage of of *KV-1* tank on the road to Opotschka. Due to the inefficiency of the *3.7cm Pak* against the heavy Soviet tanks, a battery of howitzer 150 of *IV./SS-T.Art.Rgt.* systematically supports the forerunner group of the division from the 1st July. (NA)

Another *KV-1* suffered a big blow which dislodged the turret from its tracks. Perhaps the damage was caused by a magnetic mine. (NA)

This *KV-2* was destroyed in the same area. At the beginning the Germans who did not know the existence of these heavy tanks, were unpleasantly surprised by their appearance on the battlefield. As the *KV-1* was later followed by the *KV-85*, the *KV-2* was quickly abandoned by the Soviets due to their extremely slow pace which made it an easy target for the German artillery. (NA)

In addition to the armoured vehicles, the Soviets also suffered heavy losses of all sorts of equipment. Here is a heavy machine gun *"Maxim" M1910* on a wheeled mount – which was necessary due to the heavy weight of this weapon – (right) and a farming tractor turned into an artillery one (below). (NA)

The Germans also captured lots of prisoners. Their fate is not enviable. In August 1941, while convalescing, Theodor Eicke organised at Sachsenhausen the execution of hundreds of Soviet prisoners. (NA)

The battle of Opotschka cost *Totenkopf* dearly: during only one day on the 10th July 1941, there were 164 deaths, 340 wounded and 34 missing. The toll of these losses since the beginning of the eastern campaign led to the disbanding of *SS-T.IR 2* from which the men joined the heavily affected companies of *SS-T.IR 1* and *SS-T.IR 3*. The mainstay of the division can then benefit from a brief period of rest.

A division motorcyclist pays his respect at the grave of one of his comrades before returning to his mission. Notice the difference between the tombs. The one in the background is surrounded by a basic fence: it is probably the grave of an officer or a non-commissioned officer. (NA).

A kind of scene rarely photographed by the *SS-KB*: the snaps from these ceremonies usually show the presenting of arms after the lowering of the body. (NA)

A photograph taken after the battle of Opotschka as *SS-Sturmmann* Gotthilf Weber was killed on the 29th July in the sector of Mschaga, but it gives an accurate idea about the appearance of cemeteries set up by the SS on the Russian front. (NA)

Between the 12th and 15th July, the *Totenkopf* division enjoy a few days of relative calm in the sector of Porchow. They take the opportunity to repair arms and vehicles.

Above: A soldier takes a photograph of his comrades near a field kitchen. According to the markings on the side-car, these men belong to *SS-T.IR 3*. (NA)

Left: Portrait of an *SS-Uscha.* of the *Totenkopf* division wearing shoulder traps from the *Leibstandarte*. Perhaps a vet of Hitler's pretorian guard. (NA)

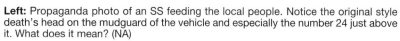

Left: Propaganda photo of an SS feeding the local people. Notice the original style death's head on the mudguard of the vehicle and especially the number 24 just above it. What does it mean? (NA)

Below: These men from the reconnaissance group, wearing black uniforms of the machine gun crew, relax reading the latest news. In the summer of 1941 these can only be good for the Germans. (NA)

Even though reading newspapers is not as enjoyable as the reading of mail from loved ones, it is nonetheless relaxing and comforting, as propaganda from Dr. Goebbels is particularly good at cheering up the troops. (NA)

On the 23rd July, the divisionel reconnaissance battalion lead the attack in the Listwjenka forest. It opens the way for *III./SS-T.IR 1*. The 750 cc side-cars (*BMW R12*) advance with difficulty on the marshy ground. (NA)

Offensive on the Mschaga river

From the 15th to the 17th July, *LVI.AK (mot.)* is harassed on its flanks and rear by the Soviet attacks coming from the south east and north west. Its lines of communications are cut between Porchow and Szoltzy. *II./SS-T.IR3* is then sent onto Baranowa where it will help *3.ID (mot.)* to resto-re the position and thus allow Manstein to resume his offen-sive on Nowgorod. On the 18th the whole of the *Totenkopf* division replaces *8.Panzerdivision* on the front line. It will stay there permanently for over a year.

The motorcyclists have just left the sheltering wood and suddenly find themselves on open ground. They have to deploy immediately. (NA)

One of them has quickly deployed his *MG 34* in order to assist his comrades. His machine gun is not belt-fed but has a 75 cartridge magazine, thus not necessitating a team-mate when firing. (NA)

The same gunner, recognisable by his helmet cover, has moved forward and opened fire towards the enemy line according to the instructions from the soldier with binoculars, seen in the background. (NA)

Thus covered, the motorcyclists launch their assault. It is usually a task performed by the infantry. (NA)

Above: A soldier got shot and his comrades pull him back with a piece of tent. (NA)

Left: Once safe, he is taken care by a nurse who has arrived in a side-car. (NA)

Below: Our man does not seem too seriously injured judging by the smile on the nurse's face. Notice that the camouflage patterns differ from one jacket to the other. (NA)

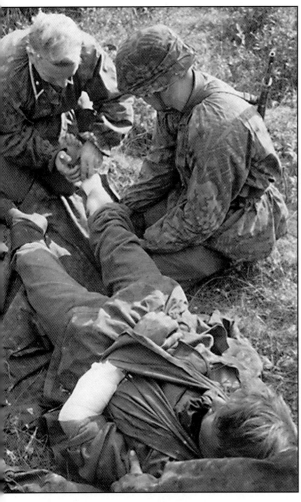

Above: The nurse has finished the bandaging; the soldier might have been injured by shrapnel, unless all this is staged, which is quite likely. (NA)

Above right: The wounded man is carefully lifted into a side-car then driven to an aid station. (NA)

Below: Picture of a campaign hospital. The wounded are laid on the floor under a mosquito net, an uncomfortable position for them and for those treating them. (NA)

Photo of a "real wounded man". He seems to be in a state of shock. Attached to his jacket is his identity tag on which his surname, first name, identification number and the nature of his wound are written. (NA)

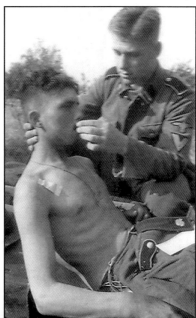

The "diplomatic" incident

On the 30th July, during a "friendly" conversation bewteen *SS-Ostuf.* Stürzbecher (Div.-02) and *Hauptmann i.G.* Schultz of *Gen.KdoXXVIII.AK*, the latter quizzes his SS colleague about the heavy losses suffered by the *Totenkopf* division since the beginning of the eastern campaign. He asks him if the attacks were launched after an artillery fire or just with "hurrahs". Their conversation is reported first to the headquarters of *SS-Brigaf.* Keppler and then to Himmler himself. *XXVIII.AK* will try to appease the SS by a letter playing down the incident.

The *Heer* officer is taken back to his Fieseler Storch aircraft. (NA)

Above: It is during a conversation like this one that the incident related on the other page took place. A *Heer* officer, accompanied by his batman, is chatting with an SS officer who does not seem annoyed by the questions. (NA)

The SS officers then talk about the previous conversation. (NA)

At the beginning of August 1941, the Germans decide to penetrate the Louga line in order to proceed to Leningrad. Bad weather delays the attack by a few days. The *Totenkopf* division launches its attack on the 10th August on the Mschaga which they managed to cross in the Sakibje sector. The Soviets tried to reduce the bridge head by launching against the SS fresh troops, high on vodka and urged on by their political commissioners. These suicidal attacks stop during the night, leaving the way open to the Totenkopf division.

Verst.III./SS-T.IR3 opened the way to the Mschaga by taking hold of the Ugorody heights at the start of the offensive. Heavy weapons – here a 3.7 cm anti-tank gun – are brought in. Notice the *MP28* of the soldier on the right hand side. (NA)

The gun has been deployed. The Soviets do not have armoured vehicles in this sector, so this *Pak 36* uses explosive shells against the enemy infantry. (NA)

The *Totenkopf* division artillery has a major role in the battle for the Mschaga. Thousands of shells have been fired within minutes to support the infantry attacks. You can see here ammunition for the *FH18* howitzer being piled ready for use. (NA)

From the Ugorody heights, the SS dominate the Soviet positions beyond the Mschaga river. These non-commissioned officers try to catch any movement from the enemy. The two white bands on the non-commissioned officer's sleeve show that he is a *Spiess* (company adjutant). (NA)

In another chapter, it was noticeable that the reports on coloured prisoners were rather frequent in the *SS-PK* archives. The same can be said about the "ethnic" coverage in the German magazines. (NA)

Another world...

When the SS, brainwashed with the racist nazi propaganda, entered the Soviet Union, they are struck by the grinding poverty. *"The miserable conditions of life in the Russian villages worsened by the war reinforce the image that they have of the Russians, that of low life. At the same time, it strengthen the soldiers' beliefs that their culture, race and direction are superior."* (in Omer Bartov, op. cit. page 224).

Left: The SS correspondents like to photograph the local customs and particularly the Russian villagers living in abject poverty. (NA)

These members of a war correspondents corps (*Kriegsberichter*) came to look at these Russian peasant families. (NA)

This newscaster asks these Russian civilians questions through a translator. The latter is probably a *Volksdeutsche* from the Baltic countries or from Russia. (NA)

The civilians gather spontaneously round the SS. During the summer of 1941 the local people are friendly with the Germans. But later when the *Reich*'s administrators start their brutal and oppressive rule, they will support the partisans. (NA)

127

On the 22nd August, the *Totenkopf* division has the task of seizing the bridges on the river Redja between Nowaje and Onufrijewa. The absence of roads in this front sector makes it difficult. Here the soldiers are making their way through a clearing. (NA)

On the march towards the river Lowat

Defeated west of the river Polist, the Soviets have trouble stopping the attacks from *LVI.AK (mot.)* towards the river Lowat. The Stavka starts to bring new troops to this front sector. These are still east of the Lowat.

Left: At the end of August 1941, it is no longer very warm in the north of Russia. The infantrymen, exhausted by long marches, get quite thirsty though. (NA)

Watching an enemy who is hiding in order to organise its defence along the next natural obstacle. (NA)

These men run carrying their *s.MG34* gun and ammunition in order not to stay exposed for too long. However, the presence of a photographer in front of them show that the danger is not as close as this photo could lead us to believe. (NA)

Clearing up a village. Here the danger is permanent. (NA)

A 4.5 ton Citroen lorry, with a 4.5 litre six cylinder engine, cautiously crosses a bridge. After the western campaign, the Germans got hold any French or British vehicles they could. (NA)

Another zone criss-crossed by waterways

Marching towards the river Lowat, the *Totenkopf* division has to cross several rivers, hurdles which slow down their advance: the rivers Redja, Porussje, Gluboka and Leuschinka.

Left: A *Krupp-Protze L2H 143* vehicle well camouflaged is pulling a 3.7cm anti-tank gun. It is followed by an identical vehicle and by a 3 ton *Opel Blitz* lorry. (NA)

A *Hanomag Sturm Modell 1937/38* 4-seater car rushes across a bridge resting on boats. This vehicle is rarely seen on the front as it is mostly used by the police or various nazi groups. (NA)

Construction of a bridge over a stream. The divisional engineer battalion has now lots of experience doing that. (NA)

The bridge over this river has been destroyed, probably sabotaged by the retreating Russian troops. The engineers have to build another one. Notice that some of them do not have shorts and have to work naked. (NA)

A difficult advance

On the 23rd August, the *Totenkopf* division reaches the river Lowat and crosses it two days later in the Kulakowa – Omytschkino – Korowitschino sector. A reconnaissance mission is sent to the river Pola.

Above: During the march towards the Lowat river, these motorcyclists ask these Russian civilians for some information during the crossing of a village. The side-car is a 750 cc *BMW R12*. (NA)

Left: A schwerer *Einheits-Personenkraftwagen Ford Typ 40 (Gruppenwagen kfz.18)* probably belonging to a gunner section moves forward with caution. Notice the *MG 34* tripods resting on each mudguard.

Gathering prisoners of the 11th or 34th Soviet army. These two great units were completely destroyed, but the Stavka have inexhaustible reserves and the *Totenkopf* division will quickly face renewed forces. (NA)

The Soviets have left behind a large quantity of equipment on the banks of the Lowat. These two SS infantry-men look at an artillery piece which appears to be in good condition. (NA)

I./SS-T.IR 3 seized Ramuschewo despite the fierce resistance from the Soviets which would be broken by the intervention of *Stukas*. These will drop a few bombs by error on the *SS*. (NA)

Spähtrupp "Gabriel"

Again on the 23rd August, the divisional reconnaissance corps which cover the left flank of *Totenkopf* at Jaswy is told that there are still strong Soviet opposition at Sytsahowa. A patrol led by *SS-Hstuf.* Elmar Gabriel has the task of destroying the artillery forces.

A radio communication vehicle (*Sd.Kfz.261*) from the patrol just before leaving to its mission. The last instructions are given to the leading officer. (NA)

Other patrol members on its way. Here is a light armoured car 4x4 (*Sd.Kfz.222*) built on a *Horch* chassia with a 3.5l and 8 valve engine. Weighing 4.3 tons, it can reach a road speed of 80 km/h and a maximum range of 280 km. (NA)

The patrol is heading toward the enemy in a dust cloud. The wooded terrain is conducive to defence. (NA)

Below: At the approach of the patrol, the Soviets open fire. The SS managed to withdraw without big losses and now has the knowledge of the enemy weaponry position. These will be destroyed a few minutes later by accurate shots from a section of *13. (IG)Kp./SS-T.IR 3* attached to the reconnaissance battalion. (NA)

Above left: A soldier watches the enemy positions with binoculars. One can see by his clothing that he does not belong to the vehicle crew. He notices that the Soviet troops at Sytsahowa are much more important than told by the prisoners. There is indeed a regiment well covered in the wood surrounding the village. (NA)

Above right: A close-up of the machine gun mount. The vehicle has a 3 men crew: a chief gunner, a radio operator and a driver. Notice the anti grenade wire mesh screen which normally has to be pulled down for battle. (NA)

During the summer of 1941, the *Totenkopf* division uses its motorcyclist troops a great deal, even creating a battalion in order to have a ready reserve. This became a necessity due to the huge areas covered. With the dissolution of *SS-T.IR 2*, the division copied its structure on the motorised infantry division of the *Heer*.

Left: The motorcyclists are mobile on the road, but not so on the Soviet Union tracks. The crew have great difficulty getting their bikes off the mud. Two men here are labouring to start their *BMW R12* side-car. (NA)

Right: A same type side-car, heavily laden. The inconvenience of that type of unit – average cross country mobility and little fire power – and going from an offensive to a defensive war – will lead to abandon the motorcycling battalions during the spring of 1943. (NA)

The new motorcyclist battalion has the help of a heavy company to give firing support to the rest of the unit. It is made up of a gun infantry section, a mortar section, a machine gun section and anti-tank section of which a 3.7cm is shown here. (NA)

The motorcyclists are also used as couriers because of difficult radio or telephonic transmissions. This courier has a NSU 251 OS bike, production of which ended in 1940. Because of heavy danger from partisans, scattered soldiers – he has a MP 28 submachine gun, based on the MP 18 designed during the Great War by Hugo Schmeisser. Capable of single shot or fully automatic, the MP 28 will be in service until the end of the conflict. (NA)

Deterioration of roads

At the end of August, torrential rains south of the Ilmen lake turn the roads into bogs. The advance, already difficult, slows down even more. This leaves time for the Soviets to reorganise and launch violent counter-attacks in the *LVI.AK (mot)* sector.

The crossing of Lithuania and Latvia wore out the vehicles through thick dust clogging the engines. (NA)

Now stuck in the mud, huge energy has to be spent trying to move the vehicles. The engines get damaged, the fuel consumption rockets, breakdowns increase. This *Mercedes-Benz Typ L3000S* lorry has trouble going up this gentle slope. (NA)

Help is needed as its cross-country capability is nil. Despite its weight, this lorry has only a 75 hp engine! The lack of the German army mobility would never be resolved and added greatly to the *Reich*'s defeat on the Russian front. Strange thing on this photo, the gas mask is used as a cover. (NA)

View of the column. Even though the identification badge painted on the mudguard of the 8 ton *Sd.Kfz.7* half-track is not clearly visible, it could be a vehicle from *3.Bttr./SS-T. Flak-Abt.* equipped with 88 guns. (NA)

These men try to clear the road to make it more usable. This task was often given to prisoners or if needed to civilians enrolled by force. (NA)

Manoeuvring in mud is very difficult for the motorcyclists. Numerous bikes and side-cars will be lost like this by the German troops. (Private collection.)

The divisional reconnaissance corps in action

Back inside the *Totenkopf* division, the reconnaissance battalion is particularly active at the beginning of September due to the menace from the 3rd division Soviet cavalry on the left flank of *SS-T.IR 3*.

Left: *SS-Stubaf.* Walter Bestmann, the divisonal reconnaissance batallion chief poses for the photographer. There is a flag with a swastika cross on the car bonnet for identification purposes for the *Luftwaffe*. (NA)

Another pose for the photographer, but this time Bestmann points in the opposite direction. The car is a *Horch Kfz.15* on which the insignia are visible: pennant of the battalion chief, pictogram of the headquarters of the reconnaissance and the death's head. (NA)

Below: From the start of the eastern campaign, the reconnaissance troops are often used to establish contact with the neighbouring divisions. This photo of an infantry formation, maybe *96.ID*, was taken around the 15th August. (NA)

Gathering of the motor-cyclists before their mission. The arms are ready and the motorbikes heavily laden. (NA)

Right: Motorcyclists from either *1.(Kradsch)-Kp./SS-T.Aufkl.-Abt.*, or the brand new *1.Kp./SS-T.Kradsch.-Btl*. In theory a motorcyclist battalion has the task of covering a division flanks by going from one sector to the other thanks to its mobility, while reconnaissance troops obtain information, even during fighting. In reality the latter are often used in missions normally assigned to the motorcyclist battalion. (NA)

Below: This side-car got deeply stuck in the mud and is damaged. It will be difficult to salvage. (NA)

141

Offensive on the Pola

On the 5th September, *Kampfgruppe "Lönholdt" (II./SS-T.IR 3)* is reinforced by 2 groups of soldiers equipped with flame-launchers, two infantry guns and a heavy section of *13.(IG)-Kp./SS-T.IR 3* and an antitank section) has the task of building a bridge head on the Pola at Stepanowa. After the artillery preparation by the 3rd group of the divisional artillery regiment, *II./SS-T.IR 3* launches the attack on the *Totenkopf*'s right flank .

Above: The left flank is held by *II./SS-T.IR 1* at Mal.Naljutschy, on the banks of a lake one kilometre from the Pola river. (NA).

Left: *SS-Gruppenführer* Karl Wolff (*Chef des Pers. Stabes RF-SS*) inspecting the front line in the company of Keppler and Kleinsheisterkamp. This photo was taken before the 9th September 1941, on which day Theodor Eicke regains the leadership of the division. (NA)

Below: This motorcyclist has taken a spare tyre; it is a wise move on the bad Soviet tracks. (NA)

Meal served from a field kitchen. The men do not often eat warm meals during the fighting. These will become even rarer during the Russian winter... (NA)

This Russian *BA-10* armoured car was guarding this road, but was destroyed and completely burned down. This armoured vehicle, while being under-powered (a 50 hp engine for a weight of 5 tons), will stay in service until 1943.

The battle for Lushno

Lushno is the first battle where the *Totenkopf* division will stand out in difficult conditions, unyielding in the face of an enemy superior in number. Before Demjanskunt, the division gains a formidable reputation of fanaticism until then unsurpassed in the German army.

Left: Mid September, the *Totenkopf* division is stopped in its advance towards Waldaï. Its sector is spread over 20 km from west to east, its positions towards the north. On the far left in the west is *II./SS-T.IR 3*, then *I./SS-T.IR 3* on either side of Lushno and Dubrowka, then *III./SS-T.IR 3* at the centre at Kamennaja and Jeruschkowo, then *II./SS-T.IR 1* at Kirillowschtschina, and last on the right side in the east, *I./SS-T.IR 1* at Chilkowo. (NA)

The division has to dig in along the banks of the Pola. The transmissions units have then the task of putting up telephone lines to allow communication between the different battalions which are widely spread due to a winding wooded and marshy front. (NA)

A artillery tractor towing a heavy field howitzer *s.FH18* crosses the Pola. Its arrival is very welcome as the division intelligence services have located large Soviet forces in front of its positions. (NA)

Fritz Christen

The nazi propaganda will turn him into a hero. In order to keep him safe, the *SS* remove him permanently from the battlefield. (NA)

Fritz Christen appears in numerous photographs and articles in the German press. He is her with pupils from the *SS-Panzerjägerschule*. (Private collection.)

Above: A combat scene. This one seems real, indeed the chamber of the *MP38* is open, which means that his owner has just emptied its magazine. (NA)

Left: A division anti-tank gun is waiting for the next assault. It is a *3.7cm Pak*, an obsolete weapon at that particular time. (NA)

At Lushno, the greatest effort is bore by the infantry which suffers from heavy losses. This portrait was taken by a reporter from the *SS-Kriegsberichter-Abteilung* emphasises that the SS soldier is determined despite everything. (NA)

Men from the division examine the drum magazine of a *Degtyerev DP* model 1928 machine gun, which was the most used light machine gun during the Second World War. (NA)

Picture of a photographer attached to the division. There were quite a few *SS-KB* in the *Totenkopf* division between 1939 and 1944. Among them were Adendorf, Alber, Apfel, Ahrens, Baumann, Cantzler, Ege, Gottschmann, Grönert, Helmersen, Merz, Pierich, Prochnow, Schoelkopf, Schreiber, Schulz, Taraba, Wiegand, Wisniewski, Wittmar and Zeymer. (NA)

The division anti-aircraft corps

The *SS-T.Flak-Abt.* is to become the anti-aircraft unit, having the best record of all the *SS* divisions. At the end of the war it would have destroyed 300 enemy aeroplanes, a hundred tanks and assault guns; although at the beginning it was made up from totally untrained personnel in that field as they were infantrymen. In September this group is heavily tested as the Soviets air attacks multiply above its sector.

A 88mm *Flak 36* gun belonging to the 3rd battery is deployed. The most famous gun of the Second World War, it was so feared by the allied troops that they seem to find them everywhere. It was indeed to be feared as it was capable of firing fifteen 11.35kg shells from 10000m in one minute. (NA)

Close-up on the gunners. The crew normally comprises of six men trained for anti-aircraft battle but also for ground fight, as the 88 has a reach on the ground of 14806m. Its use as a ground weapon was formalised during summer 1939. Indeed, in the "Procedures of attack against defences" it is stipulated that the "auxiliary assault troops, followed closely by anti-tank guns and 88 guns, would be launched against any breach in the front defences." (NA)

Hooking to an 8 ton half-track (*Sd.Kfz.7*). The use of such a heavy vehicle is necessary as the 88 gun weighs a hefty 7200kg... (NA)

From the six gunners, two are looking at optical and aiming equipment. Here one of them is using a rangefinder. (NA)

Although not often on the first line, the 88 battery sometimes suffers from firing as shown by these bullet holes on this vehicle windscreen. (NA)

Matthias Kleinheisterkamp decorate these deserving soldiers from his regiment. Coming from *SS-Verfügungstruppe* and not from the inspection of camps, he is not appreciated by Theodor Eicke who tries to get rid of him by sending a mail to *SS-Gruf.* Wolff (Chief of *Pers.Stabes RFSS*) dated 28th October telling that he is suffering from a nervous breakdown following the defeat of *SS-Ostubaf.* Heinrich Petersen. Eicke will be severely reprimanded by Himmler and Kleinheisterkamp's job confirmed. (NA)

Autumn 1941

With the autumn heavy rains turning roads into marshland, the moving war turns into a static one. The weather worsens rapidly at the end of September and the cold weather appears prematurely in this relatively temperate area of the Soviet Union.

Another decorating session in the Lushno sector. *SS-Ostuf.* Richard Pauly (*Adjutant SS-T.IR 3*) has just pinned a second class cross on an unidentified *SS-Untersturmführer*. The vehicle camouflage inidcates that the Soviet airforce is dominant in this front sector, most of the *Luftwaffe* gone to support the offensive of *Heeresguppe Mitte* going towards Moscow.

Theodor Eicke (in the centre, wearing a leather coat and hands behind his back) and officers from his headquarters watch the traffic on a grey and cold day. The car, a *Kübelwagen Adler Typ 3 Gd*, belongs to the *2.Kp./SS-T.Kradsch.-Btl*. But has kept its previous insignia, that of *15.Kp./SS-T.IR 3*. (NA)

Articles published in the 6th November 1941 issue of *Das schwarze Korps*, telling the epic events which gave Fritz Christen and Max Simon the knight cross. (Private collection.)

Für die Waffen-SS

SS-Oberführer Max Simon ausgezeichnet

Deutschlands jüngster Ritterkreuzträger

Besuch des Reichsführers SS auf der Prager Burg

SS-Hstuf. Stange, top left hand side, instructs SS.Ostuf. Dost, telephone in hand, and SS-Ostuf. Naujok, on the foreground. (NA)

An artillery observer of the divisional 1st artillery group. His work is fundamental for spotting the points to destroy. Most often placed on the front line, but this is not the case here, observers suffer heavy losses during combat. (NA)

The same observer with *SS-Ostuf.* Naujok, kneeling behind binoculars on tripod. (NA)

Relaying firing orders to an *SS-Uscha.* of a battery of the artillery 1st group. (NA)

A reconnaissance plane from the *Luftwaffe* in sync with the *Totenkopf* artillery. It is a twin-tailed *FW 189*. (NA)

This is the result: the target, a hamlet where some Soviet soldiers have been spotted, catches the fire of the divisional artillery. A thatched cabin burns releasing thick smoke. (NA)

This series of photos has been taken from a personal album belonging to a former member of *13.(IG)Kp./SS-T.IR 1*. Due to the shortage of tracked prime movers, the guns of the company are towed by lorries. One of them is seen here crossing a small stream, somewhere in Lithuania. (Courtesy Michael Cremin)

Motorcyclists of *13.(IG) Kp./SS-T.IR 1*. The man on the right is holding a camera. The death's head is clearly visible on the back of the side-car. (Courtesy Michael Cremin)

Fire ! Guns of *13.(IG) Kp./SS-T.IR 1* shown at full recoil. The photographer has perfectly timed his shot. (Courtesy Michael Cremin)

Another picture of the same guns, but taken from a different angle. The crews have settled their guns on open ground as the Soviet Air Force is not a threat anymore during the first weeks of the German offensive towards Leningrad. (Courtesy Michael Cremin)

This time, the picture was taken just before firing. The man are putting their fingers in their ears and are opening their mouth to prevent an ear-drum lesion from blast. The gun is a *s.IG 33*, a 15cm-infantry gun which was produced in great numbers throughout the war. (Courtesy Michael Cremin)

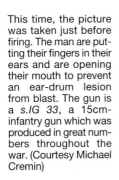

157

On the opposite, Soviet tanks are encountered in great numbers. Soviet armour tactics are disastrous and the Germans inflict considerable losses. A *T-26* has probably been abandoned by its crew since it seems to be intact. (Courtesy Michael Cremin)

An infantry gun crew on a lorry. Lithuanian and Latvian roads proved to be sandy and dusty. This can be seen on the faces of these exhausted looking men. (Courtesy Michael Cremin)

Preparations for battle! Despatch riders are going away with their messages and guns are to be uncoupled from their lorries. (Courtesy Michael Cremin)

Vehicles of *13.(IG)Kp./SS-T.IR 1* are stopping their advance to take a rest on a sandy road. No one can be seen. The SS soldiers are certainly trying to sleep somewhere on the grass beside the road. (Courtesy Michael Cremin)

Opposite above: Guns are prepared for short range firing as their barrels are nearly vertical. (Courtesy Michael Cremin)

Opposite below: The gun on the left side of the road opens fire. Notice the large flame bursting out of the barrel. (Courtesy Michael Cremin)

Men belonging to the infantry gun company are discussing a grave matter as can be seen on their faces. There are no smiles despite the photographer's presence. The fighting is harder than they could have ever imagined. (Courtesy Michael Cremin)

Bivouac by a small brook. Foxholes have been dug on a flat ground which offers no protection. In this condition, camouflage is vital. (Courtesy Michael Cremin)

Above: Autumn has come. Temperatures have plunged. Officers and men are wearing their greatcoats. Notice the impressive size of the shells and the well-prepared position. (Courtesy Michael Cremin)

Below: Close-up on the gun and its crew. Of special interest is the fact that seven soldiers are posing on this photograph though a *s.IG33* had a six man crew. Add to these the photographer, this makes eight men. The two supernumerary men must be the lorry drivers. (Courtesy Michael Cremin)

5

The Demjansk pocket

Soviet breakthrough in Staraja Russa

On the night of January the **7th 1942**, the Soviets launched a strong offensive on the left flank of *Heeresgruppe "Nord"*. Between Lakes Ilmen and Seliger, three armies managed to pierce through the German front, while the Soviets' 3rd shock army was breaking the *16.Armee*'s lines south of Lake Seliger. On the 9th, the 11th Soviet army reached Staraja Russa and then turned south. Meanwhile, the 1st shock army, attacking west of Lake Seliger, moved up along the Lowat to link up with the 11th army, thus threatening to surround the whole *16.Armee*. Aware of danger, *16.Armee* immediately ordered its best division, *Totenkopf*, to build up *Kampfgruppen* and to send them where the front showed signs of collapsing. The sector of Staraja Russa was obviously the most sensitive spot. The *"Rollbahn"* Staraja Russa - Ramuschewo - Kobylkino - Wassiljewschtschina - Demjansk, on which all the supplies for *II.AK* and *X.AK* circulated, was directly threatened by the north-east pincer movement of the Soviet offensive (11th army).

On the **8th of January**, the following elements were sent to Staraja Russa:

- *SS-Artillerie-Gruppe "Stange"*
- *SS-T.Aufkl.-Abt. (SS-Stubaf.* Kurtz)
- *SS-Kampfgruppe "Ullrich"*
- *SS-Kampfgruppe "Eichert"*
- *SS-Kampfgruppe "Bochmann"*
- *SS-Kampfgruppe "Wedenig"*
- *SS-Kampfgruppe "Becker"*
- Elements from the *SS-T.StuG-Bttr.*

Once arrived at Staraja Russa, the different *Kampfgruppen* from the *Totenkopf* were joined to *18.ID (mot.)* and immediately thrown along the Polist to face Soviet waves of assault. But the situation became tougher and tougher for the Germans, who failed to seal all the gaps. Panic was gradually overcoming most units defending Staraja Russa. On the **10th of January**, the Soviets tried to bypass the town from the west. This time, their attacks were repelled and they lost many men on the way. On the **11th of January**, *Gen.Kdo X.AK* ordered other units from *Totenkopf* (*III./SS-T.IR 3* and *9.Bttr./SS-T.Art.-Rgt.* [*SS-Kgr. "Moder"*]) to be subordinated to *290.ID*, in order to strengthen the *16.Armee*'s south flank. *SS-T.Pi.-Btl.* also got to Staraja Russa, and laid down defensive positions east of the city. South-east, the critical situation forced the Germans to attempt a counter-attack. It only resulted in a disaster, despite the destruction of 14 Russian tanks. In Mednikowa, *SS-T.Aufkl.-Abt.* And *SS-Artillerie-Gruppe "Stange"* drove back several enemy attacks. On the **13th of January**, Soviet attacks followed one another before Staraja Russa. Their assault groups went as far as the town cemetery. North-east, they cut the road to Schimsk and aimed at the *Rollbahn* to Dno. South-east of Staraja Russa, *SS-Kampfgruppe "Moder"* was sent before Beglowo, where it fought till the end of the month, with awful losses. Another *ad hoc* group

task force, made out of *SS-T.Kradsch.-Btl.* and commanded by *SS-Ostuf.* Säumenicht, was also thrown against the Soviet attack forces: it was almost completely wiped out in a few days, and survivors were to be taken in at the end of January in the sector of Welikoje Selo by men from *SS-Kampfgruppe "Becker"*, another task force made of motley elements from the *Heer,* the *Luftwaffe* and the *Waffen-SS.*

During the following days, thanks to the arrival of some reinforcements, all the Soviet attacks were repelled before Staraja Russa and the Germans managed to hold the line Dubowizy - Gutschino - Mednikowa - Lipowizy - Goroschkowa. The road to Schimsk even fell into their hands again.

On the **15th of January**, *Totenkopf* was subordinated to *II.AK* in Dobrosli. A week after the beginning of the Soviet offensive, almost half of its infantry and a substantial part of its artillery were backing up *290.ID* or fighting around Staraja Russa. In the mean time, the general situation had considerably worsened. South of *II.AK*, the Soviets had seized Ostachow, and after the retreat of the *9.Armee* (*XXIII.AK*)'s left flank on the Lowat, there was now an 80-kilometre breach on the right of before the *16.Armee*. Soviet 1st shock army was marching against Cholm. Other elements had already wheeled round towards north-west to seek contact with the 11th Soviet army. Stretched out 90-kilometre wide, *123.ID* proved unable to hold its positions. Some of its elements got isolated in Cholm. What was left of *32.ID* and *123.ID* established a new 190-kilometre long (!) defensive front line facing south. The Soviets took advantage of the breach to throw west their ski rear brigades, backed up by tanks, thus threatening the *II.AK*'s. North, the Soviets were still throwing more and more troops against *290.ID* and Staraja Russa. They managed to cut the railroad to Schimsk. South-east of the city, they rushed towards the Lowat. The encircling of *II.AK* and *X.AK* bacame increasingly menacing.

In order to stabilize front level with Molwotizy, *II.AK* took out again *Totenkopf* units from the Waldaï front. A mixed battalion commanded by *SS-Stubaf.* Kron (*Kdr. SS-T.Flak-Abt.*) was thus thrust in the furnace together with *16.(Pi.)Kp./SS-T.IR 1* (*SS-Ostuf.* Iser). Both SS units managed to repel all the Soviet attacks before Molwotizy till mid-April. Constant threat against the *II.AK*'s right flank forced it to regroup extra forces midway between Staraja Russa and Demjansk from the sector of Salutschje. *X.AK* also sent units south: thus, a motorcyclist unit from the *Totenkopf* was sent from Jaswy to the line Nikolino - Chubino – on the Robja valley.

On the **20th of January**, compelled to stay put by Hitler, *II.AK* found itself isolated around Demjansk, after the 27th Soviet army had cut one of the last land connections with the salient. Hence, the bulk of *Totenkopf* as well as *290.ID, 30.ID, 12.ID, 123.ID* and *32.ID* were trapped inside. These units were subordinated to *II.AK*. Elements from *Totenkopf* in Staraja Russa – so outside the salient – were joined to *X.AK*.

At the end of January, assault guns of *SS-Ostuf.* Meierdress and *Kampfgruppe "Ullrich"* were taken over from the sector of Staraja Russa and sent around Ramuschewo. This town was of vital importance to the Germans, since it commanded the main communication route with the salient in Demjansk. In early February, *SS-Kampfgrgruppe "Moder"* was again engaged in violent combat alongside *290.ID* in the sector of Mal. Kalinez. It was almost annihilated and its survivors joined *SS-Kampfgruppe "Kleffner"* in Wassiljewschtschina.

Combats of the Gruppe *"Eicke"* in the Demjansk pocket

At the end of January 1942, the 1st and 2nd Soviet Guard Corps penetrated south from the valleys of the Redja and the Lowat. Their aim was to cut the Wassiljewschtschina - Bjakowo - Omytschkino road in order to cut off *II.AK* from *X.AK*. The Germans had only one route left to supply *II.AK*: a road on the south going by Kobylkino and Salutschje. But it was threatened from the south as well, as strong Soviet formations were going up north-east through a territory of swamps and forests east of the Lowat, in the sector of Molwotizy. To set against them, *II.AK* and *X.AK* had only meagre and scattered companies, plus a few *Kampfgruppen* hastily formed with disparate elements. Thus German commandment found itself compelled to improvise a new defensive front facing west, to deal with the Russian troops marching towards the rear of *II.AK*. On the **1st of February**, *IR 368* lost Ramuschewo, *Kampfgruppe "Säumenicht"* got surrounded in Redzy and the situation in Wassiljevschtschina grew even more confused. On the **3rd of February**, *General* Brockdorff-Ahlefeldt decided to split the *Totenkopf*'s units inside the Demjansk salient into two groups, to use them in more threatened sectors.

Gruppe "Eicke" was sent to defend a 64 kilometre front (!) along the line Wassiljewschtschina - Bjakowo - Kobylkino - Tscherentschizy – Salutschje, in the westernmost point of the salient, as a back-up for *290.ID*. Its mission was to prevent the Russian from widening the breach between *II.AK* and *X.AK* by attacking from the west. To do so, *SS-Gruf.* Eicke had the following elements at its disposal:

- Elements from the *32.ID*'s artillery regiment and anti-tank battalion.
- A battalion from *30.ID* (*I./IR 6*)
- *SS-Kampfgruppe "Wallner"* in Bol. Dubowizy
- *SS-Kampfgruppe "Kleffner"* in Wassiljewscht-schina
- What was left of *III./SS-T.IR 3* in Gortschizy
- *SS-Kampfgruppe "Meierdress"* in Bjakowo
- Elements of *SS-T.Pi.-Btl.* in Kobylkino, commanded by *SS-Stubaf.* Ullrich
- Elements of *I./SS-T.IR 3* (*SS-Hstuf.* Hartjenstein) in Tscherentschizy.

Gruppe "Eicke" had about six thousand men. The other *Kampfgruppe* made out of the *Totenkopf*'s units inside the salient was handed over to *SS-Obf.* Simon: it was deployed in the north-east sector of the salient, where the pressure exerted by the 34th Soviet army was threatening to crush the German defensive lines. With so few men at its disposal, Eicke had to resign himself to arrange his defence in several bases of operations set apart one from the other. Perfectly aware of the situation, *II.AK* gave definite instructions: *"Bases of operation must be held till the last man standing, till the last cartridge. Combat can only be stopped or positions evacuated on formal order. The oldest officer in every base of operation will be*

held responsible for the enforcement of this order. Each house and each village evacuated will have to be burnt down. Thus shall we defeat the Russians." Theodor Eicke passed Brockdorff-Ahlefeldt's unambiguous orders in his own words: *"Hold or die!"* The *Kampfgruppe*'s six thousand men were holding in their hands the fate of the *II.AK* and *X.AK* 90.000 soldiers, and thus of the whole *Heeresgruppe "Nord"*'s. Eicke became the leading light of resistance. He ordered the garrisons of each base of operations to bury themselves. But this tactic wasn't enough to hold positions attacked by an enemy with much more troops backed up by tanks. As a matter of fact, on the **6th of February**, *SS-Kampfgruppe "Ullrich"* found itself isolated in Kobylkino, which was bypassed by the Soviets, and the battle of Tscherentschizy brought about heavy losses in the SS ranks. The Soviets tried to break through the Bjakowo - Tscherentschizy line, to go on towards Salutschje. Over the following days, the SS were to make them pay dearly every attempt at breakthrough. On the **8th of February**, vanguards from the 11th and 1st Soviet shock armies linked up in Kobylkino. In the evening, the last supply road of *II.AK* was cut. The Demjansk salient became a pocket. Hitler repeated the order to stay there until the front was stabilized west of the Lorat, so that a relief attack could be launched. Besides, Göring had claimed he could supply surrounded troops by air. But after two promising weeks, an exhausted *Luftwaffe* proved unable to see the mission through.

The lot of the German troops trapped inside the Demjansk pocket was little enviable, but the Russian people's was tragic. Since December, *II.AK* had evacuated more than two thousand civilians to clear a nine-kilometre-wide zone. Houses had been burnt down or requisitioned. The other divisions of the army corps had also taken similar measures to send the population away from the war zone. *II.AK* acknowledged though that expelled civilians didn't have enough provisions, especially in such a cold winter ? temperatures reached -50°C (-60°F), or even lower! Behind this nine-kilometre narrow strip, *II.AK* established another forbidden zone where feeding the population was impossible. Unfortunately, there isn't any data about the civilians' fate in the Demjansk pocket. But many of them probably died from lack of shelter and food.

On the **9th of February**, the front of *Gruppe "Eicke"* passed by Bol. Dubowizy - Wassiljewschtschina - Bjakowo - Kalitkino - Kobylkino - Dubki - Kulakowo - Tscherentschizy - Shelgunowo. Combat was fierce around Bjakowo, Korowitschina, Kobylkino and Tscherentschizy. On the **11th**, south front of *Gruppe "Eicke"* was attacked around Salutschje. Consequently, Eicke asked permission to evacuate Kobylkino, to send *Kampfgruppe "Ullrich"* on a counterattack, but *II.AK* turned down the request and chose to organize the defence of Salutschje instead. On the **15th of February**, the *Kampfgruppe* made of six companies and commanded by *SS-Hstuf.* Häussler was sent on Wersch. Sosnowka, south of Salutschje, to slow down the pushing of the Soviets along the road Schubino - Salutschje, and thus to allow the setting up of defensive positions in Salutschje. The Russians were unremittingly attacking the towns of Kobylkino and Tscherentschizy in what looked like inexhaustible numbers, and with the back-up of massive artillery, tanks and a very dynamic air force. In Kobylkino, the situation became more critical with each passing hour. On the **22nd of February**, after setting die-hard resistance against an enemy much superior in number, *Kampfgruppe "Ullrich"* left the town and reached Tscherentschizy. That same day, Count Brockdorff-Ahlefeldt wrote: *"Gruppe "Eicke" put on a remarkable fight. To me, men in Kobylkino* and Wassiljewschtschtina and their commandants, *SS-Stubaf.* Ullrich and Kleffner, were heroes." A bit later in the day, Tscherentschizy was deserted. The garrison thus retreated to Werjasko, before reaching the sector of Salutschje. *Kampfgruppe "Ullrich"* settled next to *Kampfgruppe "Schröder"*. SS engineerswere backed up by various units and Karl Ullrich reorganized his *Kampfgruppe* into two battalions commanded by *SS-Hstuf.* Dörner and Krauth. Then the Soviets attacked the *Kampfgruppe "Häussler"*'s positions in Werch. Sosnowka. *Kampfgruppe "Häussler"* carried out its mission there till it was ordered to reach Salutschje, on the **25th of February**. At the end of February, the Soviets increased their pressure to clear the pocket before the Germans could set up a counter-attack and break the encircling. But the besieged held on, regardless of the freezing cold that paralysed most weapons and of the intensive shelling they were subjected to. There were Dantesque combats to take Bjakowo – held for more than a month by the 120 men of *Kampfgruppe "Meierdress"* – and Kalitkino, where a few dozens of SS commanded by *SS-Ostuf.* Richter had entrenched themselves.

In early March, *Totenkopf* welcomed 540 recruits from *SS-T.Inf.Ers.-Btl.III* in Brno (Brünn), sent to the pocket by plane from Pskow. On the 12th of March, *Generalleutnant* Zorn, former commandant of *20.ID* (mot.), arrived to take charge of *290.ID*, *Arko 105* and *Gruppe "Eicke"*, that now made up *Korpsgruppe z.b.V "Zorn"*. Zorn came to find a critical situation: during the ferocious combats that were still succeeding one another in every base of operations, *Gruppe "Eicke"* had lost many men and now comprised less than two thousand fighters. Bases of operations were so isolated from one another that it had become impossible to transfer the injured to the Demjansk hospital.

Combats of *SS-Kampfgruppe "Simon"* on either side of Kirillowschtschina

The *Totenkopf* units that remained in the area of Lushno, before the heights of the Waldaï, were commanded by *SS-Obf.* Max Simon (*Kdr. SS-T.IR 1*). Since the departure of the various *Kampfgruppen* hadn't been compensated simultaneously by a shortening of the front line, Simon had to arrange infantry units out of artillerymen, drivers, mechanics and men from the supply corps. They managed to partially fill the gaps between Lushno and Kirillowschtschina. A disciplinary company (*SS-Einsatzkommando z.b.V*) was set west of Kirillowschtschina. In addition to that, fighter commandos (*Jagdkommandos*) and a skier company led by *SS-Ostuf.* Schassberger were thrown to the battle behind the front, especially from March, when the Soviets started launching airborne troops and paratroopers against Demjansk.

The only seasoned units in *Kampfgruppe "Simon"* were now *II./SS-T.IR 3* (*SS-Hstuf.* Launer), *III./SS-T.IR 1* (*SS-Stubaf.* Schubach), and the unranked companies from the two infantry regiments of the division, which was more or less equivalent to a regimental group. The Germans had five rifle divisions to face them. In January and February, the Soviets tried everyday to break through the front line or to destroy a base of operations. It seemed as though their artillery had an inexhaustible stock of ammunitions, given how their pounding never gave the Germans any respite. In mid-March, in order to synchronize their attacks with those of airborne units from inside the pocket, the Soviets intensified again their pressure on the defenders. The main target of their new offensive was *30.ID*, left of *Kampfgruppe "Simon"*. The Russian tried to cut *Rollbahn* to Staraja Russa. Thus, not only did the *Kampfgruppe "Simon"* have to keep on holding the 25-kilometre-long front line between Lushno and Kirillowschtschina, but it also had to see that the *Rollbahn* was properly secured along the twenty kilometres or so between Lushno, Ilowka, Meletscha and Tschitschilowo. The group was given this additional mission, even though its numbers were constantly decreasing.

On the **9th of April 1942**, thaw caused much flooding. Roads turned into rivers, bridges were swept along by water and bunkers collapsed one after the other. New bunkers had to be built, and roads had to be made passable again. On the 26th, after contact was established again between *II.AK* and *X.AK* (see next chapter), *SS-Kampfgruppe "Launer"* was sent to join *Gruppe "Eicke"*. Its former sector was entrusted to *Gruppe "Schubach"*. The *Gruppe "Simon"*'s right flank was now held by *Kampfgruppe "Schulze"*.

On the **5th of May**, the Soviets moved into attack in the sector of Kirillowschtschina with tanks and infantry. Situation turned critical, especially for SS advanced posts on the "height of the birches" and in Ssuschaja Niwa. *11.* and *12.Bttr./SS-T.Art.-Rgt.* thus came as direct support for infantry and managed to destroy ten tanks. Several *JU-88* were then sent to shell zones of gatherings of Soviet tanks. The front line held out. The Russians attacked again on the 8th of May, and lost six other tanks. The 10th of May marked the end of the attacks on Kirillowschtschina. The Soviets had suffered very serious losses and had to regain their breath. They took action again on the **20th of May** and managed to appropriate Hills 172 and 185. The latter was taken again during a counter-attack launched immediately afterwards by the SS. Combats resumed the next day. Late in the evening, the *Stukas* appeared at long last and shelled infantry concentration zones of and artillery positions of the Soviets. In the night of May **21st**, opponents started fighting over Kirillowschtschina again. Except for the so-called "hillock of ants", the SS lost all their bases of operations. Two companies from the *Heer* were sent as reinforcement and placed under the lead of *SS-Stubaf.* Schubach, who then took charge of the sector of Kirillowschtschina. The Russians used a heavy battery moved on railroads, which had much too long a range to be threatened by the division's pieces. Impacts were so strong that even from a great distance, heavy howitzers weighing more than five tons were lifted up the ground. Combats lost intensity on the 23rd of May. From the **30th**, *Kampfgruppe "Simon"* was gradually relieved by *30.ID*. *Totenkopf* had only 225 officers, 722 non-commissioned officers and 5779 men left (total: 6726 men), out of a theoretical strength of 638 officers, 2836 non-commissioned officers and 14.058 privates (total: 17.532). This assessment shows the extent of the sacrifices made by the division. Not only had its strength in numbers melted away, but the survivors were physically not able to keep on fighting. A report from *SS-Hstuf.* Dr Eckert, the doctor of *II./SS-T.IR 1*, showed that out of the 281 men he examined, 88 were unfit for military service, even according to the less rigorous criteria of the *Wehrmacht*. The other soldiers he examined had lost an average of 22 pounds, and were required to be put to rest before going back to front.

The first battalion from *30.ID* arrived on the 3rd of June and took over from *II./SS-T.IR 1* exhausted companies on the left flank. At the same time, hell broke loose again in the sector of Kirillowschtschina, with a new offensive from the Soviets. The "sand hill" in Borok was lost after violent combat. The relieve of *Kampfgruppe "Simon"* was only completed on the

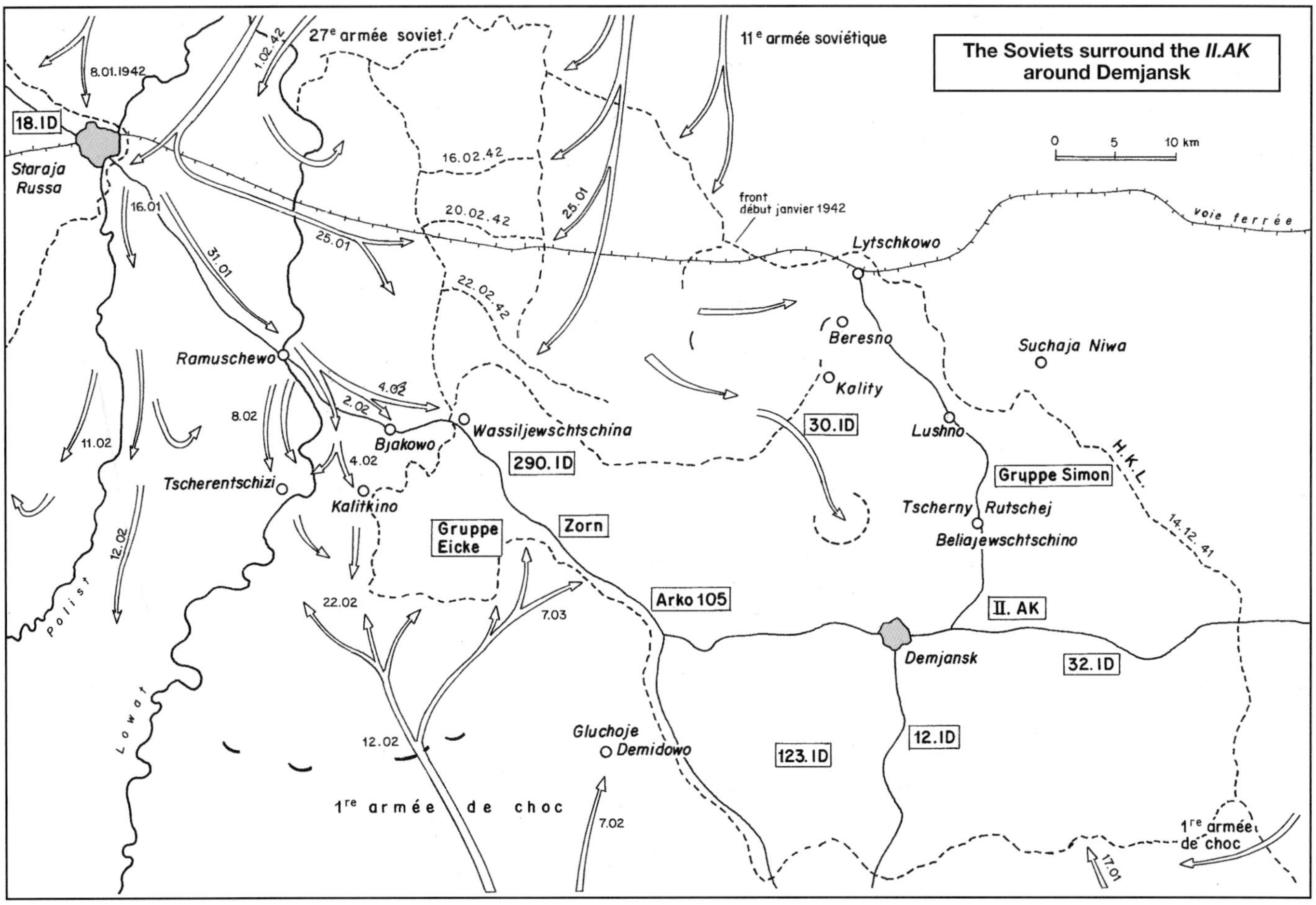
The Soviets surround the *II.AK* around Demjansk
0 5 10 km
27e armée soviet.
11e armée soviétique
8.01.1942
1.02.42
18.ID
Staraja Russa
16.02.42
20.02.42
16.01
25.01
31.01
25.01
22.02.42
front début janvier 1942
voie ferrée
Lytschkowo
Beresno
Kality
Suchaja Niwa
Ramuschewo
4.02
2.02
8.02
11.02
Bjakowo
4.02
Wassiljewschtschina
290. ID
30.ID
Lushno
H.K.L.
Gruppe Simon
Tscherentschizi
Kalitkino
Gruppe Eicke
Zorn
Tscherny Rutschej
Beliajewschtschino
14.12.41
12.02
Polist
22.02
7.03
Arko 105
II. AK
Demjansk
32. ID
Lowat
12.02
Gluchoje
Demidowo
123. ID
12. ID
1re armée de choc
7.02
1re armée de choc
17.01

20th of June 1942. However, *III./SS-T.IR 1*, elements from *SS-T.Pz.Jg.-Abt.* and *11.* and *12.Bttr./SS-T.Art.-Rgt.* kept fighting in the sector of the Waldaï, and remained joined to *30.ID* till mid-July.

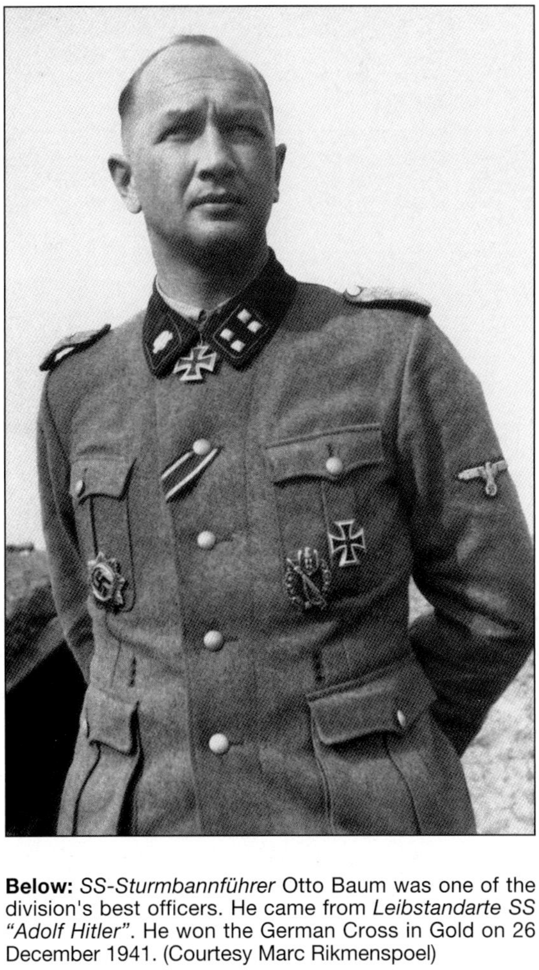

Below: *SS-Sturmbannführer* Otto Baum was one of the division's best officers. He came from *Leibstandarte SS "Adolf Hitler"*. He won the German Cross in Gold on 26 December 1941. (Courtesy Marc Rikmenspoel)

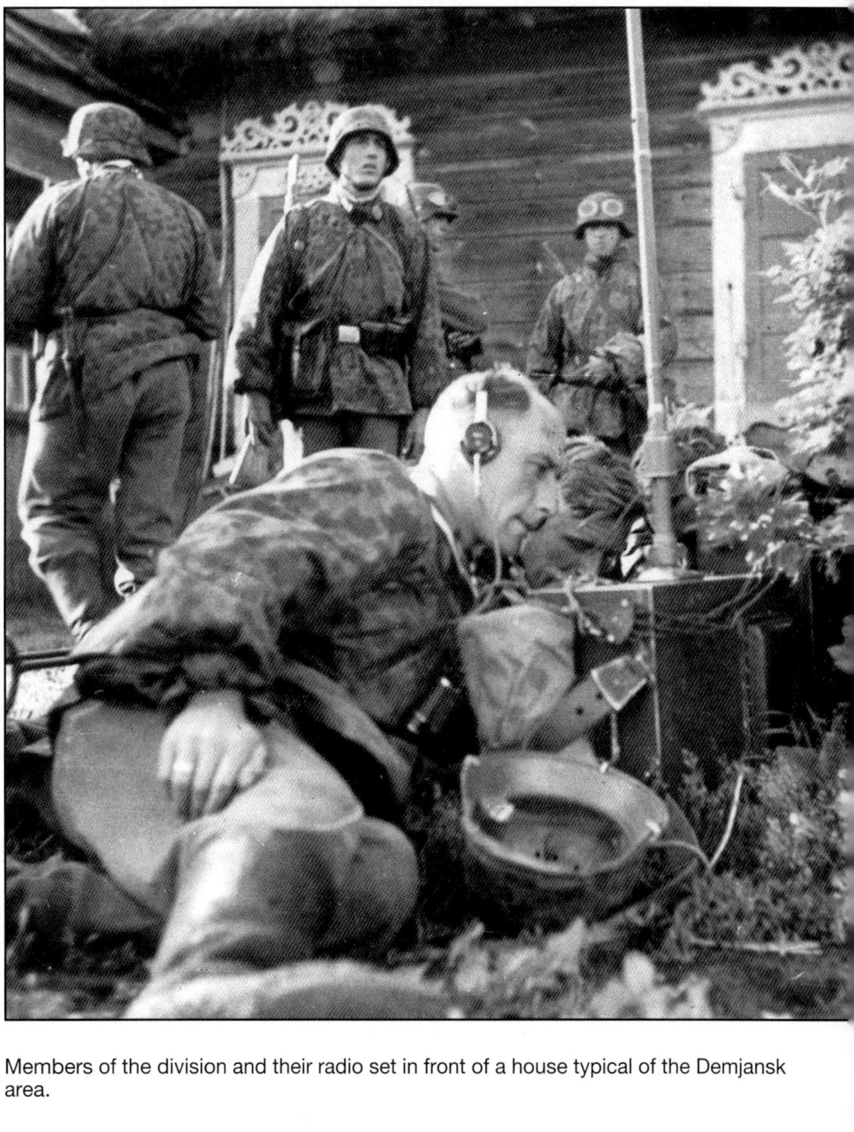

Members of the division and their radio set in front of a house typical of the Demjansk area.

The terrible winter 1941-1942

In the month of December 1941, while the German Army Group Centre *Heeresgruppe "Mitte"* is near to exhaustion at the gates of Moscow, suffering enormous losses in both men and equipment, *Totenkopf* is in a sector which appears to be relatively calm near the Valdaï plateaux. For the time being, its main concern is to survive the rigors of an exceptionally harsh winter. As a result the Soviet counter-offensive in January 1942 even more dreadful.

Unlike most of the German units engaged on the eastern front, *Totenkopf* was equipped with clothing relatively suitable for the extremely cold temperatures, sent from Dachau since it had been manufactured using garments taken from the deportees. Nevertheless, many soldiers were unable to escape frostbite. (NA)

Two men from a workshop company from the division in the snow of winter 1941-1942. (Private collection)

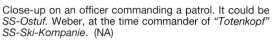

Close-up on an officer commanding a patrol. It could be *SS-Ostuf.* Weber, at the time commander of *"Totenkopf" SS-Ski-Kompanie.* (NA)

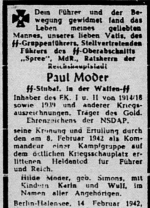

Dein Führer und der Be-
wegung gewidmet fand das
Leben meines geliebten
Mannes, unseres lieben Vatis, des
ℋ-Gruppenführers, Stellvertretenden
Führers des ℋ-Oberabschnitts
„Spree", MdR., Ratsherrn der
Reichshauptstadt
Paul Moder
ℋ-Stubaf. in der Waffen-ℋ
Inhaber des EK. I u. II von 1914/18
sowie 1939 und anderer Kriegs-
auszeichnungen, Träger des Gold.
Ehrenzeichens der NSDAP.
seine Krönung und Erfüllung durch
den am 8. Februar 1942 als Kom-
mandeur einer Kampfgruppe auf
dem östlichen Kriegsschauplatz er-
littenen Heldentod für Führer
und Reich.
Hilde Moder, geb. Simons, mit
Kindern Karla und Wulf, im
Namen aller Angehörigen.
Berlin-Halensee, 14. Februar 1942,
Kurfürstendamm 135.

Paul Moder:

Death notice of *SS-Stubaf.* Paul Moder (*Kdr III./SS-Art.-Rgt."T"*) published in *Das schwarze Korps* on 26 February 1942. (Private collection.)

Information gleaned from the population of a village in the Staraja Russa sector. The Germans often found that the men in the villages were either very old or very young, as can be seen on this photograph. Those old enough to fight had been enrolled in the Red Army or with the partisans. (NA)

Ludwig Schwermann (leader of *16.(Pi.)/SS-T.IR 3*) going on leave from Demjansk aerodrome. (Private collection S.)

The heavy snowfalls had whitened the countryside and the soldiers had to be camouflaged as well as possible to escape enemy eyes. This soldier from the rear had to paint the helmets white. (NA)

Advance observation post. The white clothing supplied during this famous winter of 1941-1942 was far from being standardised. Generally, the division's tailors made it with whatever they could lay their hands on, especially white sheets "requisitioned" on site. (NA)

This soldier is ready to fire near the entrance to a bunker. Photographers had taken the habit of only taking photographs of men warmly dressed, avoiding the thousands of soldiers in the German army who shivered with cold in miserable uniforms. (NA)

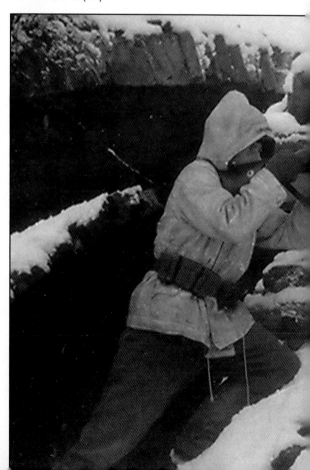

Observers at work. During the month of December 1941, the division detected renewed activity behind the Soviet lines, while the *Luftwaffe* reported numerous troop movements along the former Moscow – Leningrad railway line. Eicke kept *Totenkopf* on a high level of alert and accelerated the construction of fortifications. (NA)

Totenkopf was unusual in that it had split up its troops into numerous *Kampfgruppen* to block the increasing number of breaches along the perimeter of the Demjansk pocket. One of the most active groups was *Einsatz-Kompanie "Schiweck"*, formed from *1.Kp./SS-T.IR 3*. (NA)

Due to insufficient numbers, *Totenkopf* was unable to hold a continuous front line, especially in the west of the pocket. It therefore set up solid strongpoints which threw back countless Soviet attacks. (NA)

An *MG-34* machine gun in heavy configuration, somewhere in the Demjansk pocket. (Private collection S.)

Fighting in the Demjansk pocket

The encirclement of *II.AK* and *X.AK* around Demjansk remains an episode of the war which is relatively unknown by the general public. By ordering all units trapped east of Staraja Russa to stay in position, against the opinion of his generals, Hitler managed to draw most of the Soviet forces, thereby minimizing the enemy's tactical success. In view of this half-victory, in which the *Luftwaffe* played only a minor - but extremely amplified - role, Hitler adopted the same strategy at Stalingrad resulting in the consequences we are all familiar with.

Due to the shortage of infantry, the role played by the division's artillery proved to be of vital importance. This photograph shows an observer looking through his binoculars. No less than eleven members of *SS-T.Art.-Rgt.* were awarded the Knight's Cross or the German Cross in gold for military achievements during the battle of Demjansk. (NA)

681

No 22 · 21. Mai 1942   51. Jahrgang · Preis 20 Pfg

Berliner

Illustrierte Zeitung

Above: Max Seela (on the left) and Siegfried Müller (on the right) make the headlines of the *Berliner Illustrierte Zeitung* dated May 21, 1942. Seela came from inside the pocket, Müller from the west: they met on the banks of the river Lowat.

Opposite: A *Junker Ju-52* on Demjansk aerodrome. The *Luftwaffe* made a decisive contribution during the first days of the encirclement. Afterwards its role was drastically reduced. (NA)

Below: One of the features throughout the Soviet Union was the dreadful road network. This photograph shows a view of the Demjansk – Staraja Russa Rollbahn where a *Totenkopf* convoy is stuck in the mud. The leading vehicle is a captured Russian tractor on which a death's head and the *"SS"* insignia have been painted on the front grille. (Private collection.)

To improve the communication channels, a log road was built from October 1941. This lifeline, vital for the German, was the scene of furious fighting until the pocket was evacuated in February 1943. (Private collection.)

A well camouflaged shelter in the Demjansk forest. (Private collection.)

A look-out, somewhere inside the pocket. The soldier is from a transportation unit, hence the obsolete equipment, especially the helmet! (Private collection.)

1

2

3

4

1. Hans Ulmer (SS-Nr. 10 557) was a reserve officer who distinguished himself during the Demjansk siege by efficiently organizing supplies to the division, especially the parachute drops of food and weapons by the *Luftwaffe*. In January 1944, he replaced Hans Moser as intendant of *II.SS-Pz.Korps* and ended the war as a member of *SS-FHA*. He was promoted *SS-Standartenführer* on June 21, 1944. (Rights reserved)

2. Until May 1942, the toops holding the western sector of the pocket were under the command of *Generalmajor* **Hans Zorn**. He was awarded the Knight's cross on July 27, 1941 at the head of *20.ID (mot.)*. (Rights reserved)

3. *SS-Hstuf.* **Dietmar Prem** (SS-Nr. 49 309) had been in command of *7.Kp./SS-T.IR 1* since August 9, 1941. Injured in Demjansk in June 1942, he was to leave the division in April 1943. On January 1, 1944, he was transferred to an anti-partisan unit, *Feldjäger-Kommando III*, where he won the German Cross in gold on May 26, 1944. (NA)

4. Eduard Deisenhofer (SS-Nr. 3642) was a former member of the *SS-TV* which he had joined in 1935 after starting his career in the *Leibstandarte*, Hitler's bodyguard regiment. In 1941, after completing a PhD in law, he was appointed commander of *I./SS-IR 9* which he led in the fighting on the Finnish front. In the autumn, he rejoined *Totenkopf* and took command of *I./SS-T.IR1*. In autumn 1942, he was transferred to *SS-Junkerschule* at Bad Tölz where he acted as *Lehrgruppenkommandeur*. In 1943, he served for a short period of time with the inspectorate of the *SS-FHA* infantry before taking command of *SS-Pz.Gren.Rgt.21* of the *"Frundsberg"* division in early 1944. He was promoted *SS-Standartenführer* on April 20, 1944. On August 30, he was appointed commander of *17.SS-Panzergrenadier-Division "Götz von Berlichingen"* and one month later, was given a recruitment mission in the Carpathian Mountains. He was declared missing on January 31, 1945 while en route to Pomerania to take command of *15.Waffen-Grenadier-Division der SS*. (Rights reserved)

It is now winter and temperatures are below freezing. Snow is covering the whole land. Totenkopf had to wait before being delivered adequate clothing. (Courtesy Michael Cremin)

Without whitewashed helmets and white clothes, the German soldiers were easily spotted by the Soviet snipers and losses mounted dramatically before a few stop-gap measures were taken. (Courtesy Michael Cremin)

The gun crew has kept the same position in the Kirillowschtschina sector. The only difference is that the snow has now turned the landscape white. (Courtesy Michael Cremin)

6

The battle for the Demjansk salient

Operation *"Brückenschlag"*

In February 1942, after succeeding in stabilizing the front around Staraja Russa, *16.Armee* started to work out an offensive to restore connection between *X.AK* and *II.AK*. For what would become the *"Brückenschlag"* operation, the *OKW* gave up *5.leichte-Division*, *8.leichte-Division* and *329.ID*. *Heeresgruppe "Nord"* handed over *18.ID (mot.)*, *122.ID* and some elements from *Totenkopf* stationed in the sector of Staraja Russa. These units were strengthened by *I./Pz.Rgt.203*, *StuG-Abt.184* and *StuG-Bttr. 659*, and gathered within *Korpsgruppe "von Seydlitz"*. The attack was launched on the **21st of March** along a ten kilometre front. The territory to cover was a forty-kilometre-wide zone of thick forests and swamps. The Soviets had built a strong defence network of bunkers and trenches over it. On the **22nd of March**, IR 522 from the *329.ID* extricated an SS company from *Kampfgruppe "Becker"*, which had been surrounded for eight weeks in Podzepotschje. On the **29th of March**, all the towns located along the Redja between Welikoje Selo and Michalkino fell into the hands of the Germans anew. On the 1st of April, *Jäger-Rgt.56* freed a part of *SS-Kampfgruppe "Eichert"* which had been stuck in Sytschewo since January. But the first days of April saw the Soviet defence clearly toughening between the Redja and the Lowat. After several days of fierce combat, *Gruppe "Engelhardt"* moved on as far as Michalkino and managed to force its way through the enemy line. The road to the Lowat was cleared. The last strike was given on the **19th of April**, but the *Jäger* were finally stopped before the river Gussinez in spate. The next day, *III./IR 51* managed to besiege Ramuschewo. Its head officer, *Major* Steinhardt, known for being the first soldier from the *Heer* to ever be given the Knights' Cross, was killed in the battle for the town. On the afternoon, *I./IR 30* managed to break the Soviet resistance and to force its way as far as the Lowat, but its flooding waters remained a serious hurdle.

Operation *"Fallreep"*

In March, it was decided that *Korpsgruppe "Zorn"* should move into attack from inside the Demjansk pocket towards Kobylkino, so as to meet with *Korpsgruppe "von Seydlitz"*. *SS-Kampfgruppe "Bochmann"* was to go north. On the left was *SS-Pi.-Kp. "Seela"*, while *SS-Kampfgruppe "Kleffner"* was to move north-west through swampy ground. Indeed, since the beginning of the month, a rise in temperature had led to thaw: all the rivers were in spate, flooding trenches, bunkers and individual shelters. Wading about in the mud, soaked to the skin, the men came to miss the cold of the previous months. The Demjansk airfield had been turned into a mud field on which transport planes couldn't land, thus making the supplying of the pocket all the more difficult.
On the **14th of April**, despite such dreadful conditions, 1200 men from *Totenkopf* launched an assault on the Soviet positions. Soldiers on each side gripped each other by the throat. On the **15th of April**,

battalions moved into attack again after a fruitless first day. *Kampfgruppe "Kleffner"* besieged Bjakowo around 6.30 pm. The SS thus got a perfect starting point for their attacks to come towards the Lowat. The second phase of *"Fallreep"* started on the **17th of April**. The aim was to go through the large forest leading to the Lowat. *Kampfgruppe "Kleffner"* attacked from Bjakowo towards the river. The fighting was brutal: Soviet artillery and air force never gave the Germans any respite. Losses were excessively heavy with regard to the insignificant land captures. The next day, the two *SS-Kampfgruppen* and *Rgt. "von Borries"* resumed the attack. Men fought over every inch of land, and the log path was the focus of a fierce struggle. On the evening, Georg Bochmann's men found themselves in front of Omytschkino. The town, located on the east bank of the Lowat, fell into SS hands on the **19th of April**, thanks to a flanking movement from the south. But the river was flooding and its crossing was made momentarily impossible. Little did it matter: Georg Bochmann chose to move up north, surprising the Soviet defenders. On the **20th of April**, the SS resumed their movement towards Nowo Ramuschewo. They lost many men on the way, but finally captured the village. Meanwhile, *Gruppe "Seydlitz"* renewed its attack towards the Lowat. Caught in the crossfire, the Soviets withdrew. Around 6.30 pm, Seydlitz's men reached the west bank, thus releasing cries of joy among Bochmann's men on the other bank. *SS-Hstuf.* Seela (*3.Kp./SS-T.Pi.-Btl.*) and Müller (*1.Kp./SS-T.Pi.-Btl.*), one from the east, the other from the west, met in the middle of the river on inflatable dinghies. Thus the surrounding was over. The Demjansk pocket became a salient again! Next step for the Germans was widening the corridor by attacking northwards and southwards. The attack towards the north was launched by *Gruppe "Zorn"* on the **25th of April**. *Gruppe "Seydlitz"* attacked south of Ramuschewo and allowed to widen the corridor linking up *X.AK* and *II.AK* on either side of the Lowat, between Redzy and Kobylkino on the west bank, and between Prismorschje and Nowosselje on the east bank. This achievement marked the end of Operations *"Brückenschlag"* and *"Fallreep"*.

The defence of the Ramuschewo corridor

Despite its disastrous losses and the state of exhaustion of its soldiers, *Totenkopf* wasn't evacuated from the Demjansk salient. True, its heroism and sacrifices were rewarded by the giving of ten Knights' Crosses, but as the Soviets had resumed their offensive and were now showing signs of strangling the Ramuschewo isthmus, it was decided at higher command that *Totenkopf* should stay there to protect this umbilical cordon, on which the supplies for *II.AK* circulated. It only had a minimal number of soldiers left. Furthermore, it had been noticed from November 1943 that both the morale and the discipline of the troops were undermined. There had clearly been an increase in the acts of cowardice when facing the enemy, self-mutilation and theft. In February, when the situation had become worryingly critical, three cases of desertion had even been reported, which was extremely rare in the *Waffen-SS* at this stage of the war. Nevertheless, the victorious conclusion of the battle of Demjansk persuaded Hitler that the *Totenkopf's* presence was essential to the stability of the German front south of Lake Ilmen. He regarded it now as one of the best divisions in the German army, and he repeatedly refused to grant it some healing time off-front. He authorized though the formation of new SS units meant to strengthen *Totenkopf* as soon as they were sufficiently trained and equipped. Setting up these new units would take four months.

In early May, Theodor Eicke started reassembling the scattered units of his division. The next day, he took command of *Korpsgruppe z.b.V "Zorn"*, and *SS-Staf.* Becker took over from him as the head of *Gruppe "Eicke"*. It allowed for better cohesion of the chain of command in the most sensitive sector of the corridor. Indeed, the Soviet attacked day after day south and north of this zone. Despite the use of tanks, extra-powerful artillery and countless infantry, they just couldn't strangle this isthmus.

On the **8th of May**, *Freikorps "Danmark"* was sent to join *Korpsgruppe "Eicke"* in the salient: such reinforcements were much helpful to the Germans, and the new companies were in no time distributed between Werezniza and Zemena. At the end of May, as the Soviets were multiplying their attacks between Sutoki and Nowosselje, the Germans reacted by launching a few raids with shock detachments. But the general situation remained downright worrying for the Germans. As a matter of fact, *Korpsgruppe "Eicke"* had to defend an 84-kilometre-long front with less than eight thousand men. It was nonetheless decided that the Ramuschewo corridor should be widened by an offensive codenamed after the Danish flag: *"Danebrog"*. The order to attack was given on the **3rd of June**. *Totenkopf* was to clean out the sector north of the *Rollbahn* between Wassiljewschtschina and Bjakowo, and to set up new defensive positions on the west bank of the Pola. The Danes lost many men on their first assault (26 men killed, including their commandant, *SS-Stubaf.* von Schalburg). Their failure prevented the operations to go on as planned. Another attack was launched on the **5th of June**: this time, Bol. Dubowizy fell into the hands of the Danes and many bunkers were cleared. The following days saw a clear stabilization of the front. On the **10th of June**, at about 7 pm, the Soviets resumed their attacks after what had been a very quiet day. They took Bol. Dubowizy anew. *SS-Kampfgruppe "Kleffner"* and *Freikorps* were quickly thrown into battle, but couldn't retake the town. The Danes lost their commandant — *SS-Ostubaf.* von Lettow-Vorbeck — for the second time within a few days.

Early in July, the German staff had asked permission to evacuate the Demjansk salient to allow *II.AK* to shorten its lines so as to relieve reserves. On the contrary, Hitler decided to keep this salient, which he thought could be useful for a future offensive towards Moscow. Reinforcements were even sent there. On the **17th of July**, after a short lull, the Soviets launched another major offensive. Their artillery slashed the whole front, turning over minefields and destroying every German position one after the other. The centre of gravity of the offensive was between Dubowizy and Wassiljewschtschina. Early in the afternoon, the Soviets took Wassiljewschtschina, where what was left of two *Totenkopf* companies fought till the last man standing before it finally capitulated. *Totenkopf* was then ordered to fill in the breach at any cost. But for the first time since the beginning of the war, his commandant – at that

time Max Simon, who was standing in for Theodor Eicke for a few weeks – preferred to disobey. He informed *Korpsgruppe "von Knobelsdorff"* in quite straightforward terms that *Totenkopf* had lost 532 men since the **17th of July** in the afternoon, and was in no condition to attack. *8.Jäger-Division* was thus asked to do the job, but eventually failed. The Soviets carried on with their attack on the **18th of July**. *I./SS-T.IR 3* repelled all their assaults before Rykalowo, but due to the lack of experience of their leader, *SS-Hstuf.* Hoppe, the battalion endured disproportionate losses. On the **24th of July**, after several days of merciless combat, *Totenkopf* and *8.Jäger-Division* managed to take control of the former front line again. There were 59 skeletons of Soviet tanks scattered on the battlefield. The Danes were relieved and reached Moklokowo. Since the **20th of May**, they had had 126 men killed and more than 600 injured! On the **27th of July**, Max Simon informed Marshal von Küchler that, since the **16th of July**, *Totenkopf* had lost 40 officers and 1945 NCOs and privates.*SS-Rgt. "Becker"* only had 541 men now to defend the seven-kilometre-long front. Altogether, *Totenkopf* had only 2736 combatants left. Max Simon was thus compelled to reorganize his lines in three different sectors: the Robja front was given to *SS-Stubaf.* Baum, with 543 men for a 7 kilometre front; the sector of Welikoje Selo (west) was controlled by *Kampfgruppe "Schröder"* (from the *Heer*), with 976 men for a 13 kilometre front; and the sector of Salutschje (south) was defended by *Kampfgruppe "Glase"* (another unit from the *Heer*) with 1227 men for a 21 kilometre front. Whilst survivors in the salient fought roughly in awful conditions, Theodor Eicke, in accordance with Hitler's promise, set up a new *"Totenkopf"* division in *SS-Truppenübungsplatz "Sennelager"* with new recruits, convalescent men and soldiers on leave he preferred not to send back to Demjansk, to keep experienced officers for the rebuilding of the units. In the meantime, *SS-Oberführer* Simon managed to send 170 officers and NCOs from the main units of *Totenkopf* back to Germany using various excuses. Thus preserved, these men were to help in building the core of the new regiments and battalions of the future division.

On the **10th of August**, the Soviets tried once more to strangle the corridor. The SS were again in the heart of the battle. The Russians launched fresh troops against German positions. From day 1 of the offensive, the SS battalion fighting in the sector of the Robja lost one third of its numbers. But the Soviets also suffered cruel losses and were finally stopped after nine days of fierce combat. Sorely afflicted, *Totenkopf* only lined up 959 fit soldiers. As a supplement, 80 male nurses, 80 drivers from the service corps, 20 men from the supply corps, 40 artillerymen from *SS-T.Flak-Abt.* and 10 crewmen from *SS-T.StuG-Batterie* were used as infantrymen. On the **23rd of August**, some Russian deserters announced the imminent resuming of violent offensives. Indeed, the Soviets launched 21 attacks that day, all of which were repelled by the SS. On the **31st of August**, the Soviets attacked again in the sector of the Robja with a regiment of fusiliers backed up by tanks. They were smashed by precise fire from the *Totenkopf* artillery, and had to withdraw, leaving many casualties behind. From the 3rd of September, *Totenkopf* confined itself to the southern part of the corridor and to the banks of the Robja, where the Soviets were still fighting. What was left of the division was holding the front of the Robja along a 5.5 kilometre distance, between Sutoki and Demidowo. On the **11th of September**, *Totenkopf* had 6409 men in the salient. This total included the non-fighting staff (secretaries, drivers, cooks, nurses, etc.), the wounded and soldiers hospitalised for sickness.

SS-Sturmmann Alfred Hilger (*2.Bttr./SS-Totenkopf-Flak-Abteilung*) was decorated with the German Cross in Gold on 12 August 1942 for showing repeated personal bravery during the Demjansk fighting. (Courtesy Martin Månsson)

On the **27th of September**, *Gruppe "von Knobels-dorff"* launched operation *"Michael"* from the Robja towards the Lowat. This time, the aim was not only to widen the corridor, but also to open a second supply route for the 100.000 men still fighting in the salient. The main effort was directed by *5.Jäger-Division*. On its right, *Totenkopf* was meant to back it up with artillery fire. The infantrymen from the *5.Jäger-Division* managed to cross the Robja and to gain ground westwards. On the **30th of September**, *SS-Btl. "Baum"* and *"Reder"*, which now accommodated the whole *Totenkopf* infantry, came from Nowosselje to cover the right flank of *5.Jäger-Division*. The SS carried on with their attacks the next day, with the efficient backing of the artillery and the *Stukas*. On the **5th of October**, *SS-Ogruf.* Eicke took back the head of *Totenkopf*, that was still progressing sou-

thwards, in the direction of Schotowo and Chodyni. On the **8th of October**, *Gruppe "von Knobelsdorff"* announced it had reached all its objectives. The corridor was sufficiently widened and the second supply road was opened. Operation *"Michael"* was a substantial success.

On the **12th of October**, what was left of *Totenkopf* was at last ordered to leave the front. After almost 16 months of continuous combat on the front line in dreadful conditions, the survivors boarded in the Staraja Russa station on the **23rd of October** on a train going to France via Pskow, Riga, Tilsit, Kassel, Strasbourg and Mulhouse, leaving all their vehicles and heavy weapons behind. The convoys then reached the area of Poitiers and Angoulême, via Belfort, Dijon and Tours.

Couriers from the division in the Demjansk salient. Notice the antigas blankets slung across their shoulders. (Rights reserved)

A Soviet heavy machine gun on a captured carriage on wheels, turned against its former owners by these SS infantrymen in a quite thick wood typical of the Demjansk region. (Rights reserved)

SS-Totenkopf-Pionier-Bataillon (engineers) are laying mines. Since the lines of *Totenkopf* were stretched in the extreme, this type of defence was absolutely necessary to make up for the lack of infantry. (Rights reserved)

The Totenkopf *artillery in the pocket of Demjansk*

In keeping with the infantry fighting in the multiple *Kampfgruppen* following the needs and the circumstances, the divisional artillery get organised in *Artillerie-Gruppen* mixing batteries belonging to different *Abteilungen*. For example, *SS-Hstuf.* Martin Stange's one which is formed by the headquarters of the 1st artillery group with the 4th and 10th ones in January 1942, then with the 1st, 2nd, 3rd and 7th ones in the following May.

The Demjansk aerodrome is mainly used by *Ju-52* supply planes under the command of the *Oberst* Morzik (*Lufttransportführer der Luftflotte1*) and belonging to *Kampffl.Gr.z.b.V.1, 105, 500, Öls* and *Posen*. This set of photographs show the unloading of spare parts, here wheels for the carriage of a *21cm Mörser 18* howitzer. The impressive size of these wheels foretell the size and weight of the whole piece: 6.51m long, it weights more than 16 tons when set up and 22 tons on the road to pull an explosive shell of 121kg at 16.7 km. In the pocket, *3 Bttr./Art-Rgt.636* is with such weapons equipped. The aerodrome is also used for the evacuation of wounded and on leave personnel, in order to make the most of the planes leaving the pocket. In one year, the *Luftflotte 1* would have carried 64844 tons of equipment and 30500 soldiers to the pocket, losing 265 aircraft and consuming 42155 tons of fuel. (NA)

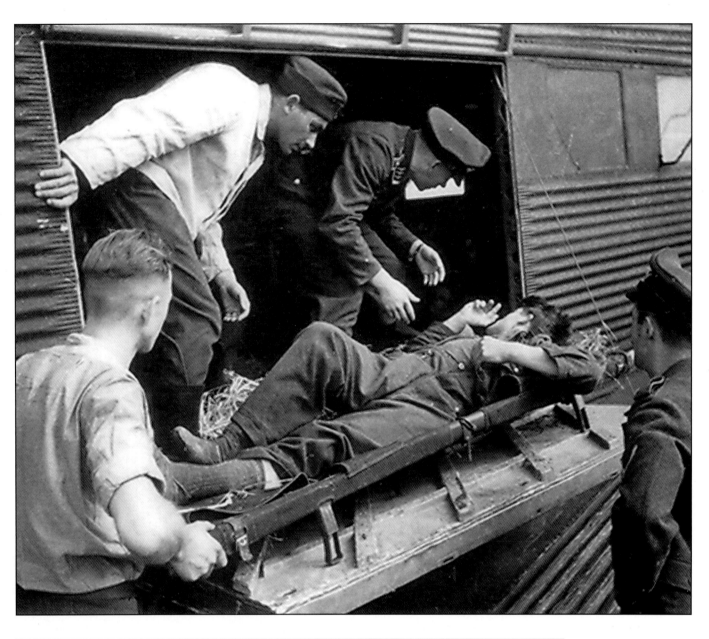

The anti-aircraft artillery of the *Totenkopf* division is widely used during the battle for the pocket, either against terrestrial targets or against the Soviet airforce. Here is a 3.7cm gun with its sight instrument without an aiming corrector. (NA)

In 1942, 3.7 *Flak 36* are used by the 2nd battery of *SS-T.Flak-Abteilung*. Until the 10th May this unit is under the command of *SS-Hstuf.* Siegfried Grässler, formerly *Adjutant* of *SS-T.IR 2*. His successor will be the *SS-Ostuf.* Erhard Lehmann. (NA)

War of the positions in the pocket

In April and May 1942, while the hard fight to open and maintain a corridor near Ramuschewo continues, a war for positions is taking place in the remaining pocket. Hand to hand combats, artillery firing and patrol activities happen on a daily basis with heavy losses.

The sector of Kirillowschtschina is held by *II./SS-T.IR 1* led by *SS-Stubaf.* Wilhelm Schulze seen here talking with *SS-Ostuf.* Backe, in the centre. In May 1943, Schulze will be incarcerated for four months for ill-treating his subordinates. Indeed, in December 1942, in front of his assembled battalion, he slapped three young recruits guilty of petty thefts. (NA)

Even train drivers have to live in holes. (Private collection.)

The division engineers have also the task of making safe booby traps and unexploded ammunition. This shell has been marked to avoid any accident. (NA)

On the 10th June 1942, a Soviet infantry battalion, supported by 18 tanks, succeeded in breaking through the SS lines north of Dubowizy. Although his right flank is now exposed, SS-Ostuf. Schwermann (16./SS-T.IR 3), already known for being one of the most daredevil officers of the division, counter-attacks with a handful of men and prevent the Russians from cutting the Wassiljew-schtschina-Bjakowo road. (NA)

A heavy machine gun is set up in a quiet sector, if you consider the casual attitude of the men in the background. (NA)

8.1cm (*8cm m.Gr.W.34*) mortar gunners in action. It is the standard mortar used by the infantry. From 1942 the Germans abandon the 5cm light mortars which had a low firing power. (NA)

Ammunition supply. The soldier in the centre of the photograph is wearing what looks like training gear. (NA)

A *StuG.III* with short gun (*7.5cm-StuK.L/24*) of *SS-StuG.-Bttr. "Totenkopf"*. One of the crew member is drawing a 5th victory circle. (Private collection S.)

The assault group of the SS-Oscha. *August Zingel*

East of Nowosselje, the Soviets have an observation post which allow them to direct their batteries fire onto the Rollbahn. *SS-Hstuf.* Krauth gives then *SS-Oscha.* August Zingel the task of eliminating the enemy position which inflict heavy losses to the German supply convoys.

SS-Hstuf. Heiner Krauth (*Kdr.II./SS-T.IR 1*) talking with non-commissioned officers from his headquarters. Notice the mosquito net pulled back over his cap, a very useful accessory in this swampy area. (Private collection S.)

Zingel then receives his new instructions directly from Krauth. The latter wears the German cross in gold won on the 29th April 1942. (Private collection S.)

SS-Hstuf. Zech (*Chef 15.Kp/SS-T.IR 1*) thus organises a shock section which *SS-Oscha.* August Zingel (facing) will lead. He will have three squads led by *SS-Uscha.* Marx, Eschenbach and Kellermann. (Private collection S.)

Zingel prepares his section for combat. Although this will take place during the night, Zingel has taken with him a face mask. Tension can be seen on their faces. (Private collection S.)

Morning of the 9th September 1942. August Zingel's section come back from their mission, crossing the Robja in inflatable dinghies. (Private collection S.)

One of the squads is ready to step onto the bank. The mission is a total success: for one dead and nine wounded, the "Zingel" section has destroyed 32 bunkers, 4 mortars and five 76.2 guns. (Private collection S.)

The dinghy is coming near the photographer. The fight was hard and the faces are marked by true tension. (Private collection.)

Main field hospital

The division medical services are well organised and benefit from qualified personnel who have learned from the French campaign. During the winter of 1940-1941, doctors and nurses went on several training courses in order to learn war medicine, which few of them were familiar with as they mostly came from concentration camps sanitary services.

A Hanomag car from a division motorcyclist company brings a wounded man to the *Truppen-Verband-Platz III* where he is taken in by some stretcher bearers. (NA)

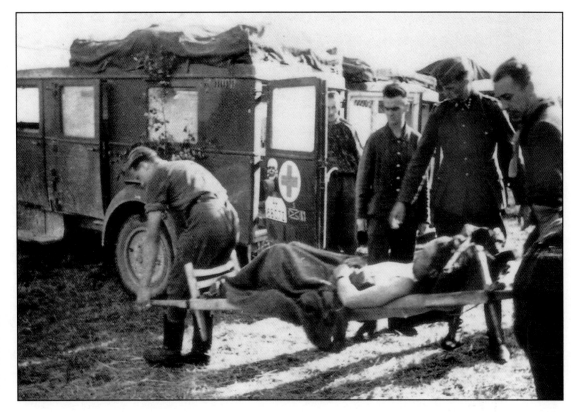

Another wounded man is carried to a vehicle of the 1st section ambulance. It is a *Phänomen Granit 2500H*, the oldest version of the *Kfz.31*, built from 1936 to 1939. (NA)

These two photographs show a detailed view of the inside of the ambulance, which the model makers would appreciate. (NA)

Considered a "heavy" ambulance, the *Granit 2500H* could carry four wounded people on stretchers. (NA)
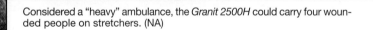

The wounded soldiers are carried to the field hospital by any means possible. This vehicle coming back from the rear echelon lines took the opportunity to bring back bread loaves from the baker section. (NA)

Right: The first aid and field hospitals during the summer of 1942 are crowded with the wounded. (NA)

Combats for the "Finger-Stellung"

This position, so called because it is shaped as a glove finger towards the Soviet lines west of Bol. Dubowizy, is the stage for relentless fighting during the summer of 1942.

Under the leadership of *SS-Ostuf.* Endress *(Adjutant SS-KGr. "Kleffner")*, some men from the motorcyclist battalion and the division disciplinary company are holding on despite being bombarded every day by artillery fire and mortar attacks dozens of time from the Soviet infantry and tanks. (NA)

A photograph of this non-commissioned officer from the division was published many times. Here are photos issued from the same film. Notice the skull on each side of the collar, practice which makes the identification of grade impossible when the jacket, like here, is covered by a camouflage overall. (NA)

Counter-attack east of Korowitschino

On the 5th July 1942, the *I./SS-T.IR 1 (SS-Stuf. Eckert)* has a mission to destroy the Soviet positions in the "Egg Wood", with the help of a battalion of the *Heer* on its left, and to establish a new defensive front towards the north and the east.

An *SS-Obersturmführer* decorated with an iron cross 2nd class cross is resting. Even though for propaganda reasons the photographs do not show exhausted soldiers, it is obvious that holding the front line by the *Totenkopf* division has pushed its men to their physical and psychological limits. (NA)

The operation was a success after hand to hand combats, but with heavy losses. (NA)

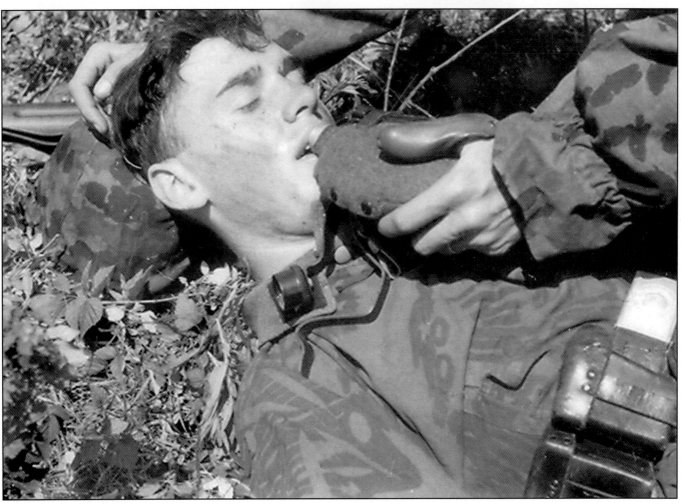

Picture of a division motorcyclist. The tension from the fighting can be seen on his face. (NA)

Below: *SS-Oberführer* Max Simon in the company of Karl Stieglitz and Otto Baum in the Kirillowschtschina during the summer of 1942. (Rights reserved).

A prisoner is being interrogated. The interpreters of the division were mostly ethnic Germans from the Baltic countries. (NA)

The entrance of this bunker was bombed and this soldier is about to do the necessary repairs. This photo was taken during a heat wave according to what this SS is wearing; the camouflage shirt is worn just over a vest, which is not a regulation practice but is often authorised. (NA)

Above right: Theodor Eicke inspects the front on board a *Kübelwagen*. The holder of the knight cross who is saluting him is *SS-Stubaf.* Franz Kleffner. (Private collection S.)

Below: A *2cm-Flak* gun on a *Sd.Kfz.10* chassis. It probably belongs to *1.Bttr./SS-Flak-Abt."T"* (*SS-Hstuf.* Knöchlein). (NA)

SS infantryman watching the enemy lines with binoculars. Notice the round magazine of the *MG-34* gun. (NA)

A welder, duly protected. (NA)

Reporting on the division vehicle maintenance workshop

At the start of the war in 1939, the *SS* units were well behind their *Heer* colleagues regarding the logistics support. This is still the case for the *Totenkopf* division in the summer of 1942, as the decisions made in May by the *SS-FHA* to reinforce theirs would not apply until the autumn. The vehicle maintenance workshop is not functioning independently from the division train's one.

Left: A hoist on an unidentified vehicle can lift up the engine of a *Opel Blitz* lorry. Notice the death's head painted on the side of the vehicle, which is an unusual practice. (NA)

A mobile workshop cannot function without its own power supply. This one is on a trailer. (NA)

A soldier from the workshop distilling fuel – is it alcohol? The equipment used is rather primitive. (NA)

Working on an engine. On the foreground, a crankshaft with its axle. (NA)

Left: Checking the suspension of a vehicle. (NA)

The workshop also owns a sewing machine: here a motor-bike saddle is being repaired. (NA)

A train driver built a makeshift desk in the Demjansk forest. (Private collection.).

This lorry is being attended to in the workshop. It has a press (unless it is a column drill) and oxygen and acetylene bottles for welding. (NA)

Above right: This lorry is used for storing spare parts. In the foreground, a storage cabinet is ready to go.

Right: An unidentified *SS-Hauptsturmführer*, probably the leader of the three division workshops, maps the vehicles to be recovered.

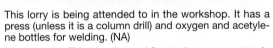

A damaged Mercedes Benz ambulance is coming to the workshop. During the Second World War, the Red Cross flag is not always a guarantee of protection. (NA)

Above: *SS-Oberscharführer* Ernst Stäudle was decorated with the Knight's Cross on 10 April 1942 as an artillery forward observer within *8.Bttr./SS-Totenkopf-Artillerie-Regiment*. He can be seen here as an *SS-Unterscharführer* serving within *SS-Totenkopf-Standarte 1 "Oberbayern"* just before the outbreak of the war. Notice the number "I" on his left shoulder trap. (Courtesy Martin Månsson)

Opposite: *SS-Oberscharführer* Ernst Stäudle.

Ernst Stäudle with his family. His brother is a *Luftwaffe* NCO. Ernst was promoted to *SS-Untersturmführer* on 1 September 1943 and to *SS-Obersturmführer* on 21 June 1944. He died in Soviet captivity on 11 July 1946. (Courtesy Martin Månsson)

Ernst Stäudle is photographed shortly after his promotion to *SS-Untersturmführer*. He was awarded the Knight's Cross for outstanding deeds during the night battles of 26/27 February 1942. Thanks to their overwhelming numbers, the Soviets came to within 50 meters of the German positions in Schumilkino which were manned by just a few defenders. A German construction battalion, which had been sent in as reinforcement, fled when it was attacked by the Russian soldiers. In those dramatic conditions, despite a severe wound, Stäudle gathered the last survivors of the German garrison and, with only an *3.7cm-Pak 36* available, managed to keep the enemy at bay, at times fighting at very close range. His action had prevented a Soviet breakthrough behind the German positions in Salutschje. (Courtesy Martin Månsson)

Ernst Stäudle is seen here as an *SS-Obersturmführer* and training officer within *SS-Artillerieschule "Beneschau"* (Benesov). On 30 April 1945, the elements of the school who had not yet been engaged were regrouped in Prague and Stäudle was named *Kompanie-Chef* in one of the *Kampfgruppen* formed with the school personnel. He was captured by the Americans who handed him over to the Soviets. Working in a coalmine in Silesia, he died of pneumonia in a prisoner camp, south of Kattowicze. (Courtesy Martin Månsson)

Angoulême, autumn 1942. *SS-Unterscharführer* Hans Hirning is being decorated by Max Simon with the Knight's Cross he won on 23 October 1942 as *SS-Rottenführer* and *Granatwerfer-Truppführer* in *6.Kp./SS-T.IR 1*. (Courtesy Martin Månsson)

Hirning is congratulated by an *SS-Sturmbannführer*. The former typifies the fanatic attitude of a great number of members of *Totenkopf*. Despite a first failure while trying to silence a Soviet antitank gun, he did come back a few minutes later with two hollow charges and managed to destroy the gun and its crew. (Courtesy Martin Månsson)

Hirning parades in front of men of his company, just after the award. The unidentified *SS-Sturmbannführer* of the previous photo is now visible from the front: he is Wilhelm Schulze, his battalion commander. (Courtesy Martin Månsson)

Above left: Notice that Hirning is not wearing a wounded badge. Despite his daredevil deed which had earned him the Knight's Cross, he escaped unscathed after having destroyed the enemy antitank gun that was threatening his unit positions. (Courtesy Martin Månsson)

Above right: Hirning is taking a well deserved leave. He is seen at his home town station where he is welcomed with flowers. (Courtesy Martin Månsson)

Opposite: Studio portrait of Hans Hirning, dated from 2 June 1943. He was killed on 30 April 1945 near Prague as an *SS-Oberscharführer* and section leader within *SS-Kampfgruppe "Böhmen und Mähren"*. (Courtesy Martin Månsson)

A well known portrait of Hans Hirning but this particular one bears his signature. (Courtesy Martin Månsson).

Summer is back. New positions are dug. Many veteran accounts insist on the time devoted to repeated and exhausting trench-digging. (Courtesy Michael Cremin)

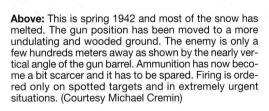

Above: This is spring 1942 and most of the snow has melted. The gun position has been moved to a more undulating and wooded ground. The enemy is only a few hundreds meters away as shown by the nearly vertical angle of the gun barrel. Ammunition has now become a bit scarcer and it has to be spared. Firing is ordered only on spotted targets and in extremely urgent situations. (Courtesy Michael Cremin)

Opposite: *SS-Standartenführer* Hellmuth Becker (*Kdr. SS-T.IR 3*) is shown before a meeting with the *II.AK* commander inside the Demjansk salient. (BA)

208

Above: *SS-Unterscharführer* August Zingel (seen here as an *SS-Oberscharführer*) won the Knight's Cross on 4 October 1942 as Stosstruppführer within *SS-Kampfgruppe "Krauth" (15.Kp./SS-T.IR1)*. He ended the war as an *SS-Untersturmführer, Div.-05* and commander of *Divisions-Sturmkompanie.* (Courtesy Martin Månsson)

Above: Portrait of Max Seela, taken shortly after he was awarded the coveted Knight's Cross. (Courtesy Martin Månsson)

Totenkopf is leaving the Eastern Front. After fifteen months of continuous and bitter fighting, the division is heading towards France for a complete refitting. (Courtesy Michael Cremin)

7

Reffiting in France

Conversion into a *Panzergrenadier-Division*

On the **26th of July 1942**, the *Totenkopf* depot units altogether had 635 men at the *Sennelager*, in Paderborn. They were joined by *SS-IR 9 (mot.) "Thule"*, with its 950 men on leave. At the end of the month, the first 1130 recruits, coming from *SS-T.Inf.Ers.-Btl.I* (in Warsaw) and *III* (in Brno), were registered by *Aufstellungsstab*, headed by *SS-Ostubaf.* Lammerding. These young soldiers – most of whom were barely eighteen – had followed a five to eight week military training. Until the **1st of October**, 2930 extra recruits arrived at the *Sennelager*. *Totenkopf* then lacked 11.000 men compared to its theoretical strength. The *SS-FHA* tried to solve the problem by transferring to the division 5000 extra men. *SS-Hstuf.* Schulze-Kossens, who was then the *Führer*'s adjutant, reported this poor outcome to Hitler, whose reaction was immediate: on the **26th of August**, 60.000 recruits from the *RAD* were handed over to *Totenkopf*. But short numbers wasn't the only problem the *Aufstellungsstab* was facing: it sorely lacked experienced officers. Their were no instructors for sappers and infantry guns companies, and for the rebuilding of the antitank battalion, there was a single platoon major to instruct 150 new recruits!

On the **7th of October**, after the end of operation *"Michael"*, what was left of *Totenkopf* left the Eastern Front at last. This core of experienced fighters was essential to the new division. They were taken much too late from the front though, and there were now too few of them to fully play their part. The *Aufstellungsstab* and the training units were transferred from the **12th of October** to the region of Angoulême, the new sector allocated to the division. There, they were subordinated to the *AOK 1*. On the **13th of October**, Eicke went to Rastenburg, where Hitler in person ordered him to have his division operational on the **10th of January 1943**. It was obviously too short a time, but Eicke didn't complain, because he was given the promise that a second armoured battalion would be created (a first one had been in January), as well as an assault gun group. Of course, this decision met with much reluctance within the army. During the summer, the *OKH* had already decided that it was out of the question that tanks would be delivered to the armoured battalions from *Totenkopf*, since the absolute priority was to equip divisions from the *Heer* that were fighting on the Eastern Front. Still the task remained difficult, as the losses exceeded by far the production of tanks from the *Reich* factories.

Till the end of the month, 31 convoys from the Eastern Front called at the stations of the Charentes region. Units from the division then depended upon *AOK 1* as far as logistics were concerned, and upon *Gen.Kdo. SS-Pz.Korps* on military level. With the return of the veterans from Demjansk, the *Aufstellungsstab* and most instruction units were dissolved. Drill was carried out at a furious pace. But the setting up of the division went off with much difficulty, because of staff and equipment shortage.

One of the first units to get set up was the *SS-Schützen-Regiment "Thule"*: it was made out of what was left of *SS-IR 9 "Thule"* and *SS-T.Kradsch.-Btl.*. This motorcycle regiment was headed by *SS-Ostubaf.* Lammerding and his battalion commanders, *SS-Stubaf.* Kleffner (*I.Btl.*) and Bochmann (*II.Btl.*).

SS-Sturmgeschütz-Abteilung 3 was formed from the **14th of October 1942** in the Debica camp, in Poland. Its core was made out of *SS-StuG.-Bttr. "Nord"*. At the end of October, the 36 survivors from *SS-T.-StuG.-Bttr.* arrived at Angoulême and were, against all odds, used for the setting up of *SS-Pz.Rgt.3*. True, the *Panzerwaffe* from the SS had to be created *ex nihilo*. Thrown into it were scouts and assault gun crews with a certain experience in driving tanks – even if, as far as tactics were concerned, they were quite different weapons – as well as staff specialised in antitank fighting. The rest of the men came from the infantry. Only at the end of November did *SS-StuG.-Bttr. "Nord"* reach at last the Debica camp. It stayed there for a mere few days, because it had to be on the Eastern front as early as on the **4th of December**. It was then necessary to create another core to set up *SS-StuG.-Abt.3*. This time, soldiers came from the antitank battalion, from gun companies of the infantry and from the artillery regiment. Some infantrymen who had had frostbite and were now unfit for infantry work joined them. Finally, a few men from *SS-T-StuG.-Bttr.* joined them as well because of their experience. The assault guns, 22 *StuG.III Ausf. F*, were only delivered from the 20th of January 1943.

The armoured regiment (*SS-Pz.Rgt.3*) was formed on the **14th of October 1942** out of *SS-Panzer-Abteilung 4*. The latter had been created on the 1st of June 1942 with volunteers coming for the most part from *SS-Pz.Jg.Ers.-Abt.* in Hilversum. The new regiment (*SS-Stubaf.* Leiner) was stationed at the La Braconne camp. The conditions of the drill were awful: the exercise field was only three kilometre long and 500 metre large! Moreover, the panzers delivered were in bad condition: there were many breakdowns, and manufacturing defects revealed themselves in the middle of manoeuvres. A month later, on the **13th of November**, order was given to set up a company equipped with *Pzkpfw.VI "Tiger"*. It was created in Fallingbostel; officers from *s.Pz.Abt.502* carried out the drill, and commandment was given to *SS-Hstuf.* Mooslechner. The drill was first carried out on *Pzkpfw.III*, since production was insufficient and the *"Tiger"* were to be delivered in January only. It only left a very short time for the company to master all the technical difficulties of such complex tanks.

SS-Totenkopf-Artillerie-Regiment was still commanded by *SS-Staf.* Hermann Priess. It got rebuilt in the sector of Saint-Maixent with new recruits from *SS-Art.-Ers.-Rgt.* in Munich. Contrary to the other units of the division, it was well fitted out.

As for *SS-Flak-Abt. "Totenkopf"*, it was trained in Saint-Jean-d'Angely. It was led by *SS-Stubaf.* Otto Kron and it welcomed many recruits from *SS-Flak-Ers.-Abt.* in Arolsen.

Infantry regiments were renamed *SS-Totenkopf-Grenadier-Regimenter 1* (*SS-Obf.* Simon) and 3 (*SS-Staf.* Becker) on the **15th of October 1942**. Their out-ranked companies were:

- 13.(s.IG)Kompanie (infantry guns)
- 14.(Fla)Kompanie (anti-aircraft defence)
- 15.(Kradsch.)Kompanie (motorcyclist)
- 16.(Pi.)Kompanie (sappers from the Engineers)

I./SS-T.-Gren.Rgt.1 had to be given 90 *SPW (Sd.Kfz.251)*. It was then trained north of Bordeaux, on the mouth of the river Gironde.

SS-Pionier-Bataillon "Totenkopf" was in Saintes. From the **27th of October**, it was led by *SS-Stubaf.* Max Seela.

Totenkopf also got itself a supply corps battalion; until then, bakers, butchers and outfit units didn't have a corporative structure. The new battalion (*SS-Wirtschafts-Bataillon "Totenkopf"*) was led by *SS-Stubaf.* Hans Ulmer.

The setting up of the different units of the new division was carried out restlessly. Time and equipment were lacking. Besides, not only did *Totenkopf* have to get back on its feet, but also to keep watch over the Atlantic coast and the demarcation line.

Occupation of the French "free zone"

On the **7th of November**, because of the threatening presence of Ally convoys in the Mediterranean, Hitler ordered the launching of Operation "*Anton*", in other words the takeover of the French free zone. *Totenkopf* must cross the demarcation line east and north-east of Angoulême with all its motorized elements, to seize an important weapon depot in Limoges. The Allies landed in North Africa ("Torch" operation) on the **8th of November**. The next day, Pierre Laval, who was at the same time the Home Secretary, the Minister of Information and the Minister of Foreign Affairs in the Vichy government, headed for Hitler's head-quarters. Their meeting didn't bring about the guarantees required by the Germans. In North Africa, Darlan ordered a ceasefire. These events hastened the invasion of the free zone by the Germans.

On the **11th of November**, *SS-Panzergrenadier-Division "Totenkopf"* (a denomination it was given on the 9th) crossed the demarcation line. Limoges was taken quite smoothly. Units radiated from there towards Mende, Aurillac and Brive. The next day, *Totenkopf* was ordered by *AOK 1* to move towards Montpellier and to act friendly with the units of the French army.

On the **14th**, Theodor Eicke thundered forth about the scattering of his division and the interruption of training. However, most units quickly started to go back to the area of Angoulême. But on the **16th of November**, French forces in North Africa chose to join the Allies on their fight against the Axis. As a consequence, the return of the division to Charente was no longer possible: on the **18th**, the Germans decided to disarm the French forces and to seize their fleet anchored in Toulon to prevent it from fleeing to Africa. Several units from the division were then sent towards the coast of Languedoc, from Narbonne to the Spanish border. Eicke requested again that his division be sent back to Charente to resume instruction. But, after disarming the garrisons in Castres, Albi and Carcassonne, the division's *Kampfgruppen* was ordered to stay and keep watch over the Mediterranean coast until mid-December!

End of the training period

In December, new recruits arrived every day as *Totenkopf* still lacked about 6000 men as compared to its theoretical numbers. News from the Eastern Front were far from good. Operation "*Wintergewitter*", led by Hoth's *4.Panzerarmee* to free *6.Armee* surrounded in Stalingrad, came to nothing. North-east, the Soviets crushed the 8th Italian army, *Armee-Abteilung "Hollidt"* and the 3rd Romanian army. A huge breach was opened in the already much weakened layout of *Heeresgruppe "B"* along the upper Don, and was showing signs they were trapping the German armies which had ventured into the Caucasus. On the **22nd of December**, the breach between *Heeresgruppe "B"* and *Heeresgruppe "Don"* was more than 300 kilometre wide. On the **28th**, Hitler authorized retreat of *Heeresgruppe "A"* from the Caucasus towards the line Mostowskoje - Armavir - Salsk and the *OKH* gave the following order: "*In order to be able to carry out the freeing of 6.Armee, a strong group of armoured units will have to gather until mid-February in the sector south-east of Charkow. In order to do so, the following will be transferred west as soon as possible:* SS-Adolf-Hitler, SS-Reich, SS-T, *and from Heeresgruppe "Mitte", the* Grossdeutschland *division.*"

On the **30th of December**, *Gen.Kdo. SS-Pz.Korps* transmitted to *Totenkopf* the following order: "*By order of the Führer, the* SS-Totenkopf-Division *must be ready to move east. To that effect, the division is immediately joined to* SS-Gen.Kdo. (Pz.)." Theodor Eicke protested vehemently. On the **2nd of January 1943**, he sent a telex to Himmler: "*The last elements from the division coming from the Eastern Front only arrived in France at the end of October. Since then, the division has had 75% of untrained recruits in its ranks. The occupation of the free zone necessitated the setting up of intervention groups with experienced cores, setting aside fresh recruits. I was only given back these cores for training on the 20th of December. I repeat: it is impossible, in such conditions, to enforce the Führer's order.*

SS-Panzerkorps *gave me order to make Totenkopf-division ready to reach the Eastern Front on the 8th of January. This order is jeopardized by the following facts:*

1) 60% of the division's drivers are missing. They stayed on the battlefield. Despite several complaints, I was never granted the petrol necessary to the training of new drivers. As a result, 60% of my vehicles cannot be mobilized.

2) 70% of our strength (the recruits) don't know how to use their weapons, because there hasn't been time or opportunity to teach them. I need 8 weeks to train these men. Collective exercises won't be possible.

3) Today, 50% of the vehicles are still missing. Even the armoured regiment only has half its tanks.

4) There is a dire lack of staff in the signal corps (radio operators), because of the heavy losses they underwent on the Eastern Front. 40% of the radio transmitters are missing, as well as much of the transmission equipment..."

This complaint bore fruit, as Hitler finally authorized *Totenkopf* to carry on with the drilling as long as possible. Missing staff arrived at last, which allowed for more intense drilling. Regarding equipment and vehicles, priority was given to *Totenkopf*: all the supply to other units were stopped and redirected to it. However, on the **19th of January**, Theodor Eicke received order to have his division transferred to the Soviet Union by the **31st of January**.

Heinz Lammerding (here as an *SS-Brigadeführer*, when he headed the *"Das Reich"* division in 1944), commands the new *"Thule"* motorcyclist regiment. (Rights reserved)

A mixed column, composed of motorcyclists, motorized infantry and tanks (*Pzkpfw.III Ausf.J*) are moving southwards. The invasion of the french Free Zone did disrupt the units' combat training but allowed Theodor Eicke to test his division's mobility in a real size exercize. (Collection J.L. Roba.)

Elements of the division are leaving the Roussillon region to go back to the Charentes by rail. The nearest vehicle is a *Horch Kfz.15*. (Collection J.L. Roba.)

Alfred Arnold can be seen on the right. Facing the camera is his battalion commander, *SS-Sturmbannführer* Georg Boch-mann. (Courtesy Tim Willemsen)

SS-Hauptsturmführer Alfred Arnold (commander of *7.Kp./SS-Kradsch.-Rgt. "Thule"*) is giving instructions to his men prior to the trip back to the Eastern Front. He was severely wounded on 20 February 1943 and stayed in hospital till November 1943. He then took command of a company within *SS-Pz.Aufkl.-Ersatz-Abt.* He died on 10 October 1944 from another severe wound caused by caused by mortar fire while commanding *SS-Infanterie-Bataillon 1 (mot.)* within *SS-Panzerbrigade "Gross"*. He received the German Cross in Gold posthumously on 6 January 1945. (Courtesy Martin Månsson)

Creation of the "Thule" motorcyclist regiment

While there is a debate regarding the tactical benefit of such a unit, particularly the great number of vehicles delaying its movement and readiness for combat, which is contrary to the aim of its use, the *Totenkopf* divison and the *SS-FHA* organise nevertheless its formation, maybe with the idea of making it into a future third motorised regiment.

Above: This motorcycle regiment must have some amphibian vehicles *(Schwimmwagen)*. The first ones are carefully examined. Notice that the death's head, the division insignia, has already been painted on the boot. (Collection Jean-Louis Roba)

Formation of *SS-Kradschützen-Regiment "Thule"*. On the right hand side its commander Heinz Lammerding walks along the 2nd battalion chief, the *SS-Stubaf*. Georg Bochmann, who wears the knight cross earned during the battle in the *Demjansk's pocket*. (Collection Jean-Louis Roba)

Above: View of the barracks inner courtyard which has been turned into a parking lot for *Schwimmwagen* equipping the unit. (Collection Jean-Louis Roba)

Above: The amphibian capability of these new vehicles are being tested. The driver, wearing civilian clothes, may be an engineer from the Volkswagen company. (Collection Jean-Louis Roba)

Right: The engineer has changed position with a soldier of the regiment and instruct him under the scrutiny of another *SS*, sitting in a boat. (Collection Jean-Louis Roba)

The *Schwimmwagen* can only carry four men, so quite a few are needed to transport a company, to have enough vehicles to move a standard motorised infantry battalion. In the end, for a similar time, the theoretical speed to the *Schwimmwagen* being slowed down by having to wait for the tracked vehicles pulling the heavy equipment, the motorcyclist regiment would have only put on the line one company instead of a whole battalion for a motorised infantry regiment. (NA)

Deprived from heavy arms, *"Thule"* must rely on batteries that the artillery regiment will tactfully supply them. Here is a 105 howitzer (*le.FH18*) and its crew being trained in the Charentes. (NA)

Exercise in the forest

The reformation of the division began well before autumn 1942. At the start of October 1941 Theodor Eicke who wanted to get rid of Matthias Kleinheisterkamp, wanted him to go back home to supervise the reformation of the third infantry regiment for the division. The idea of restoring most units started in the spring of 1942, while keeping in Germany officers and non-commissioned officers convalescing after being wounded or sick. So instead of being sent for reinforcement on the Demjansk front, most of the new recruits were assigned to units being reformed. The engineer battalion, nearly destroyed in Russia, was consequently re-established with inexperienced volunteers. Here is an engineer company training in a forest in western France.

Exercise to clear a road blocked by tree trunks. Before starting the clearing, the engineers have to secure the area. The trunks are cut then put on the side to allow the passage of motorcyclists. Notice the young age of the recruits – most are still 18 year old adolescents from the Labour Service of the *Reich* – and the brand new uniforms. (NA)

Training with collective and individual weaponry

More than half the combat personnel in the autumn of 1942 are totally inexperienced and have to be trained from scratch on heavy or light weapons.

Training on an 3.7cm anti-tank gun which is obsolete since 1940. But maybe this *Pak 37* is only used here for training purposes and not for operational ones. (NA)

Firing a 8.1cm mortar *m.Gr.W.34*. The *SS-Uscha.* wearing a white armband is supervising the exercise. (NA)

Last checks before a training day. It is cold and foggy, the men are wearing coats. (NA)

Below: Working with a range-finder. It is an indispensable tool to the artillery, anti-aircraft and mortar units to measure distances. This is how it works: form a triangle with a given base and the subject as its top. Knowing the length of the base and the angle under which the subject can be seen, you can work out the distance. (NA)

The logistics units are also training, like the medical services here. These will be totally reorganised in the autumn of 1942, with their integration within a battalion and a marked increase of their human and equipment resources. (NA)

The *Totenkopf* division, like the other divisions of *SS-Pz.Korps*, is particularly favoured by Hitler for the allocation of new weapons. Among those, a few 2.8cm anti-tank tapered bore-guns *(s.Pz.B.41)* which fire tungsten shells, have a superior performance to the *Pak 37*, are delivered at the end of 1942. Due to the short supply of tungsten and also to its high cost, the production of this weapon will cease in 1943. (NA)

1. Theodor Eicke entrusts the formation of the divisional armoured regiment to his son-in-law, *SS-Stubaf.* Karl Leiner, seen here with an officer from the *Heer* division coming to supervise an exercise. (Private collection S.)

2. Max Seela commands the division engineer battalion. He is seen here posing on one of the armoured vehicles type *Sd.Kfz.251/7*, part of his unit equipment. (Private collection).

3. Some division personnel are billeted locally. *SS-Uscha.* Richard Doll, of the transmissions battalion, was lucky to be lodged in a castle near Angoulême. (Private collection)

Himmler's visit

Himmler has always kept a close eye on his older divisions and particularly the *Totenkopf* due to Theodor Eicke making his own decisions, ignoring orders from the *SS-FHA*, concerning personnel or the organisation of his own units. In the autumn of 1942, the reasons of his visit are manifold: greeting the unit which distinguished itself on the eastern front, nominal transformation of the division into a motorised one (but in fact into an armoured one), Theodor Eicke's increased prestige and political ambitions.

Accompanied by some officers from his headquarters, Himmler inspects a radio vehicle. In the background is the typical landscape of the area north of the Gironde. (NA)

Himmler next to a *StuG.III*. Until now the division had only one battery. The new organisation allocates it a whole group of three batteries. Moreover, The *StuG.III* with a short gun (*KwK. 7.5cm L/24*) have been replaced by more recent models with long guns (*KwK. 7.5cm L/43*), more efficient against the Soviet heavy armoured vehicles. (NA)

A company parades before Himmler. Its men, wearing training clothing, sing while marching. Some are quite small and none of them are carrying automatic weapons. Is it a logistics support unit? (NA)

The visit is over. Himmler is talking to a young *SS-Untersturmführer*, visibly impressed by having to converse with his *Reichsführer-SS*. (NA)

8

The battle for the Donets basin (February 1943)

Back to the Eastern Front

On the 31st of January 1943, the first *Totenkopf* unit to leave Angoulême was *I./"Thule"*, now headed by *SS-Hstuf.* Ernst Häussler, taking over from *SS-Stubaf.* Franz Kleffner, who had been dismissed after one of his many verbal affronts. The convoys passed by Görlitz and reached Kiew on the **7th of February**. Men set their quarters on the eastern bank of the Dniepr.

On the front, the situation was most worrying. *SS-Pz.Korps* were repelled from the banks of the Oskol towards Charkow: *Leibstandarte SS "Adolf Hitler"* fought on either side of Tschugujew and *Das Reich* in the sector of Woltschansk. The *OKH*, who had planned to launch *SS-Pz.Korps* on a counterattack, thus was thwarted by the Soviet advance. *SS-Pz.Korps* had no connection with the German units stationed on its south flank. North of Charkow, the situation also worsened: on the **8th of February**, *168.ID* was driven back from Bjelgorod, which caused the withdrawal of the division *"Das Reich"* to the west bank of the Donets. Division *"Grossdeutschland"* was now protecting the north flank of *SS-Pz.Korps* between Rogan and Solotschew. *SS-Pz.Korps*, that was facing four Soviet armies, was expected to keep holding a front more than 100 kilometre wide, plus to launch an attack southwards, towards Losowaja, by the 10th of February! *Totenkopf* was needed more than ever, and it was thought that its 120 convoys would be there in 10 days. For now, only the *SS-Rgt. "Thule"* was available; it gathered in Poltawa.

However, on the 10th of February, the situation wasn't as bad as it looked for the Germans. Indeed, *1.Panzerarmee* was still holding Slawjansk, *Armee-Abteilung "Hollidt"* had managed to withdraw behind the Mius and, last but not least, the *Stavka* had misinterpreted the withdrawal of *4.Panzerarmee*: the Soviet staff was sure that the Germans were preparing a general retreat behind the Dniepr and its optimism blinded it to any contemplation of an offensive return from the *Wehrmacht*. For General Vatoutine, the *Panzerdivisionen* that had arrived in numbers these last few days were only there to cover the retreat. This misunderstanding of the German intentions was to lead the Soviets right into the trap von Manstein (*OB Heeresgruppe "Don"*) was devising for them. Indeed, they rushed towards the breach between Charkow and Slawjansk.

On the **13th of February**, *SS-Rgt."Thule"* settled for defence around Krasnograd. Until now, all the patrols had come back without meeting the enemy. Southwest of Nowaja Wodolaga, contact was made with some elements from the *Leibstandarte*'s reconnaissance force. The German attack, led by *SS-Kradsch.-Btl. "Das Reich"* and *Kampfgruppe "Kumm"*, allowed for the seizing of Nowaja Wodolaga and carried on southwards as far as Stanitschnyj. However, in the sector of Charkow, the situation remained difficult for *SS-Pz.Korps*, which was assailed by three Soviet armies. The surrounding of the town further materialized: the Russians were threatening Dergatschi in the north and Olschany in the west. East of the area, they had just managed to break through the *Das Reich* lines

Marshall Erich von Manstein is the brilliant chief of the German counter attack in the Donets basin. This will be the last time for the Wehrmacht to show their manoeuvring capabilities. (R.R.)

in the sector of Rogan and Satischje. So Paul Hausser gave orders to prepare the destruction of bridges and the mining of roads in expectation of the evacuation of Charkow. *General* Lanz, following Hitler's instructions, ordered *SS-Pz.Korps* to stop destroying bridges and roads systematically. *Korps "Raus"* was in charge of defence north and west of Charkow. Its mission was to establish a strong front line in Olschany to stop the Soviets' progress towards the east, which was threatening to surround Charkow from the west. In this perspective, at 6 pm, *Armee-Abteilung "Lanz"* ordered *Totenkopf* to send all its elements available to the sector of Poltawa towards the road to Walki, in order to repel the Russians attacking north of the road Walki - Charkow.

On the **14th of February**, at midnight, *Armee-Abteilung "Lanz"* was subordinated to *Heeresgruppe "Don"*, which was renamed *Heeresgruppe "Süd"*. While *Angriffsgruppe SS-Pz.Korps* was carrying on with its attack southwards, things were getting worse around Charkow, and Hitler ordered again that the town hold at any cost. Nevertheless, seeing that the complete surrounding of the town was bound to happen, *Armee-Abteilung "Lanz"* commanded the destruction of supply depots and military installations. Given the circumstances, *SS-Ogruf.* Hausser let *Armee-Abteilung "Lanz"* and *Korps "Raus"* know his intention to evacuate Charkow on the night of February the 14th, and to withdraw the *SS-Pz.Korps* beyond the Udy, even though it went against the *Führer*'s orders. Lanz was scared of disobeying Hitler, but knew Paul Hausser was right. He put off transmitting the news to his superior, knowing that once the evacuation of Charkow was under way, there was no stopping it.

In Charkow, combat started in the south districts of the town. A narrow corridor was the only communication route left with the south-west. Convinced that *Totenkopf* would not be there soon enough to free the town, Paul Hausser ordered the troops to evacuate at 1 pm. Such an act of disobedience to Hitler was all the more exceptional coming from an SS officer! In the "Wolf's Lair", the *Führer*'s headquarters, Hitler showed no reaction. True, the new situation was in many ways advantageous to the Germans: they now had a complete armoured corps at their disposal, ready to counter-attack with the backup of *"Grossdeutschland"* and *320.ID*! Besides, the Soviets saw in this retreat a confirmation of the Germans' intention to withdraw completely. As a matter of fact, the *Stavka* ordered the 6th army and the armoured group *"Popow"* to rush towards the Dniepr as quickly as possible, without caring about their flanks.

On the **15th of February**, a day which had such an influence on things to come, the units from *Totenkopf* kept on flocking around Poltawa. In Walki, *SS-Kampfgruppe "Schulze"* and *II./"Thule"* were placed under the command of *SS-Ostubaf.* Lammerding. He was given orders to repel the enemy moving on towards the Mertschik. There, *II./"Thule"* was to attack northwest towards the Bairak, and *SS-Kampfgruppe "Schulze"* north-east towards Udarnyj. The aim was to secure the north flank of the counteroffensive to be. *SS-Rgt. "Thule"* was thus to fight apart from the bulk of the division. Its mobility and fire power constituted a much appreciated support for *Korps "Raus"*. On the evening of February the 16th, *SS-Kampfgruppe "Schulze"* managed to make contact with the *"Grossdeutschland"* division east of Udarnyj.

On the **17th of February**, von Manstein decided to launch *SS-Pz.Korps* in a counterattack from Krasnograd towards south-east, in the direction of Pawlograd. Afterwards, together with *4.Panzerarmee* (*XLVIII.Pz.Korps* et *LVII.Pz.Korps*), *SS-Pz.Korps* was to annihilate the Soviet forces which had rushed inside the breach opened between *1.Panzerarmee* and *Armee-Abteilung "Lanz"*. After restoring a coherent front on its right flank (*Armee-Abteilung "Hollidt"* and *1.Panzerarmee*), *Heeresgruppe "Süd"* resumed its offensive towards Charkow. Control over operations on the left flank was given to *4.Panzerarmee* (*Generaloberst* Hoth).

SS-Pz.Korps moved into the counterattack

The **19th of February** was marked by the dismissal of *General* Lanz, Hitler's scapegoat for the loss of Charkow. He was replaced by *General* Kempf. In *SS-Pz.Korps* offensive sector , *III./"D"* took Pereschtschepino; it crossed the Orel and resumed its attack southwards, thus entering deep inside the right flank of the Soviet 6th army. At 10.40 am, by order of *Armee-Abteilung "Lanz"*, *Totenkopf* was subordinated to *SS-Pz.Korps*, and had to reach the sector of Krasnograd - Karlowka. There was a risk in reaching a rallying sector, as the Soviet units were already stationed further west. Indeed, *IV./SS-Art.-Rgt.3 "T"* was attacked on the way, west of Krasnograd, by a whole Soviet battalion. On the night of the **20th**, *Das Reich* crossed the Samara east of Nowomoskowsk, seized Pestschanka and started to besiege Pawlograd. Its attack crushed the forefront of the Soviet offensive towards Dniepr. Advanced elements from the Soviet 6th army were cut off from their rear. At noon, *SS-Pz.Korps* and *Totenkopf* were joined to *4.Panzerarmee*, while *Leibstandarte* was subordinated to *Armee-Abteilung "Kempf"* (ex *"Lanz"*). Theodor Eicke and his Ia, *SS-Stubaf.* Rudolf Schneider, were received at the *SS-Pz.Korps* headquarters, where they were given the order to attack Pawlograd from the north, backing up *Das Reich*, that was attacking from the west. First combats occurred against the Russian infantry in the sector of Konstantinoda. These fights were only brief skirmishes that didn't delay the setting up of the units.

On the **22nd of February**, while the assault groups of *Totenkopf* were gathering in Pereschtschepino, coming from the west and the north-west, the 106th fusilier brigade attacked the town by surprise, taking advantage of the thick fog that enveloped the whole plain. Its objective was simple enough: to break through the German lines to reopen the communication routes of the 6th army. *III./SS-Pz.Gren.Rgt.1 "T"* managed to repel the attack, and the Soviets withdrew, leaving 150 killed and 60 prisoners behind. Around noon, the battalion moved along the Samara and settled before Andrejewka. Meanwhile, the *"Schulze"* battalion seized Michailowka and Pawlowka. During the day, *Totenkopf* managed to make contact with *Leibstandarte* in Otrada, and *Das Reich* with *XLVIII.Pz.Korps*, east of Pawlograd.

On the night of the **22nd**, *Totenkopf* attacked from the line Andrejewka – Pawlowka towards south-east. Opposite was the 1st armoured corps from the Guard. After initially promising progress, the SS were stopped before Wjasowok. This failure prevented the division from making contact with *Das Reich* in Pawlograd. In the evening, the division transmitted to *SS-Pz.Korps* the number of its tanks available: 62 *Pzkpfw.III,* 18 *Pzkpfw.IV,* 9 *Pzkpfw.VI "Tiger"*. Actually, they hadn't lost a single panzer in combat yet, but many breakdowns and accidents had considerably reduced the number of vehicles in working order.

On the 24th of February, *Totenkopf* had to seize the crossing points of the Samara in Werbki and to take Orelka, so as to be able then to move further towards Losowaja. The division gathered its forces before the attack: *I.(gep.)/SS-Pz.Gren.Rgt.1 "T"* was called back from Pereschtschepino, as well as *SS-Pz.Rgt.3. Totenkopf* moved into the attack at 9.30 am. It succeeded in seizing Wjasowok, and then methodically cleaned out the Soviet bases of operations one after the other. The town fell into its hands at 1.45 pm. The division's armoured force, preceded by an impressive artillery barrage, moved into two waves and cleaned up the heights north and north-west of the town, inflicting heavy losses on the Soviet infantry, who made the mistake of running away in open country. *II./SS-Pz.Gren.Rgt.1 "T"* seized the opportunity and rushed towards Werbki to take the Soviet units facing *Das Reich* from the rear. Contact was quickly made between the two SS divisions: the crossing points on the Samara were thus open and *Das Reich* could now wheel round its offensive northwards in the direction of Losowaja. Meanwhile, *SS-Pz.Gren.Rgt.3 "T"* was strengthening the protection of *SS-Pz.Korps*'s north flank and the situation became really favourable to the carrying out of the offensive towards north-east. As for *SS-Rgt. "Thule"*, it was still fighting alongside *"Grossdeutschland"* division between Poltawa and Ljubotin.

For the last few days, the fierce attacks of *SS-Pz.Korps* had allowed to fill in the breach that was setting it apart from *Heeresgruppe "Süd"*. This first phase of the German counterattack was a complete success. However, the Soviet elements cut off from their rear remained a looming threat for the supply routes of *SS-Pz.Korps*.

On the **25th of February**, *Totenkopf*'s armoured group set off towards Panjutina. East of Orelka, *Angriffsgruppe "Becker"* (*SS-Pz.Gren.Rgt.3 "T"*) was facing powerful Russian formations backed up by some *T-34*. The progress of SS grenadiers stopped dead. At 2.15 pm, the vanguard of *SS-Pz.Rgt.3* arrived at Alexejewka, a village north of the road Orelka – Losowaja, thus an objective of paramount importance. A tank battle began. The Soviets got the upper hand, forcing Karl Leiner to order the withdrawal of his tanks, which were apparently short of gas and ammunitions. The next day, on the 26th, the *SS-Pz.Korps*'s mission was to seize Losowaja, the cornerstone of the Soviets' defence in this sector of the front. *Totenkopf* had to get rid of the threat that was hanging over its rear while keeping on attacking northwards in the direction of Panjutina. There were tough combats south of Orelka. This situation disrupted the *Totenkopf*'s offensive, which had to send two battalions to attack the Soviet units that were trying to cross the Orel. As for *SS-Pz.Rgt.3*, it tried to force its way north of Strastnoj. At 10 am, it came across a strong barrage of anti-tank guns and *T-34* north-west of Losowaja. The battle was fierce, but its localization remained imprecise. Indeed, contact between the divisional headquarters and *SS-Pz.Rgt.3* was cut between 12 and 1 pm. Seemingly worried about his son-in-law, Eicke decided to go and appraise the situation himself, and thus climbed aboard a *Fieseler Storch* with *SS-Hstuf.* Otto Friedrich (*Div.-01*). At about 1 pm, he left Orelka and reached some advanced headquarters of the reconnaissance group. He was welcomed there by *SS-Ustuf.* Kohlig who informed him that the Soviets had set barrages on the road and had some *T-34*. Eicke then joined the elements of the reconnaissance force whose positions were

SS-Obergruppenführer Paul Hausser will not be sacked from his post despite his disobedience to Hitler's orders. Few generals could afford to do so. (RR)

The *II./ "Thule"* is headed since its formation by the *SS-Stubaf.* Georg Bochmann (SS-Nr. 122632). Previously he was in command of the *14. (Pz.Jg)Kp./SS-T.IR 1* and replaced *SS-Stubaf.* Frimmersdorf as the leader of the anti-tank battalion. In July 1943 he will succeed to Eugen Kunstmann as the chief of the *SS-Pz.Rgt.3*, then in the autumn of 1943, he will take the lead of the *SS-Wirtschafts-Verwaltungs-Schule* of Arolsen until the end of summer 1944 when he will replace Otto Meyer at the *SS-Pz.Rgt.9*, but only for a few days. In between he was made *SS-Obersturmbannführer* on 09.11.43 then *SS-Standartenführer* on 09.11.44. The 3rd January 1945, he will take leadership of the *18.SS-Pz.Gren.Div. "Horst Wessel"*. He will then be transferred to the head of the *17.SS-Pz.Gren.Div. "Götz von Berlichingen"* with which he will surrender to the US troops on the 8th May 1945. (RR)

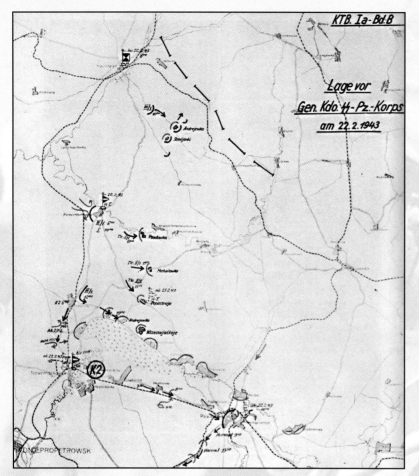

Counter attack of the *SS-Panzerkorps* towards Pawlograd. Status on the 22nd February 1943.

even more advanced north-east of Orelka. The *Fieseler Storch* made the most of a small field to land but the scouts didn't have any information about the whereabouts of the armoured regiment, as radio contact hadn't been re-established yet. The plane took off again for the last time to search for the panzers. It was shot down at about 4 pm by the Soviet anti-aircraft defence near Artelnoje. The news of Theodor Eicke's death spread quickly throughout the units of the division and *SS-Pz.Korps*. Paul Hausser notified Himmler of it in a telegram at 10.50 pm. Himmler told Hitler himself a few minutes later. The official announcement of his death was delayed to the 1st of March though, since the *Reichsführer-SS* wanted to know all the details before telling the press. Messages of condolence then flooded in from all parts at Himmler's office. Written in a pompous style, so typical of the official communiqués of the Third Reich, they cannot conceal an obvious lack of sincerity. Indeed, Eicke would be missed for his exceptional capacities as an organizer and a born leader, and for his unique status inside the Nazi Party; but few were those who could call him a friend. However, in spite of his severity and his drastic methods, his death was perceived as a tragedy in the ranks of the *Totenkopf* division. True, he

was close to his men, he shared the same rations and trenches, and he often came to visit them in the toughest of combats. From a military perspective, his death didn't really affect the fighting capacities of the division, even if he had clearly left his mark on it. A general of average competence, he had made up for his lack of training and tactical imagination with a constant determination, for attack as well as for defence, leading his division as he had once ruled concentration camps. Therefore, his replacement wasn't really an issue for the *Totenkopf*'s staff, which had a whole corps of officers of the same calibre. In the main, staff had gotten out of the Demjanks ordeal more experienced and hardened, and the troops, physically above average, remained highly motivated. *SS-Obf.* Max Simon was made head of the division. *SS-Ostubaf.* Otto Baum took charge of his former regiment.

On the **27th of February**, *Totenkopf* was to surround the Soviet forces by attacking north of Losowaja. The seizing of Zaredarowka was to allow the cutting of the Soviets' main retreat route. As for *Das Reich*, it was to eliminate the enemy troops gathered in the sector of Losowaja – Panjutina, and to pursue them northwards, thus pushing them against the *Totenkopf*'s positions. *SS-Kampfgruppe "Leiner"* managed to take Zaredarowka as soon as 7.40; then it kept going northeast, towards Panjutina. At 11.35, it blocked all its issues. *Gruppe "Baum"* wrapped Panjutina from the north. Despite the backup of panzers, the town centre was only reached in early evening, after each base of operations had been eradicated with guns and grenades. In Krasnopawlowka, the Soviets hung on to every inch of land. The last bases of operations were cleaned out during the night. It was a major success, but the SS had suffered heavy losses. In the evening, *Totenkopf* announced it still had 112 tanks in working order, including 61 *Pzkpfw.III*, 15 *Pzkpfw.IV*, 9 *Pkpfw.VI "Tiger"* and 18 *StuG.III*. As for *Das Reich*, it had taken Losowaja at last.

The next day, *Totenkopf* went in pursuit of the Soviet elements retreating northwards. The initiative had obviously changed camp. The division didn't fully capitalize on its success, as Max Simon had difficulty gathering the *SS-Pz.Rgt.3* tanks that were scattered around Panjutina. Without waiting the panzers' backup, Otto Baum launched his regiment into assault along the course of the Orel. In the evening, *4.Panzerarmee* announced that: *"After eight days of tough offensive combat against a powerful and much determined enemy, the units from 4.Panzerarmee have contributed not only to eradicate the threat that was looming over the Heeresgruppe's rear, but also to get a 120 kilometre long and 100 kilometre wide sector back... From the 21st to the 28th of February, the followings were captured or annihilated: 156 tanks, 24 armoured cars, 178 pieces of artillery, 284 anti-tank guns and 40 pieces of anti-aircraft defence. 4643 prisoners were gathered and about 11.000 enemy corpses counted."*

SS-Pz.Korps was now to carry on its offensive in the north, towards the heights of Jefremowka.

Theodor Eicke: his death marks a turn in the history of the *Totenkopf*. It is a big loss, as the division would not be what it is without his political support and his unusual methods. For instance, during a discussion regarding the allocation of weapons for his division, he took his pistol out and threatened to shoot himself on the spot should his colleagues continued objecting to his demands. (RR)

The armoured troops have a major role in the battles south of Charkow, but the SS infantry is indispensable to clear the lines where numerous Soviet units, overwhelmed by the German counter-attack, are trying to retreat to their lines. (NA)

Outstanding photograph of *MG* gunner. His parka jacket is new, notice the details, in particular the cartridge belt. (Rights reserved)

231

Arrival of *Totenkopf* division west of Char-kow

SS-Kradschützen-Regiment "Thule" was the first division unit to be operational in the sector of Poltawa. In the evening of the 11th February 1943, it is ordered to rejoin Krasnograd. Its mission is to guard the station and the road, to establish contact with the Leibstandarte at Nowaja Wodolaga, while sending reconnaissance patrols towards Pawlograd, Losowaja and Charkow.

From the 19th February, SS-Kampfgruppe *"Peiper" (verst.III.(gep)./SS-Pz.Gren.Rgt.2 "LSSAH")*, after providing cover for the withdrawal of Charkow, rejoins the Krasnograd sector where it has to give cover to the rear echelon lines of *Totenkopf* towards the north east. (NA)

SS-Kampfgruppe *"Schultze"* which comprises a *Panzergrenadiere* company on SPW *(4/SS-Pz.Gren.Rft.1 "T")* and the divisional assault gun battalion, is also operational from the 14th February. This *Sd.Kfz.251 Ausf.C* had not had time to be painted in white, and its crew, being too cramped, has put their supplies, ammunition and a fuel can on the outside. (NA)

Superb shot of an *8.8cm-Flak 36* crew, somewhere south of Charkow. The second man starting from left shows Asiatic traits. It must be because of his slight grin as he cannot be a *Hiwi* since he wears an *SS-Sturmmann* tunic. (Courtesy Michael Cremin)

A group of grenadiers advance in the snow. Notice the variety of the clothing. (Private collection)

Waldemar Riefkogel (*1.Kp./SS-Pz.Rgt.3*) is also wearing a leather jacket. Tank in the background is a *Pzkpfw.III Ausf. L*. (private collection S')

SS-Pz.Rgt.3 disembark at Poltawa just after the *"Thule"* regiment. Here is a *Pzkpfw.IV Ausf.G* followed by a *Pzkpfw.III Ausf.J* soon after their arrival. The front is far away and the guns are still covered. (NA)

SS-Hstuf. Erwin Meierdress. comes to coordinate its action to the infantrymen's. Coordination between tanks and infantry was essential both for defence or attack. (NA)

Armoured vehicles (*Sd.Kfz.251*) and assault guns (*StuG.III Ausf.F*) are moving ahead on the vast Ukrainian plains. The battle of the Donets basin is a perfect example of a blitzkrieg where static forces are doomed to destruction. On this point, the Germans show that they have more tactics skills than the Soviets. (NA)

A Marder column of *SS-Panzerjäger-Abteilung "Totenkopf"* on its way to the front. (NA)

I.(gep.)/SS-Pz.Gren.Rgt.1 "T" (*SS-Ostubaf.* Baum) advances with difficulty on the 24th February towards Wjasowok due to a sudden thaw. Here are its *SPW* on the assault on the heights north of the place. (NA)

Two assault tanks (StuG.III) in a snow storm. From one day to the next the weather is very changeable. During the six weeks of the Donets basin battle, snowfalls, intense cold and sudden mild weather would alternate until spring. (NA)

On the 25th February, after breaking the Soviet resistance west of Kondratjewka, the armoured vehicles of the division – here a Sd.Kfz.252 carrying grenadiers – are heading to the north east via Marinskoje and Nikolajewka. (NA)

The Soviets suffered heavy losses, but the crushing of their units south of Orelka delay by 48 hours the Totenkopf division resuming their offensive to the north. (NA)

At the end of the battle of Orelka, the division armoured group round up west of Zaredarowka. (NA)

On the 27th February, the division has eighteen *StuG.III* still running. Here are two with a le.*SPW Sd.Kfz.250* (in the foreground) and a m.*SPW Sd.Kfz.251*. (NA)

Grenadiers on the plains of Donets. They are wearing the white side of their parka jackets due to the snow. (NA)

The *Totenkopf's* left flank is covered by its reconnaissance group. On the 25th February it marches onwards to Artelnoje then Orelka and reaches the next day the southern outskirts of Krasnopawlowka. One of its companies is equipped with *Sd. Kfz.250*, here is one with a visible radio antenna. (NA)

9 — The battle of Charkow

The Jeremejewka pocket

As *4.Panzerarmee* attacked the 6th army and the 1st Guards army in the south, *Armee-Abteilung "Kempf"* was carrying out a moderate withdrawal, while containing the Soviet 3rd armoured army's thrusts. The latter had suffered severe losses, and the threat to see the German front crumble before Krasnograd was now lifted. However, the Soviets kept some offensive impulses, and their 3rd armoured army gathered around Kegitschewka and Jefremowka on the 27th and 28th of February. Indeed, Rybalko had decided to launch his tanks southwards against *SS-Pz.Korps*, east of positions that were held by *Leibstandarte*. Short of gas and ammunitions, he had to postpone the attack to the 3rd of March. Only that was two days too late, for a new battle started on the **1st of March**: *SS-Pz.Korps* carried on its offensive, this time towards north-west. Its objective was to take the heights of Beraka and Jefremowka to line up its front with the *Leibstandarte*'s, that was holding the east wing of *Armee-Abteilung "Kempf"*. The *Totenkopf*'s mission was to break through the lines of the 3rd armoured army east of Kegitschewka, and then to wheel round westwards and thus cut the Soviet units' supply routes. Meanwhile, *Leibstandarte* and *Das Reich* were to meet up north, in the sector of Starowerowka. This offensive was aimed at surrounding the 12th and 15th Soviet armoured corps. At 7 am, *Totenkopf* moved into attack along the river Orel. Caught unawares, the Soviets were driven back. Towards the end of the day, the division was controlling the line going through the heights of Semenowka, Timtschenko, and the Orel. That same day, Himmler decided to give *SS-Pz.Gren.Rgt.3 "Totenkopf"* the honorary title of *"Theodor Eicke"* ("*TE*"in abbreviated form).

On the **2nd of March**, the division seized the Schljachowoje station: it was a major capture, since the station was set on the line Krasnograd - Panjutina, on which most of the supply to Soviet units in Kegitschewka circulated. The loss of Schljachowoje only left the Soviets with a small corridor towards the north. Thus was the fate of the 12th and 15th armoured corps virtually sealed. But oddly enough, Rybalko sent again some reinforcements to Kegitschewka from the north, most likely to prepare for his offensive due on the **3rd of March**. But these only threw themselves in a pocket whose closing was just a matter of hours, and on the way came across retreating columns from the 6th army fleeing from the opposite direction! Early in the afternoon, *I./SS-Pz.Rgt.3* and some elements from the *Das Reich* managed to establish contact with *Leibstandarte* near Berestowaja. More than 50.000 men from the 3rd Guards army were trapped. However, *SS-Pz.Korps* didn't have enough troops at its disposal to close hermetically the pocket around Jeremejewka. Some Soviet units took advantage of it to escape.

On the 3rd of March, *Totenkopf* was commissioned to annihilate Soviet units in the sector of Losowaja - Kegitschewka. Some Russian units, threatened by strong-minded officers and political commissars,

tried to extricate themselves from the pocket. The situation was chaotic. Combat was fierce and there were heavy losses in both camps. The 15th Soviet armoured corps finally broke up, abandoning all his tanks and heavy weapons inside the pocket. Only a few groups of isolated soldiers managed to escape. At 11 am, Jeremejewka fell into SS hands. The SS reported that there were piles of Russian soldiers' corpses in the streets. On the 4th of March, the 3rd Soviet armoured army didn't exist as such anymore. More than 3000 soldiers were killed on the Jeremejewka plain. 36 tanks, 11 armoured cars, 159 guns, 520 trucks and 352 vehicles of all kinds were captured or destroyed by *Totenkopf*. Towards the end of the day, *Totenkopf* gathered along a line going through the heights west of the Orel. It only had 41 *Pzkpfw.III*, 11 *Pzkpfw.IV*, 6 *Bef.Pz.*, 6 *Pzkpfw.VI "Tiger"* and 17 *StuG.III* (total: 81) in working order left. Its anti-tank equipment was overabundant, though, with fifty seven 5 or 7.5 cm towed or self-propelled *Pak*.

The recapture of Charkow

On the **8th of March**, *SS-Pz.Korps* carried on its offensive aiming at surrounding Charkow (a.k.a. Kharkov) from the west. The bulk of *Das Reich* managed to cross the Msha and went on beyond the Odrinka, as the *Leibstandarte* took Staryj Ljubotin. Reports from *SS-Pz.Korps* indicated that the Soviets weren't battling with their usual drive anymore; as soon as the Germans made a breakthrough, they stopped holding to their territory and withdrew straight away, almost without fighting. True, they had been subjected to massive pressure for several weeks, and they only had a few tanks left. However, in the west, *XLVIII.* and *LVII.Pz.Korps* were facing an extremely strong and determined defence. *Totenkopf* received order to cross the railway Poltawa - Charkow and to seize Stary Mertschik, a town west of Ljubotin. *SS-Rgt."TE"* reached its objective at 5 pm, which was far from easy because of the bad condition of the roads. Untracked vehicles had to go through a lot of trouble to get going. The regiment then met with the units of *Panzergruppe "von Strachwitz"*, north-east of Walki. The *Totenkopf*'s mission was now to protect the *Leibstandarte*'s flank in its attack against Charkow from the north. On the night of January the 8th, the regiment "*Totenkopf*" (*SS-Rgt."T"*) moved into attack from Walki and reached Olschany at 4 am. Strangely enough, this strategic crossroads for rail or road communications wasn't protected by any Soviet troop. The regiment then kept moving without delay towards the Udy, and made contact with *SS-KGr."Witt"* and *Leibstandarte* north of Peressetschnaja. Otto Baum's men settled in the evening along the line Tschepelin - Siseny. In the other sectors of *SS-Pz.Korps*, *Das Reich* and *Leibstandarte* were fighting for Korotitsch and Ljubotin. At 12.15 am, *4.Panzerarmee* asked by radio to *SS-Pz.Korps* if Charkow could be taken in a single strike. Hausser's answer was clear: "*Strike possible on the 10th at best*". At 5.05 pm, since he hadn't received any counter-order for the next day, Paul Hausser decided to seize Charkow. Most historians have claimed that Paul Hausser had acted without orders and launched *SS-Pz.Korps* in Charkow on the 10th to take personal revenge on the previous evacuation of the town, and to enhance the prestige of the *Waffen SS*. But this is to ignore documents from von Manstein himself. Indeed, on the **10th of March**, at 7 pm, *Heeresgruppe "Süd"* had sent a telex to *4.Panzerarmee* mentioning quite clearly the possibility to take Charkow if Soviet resistance were to fail.

The centre of gravity of the *SS-Pz.Korps'* offensive was now on its left flank, with *Leibstandarte* and *Totenkopf* attacking north-east to surround Charkow from the north. On the 10th of March, *SS-KGr. "Baum"*, backed up by the *"Tiger" Kp.* (*SS-Hstuf.* Richter), leaped to the assault from Golowaschtschewka. The *"Tiger"* destroyed the Russian anti-tank positions one after the other, the 45 mm shells having no effect on their thick front armour plating. The *Kampfgruppe* seized the north districts of Dergatschi; the town was also attacked by the tanks of *Leibstandarte*, albeit without any real coordination. Driven back to the town centre, the Soviets fled north-east. It allowed *Leibstandarte* to turn off south towards Charkow. But Russian resistance hardened around the great Ukrainian city. In the afternoon, *SS-KGr. "Baum"* attacked eastwards, just north to the progression path of *SS-KGr."Witt"*. At 4 pm, *15.Kp./"T"* seized Russkaja Losowaja with an audacious strike. The road to Charkow was thus secured and this success was all the more important as it was one of the rarest cobbled roads in the whole region. Hence, in the evening of Mars 10th, *SS-Pz.Korps* was ready to besiege Charkow.

On the 11th of March, *SS-Pz.Korps* was to take the city with *Totenkopf* backing up its north flank along the line Russkoje - Dergatschi - Olschany. Therefore, *Totenkopf* was in charge of a 28 mile front, while *Das Reich* and *Leibstandarte* moved into attack respectively from west and north. In the afternoon, *4.Panzerarmee* ordered *SS-Pz.Korps* to gather: *Das Reich* must take over from *Totenkopf* north of Charkow, allowing it to thwart any Soviet disengagement towards east, and to send a *Kampfgruppe* to Tschugujew. This order was a consequence of the failed attack of *XLVIII.Pz.Korps* south of Msha. Paul Hausser protested against this change in direction of the offensive: *Das Reich* had just broken through the Soviet defensive lines west of Charkow, and *Leibstandarte* was already involved in a tough battle around the city centre. Given the situation and the state of the roads, Paul Hausser assumed it would take the *Das Reich* one and a half day to relieve *Totenkopf* north of Charkow. Consequently, he announced his intention to carry on with the attack as planned, and to gather his divisions only when Charkow was in the hands of *SS-Pz.Korps*!

On the **12th of March**, *SS-KGr. "Baum"* took over Bairak and settled a defence zone. The rest of *Totenkopf* was also holding several bases of operations along a line going through Russkaja Losowaja, Dolshik and Rogosjanka. The Soviets launched a number of attacks and took Zirkuny again. At 2 pm, *I./"TE"* took it back anew after some most violent street fights. On the 13th of March, after the division *"Grossdeutschland"* got moving towards Bjelgorod, *Totenkopf* was ordered at 7.10 am to widen its sector westwards, beyond the road Charkow - Bjelgorod. At sunrise, *SS-KGr. "Baum"* moved towards Rogan with much difficulty, first because of the lack of roads from the west to the east, and second because of an obdurate Soviet resistance. Reinforced by *I./SS-Pz.Rgt.3*, it kept going south towards the road Charkow - Tschugujew. At dusk, it besieged

Rogan. Contact with *Das Reich* was established north of the tractor factory.

In the evening, *SS-Pz.Korps* announced that it had seized two thirds of Charkow. *Totenkopf* was then holding the line Russkaja Losowaja - Zirkuny - Rogan.

On the **14th of March**, the SS moved back into assault towards Tschugujew. At 11 am, *Pz.Gren. Rgt.1 "T"* reached the heights seven kilometres east of Rogan. Before Kamennaja Jaruga, they came across the 3rd Guard fusilier division, recently sent as reinforcements by the Soviets. The battle was furious. Soldiers had to fight for every house. The Germans' devastating fire power allowed them to win. With the help of *Stukas* crushing each and every base of operations, the SS managed to take the town in the middle of the night. On the night of March 14th, *III./"T"* seized Tschugujew: the surrounding of Charkow was completed on the east. Now *Totenkopf* was to widen its right wing as far as Nwedenskoje and to make contact with *6.Panzerdivision* in the Udy valley.

The *SS-Pz.Korps'* offensive was now to keep going towards the Donets and settle there as defence, all of which during the mud period. Therefore, the three divisions from the corps must attack side by side towards north and north-east with *Totenkopf* in the sector of Tschugujew - Werchnij Saltow, *Das Reich* on its left and *Leibstandarte* for backup on the north flank towards Bjelgorod. On the **16th of March**, *Totenkopf* was attacked relentlessly by Soviet units trying to escape surrounding from south, west, south-west and north-west! All these attacks were repelled, but the division remained nail to the spot for almost twenty-four hours. On the **17th of March**, *KGr. "Oppeln"* and *6.Panzerdivision* (*XLVIII.Pz.Korps*) arrived south-east of Tschugujew and made contact with *SS-KGr. "Baum"*. The latter finished to clear up the town and could then start to gather south-east of Nepokrytaja to cover the *SS-Pz.Korps'* right flank during its attack towards Bjelgorod.

Attack towards the north

On the **18th of March**, following upon the successful progress of *Das Reich* and *Leibstandarte* towards Bjelgorod, *SS-Pz.Korps* proposed *Pz.AOK 4* to send *Totenkopf* to Murom and to repulse beyond the Donets the Soviet troops that were still on the west bank. Thus the division received order to move its units northwards. On the **19th of March**, the capture of Bjelgorod and the almost complete cleaning up of the Donets' west bank north-east of Charkow marked the end of the victorious *Heeresgruppe "Süd"* counteroffensive. Still, it was no absolute success, since all the objectives von Manstein had set himself weren't reached, far from it. First, even if the Soviets had suffered substantial losses, they hadn't been annihilated and their almost inexhaustible reserves were to allow them to refill their front again quite soon. As for the Germans, their losses were significant too: *SS-Pz.Korps* had lost 365 officers and 11.154 NCOs and men (killed, injured or missing) during the battle. Between the 10th of February and the 20th of March 1943, *Totenkopf* alone had lost 94 officers and 2.170 NCOs and men, killed injured or missing. These were terrible losses on a quality level, since the SS divisions could only compensate for them with fresh recruits of lower value as regards training and experience in combat, and above all much less motivated ideologically. Actually, most of those who would fill in the ranks of divisions *"Leibstandarte"*, *"Das Reich"* and *"Totenkopf"* weren't volunteers. Last but not least, the German counteroffensive had left a huge salient around Koursk, because of the *Heeres-*

gruppe "Mitte"'s inability to support von Manstein's efforts. The elimination of this salient would have allowed to shorten the front and to extricate some reserves. The attempt to reduce the salient during the following summer was to wipe out the Germans' hopes of victory on the Eastern Front.

The refit of the division

On the **1st of April**, *Totenkopf* was released on either side of Stariza by *6.Panzerdivision*. It then came to set under the commandment of *Korps z.b.V "Raus"* in Bjelgorod, where it was reinforced by *SS-Korps-Werfer-Abteilung* (*SS-Hstuf.* Neitzel) and the 2nd section of *3.SS-Wehrgeologen-Kp.* (*SS-Ostuf.* Wasmuth). The latter was commissioned to supply the division with water. On the **10th of April**, Max Simon left the division to have his wounds treated in a German hospital. *SS-Obf.* Hermann Priess stood in for him at the head of the division. Another noteworthy change: in the armoured regiment, *SS-Stubaf.* Leiner, who had proven his inability to lead such a unit, was transferred to the *SS-FHA*. *SS-Stubaf.* Kunstmann took over from him. The artillery regiment was now headed by *SS-Stubaf.* Swientek, after Hermann Priess' departure. As soon as he had taken up his post as head of division, Hermann Priess quickly organised training periods for NCOs and NCO candidates to offset the staff shortage. Sharpshooters and vehicle drivers were also trained. Several changes occurred in the structure of division command: new quartermaster (*Ib*) was *SS-Hstuf.* Stürzbecher, the reconnaissance battalion was given to *SS-Hstuf.* Kron, who used to lead the anti-aircraft defence battalion, now ruled by *SS-Ostubaf.* Fuhrländer. In June, *SS-Stubaf.* Baldur Keller came to be chief of staff for the division, and *SS-Stubaf.* Sander, transferred to *10.SS-Panzergrenadier-Division*, was replaced at the head of *IV.(s)/SS-Art.-Rgt."T"* by *SS-Hstuf.* Messerle.

SS-Kradsch.-Rgt. "Thulé" had suffered so many losses in men and equipment that the *SS-Pz.Korps'* chief of staff decided to dissolve it on the 19th of April. The regiment was reduced to one mere battalion, which was in the end dissolved as well on the 20th of May, and integrated to the reconnaissance battalion.

Totenkopf started to be relieved from its positions north of Bjelgorod by *168.ID* from the **24th of April**. The bulk of the division settled north-east of Charkow where it began to be refitted. Weapons and vehicles were delivered in large quantities in May and June. Thus, *I./SS-Art.-Rgt."T"* was to be equipped with self-propelled guns (*Sd.Kfz.124 "Wespe"* for the *1.* and *2.Bttr.*, and *Sd.Kfz.165 "Hummel"* for the *3.Bttr.*). Drill was going full swing: officers and NCOs were sent in training camps, new drivers and transmitters were trained. Since the division wasn't expecting any reinforcement from *SS-Nachr.-Ersatz-Abt.*, the missing troops were recruited in Ukrainian towns populated with *Volksdeutsche*. These new recruits were to become good soldiers but terrible radio-telephonists, due to their poor mastery of the German language! By the **1st of June**, thanks to the arrival of reinforcements, the division had (*Ist-Stärke*) 586 officers, 2.964 NCOs and 16.567 privates (in total 19.999 men). It was to keep on receiving extra reinforcements, which brought the total to more than 21.000 men at the end of June.

This resting period north-east of Charkow was much appreciated since the division had come out of the German counteroffensive completely exhausted. Besides, with the experience of combat, training started on new foundations.

On the **26th of June**, *SS-Brigaf.* Simon said his final farewells to *Totenkopf*. Hermann Priess, who was till then standing in for him, was officially nominated as division head. The next day, its different units got moving to meet with the start positions they were assigned for operation *"Zitadelle"*. *Totenkopf* was to fight on the *SS-Pz.Korps*'s left flank, between Blishnij Iwanowskij and Jachontow.

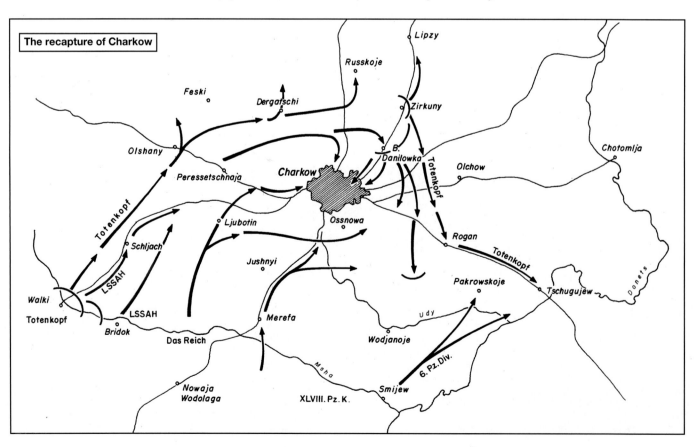

The recapture of Charkow

244

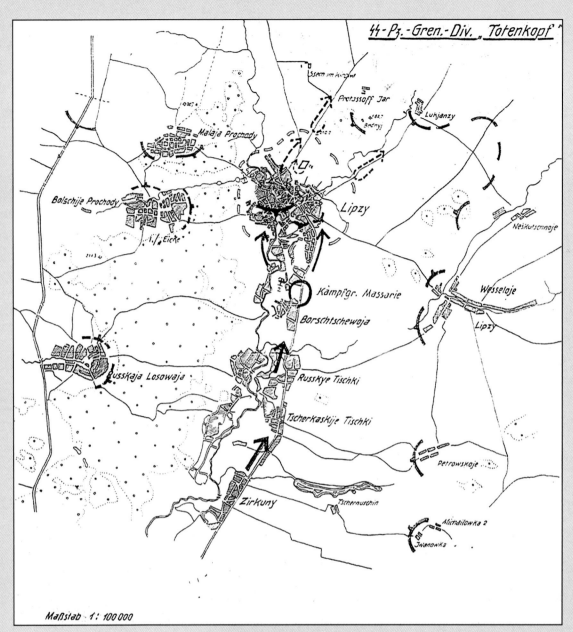

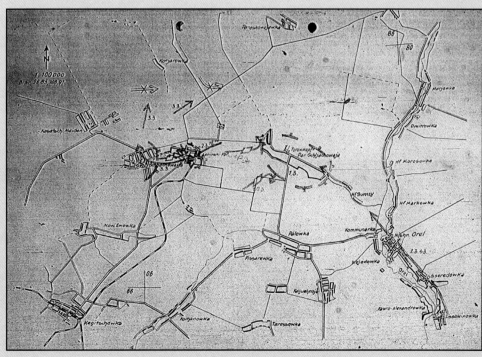

The pocket of Jeremejewka.

On the 1st March, *I.(gep.)/SS_Pz.Gren.Rgt.1 "T"* captures Oleiniki. The sudden thaw has turned the roads into bogs, with the exception of connecting carriageways made usable by *SS-Pi.Btl.3* thanks to seven cubic metres of gravel. (NA)

The pocket of Jeremejewka

The counter attack of *SS-Pz.Korps* from Krasnograd to Pawlograd grind the 1st and 6th army of the Soviet Guard. The others try to retreat towards the north with the help of the 3rd armoured army. The latter ventured south and found the *Totenkopf*, the *Das Reich* and the *Leibstandarte* divisions. Surrounded at Jeremejewka, they are crushed in four days in bloody battles. The Germans have now the upper hand.

16.(Pi)Kp./SS-Pz. Gren.Rgt.3 "T" seizes Mariewka with the help of a battery of assault guns. Here is a *StuG.III* sheltering near a house. (NA)

The battle of Jeremejewka ends on the 4th March with the destruction of the Soviet 12th and 15th armoured corps. A large number of Russian soldiers are captured by the SS. (NA)

Assault guns and *SPW* of *Kampfgruppe "Reder"* criss-cross the pocket of Jeremejewka to eliminate the last Russian troops left there. (NA)

Walter Reder, seen here with the grade of *SS-Sturmbannführer* during a ceremony awarding the iron cross to the men of *SS-Pz.Aufkl.-Abt.16* in Grosswardein, inflicts heavy losses to the Soviets. (Rights reserved)

The recapture of Charkow

After the destruction of their 3rd armoured army, despite reinforcements sent by the *Stavka* south of Charkow, the Soviets can no longer contain the *4.Panzerarmee* offensive towards the Donets basin city. The town falls into the hands of the Germans on the 15 or 16 March (the date of the end of the battles in the town cannot be determined precisely, as a few isolated groups of Russian soldiers tried for several days to rejoin their lines), that is a month after being abandoned by Paul Hausser.

Right: The only division troops fighting in Charkow itself are units from *Kampfgruppe "Kunstmann"*. *7.Kp./SS-Pz.Rgt.3* is part of it. Its chief, *SS-Ostuf.* Behr, is on the left with headphones. One of his section chiefs share a brief respite with him. (NA)

A battery of assault guns of *SS-StuG.-Abt. "Totenkopf"* stopping on a road north of Charkow. (NA)

On the 10th March, the *SS-Kampfgruppe "Baum"* seizes Dergatschi and starts to surround Charkow from the north, headed by its *Sd.Kfz.251*. On its right the *Leibstandarte* turns to the south towards the great Ukrainian city. (NA)

The *Pzkpfw.IV* of Hans Behr goes through a street in Charkow. In the evening of the 12th March, *SS-Pz.Korps* let it know that for the past ten hours the Soviets have been defeated. These have started to retreat towards the north east. Behr will be killed the next day in Rogan. (NA)

A series of well known photographs showing grenadiers from *II./SS-Pz.Gren.Rgt.1 "Totenkopf"* on *Pzkpfw.IV* belonging to *7.Kp./SS-Pz.Rgt.3*. (NA)

SS-Hauptsturmführer Erwin Meierdress is proudly wearing his Knight's Cross. He is now in charge of *I.Abt./SS-Pz.Rgt.3* and can be seen here with two of his staff officers. (Courtesy Tim Willemsen)

Waldemar Riefkogel with two of his comrades from *1.Kp./SS-Pz.Rgt.3*. All three are enjoying the rest period prior to the Kursk offensive. (Courtesy Tim Willemsen)

View of the Red Square. This photograph was taken well after the end of the battles. (NA)

Grenadiers from *Leibstandarte* and tanks of *Kampfgruppe "Kunstmann"* fighting side by side in Charkow. Here is a *Pzkpfw.III* probably from *5.Kp./SS-Pz.Rgt.3*. (NA)

Pzkpfw.III of *Kampf-gruppe "Kunstmann"* in Charkow. (NA)

Well known photo from *Wochenschau*, the caption of which was incorrect. It is not a *Pzkpfw.IV* from *Leibstandarte* but from *Totenkopf*. Indeed, the number on the tank is painted in white with a black border, which is a characteristic of *II./SS-Pz.Rgt.3.* (NA)

Grenadiers and gunners side by side in the town. Notice the non regulation sheepskin jacket. (NA)

The *Totenkopf* division completes the encirclement of Charkow from the east

From the 13th March, the Soviet troops (1st and 2nd armoured corps of the Guard, 19th, 104th, 305th and 307th fusiliers divisions) start to evacuate Charkow from the north east. The main of the *Totenkopf* division tries to stop them by heading towards Rogan and Tschugujew.

Right: A *Pzkpfw.IV* of *3.Kp./SS-Pz.Rgt.3* (*SS-Ostuf.* Riefkogel) support the grenadiers from the *Totenkopf* regiment towards Rogan. Notice that the markings of *I./SS-Pz.Rgt.3* differ from those of *II./SS-Pz.Rgt.3*. The numbers here are entirely painted in black. (NA)

Left: Grenadiers of *Kampfgruppe "Baum"* in Rogan. Their parka jackets come from the clothes factory in Dachau where the workforce is made of concentration camps prisoners and where the textiles were retrieved from those who were executed. (NA)

Below: A *Pzkpfw.III* of *Kampfgruppe "Kunstmann"* going to Lipzy which they will reach in the afternoon of the 17th march. In the foreground an anti-tank 75 (*Pak 40*) gun. (NA)

This gunner from one of the *SS-Pz.Korps* divisions is smiling: Charkow has been recaptured and several soviet armies have been almost entirely destroyed. This will be the last major German victory. (NA)

A *Befehls-Pz.III* (a commander tank) from the headquarters of *I./SS-Pz.Rgt.3. Kampfgruppe "Kunstmann"* leaves the town on the 12th March to rejoin the bulk of the division north of Charkow. (NA)

The armoured regiment celebrates the summer solstice.
On the right hand side photograph are *SS-Ostuf.* Riefkogel
and *SS-Hstuf.* Meierdress. The
SS-Ostuf. seated on the right
could not be identified by the
author. (NA)

Shooting exercise led by *SS-Hstuf.* Meierdress *(Kdr. I./SS-Pz.Rgt.3)*. He wears with pride the knight cross. The target is a British made *Tetrach* tank. (NA)

The armoured regiment has still got five 75 cm short gun *L/24 Pzkpfw.IV* which were not effective against the *T-34*. (NA)

SS-Stubaf. Georg Bochmann (*Kdr. II./SS-Pz.Rgt.3*) practices shooting. His knight cross is hidden by a non regulation neck scarf. (Private collection S.)

28th May 1943: Sepp Dietrich (back turned) who is leading for a few more days the Leibstandarte, celebrates his birthday in the company of officers from *SS-Pz.Korps*. From left to right: Hermann Priess, Albin von Reitzenstein *(Kdr.SS-Pz.Rgt.2)*, Otto Baum and Walter Krüger *(Kdr. SS-Div. "Das Reich")*. (NA)

Most of the *Pzkpfw.IV* are equipped with a 75 cm canon *L/43* with superior firing performance than the previous gun. It must be mentioned that they are not all fitted with *Schürzen*, additional steel armoured skirts. (NA)

While many division soldiers are billeted locally during the spring of 1943, this is not the case of the gunners of *SS-Pz.Rgt.3* who have to rough it in the Ukrainian countryside. These men, however, managed to build rather cosy shelters. (NA)

The maintenance of arms and vehicles is essential in order to keep the units ready for combat. This *Pzkpfw.IV*, with eight kills, is stationed in this dense wood to avoid being detected by the Soviet spotter planes. (NA)

Picture of an unidentified *SS-Hauptsturmführer*. He has put up photographs of German actresses behind him to cheer him up. (NA)

Cleaning of the formidable 88 gun of the *Pzkpfw.VI "Tiger"*. The division, on the eve of operation "Zitadelle", owns eleven ones.

The difference in size between a *Pzkpfw.III* and a *Tiger* is noticeable. One weighs 22.3 tons, the other 56... (NA)

Tiger and *Pzkpfw.III* in a repair workshop. The crane, seen in the background, is to remove the tank turrets. (NA)

Report from the first line

An *SS-KB* is giving a coverage on a division unit on the first line in a quieter sector. During the spring of 1943, the soldiers from both sides are recuperating and prepare for the huge battle in the summer.

This mortar crew (*m.Gr.W.34*) are casually posing for the photographer. It is unlikely that they have actually fired the shell. (NA)

Left: An *SS-Obersturmführer* among his men. Their unease is unusual for reports generally done by propaganda groups. (NA)

Series of photographs of officers and soldiers. The *SS-Obersturmführer* on the previous group photograph does not wear any decorations, which is unusual at that point in time. (NA)

A more convincing photograph of soldiers cleaning the mortar barrel. There are boxes of ammunition on the right. (NA)

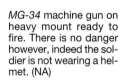

MG-34 machine gun on heavy mount ready to fire. There is no danger however, indeed the soldier is not wearing a helmet. (NA)

Another heavy machine gun on the Ukrainian plain. On such open ground, it is vital to dig in. (NA)

Above: Observation of the enemy lines with binoculars. (NA)

Right: Anti-tank 5cm gun (*Pak 38*). The enemy must be far away, as the men are in the open. But there are a few stick grenades on the ground, just in case. (NA)

Above: The occupants of a bunker pose for the photograph. Such shelters allow to protect from heavy shelling, except when these reach their targets. (NA)

The *climb towards* the front

At the beginning of July *Totenkopf* was attached to *II.SS-Pz.Korps*, which was itself under the command of *4.Panzerarmee*. This army, along with *Armee-Abteilung "Kempf"*, formed the southern claw of the pincer attack led by the *OKH* against the Kursk salient. The northern claw was formed by General Model's *9.Armee*. This salient, about 100 miles (160 km) wide at its base, delved about 75 miles (120 km) west into the German lines. The Soviets, who had been extremely well informed about the *Wehrmacht's* intentions, gathered considerable forces to defend it. Facing the 36 German divisions available for this offensive were no less than eleven Soviet armies, armed with 20 000 guns and mortars and more than 3600 tanks.

II.SS-Pz.Korps, renumbered by order of the *Reichsführer-SS*, estimated that the Russians had two infantry divisions on their first line of defense between Schopino and the Worskla and two more divisions on the second fortified line between Lutschki and Pokrowka. In order to find out if the Russians had brought in new soldiers to the first line, *Totenkopf* was ordered to take prisoners in the Jerik sector.

On **July 3**, the Soviet artillery shelled the German positions, making the work of the division's sappers much more difficult. The engineers had in fact been ordered to remove the mines placed in April. Their mission was to secure routes and mark them out. Unfortunately for them, the earth in this sector contained large quantities of iron, making their detectors useless. Probing for mines had to be carried out using small sticks made from cables. Although this mission was extremely dangerous, there were no casualties.

During the night between July 3 and 4, the Soviets continued their harassing fire. They had been at their posts since the day before and were just waiting for the German attack: all the trenches and strongpoints were occupied. The heavy rain had transformed the roads into a quagmire, slowing down the *Totenkopf's* move to its starting positions. Nevertheless, despite the inclement conditions, the units reached their sectors on time on the left flank of *II.SS-Pz.Korps*. The troops were then ordered to keep radio silence until zero hour.

SS-Pz.Rgt. "T" was located at Rakowo, ready to intervene at any moment. It disposed of:

- 59 *Pzkpfw.III* (with *Kwk 5cm L/60*)
- 5 *Pzkpfw.IV* (with *Kwk 7.5cm L/24*)
- 42 *Pzkpfw.IV* (with *Kwk 7.5cm L/43 or L/48*)
- 11 *Pzkpw.VI "Tigers"*
- 8 *Bef.Pz.III*

Generaloberst Hermann Hoth is the commander of 4.Panzerarmee since 1 June 1942. Hitler dismisses him in November 1943 after the loss of Eastern Ukraine. (Rights reserved)

Making a total of 125 tanks in running order. *SS-StuG-Abt. "T"*, had 28 *StuG.III* and *SS-Pz.Jg.-Abt. "T"*, 11 self-propelled guns (of the *Marder II type*) at its disposal. The day before the offensive, the division had 164 operational armored vehicles.

II.SS-Pz.Korps gave its attack orders for the next day: after the enemy's advanced posts had been taken,

in the forests to the North of Hill 227,4 and on Hill 218 by *"Totenkopf"* and on Hill 228,6 by *"LSSAH"*, and following the planned artillery preparation, *LSSAH* and *Das Reich* had to break through the enemy's first line of defense (Jerik valley, Beresoff, Hill 220,5 and Sadelnoje), progress to the sector between Shurawlinyj forest and the Worskla to the north and once there attack the second enemy line of defense (Lutschki - Jakowlewo). The *"Totenkopf"* division, reinforced by *Gren.Rgt.315*, had to protect the rear and the eastern flank of *II.SS-Pz.Korps*.

Operation "Zitadelle"

On **July 5** *5.Kp./"TE"* was the division's first unit to go into action. At about 02h30, they succeeded in taking control of the enemy's advanced posts situated on Hill 218, south east of Beresoff, supported by the guns of *4.Bttr./SS-Korps-Werfer-Abt.*. The Russian artillery immediately reacted to the loss of this position and shelled it heavily, cutting all telephone links. This bombardment was followed by an assault, launched at 03h00 by the Soviet infantry from "Lizard Woods" to the north of the hill. This attack was held off, but forebode the difficulties that the Germans would have to face in their offensive against tightly packed defensive positions held by soldiers ready to fight.

At 03h15, hundreds of artillery pieces opened fire. At 04h00, supported by the *Stukas* and massive bombardment of the enemy positions, the *"Leibstandarte"* and *"Das Reich"* divisions attacked. They came up against an extremely well organized defensive network. In addition, the Soviet artillery fired salvo after salvo, making any progression very costly. The Russian aviation was also very present, strafing the German assault formations and the reinforcement columns moving up to the front. Beresoff was the center of the fighting. Paul Hausser did not want to engage *Totenkopf* on the right flank of *II.SS-Pz.Korps*. until the city had fallen. But *Generaloberst* Hoth ordered him to send the division into battle without delay. *SS-Rgt. "T"* had to force the decision: its mission would be to penetrate the enemy defenses to the south of Beresoff. At 09h15, they attacked Hill 218 with the support of assault guns and panzers. The *Nebelwerfer* shelled the enemy positions for one hour, between 10h10 and 11h10. Despite this intensive shelling, the grenadiers progressed with great difficulty because of the mine fields and the massive barrage fire. The SS captured the antitank trench to the south-east of Beresoff in hand to hand combat. It was then 12h30. After a final dive-bombing run by the *Stukas*, *III./"Deutschland"* was able to take Beresoff at 11h30. *Das Reich* continued its advance to the north towards Hill 233,3. On its left, *Leibstandarte* reached Bykowka in the early afternoon. The first Soviet line of defense had just been crossed. By the end of the afternoon, most of the division had reached the south-eastern edge of Shurawlinyj forest along the Gremutschi Valley. The results of this first day of offensives were mixed: the Soviets' first line of defense had been broken, but at a very high price (31 killed, 119 wounded, and 2 missing), and not all the objectives had been reached. In the morning of **July 6**, *Totenkopf* was split up into three groups, one which would fight to the west of Schopino, another to the west of Ternowka and the last to the west of Nepchajewo. At about 12h30 they received orders from *II.SS-Pz.Korps* to send a mechanized group towards Lutschki to make contact with *SS-Rgt. "Der Führer"* of *Das Reich*. In the afternoon, *Das Reich* succeeded in breaking through the Soviet second line of defense. The Russians reacted immediately, sending their 2nd armored corps across the Lipowyj Donets. At the same time *III./"TE"* and *III./"T"* attacked Jerik from the south-west and the north-east. The two battalions joined up and a small pocket was formed near Jerik, where the Soviet troops fought with determination. It took the SS many hours to take control of the area. At the end of the afternoon *SS-Staf's SS-Rgt."TE"*. Becker took up position on the heights located along the western bank of the Lipowyj Donets against the areas where the Soviet troops were firmly entrenched (Schopino, Ternowka and Wissloje). Around 17h00, the Soviet 2nd armored corps began to threaten the right flank of *II.SS-Pz.Korps*: aerial reconnaissance planes spotted 33 Soviet tanks crossing the Donets at Soschenkoff. *Totenkopf* then received its orders from the army corps *"to set up a Sperrverband turned eastward, lock the bridgehead and prevent any enemy advance."* *5.Kp./SS-Pz.Rgt.3* was engaged against the enemy armored spearhead. The Soviet tanks reached Smorodino. The battle was raging there. At 19h10, *Totenkopf* announced that it had destroyed 15 tanks, including 12 *"Churchills"*. The day's casualties amounted to 52 killed, including *SS-Stubaf.* Schneider (*Kdr. I./"T"*) and 234 wounded.

On **July 7** at 04h30, *Totenkopf* attacked the concentrations of Soviet tanks located on the western bank of the Lipowyj Donets. At about 10h30, Otto Baum's men reached the heights situated just over a mile (2 km) west of the river. Eleven Soviet tanks were destroyed in the course of this battle. Although this day had been relatively uneventful, it still cost 39 men killed (including 3 officers) and 112 wounded.

At 23h50, *II.SS-Pz.Korps* gave its orders for the following day: *"Das Reich"* and *"Leibstandarte"*, supported by *XLVIII.Pz.Korps,* had to eliminate the soviet armored units located to the south of the Pena. *Totenkopf* had to be relieved by *167.ID* to take up position on the left flank of the corps, since it now seemed impossible for *Das Reich* and *Leibstandarte* to break through the enemy lines without its support.

During the morning of **July 8**, *Das Reich* and *Leibstandarte* attacked to the north and north-east. The Soviets reacted by sending strong armored forces against the *II.SS-Pz.Korps* right flank, threatening to cut off two the SS divisions from their rear lines. At 12h45, *Totenkopf* announced: *"Enemy attack with 30 to 40 tanks and some weak infantry units from Wisloje and Ternowka to the west."* The division sent its tank regiment to counter-attack. Near Wisloje it came under antitank fire. *SS-Stubaf.* Kunstmann was killed in his panzer. Command of *SS-Pz.Rgt.3* was then given to *SS-Stubaf.* Georg Bochmann, who was replaced at *II.Abteilung* by *SS-Hstuf.* Biermeier.

West of Wisloje the Soviet troops were pushed back beyond the Lipowyj Donets with heavy losses, despite the support of thirty or so tanks. *Totenkopf* was not the only unit that had to deal with counter-attacks from the Soviet tanks: *Das Reich* was heavily engaged on its eastern and north-eastern flanks and the strongpoints held by *Leibstandarte* were being fiercely assaulted. During the afternoon of July 8, the entire *II.SS-Pz.Korps* had to pull back into a defensive position. The Soviet objective, to stop the *II.SS-Pz.Korps* advance, had therefore succeeded. It had even had

to call in reserves to contain the Russian counter-attacks. During the afternoon, the first *167.ID* units finally arrived to relieve *Totenkopf*, which was then available to give new momentum to the attack by *II.SS-Pz.Korps* towards the north-west.

On **July 9** *Totenkopf* set up base in the Teterewino - Lutschki sector. At 07h55, the Soviets attacked its lines to the north-east of Teterewino with about thirty tanks. They were held off by *III./"TE"*. At 08h10, *SS-KGr. "Baum"* finally reached its assigned positions in the Lutschki sector. They started their attack at 10h00 in the direction of Kotschetowka. Its leading units reached Wesselyj at 11h15 without encountering any serious resistance. At 12h50, the *Totenkopf's* tanks found themselves engaged with 70 (?) Russian tanks from the Guard's 24th armored brigade to the west of Gresnoje. Fourteen of them were destroyed by *SS-Pz.Rgt.3*. At 15h30 *SS-Rgt."TE"* attacked from the Teterewino sector towards Krasnyj Oktjabr in order to establish a bridgehead on the Psel, the last natural obstacle on the road to Kursk. At 18h45, *I./"TE"* took Koslowka, but the Russian resistance became stronger as the SS progressed towards the river. In addition, the poor condition of the roads and terrain caused by heavy rainfall the night before was making the advance difficult. The decision was made to wait until dark before trying to cross the river. In the evening, the division reported that it still had 48 *Pzkpfw.III*, 28 *Pzkpfw.IV* (including 7 with short guns - 7.5cm L/24), 1 *Pzkpfw.VI "Tiger"*, 5 *Bef.Pz.*, 21 *StuG.III* and 11 *Marder II* in working order, a total of 114 armoured vehicles.

On **July 10** at 10h00, the regiments started their attack, *"Eicke"* on the right and *"Totenkopf"* on the left. They came under heavy shellfire from the soviet artillery. The SS suffered terrible losses. At 15h00, *Totenkopf* attacked again. *I./ "TE"* succeeded in crossing the Psel to the north of Prochorowka. At 15h42, with massive support from the artillery, the grenadiers of *SS-Stubaf.* Knöchlein took control of the first Russian positions in hand to hand combat. They fought for every foxhole and every trench. At 17h00, *SS-Rgt."TE"* managed to advance nearly 900 yards north of the Psel, giving a little breathing space to its bridgehead. *Totenkopf* were expecting a strong Soviet reaction. General Vatoutine, commander of the Woronesch Front, had in fact given orders that any German advance in the direction of Obojan had to be stopped.

In the night between July 10 and 11, several attacks were launched against the German bridgehead, first by companies, then by battalions, each time supported by a barrage of artillery fire. The situation of the SS grenadiers was very difficult because they were running out of munitions. It had been pouring with rain for hours. The torrential rainfall of the last two days had turned the terrain south of the Psel into a veritable quagmire over 500 yards wide. It was practically impossible for vehicles to move. Under these conditions, the attack planned to enlarge the bridgehead was postponed until the following day.

On **July 12**, in order to break the *II.SS-Pz.Korps's* offensive, the Soviets called in the Guard's 5th armored army, which had been held until then in reserve with the Steppe Front. This army was made up of two armored corps and one mechanized corps, a total of more than 700 tanks and assault guns. The battles had reached a new stage. During the night, the Soviet aviation and artillery had bombed and shelled the entire *Totenkopf* bridgehead. At 03h15 a Russian battalion attacked the positions of *I./"T"* to the west of Kljutschi. At 05h00 *Leibstandarte* announced that the lead units of its armored regiment had fallen upon large tank formations. The main battle had just started to the south of Prochorowka.

Ernst Häussler (SS-Nr. 217 862) commander of *II./SS-Pz.Gren.Rgt.1 "T"* from autumn 1942. He has been promoted *SS-Sturmbannführer* on 21 June 1942. From February to April 1943 he is the temporary commander of *I./SS-Kradsch.-Rgt. "Thule"*. He is then transferred to *17.SS-Panzergrenadier-Division "Götz von Berlichingen"*. He is the commander of *I./SS-Pz.Gren.Rgt.37* from 6 December 1943 until June 1944. In September 1944, after regiment commander training, he is appointed commander of *SS-Pz.-Gren.Rgt.5 "Totenkopf"*, after promotion to the rank of *SS-Obersturmbannführer* on 1 September 1944. Wounded in combat, he will only regain active command at the end of the war. (Rights reserved)

Otto Kron (SS-Nr. 31 441) has spent his career within *SS-TV* and *Totenkopf*. He was the *Flak* Battalion commander before leading the Reconnaissance Group, an altogether different sort of activity. In the *Waffen-SS* military leaders with a daredevil reputation were favoured at the expense of men with better mastery of military science. (Rights reserved)

At 06h30, I./SS-Pz.Rgt.3 "T" counter-attacked to the west of Kljutschi. The Soviets pulled back towards Michailowka. But one hour later, the attacks came thick and fast: at 07h30, an attack to the west of Kljutschi; at 07h40, a Russian battalion attacked from Ilinski towards the Psel; at 07h45, two Soviet regiments, supported by forty or so tanks, attacked SS-Rgt."TE" to the east of Wassiljewka.

By 09h00, the entire SS-Pz.Rgt.3 "T" had crossed onto the northern bank of the Psel: a terrible tank battle began. The SS suffered heavy losses during the fighting. The Soviets continued to send their forces into the battle. At 11h00, the division announced that the attack launched from Wassiljewka with two regiments and 50 tanks had been repelled. New Russian units were observed marching to the front from Obojan by aerial reconnaissance. At 11h15, II.SS-Pz.Korps ordered Totenkopf to "try to cross the Psel at Michailowka and encircle the enemy forces south of the river from the rear." The division, which was still under strong enemy attack on its left flank, suffered numerous casualties. Most of the grenadier companies were now down to less than 100 men each. The general staff of the division then decided to bring them up to strength with new recruits from the depot battalion, which was south of Snamenka at this time. The unit was practically dissolved. At 16h45, I./"TE", on the right flank of the division, managed to take Andrejewka. At the end of the afternoon, Totenkopf simply reinforced the positions taken. These battles cost them dearly: 69 killed, 231 wounded and 16 missing. 27 tanks had been destroyed and 238 Russian soldiers captured. In the evening, the mechanized group continued its advance, but once again came up against a perfectly camouflaged Russian position. The Soviet artillery did not hesitate to open fire on its own infantry in order to stop the advance of the panzers. Soviet tanks arrived on the scene and another battle took place on the heights situated about half a mile (1 km) to the north west of Poleshajew. The Soviet 31st armored corps was cut to pieces during the battle and the Totenkopf mechanized group continued advancing to the north-east. At 22h45, it reached the Beregowoje - Kartaschewka road and set up its

defense there. General Hoth (OB 4.Panzerarmee) then expressed his gratitude to the division for this decisive success which would allow the offensive to continue in the direction of Kursk. Von Manstein also congratulated the II.SS-Pz units.Korps for have wiped out the Guard's 5th armored army near Prochorowka, even though it had been impossible to make use of this victory due to the bloody failure of III.Pz.Korps against the Guard's 69th and 7th armies on the right flank of Paul Hausser's troops. Das Reich was unable to help Leibstandarte take Prochorowka and complete the destruction of the 5th armored army, a move which would have put the Soviet units located to the north of Psel, facing Totenkopf, in a difficult position. This day had been a turning point in the battle, because in the Orel sector the Brjansk Front went on the offensive against 2.Panzerarmee, threatening the rear of Model's 9.Armee. 9.Armee was obliged to go on the defensive to send reinforcements to 2.Panzerarmee. Operation "Zitadelle", whose objective was to encircle the Soviet forces in the Kursk salient, could now be considered a failure with its northern claw finally abandoned. To the south, the Germans still had the perspective of destroying the Soviet armies lined up against 4.Panzerarmee and Armee-Abteilung "Kempf".

The night between July 12 and 13 was relatively calm. The troops on both sides were still "shell-shocked" from the dreadful battle the day before and needed to muster their forces. At 09h45, the Soviets attacked the positions of SS-Rgt."TE" supported by just 8 tanks, proof that they had lost numerous tanks during the battles of July 12. During the day, II.SS-Pz.Korps decided to now concentrate its efforts on its right flank by sending Das Reich to the attack, since continuing to attack north of the Psel was pointless as long as the Leibstandarte had not taken Prochorowka. The Soviets, on their part, wanted to annihilate the bridgehead and were constantly sending new troops into the fight. All their attacks were held off. 2.Kp./SS-Pz.Jg.-Abt."T" (SS-Ustuf. Jendges), in particular, distinguished itself by destroying 38 Russian tanks in less than 20 minutes. At 14h25, the Soviets sent their troops to attack the division's positions once more, apparently unconcerned by their losses.

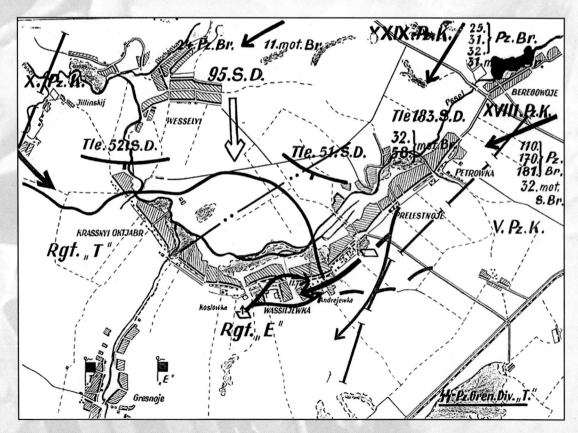

The head bridge on the Psel.

SS-Pz.Rgt.3 "T" was called in to the rescue. The Soviet attack was stopped, but *SS-Pz.Rgt.3 "T"* paid heavily for this victory. The ten *"Tiger"* tanks engaged in the battle were knocked out, as well as two command tanks (*Befehlspanzer III*), twenty-one *Pzkpfw.III*, and thirteen *Pzkpfw.IV*! However, the Soviet attacks had come up against a ferocious SS defense. 61 tanks had been destroyed by *Totenkopf* during the day, out of a total of 249 claimed by *II.SS-Pz.Korps*. *Totenkopf* had 32 *Pzkpfw.III*, 17 *Pzkpfw.IV* and 5 *Befehls-Pz* left.

At this time, Manstein still had more than 500 tanks available and could count on the support of *XXIV.Pz.Korps*, held in reserve in the Isjum region. Even though his *Heeresgruppe "Süd"* had made slow progress until then, he believed that the three Soviet armies facing him no longer had the resources to stop it. Von Manstein was convinced that he could destroy the rest of the Guard's 1st armored army and 6th army, and threaten the rears of the 40th, 60th, 65th, and 38th soviet armies. In view of the general situation, however, Hitler decided to end Operation *"Zitadelle"* and send a strong political message to his wavering ally by transferring *II.SS-Pz.Korps* to Italy, a move supported by *GFM* von Kluge, whose armies were having difficulty in the Orel region.

On **July 14**, the Soviets once again shelled the Psel bridgehead throughout the morning. Numerous attacks followed this bombardment. The attacks were countered by the combined action of the *Totenkopf's* heavy guns. On the morning of **July 15**, the Soviet artillery started to shell the division's positions on the bridgehead again. The day was exactly the same as the day before. At 22h00, the division received the following order from *II.SS-Pz.Korps*: *"The "Totenkopf" division should immediately start to pull back to the south bank of the Psel all its heavy weaponry and all non-essential vehicles. The division should be ready to evacuate its remaining units from the bridgehead on the night between the 17th and the 18th ..."*

On **July 17** from 22h10 *SS-Pz.Rgt.3 "T"* crossed back over the Psel. The retreat was punctuated by harassing fire from the Soviet artillery. The decision to abandon the bridgehead provoked anger and incomprehension among the *SS* soldiers who had fought there an entire week and lost a good number of their comrades in the fighting. The last to retreat were the sappers, who blew up all the houses, bridges and roads in the sector. There were only a few skirmishes as the Germans pulled back, since the Soviet infantry were loath to follow the Germans too closely. On **July 18** at 04h45, *Totenkopf* announced that it had reached its new positions. Around 18h00, *XLVIII.Pz.Korps* took over the sector from *II.SS-Pz.Korps*, which had received orders to go to the Stalino region. In the meantime, *Heeresgruppe "Süd"* had decided to withdraw *4.Panzerarmee* back to the front line existing before operation *"Zitadelle"*.

During the night between the 19th and the 20th, *Totenkopf* established new positions south west of Lutschki. Once again, the retreat took place under fire from Soviet artillery. It received orders to go to Barwenkowa, a town situated more than 125 miles (200 km) away as the crow flies. The division's mission in the Bjelgorod region had come to an end. The damage inflicted on the Soviets between July 5 and 18 was the following:

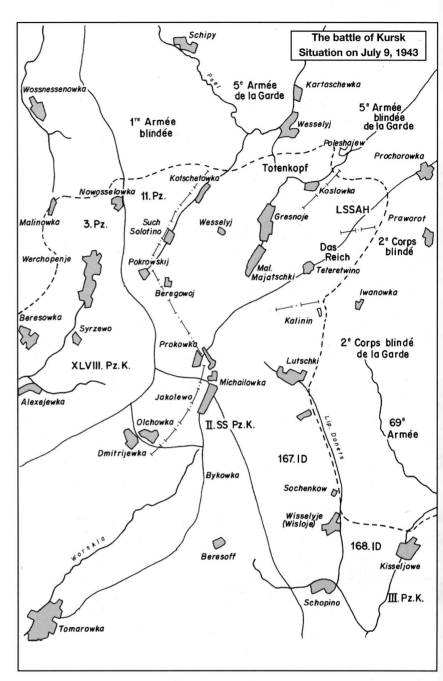

The battle of Kursk
Situation on July 9, 1943

- Prisoners:	1 547
- Deserters:	166
- Tanks:	214
- Armored cars:	1
- Planes:	14
- Antitank guns:	66
- Antitank rifles:	146
- Machineguns:	257
- Artillery pieces:	10
- Anti-aircraft guns:	1
- Trucks:	14
- "Stalin's Organs":	27

Its own losses for the period between July 5 and 19 were: 512 killed, 2118 wounded, and 38 missing (total: 2668).

Operation "Zitadelle"

On 5 July 1943, the biggest ever armour battle starts. The Germans launch 1650 tanks, assault-guns and tank-hunters against mighty Soviet fortifications. The Red Army has massed 3600 armoured vehicles behind its defensive lines. This offensive goes against all the principles of armoured warfare. Despite very strong opposition from Guderian and to a lesser degree, from Model and Manstein, Hitler, urged by the necessity of a swift and decisive victory on the Eastern Front before the Allied landings in Italy, decides to launch his panzerdivisions into a battle they will not recover from. Most of the photographs in this chapter were taken by *SS-KB* Büschel, King, Grönert et Merz. Büschel and King were normally attached to *Leibstandarte* but they took shots of *Totenkopf* units as well. Grönert and Merz belonged to *Totenkopf* but we owe them photographs of *Das Reich* units. This fact has made unit identification difficult and even uncertain at times, for which we apologise to the reader.

Opposite : it is quite exceptional for a *Waffen-SS* soldier to make the cover of *"Die Wehrmacht"*. This issue is dated 5 July 1943, the day "Zitadelle" starts. (Private collection.)

SS-Staf. Hellmuth Becker inspects troops on the frontline on the eve of the offensive. Behind him is *SS-Stubaf.* Knöchlein and on the right is *SS-Ostuf.* Kallert. The officer extending is *SS-Hstuf.* Kaddatz. (Private collection.)

A very dusty motorcyclist. On the eve of the offensive, the three divisions of *II.SS-Pz.Korps* are even more powerful than they were in January, when they arrived on the Eastern Front. *Totenkopf* has more than 21000 men on strength and 164 tanks in fighting order. (NA)

A soldier, heavily laden with ammunition, marches to the the front under the clouds of an impending storm. (Private collection.)

The first *Totenkopf* unit to reach the frontline is the third battalion of regiment *"Eicke"*. A combat platoon marches towards positions previously held by *Gren.Rgt.331* north of Rakowo. Note that the *MG-34* has not yet been totally supplanted by the *MG-42*. (NA)

A 75mm anti-tank gun (*Pak 40*) in firing position. It can penetrate 98mm of armour at 1000m and it is the anti-tank gun the German infantry has long yearned for. Production of the gun, notoriously insufficient, never met the requirements of fighting units. (NA)

Couriers on their motorcyclies wait for messages. They look fresh, well-rested and brimming with confidence. Morale is at its highest.(NA)

A *SS-Rttf.* from a staff unit poses for the photographer with a captured *PPSh 41*. (Private collection..)

A *Pzkpfw.IV* partially camouflaged with foliage on its way to the front. To confuse Soviet intelligence, the death's head markings of the division have been replaced on all vehicles by three vertical bars, a tactical sign shared with *6.Panzerdivision* of the *Heer*. (Private collection..)

The Totenkopf goes on the offensive

On 1 July, *II.SS-Pz.Korps* transmits the orders for the offensive to Totenkopf : *"Behind the right flank of SS-Pz.Gren.Div."Das Reich", Totenkopf attacks at H+2 the enemy positions on hill 216,5 and in the area of Shurawlinyj and opens a passage towards the Kursk-Bjelgorod road, between Schopino and Gluschinskij. Enemy positions in Jerik must simultaneously be attacked from the rear and from the south. The sector between the Lipowyj Donets and the Kursk – Bjelgorod road must be cleared in the same breath. The division must then remain at the army corps disposition in the sector of Smorodino."* (KTB Nr.6 II.SS-Pz.Korps, Korpsbefehl Nr.17 v. 1.7.1943)

1. A machine-gunner with his *MG-42* before the start of the attack. It is a formidable weapon which is now being delivered in quantity to the units. It has a high rate of fire (1500 rounds per minute), it is reliable and it is easy to produce which explains it is an immediate success. It is today still widely in use with a number of armies, among them the *Bundeswehr*, with few modifications, as the *MG-3*. (NA)

2. A very thirsty grenadier drinks from a bucket. The offensive is launched in summer weather, with intense heat and storms. (NA)

3. Nice picture of a *Totenkopf's Schwimmwagen*. A point of view of the *Panzerschütze* Suwe during the first phases of the battle. It is possible that the officer with the map is *SS-Ostubaf.* Baum. (Courtesy W.Suwe via P.Tiquet)

2

1. Grenadiers get a lift to the frontline on a *Pzkpfw.IV Ausf.H* which looks factory fresh. In the summer of 1943, the tanks of the division are easily recognisable by the black outline of their identification numbers. (Private collection.)

2. Soviet aircraft are very active on 5 July 1943 and mainly target artillery positions and supply units. The divisional Flak (*SS-Flak-Abt."T"*) shoots four, one of them this *Yak-9*. (NA)

3. *Panzerkampfgruppe !* During the battle of Kursk, firepower enabled the mixed formations of tanks and mechanised infantry to deeply penetrate the seemingly impregnable Soviet defenses. (Copyright)

4. Elements from a staff unit discuss pursuing their advance after they have cleared up a soviet position with the support of the assault gun visible in the background. Communication equipment is at the ready. (NA)

Above: conversation atop a *Pzkpfw.III Ausf.L*. Black identification numbers are typical of *Totenkopf*. Unlike the previous day, the armoured regiment is thrown into action to
pierce Soviet lines. (NA)

Opposite: Officers of regiment *"Eicke"* : right, Wolfram
Schneider (*II./E*) and middle, Max Kühn (*III./E*). Who is the
third man ? (Private collection S.)

SS-Stubaf. Kunstmann, commander of the division armoured regiment. This shot was taken only hours before his death (Private collection.)

A *Tiger* tank returns from the frontline maybe because of battle damage. Smoke from artillery fire is visible in the background. Infantry from *Gren.Rgt.315* and *Totenkopf* are heading straight into that hell. (NA)

1. A battery of *s.FH18* heavy guns in firing position. The crew have attempted to camouflage the guns with foliage which may seem inadequate since the open nature of the terrain offers no protection. (NA)

The artillery of *II.SS-Pz.Korps* during "Zitadelle"

During the battle of Charkow, operations were characterised by extreme swiftness and mobility and artillery only played a minor role. At Kursk, the importance of artillery is self-evident because of the need to break through heavily fortified positions and the impossibilty of a surprise attack. On both sides, the concentration of artillery is awesome and shells rain on the battlefield. Infantry pays a heavy tribute.

2 and **3.** Grenadiers walk past a 150mm howitzer. On 5 July *IV./SS-Art.-Rgt."Totenkopf"* had at its disposal 512 150mm shells for its eight *s.FH18* and 256 105mm shells for its four *s.FK52. II.SS-Pz.-Korps* had 24 464 shells and 9270 *Nebelwerfer* rockets for that sole day. (NA)

3

4. During "Zitadelle", the *Totenkopf* is reinforced by three artillery groups and a group of *Nebelwerfer* rocket-launchers from *II.SS-Pz.-Korps*. Shown here is a *30 cm-Werfer* of the group heavy battery. (NA)

5. *30 cm-Werfer* firing. Launch is electrically activated. (NA)

6. The telltale large smoke trails left by the rockets are the main drawback of the *Nebelwerfer*. They allow the enemy to locate the launchers making it necessary to evacuate position as quickly as possible after firing. (NA)

4

5

6

Another defect of the *Nebelwerfer* lies in its lack of precision despite constant amelioration to the design by german engineers. However, this is greatly counterbalanced by the volume of firepower afforded by the rocket-launchers which can saturate a large area. They are also cheap to produce, costing six times less than a 150mm howitzer, which allows great numbers. (NA)

In the Kursk salient, the Soviets have massed artillery in even higher density than the Germans. Every German move is greeted by artillery salvoes.This column has been stopped in its tracks. (NA)

A *15 cm-Werfer 41* is ready to fire. In the background, an apparently factory fresh *StuG.III F* advances just behind the frontline. Because of their short range, *Nebelwerfer* are never far from the frontline. (NA)

Massive armour assault

On 7 July, *Totenkopf* must remain on the right flank of *II.SS-Pz.Korps* because of the failure of *Armee-Abteilung "Kempf"* to make any ground to the east. *Leibstandarte* and *Das Reich* get ready to continue their advance towards the northeast after breaking through the Soviet second line of defense between Lutschki and Jakowlewo. During the afternoon, they have to face violent counter-attacks by Soviet armour in the Kalinin – Teterewino sector.

Opposite: *SS-StuG.-Abt.3* sustains very heavy losses on 6 and 7 July. The soviet threat on the right flank of *II.SS-Pz.Korps* means it must be reengaged the following day, west of Wisloje. (NA)

Below: by launching hundreds of tanks against *II.SS-Pz.Korps* on 8 July, the Soviets momentarily stop the German advance. Many tanks, like this *T-34/76*, are destroyed during the fighting. Note the hull machine-gun has already been removed. (NA)

Smoke billows from this burning *T-34/76*. The situation has taken a critical turn for the Soviets who must use the 5th Guards army and the 1st armoured army which had been kept as strategic reserves to stop the advance of *4.Panzer-armee* south of the Psel. (NA)

On 9 July, the Soviet Air Force flew three times more sorties than the *Luftwaffe* above the Kursk salient. This *Yak-9* was probably shot down during an attack on the *Totenkopf* columns advancing towards Lutschki. (NA)

A *Horch Kfz.15* heavy car rolls past burning wreckage. The transfer of *Totenkopf* from the south-east flank to the north-west side of *II.SS-Pz.Korps* marks a first turning point in its offensive towards Obojan and Kursk. (NA)

Often published but still very impressive photograph of tanks and infantry from *Totenkopf* advancing south of the Psel. Of note are the three vertical bars painted on the rear of the *StuG.III* which temporarily replace the deathhead. (NA)

Tiger, StuG.III and SPW of Totenkopf move forward on the steppe under the fire of Soviet artillery. On a terrain which offers no protection, speed is essential. (NA)

Grenadiers advance along an anti-tank ditch. Engineers, with the help of Soviet prisoners, start filling in part of it to allow armour to pass through. (NA)

10 July. Regiment "Totenkopf", supported by tanks and assault-guns, attacks towards Kljutschi. It is a decisive day indeed since the division succeeds in establishing a bridge-head on the Psel. (NA)

On 11 July, *SS-Pz.Rgt.3* begins the crossing of the Psel which will be completed the following morning. The whole regiment is now established on the north side of the river. These *Pzkpfw.IV Ausf.G* are shown during transfer. Note the three black vertical bars. (NA)

Prochorowka : battle of the titans

The bridgehead established on the north side of the Psel by *Totenkopf* and the slow but inexorable progress made by *Leibstandarte* and *Das Reich* to the east, force the Soviets to launch the 5th guards armoured army against *II.SS-Pz.Korps*. On 12 July, more than one thousand tanks fight south of Prochorowka and north of the Psel. With total disregard for their own losses, the Soviets take advantage of poor visibility due to the dust over the battlefield to attack the Panzers from short range. Contrary to what has often been written, the battle at Prochorowka was not *4.Panzerarmee* "deathride". *II.SS-Pz.Korps* certainly suffered losses and the Soviet counter-attack has instantly stopped its progress, but it still remains a powerful fighting force and is well capable of advancing to the north. The failure of the northern pincher of operation "Zitadelle" and *Armee-Abteilung "Kempf"* on the eastern flank as well as major events on other theaters of operations, put an end to the german offensive.

A *Pzkpfw.III Ausf.J* passes a *Sd.Kfz.251/4 Ausf.C* towing a *5.cm Pak 38* on a dusty and sloping track (NA)

A gathering of armour – on the foreground a *Pzkpfw.IV Ausf.G* – in the sector of the Psel. (NA)

Unlike the dry and dusty terrain on the plateau, the Psel valley is quite marshy. Many Panzers will get bogged down as the commander of this *Pzkpfw.III* can testify at his expense. (NA)

A *Pzkpfw, IV Ausf. G* partially camouflaged with foliage on its way to the front. Note the *Tarnschema* of his *Schürzen*.

The Psel is overlooked by high hills making excellent observation posts for Soviet artillery. This hill has certainly been secured since this *Pzkpfw.III Ausf.M*, with side-skirts missing, seems to move undisturbed. (NA)

This *Pzkpfw.III*, lying destroyed on the battlefield, is testimony of the of the intensity of the fighting. (Private collection.)

The *Totenkopf's* bridge-head on the Psel is the object of numerous attentions from the Soviet Air Force. This twin *MG-13* is very unlikely to shoot down any of the aircraft the Soviets are now operating. (NA)

This village where firing was coming from has been destroyed by the german artillery. It is a common sight all over the eastern front. (NA)

One of many *SS-KB* reporting the battle. They are frequently on the frontline among the combatants and pay a heavy tribute during the war. (NA)

1. A motorcyclist, recognised by his goggles, during the fighting. His helmet cover and his camouflaged smock are torn and nervousness is visible in his eyes. Kursk is a titanic battle with a high cost in equipment but also in human lives. (NA)

2. An SS tank crew in a uniform which is typical of the summer 1943. He looks tired but attempts a slight smile for the photographer.

3. Young SS grenadiers at rest. It is difficult to know which division they belong to because the lack of identifying insignia –a current practice during the summer of 1943- and because the photographers attached to a given unit also report on neighbouring ones. (NA)

4

5

6

4. SS grenadiers in a trench after combat. Tension and fatigue show on their faces. (NA)

5. Discussion aboard a *Sd.Kfz.251. I.(gep.)/SS-Pz.-Gren.Rgt.1 "T"* lost two commanders in succession during "Zitadelle": *SS-Ostubaf.* Schneider and his replacement, *SS-Hstuf.* Rosenow. (NA)

6. An *SS-Grenadier* observing enemy movement from his trench. On 12 July, the Soviet attacks are unrelenting and leave little respite to the divisions of *II.SS-Pz.Korps.* (NA)

1 and **2.** *"Fliegeralarm !"* A machine-gun team improvising anti-aircraft riposte. In that role, the *MG-34* can only hopefully keep spotter aircraft at bay. (NA)

3

4

3. Although he carries a headwound, this *SS* soldier keeps a high morale. It is a permanent feature among the elite formations of the *Waffen-SS* until 1944 despite the hardship and very sombre prospects. (NA)

4. From his trench, a grenadier observes a *Pzkpfw.IV* advancing on open field. One can measure how vulnerable vehicles are when advancing on such terrain. (NA)

5

6

5. Although this shot was taken by an *SS-KB* attached to *Totenkopf*, it shows *Pz kpfw.III* and grenadiers probably belonging to the *Das Reich* since the identification numbers on the tank have white outlines which was not the practice within *Totenkopf*. (NA)

6. *SS-Obf.* Hermann Priess, right, in the company of *SS-Ostubaf.* Otto Baum, ponders a situation which is becoming more critical by the hour. (NA)

SS-Oscha. Hans Hirning, bearer of the knight's cross, on an assault-gun of *SS-StuG.-Abt.3.* (NA)

The same man now poses for the photographer with his helmet on. Of note is the perfectly visible knight's cross and the sniperface veil. (NA)

An officer of *SS-StuG.-Abt.3* on his assault-gun. He wears the iron cross first class. (NA)

Spectacular photography of two machine-gunner with *MG 34* well camouflaged with foliage and wearing facial masks.

1

SS-Ostubaf. Otto Baum, commander of *SS-Pz.Gren.Rgt.1 "Totenkopf"*, in discussion with an officer from the *Heer* probably belonging to *XLVIII.Pz.Korps.* (NA)

2

2.and **3.** *SS* soldiers dig in protected by the wreckage of a destroyed Soviet tank. It is barely identifiable because of the extent of the battle damage. It could be a Lee tank, the infamous 'coffin for seven brothers'. (NA)

4

4. The battle is over. A *Tiger* tank, bearing the scars of the fighting, rolls towards Charkow. Contrary to affirmations in numerous books inspired by accounts in the "Great Patriotic War", *II.SS-Pz.Korps* lost very few *Tiger* at Prochorowka. Proof is that *Totenkopf* lost only one during the whole duration of operation "Zitadelle". (Private collection.)

3

Counter-attack on the Mius

The *II.SS-Panzer-Korps* counter-attacks

On **July 26**, after being transferred 250 miles (400 km), *Totenkopf* returned to the Gorlovka sector in order to participate in the *II.SS-Pz.Korps* attack on the bridgehead established by the Soviets on the Mius in the Kuibyschewo–Dmitriewka sector facing the lines of the *6th Army*. *Totenkopf* established its position between Remowka, Sneschnoje and Boldyrevo. *Leibstandarte*, which was supposed to leave for Italy, left all of its tanks at the site. *Totenkopf* thereby "acquired" 4 *Pzkpfw.III*s, 30 *Pzkpfw.IV*s and 8 *Pzkpfw.VI "Tigers"* at Artemowsk. *II.SS-Pz.Korps* nevertheless still controlled three divisions because *Leibstandarte* had been replaced by *3.Panzerdivision* the day before.

Totenkopf finished setting up its position on **July 29** at 09h00. The plan of attack of *AOK 6* (Hollidt) was simple: it consisted in breaking through the Soviet lines as fast as possible to a depth of 7.5 miles (12 km) in order to reach high ground, and cutting off the Soviets from their rear lines. Because of the nature of the terrain, and in order to economize their armored forces, the Panzer attack only took place from the north and the north-west on an axis parallel to the three series of heights bordering the bridgehead. The mission of the corps was to take possession of the central group of peaks in order to dominate both valleys and to have at their disposal optimal observation conditions for the artillery. This attack, which was too academic and unimaginative, could not hope to surprise the Soviets. On July 19, *6.Armee* had already attempted this very operation with disappointing results. In addition, the Soviets had considerably reinforced their bridgehead and it was going to be even more difficult to dislodge them from this position. Hill 213,9 formed a formidable defensive breakwater, with minefields, barbed wire, artillery, and dozens of fully camouflaged antitank guns blocking the approach. Any frontal attack on this position was doomed to fail: nevertheless, this was the mission that was assigned to *Totenkopf*. The division had 76 tanks in working order at its disposal on the evening of July 29. The attack was launched the following morning at 08h10. The armored regiment, with the Tiger company at its head, was closely followed by the men of *SS-Pz.Gren.Rgt.1 "T"*. The members of *SS-Pz.Gren.Rgt.3 "TE"* crossed the front line to the south-east of Remowskij-Grube. The first line of defense was quickly overcome by the two SS formations. To the left, Hellmuth Becker's forces reached the sector situated to the north-west of Gerassimowa. The area stretches along the banks of a small river of the same name which rejoins the Mius at Dmitriewka. The Soviets toughened their resistance and then, at 17h30, the *"Theodor Eicke"* regiment stopped its progression.

As far as the main attack was concerned, the SS at first encountered no serious resistance. Suddenly, as they approached Hill 213,9 everything became complicated. The Panzers came upon a veritable antitank wall, protected by an inextricable minefield. Several Panzers were thus immobilized and became easy targets for the Soviets. Fire was coming from the hilltop itself, but also from the north-east of Stepanowka. Furthermore, the Soviet artillery was bombarding the terrain by shelling from Hill 191,3. At 08h40, engineers were called in to clear the minefields. The Panzers launched another attack. At 09h00 they reached the foot of the hill. But they fell upon new minefields, and this time the Soviets chose to die rather than retreat. In addition the Russian air force was very present in the skies above. Swarms of 20 to 40 planes dropped fragmentation bombs on the SS grenadiers. The entire battlefield disappeared in the smoke of the explosions. The SS were held at bay three times in front of the hill. At nightfall, the division reported to the Army corps that the losses amounted to 75 % of the armored regiment and 50 % of the *"Totenkopf"* regiment: 48 Panzers had been destroyed or damaged, as well as 12 *StuG.III*s and 8 *SPW*s. The day's toll was catastrophic. The *Totenkopf*'s total losses were: 49 dead and 463 wounded. At 19h45 *II.SS-Pz.Korps* continued to uphold its orders: Hill 213,9 had to be taken during the night. Paul Hausser specified: *"This is the last chance, otherwise the entire offensive will fail."* The frontal attack was again chosen even though the day's events had shown that it was suicidal to send Panzers into such a narrow corridor, open on three sides to fire from artillery and antitank guns.

Totenkopf was not the only *II.SS-Pz.Korps* unit to be held at bay: in total, the losses of the army corps amounted to 915 dead, wounded or missing in action; 91 tanks were destroyed (out of a total of 211); *Das Reich* had not been able to accomplish any of its goals: its setback was deeply felt in front of Hill 213,9 by the men of *Totenkopf*, who had endured Soviet artillery fire directed at them with precision from Stepanowka and Hill 203,9, which constituted major objectives. On the northern flank, *3.Panzerdivision* had remained blocked in the minefields in front of Hill 211,5, and had lost 19 of the 37 tanks that had taken part in the attack! The following day, in the central sector of the *II.SS-Pz.Korps* offensive, would once again turn out to be unfruitful. In order to minimize the handicap of the frontal attack which was ordered, *SS-Pz.Gren.Rgt.1 "T"* tried to take Hill 213,9 at one o'clock in the morning to take advantage of the dark. The assault groups attacked without artillery preparation in order to retain the element of surprise and they succeeded in penetrating the first line of Soviet defense and defeating them in close combat. But the Russians recovered quickly and resisted with determination from their second position. Despite the supporting fire from the *Nebelwerfer* and the artillery, the grenadiers remained locked in a position 500 yards from the main line of defense. At 10h00, the grenadiers and Panzers launched a new attack on the hill. The SS stayed near the artillery barrage but at the foot of the hill found themselves in dense fields of corn and sunflowers in which the Russians were fully entrenched. Many SS were mowed down by the sudden fire that sprang from machineguns hidden among the stalks. It became impossible for the assailants to advance deeper into the Russian defense network. During the previous 24 hours the division's losses were: 74 dead, 310 wounded, and 20 missing in action. The armored regiment now had only 5 *Pzkpfw.III*s, 9 *Pzkpfw.IV*s, 1 *Pzkpfw.VI "Tiger"* and 5 *Befehls-Pz*s in working order. *SS-StuG-Abt. "T"* had a total of 14 operational *StuG.III*s. At the end of the day General Hollidt finally acknowledged that the frontal assault would lead nowhere and that the Soviets were still too powerful around Hill 213,9, despite their considerable losses (6000 prisoners, 68 tanks, 64 pieces of artillery and about one hundred antitank guns in the *II.SS-Pz.Korps* sector alone). He decided that the center of the attack would be transferred to the juncture between *II.SS-Pz.Korps* and *XXIV.Pz.Korps*

On **August 1**, the *6.Armee* attack began at 08h30. At the right wing of *II.SS-Pz.Korps*, *SS-Rgt. "Der Führer"* succeeded in taking Hill 203,4 and reached Fedorowka near noon. The armored group of *Das Reich* succeeded in penetrating in the Olchowschik valley to the south of Marinowka. The lead units then threatened the western slope of Hill 213,9. The Russians had already began to retreat towards the Mius and several artillery units were crossing the river in the direction of its eastern bank. At 11h15, these eminently favorable conditions for the Germans dictated the orders of *II.SS-Pz.Korps*: *Totenkopf* was to take Hill 213,9. In his log, Herman Priess declared that he was going forth for the honor of his division. At 13h30, the attack was commenced by *SS-Pz.Aufkl.-Abt. "T"*, *SS-Pi.-Btl. "T"*, *II./"TE"* and the rest of *SS-Rgt. "T"*. The attack was no sooner begun than the Soviet artillery unleashed a terrible barrage of fire. Losses were heavy but the attackers, placed under the sole command of Otto Baum, pushed forward nevertheless. Unaware of the terrible enemy bombardment, Max Seela's engineers succeeded in neutralizing 1200 mines during the course of the assault. This exploit was one which *AOK 6* hoped to see published in the *Wehrmacht* bulletin. At 14h50, the division asked *Arko 122* to direct its fire on Hill 213,9, as well as Hills 140,3, 191,3, and 194,3, where the majority of Soviet batteries were located. The capture of the high ground in the Olchowschik sector by *Das Reich* then gave the artillery observers an ideal position from which to view the enemy batteries. Five artillery groups then fired approximately 600 shells during the next few minutes. The Russian guns fell silent one after another and from then on the *Totenkopf* soldiers advanced on Hill 213,9 with far less difficulty, even though the machinegun and mortar fire remained deadly. The division's tanks, which until then had been kept in reserve waiting for the Soviet antitank guns to be neutralized, were then engaged. Some of the Soviet infantry began to flee, yet many chose to die where they stood. At 17h00, the division announced to *II.SS-Pz.Korps* that Hill 213,9 had fallen into its hands. The Soviet front began to fall apart. The Russians had lost a lot of its force over the previous three days (more than 10 000 men had been captured by *6.Armee*), and the loss of its key positions forced them to evacuate the bridgehead. At the end of the afternoon, the Germans finally severed the communication lines between the Soviet units fighting in the Stepanowka - Marinowka sector and in the Mius. At the end of the day, the *II.SS-Pz.Korps* staff received orders to leave the Russian front, and *"Das Reich"* and *"Totenkopf"* were then to be attached to *III.Pz.Korps* (Gen.d.Pz.Tr. Breith) from August 3. Early in the morning, on **August 2**, the *Totenkopf* patrols reported that the Soviets were in the midst of evacuating their positions. At 05h20, the SS attacked from Hill 213,9 towards the south-east. They did not face any serious resistance and captured Hill 191,3 at 06h30 and, a few minutes

later, Hill 194,3, which had caused *"Das Reich"* so much trouble during the previous 48 hours. The Soviet artillery tried to block the advance of the *SS* by firing from the eastern bank, but the *SS* ended up reoccupying the former front line during the course of the afternoon. The last remaining pockets of resistance were cleaned out. The next day all the Soviets were pushed back to the banks of the Mius. The *Totenkopf* units began to be relieved from their positions by units of *23.Panzerdivision*. The overall tolls for the fighting that took place between July 30 and August 3 is the following: the Soviets lost 13 790 prisoners, 144 tanks, 506 antitank guns, 180 artillery pieces, 5 anti-aircraft guns and 384 mortar units against the units of *6.Armee*. The number of soldiers killed is unknown, but it is probable that it far exceeds the number taken prisoner.

Gliederung of the division on August 19, 1943.

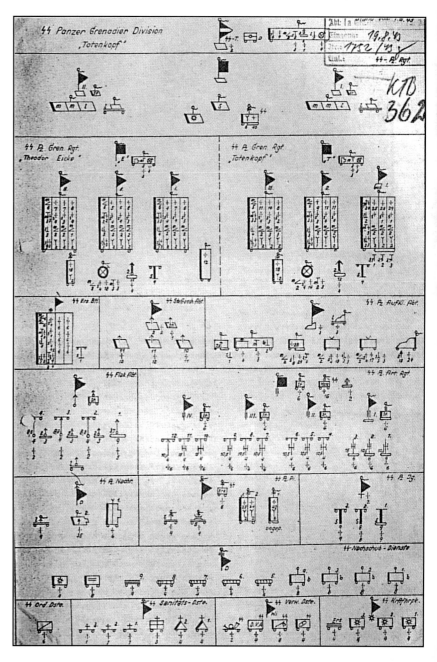

The *Totenkopf* moving into attack on the Mius front

Following the titanic battle of Kursk, *II.SS-Pz.Korps* was called on the Mius, where the *6.Armee*'s front was threatening to crumble after the setting of a solid Soviet base of operations around Stepanowka. Those who were now called the "Führer's firemen" were thus sent to reduce it and so protect access to the Dniepr and Crimea.

In the sector of the Mius, even though terrain is hilly, it doesn't provide much shelter and the losses are inevitably heavy. (NA)

July 30th. Hermann Priess and Otto Baum are watching the Soviet positions before launching their troops into attack. Since the 1st of July, *Totenkopf* has had 684 men killed, 3751 injured and 42 missing. It is thus a weakened division that must move into assault. (All rights reserved)

Above: The division reconnaissance battalion has suffered heavy losses in Kursk. This is why commandment kept it as a reserve during the first two days of attack. This light *Sd.Kfz.222* armoured car must be south-east of Perwomaisk. (NA)

SS Grenadiers caught under the fire of an enemy who's a master in the art of camouflage, even on a terrain that seems quite exposed. (NA)

It seems that the enemy has been reduced to silence, judging by the much more relaxed attitude of these SS soldiers, who are waiting for orders to resume progress. (NA)

A little bit further, a machine gun opens fire on the woods from where enemy fire probably came. (NA)

A *Befehls-Pz.III* from *5.Kp./SS-Pz.Rgt.3.* It must belong to the commander of the company, *SS-Hstuf.* Wilhelm Flohr. He served previously in the division's anti-tank battalion. He's to be killed on the 30th of July in the afternoon. (NA)

A *Pzkpfw.IV* in approach march towards the front the day before the offensive. Clearly noticeable is the 3.22 metre barrel of the 75-mm tank gun, with a bore 43 calibres in length the version "G" was equipped with. (NA)

Inside view of the *Pzkpfw.IV* from the side hatch of the turret. (NA)

Opposite: The tank crew chief is posing proudly for the photographer. On the gun were painted eight circles standing for as many destroyed enemy tanks. (NA)

The *SS-Pz.Rgt.3* on the Mius.

On the day of the attack, the *Totenkopf* armoured regiment only lined up 68 panzers in working order, when it had 125 on the 4th of July. These figures don't take into account the 4 *Pzkpfw.III*, 30 *Pzkpfw.IV* and 8 *Pzkpfw.VI* "*Tiger*" which were given up by *Leibstandarte* and were waiting for their transfer from Artemowsk. But the battle of the river Mius was to cost the division many tanks, many more per day proportionally than operation "Citadel".

Four out of the five crew men of this *Pzkpfw.IV* with their mascot. Notice how the tank crew chief is wearing a double-breasted jacket, which is normally for assault gun troops. (NA)

307

A tricky terrain for assailants.

Next photographs show how tricky such a terrain was for any assailant: a bare plain offering hardly any shelter, where each approach was easily noticed by the enemy. In such conditions, no wonder *II.SS-Pz.Korps* suffered such heavy losses during this battle.

Motorcyclists driving along a dusty road. Houses are typical of this Ukrainian region. (NA)

Grenadiers progressing in the endless Ukrainian steppe. Given the equipment men are carrying with them, this march precedes combat. (NA)

Motorcyclists are looking at a hamlet built at the bottom of a hill. Apparently, all houses are intact; there was no fighting. (NA)

A 37mm anti-aircraft defence gun on a 5 ton *Sd.Kfz.6* under-frame. On the left is another Soviet 45mm anti-tank gun abandoned there by its crew. (NA)

Another *Flak 37* on an *Sd.Kfz.6* chassis in a cereal field. When *Totenkopf* became a mechanized division, the anti-aircraft force was given two extra 88mm gun batteries and got rid of its light battery. 37mm pieces now belonged to *4.Bttr./SS-Flak-Abt.3*. (NA)

The battery is reemployed here against an on-land objective: the shells that were fired burned down a few houses whose thatched roofs blazed up in no time. (NA)

This piece has just opened fire and on the left a server is bringing another shell. Notice how the soldier operating the range-finder on the right is standing on the vehicle, and thus exposed to enemy fire. Only the three direct servers of the gun are protected by its shield. (NA)

Missions of the II.SS-Pz.-Korps and Totenkopf

By the 30th of July, the II.SS-Pz.-Korps' first objective is to reach the line going through Hills 223.7 (near Stepanowka) 213.9 and 173.4. Once these heights were taken, the corps was to repel the Soviets towards positions of XXIX.AK (17.ID, 111.ID, 336.ID, 15.Lw.Felddiv.), in the southern limit of the Olchowschik valley. The success of the whole operation depen ded on how quickly Totenkopf could seize Hill 213.9 and on the XXIV.Pz.Korps (16.Pz.-Gren.Div., 23.Pz.Div.)'s capacity to cut Soviet communication and supply routes in the Olchowschik valley.

Last briefing before the attack. Faces are solemn, weapons are ready. How many of these men are to be killed in action today? (NA)

A German trench on the start positions of the II.SS-Pz.Korps units. Notice the stones on the edges, a quite rare feature on the Eastern front, where the ground was seldom as chalky. (NA)

View of the Soviet lines before the offensive was set off. This soldier has carefully camouflaged his helmet with some quite thick greenery. (NA)

Two grenadiers are huddling up into their hole during under harassing fire from the Soviet artillery. (Private collection)

I.(gep.)/SS-Pz.Gren.Rgt.1 "Totenkopf" moves up in line. Head vehicle is an Sd.Kfz. 251/10 Ausf.C equipped with a Pak 37 whose right shield has been removed. (NA)

Above: A heavy *Sd.Kfz. 232* armoured car from the reconnaissance battalion goes through a village raising clouds of dust. Reaching up to 85 km/h, with a range of 270, it is then the best in its category. His main defect is its much too complex making. (NA)

Opposite: Judging by the smoke of explosions in the background, the battle has begun. An *Sd.Kfz. 250/1* from the reconnaissance battalion is going east, followed by two *Sd.Kfz. 250/8*. It's midday, because there are virtually no shadows. (NA)

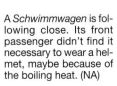

A *Schwimmwagen* is following close. Its front passenger didn't find it necessary to wear a helmet, maybe because of the boiling heat. (NA)

Some soviet soldiers were captured on top of a hill overlooking the whole sector. It's probably not Hill 213.9, since this one has been pounded so much that its surface must look like the battlefields of Verdun. (NA)

These Russian soldiers are being taken away by a small escort. One of them is carrying ammu-nition boxes. (NA)

1. Careful progress at the edge of some woods. Russian soldiers are masters in camouflage, and often let themselves be passed by, to attack the assailant's rear by surprise. (NA)

2. This SS grenadier is firing a coloured rocket to reveal the presence of his unit. True, German and Soviet lines are really close, and they must avoid being bombarded by the *Luftwaffe*. (NA)

3 and 4. A young *SS-Untersturmführer* wearing a jacket that doesn't conform to the regulations (?) and a *Wehrmacht* belt is showing the way. Within the division, losses were so heavy that companies are often headed by mere second lieutenants like this one. (NA)

5. This *SS-Unterscharführer*, exhausted by combat, sat down on the edge of a summarily dug shelter. (S.' private collection)

Vue of the Gerassimowa valley. The chalky nature of the ground in the Mius region is quite evident here. (NA)

The reconnaissance battalion has been commissioned to seize Hill 213.9 after regiment *Totenkopf*'s failure. Some *Sd.Kfz.250* are moving towards the Mius on a land scattered with Soviet soldiers' corpses. (NA)

A *21 cm-Mörser* 18 battery from the *Heer* is backing up the *Totenkopf*'s attack on Hill 213.9. This howitzer weights 16.7 tons and can launch a 121 kg explosive shell 16.7 km away! It is a fearsome weapon operating on batteries and autonomous forces directly subordinated to army corps or armies. (NA)

Remarkable photograph of a *Sd.Kfz.*251/3 equipped with a portable heavy machine gun. It is a 12.7 mm *DShK 38/46*, the Soviet copy of the Browning *M1921*. (S.' private collection)

Stepanowka falls into the hands of *II.SS-Pz.Korps* on the 1st of August. It is a Pyrrhic victory, as *Totenkopf* has lost 1458 men between the 30th of July and the 2nd of August, and only has about forty tanks in working order left, while the front has just flared up north of Charkow. (NA)

Counter-attack to the west of Charkow

Operation "Polkowodets Rumjantsew"

At 10h30 on **August 1**, whilst the battle of Mius was at its critical stage, the *II.SS-Pz.Korps Ia, SS-Stubaf.* Stolley received orders from *Heeresgruppe "Süd"* to prepare for the withdrawal of *Das Reich, Totenkopf* and *3.Panzerdivision* in order to transfer them to the Charkow region as soon as possible. The German intelligence services had in fact just identified high concentrations of Soviet troops between Bjelgorod and Tomarowka. In this sector barely 25 miles (40 km) wide, the Soviets had four armies under the command of the Woronesch Front: the Guards 5th army, the Guards 6th army, the 1st armored army and the Guards 5th armored army. Germans fears were confirmed: on August 3 the Soviets launched their offensive, Operation "Polkowodets Rumjantsew": the Woronesch Front attacked between Bjelgorod and Tomarowka and the Steppes Front attacked to the east of the Donets. The German front was shattered and a wide breach opened between *4.Panzerarmee* and *Armee-Abteilung "Kempf"*. On August 5 Bjelgorod fell into the hands of the Woronesch Front. In addition, three additional armies joined the attack to the west of Tomarowka. The following day the Germans fell into a general retreat. The 1st armored army pressed on in the direction of Bogoduchoff, a vitally important railway hub, with the intention of cutting the link between *4.Panzerarmee* and *Armee-Abteilung "Kempf"*.

Fighting to the west of Charkow

The mission of *Totenkopf* was to close the 25 mile wide gap which separated *Armee-Abteilung "Kempf"* from *4.Panzerarmee (XXIV.Pz.Korps)* between Udarnyj and Kolontajew. On August 8, the bulk of the division regrouped between Ogulzy and Walki. The first *Totenkopf* units to reach the Mertschik river sector immediately took up positions along a line passing along the Suchoj Mertschik (*SS-Rgt."TE"*) and to the south of Mertschik on either side of Alexandrowka (*SS-Rgt."T"*). *SS-Pz.Aufkl.-Abt. "T"* was stretched out in defense over the 12 or so miles (20 km) (!) between Scharowka and Krasnokutsk. During the nights of August 9 and 10, the Soviets went on the offensive along the entire front, against the three divisions of *III.Pz.Korps* (Breith). Elements of the 3rd mechanized corps crossed the Mertschik to the west of Alexandrowka and surrounded Kowjagi, thus posing a threat to the rear of *Totenkopf*. Elements of *I./SS-Pz.Rgt.3 "T"* in Walki were immediately rushed into position. During this time the Soviets were massing new forces to the south of the Merla. Further west the Soviets crossed the Mertschik at Murafa. On **August 11** the situation was becoming more and more difficult for *Totenkopf:* the Soviets sent units to the south beyond Mertschik, between Alexandrowka and Murafa. They easily broke through the overstretched lines of the *SS-Rgt."T"*. One group, comprised of infantry and armored units, succeeded in taking Nowyj Mertschik while thirty tanks pressed southwards, threatening Alexejewka. *Totenkopf*

received the order from *III.Pz.Korps* to *"remedy the situation using all available means"*. Elements of *SS-Rgt."T"* supported by panzers and assault guns launched a counter attack. Towards midday, after very heavy fighting, the SS had retaken the south bank of the Mertschik between Alexandrowka and Scharowka. At Murafa, the situation was more difficult: the Soviets crossed the Mertschik in force and started towards the south, forcing the *Totenkopf* reconnaissance group to withdraw its left flank to Katschalowka. At the end of the day the division was extended over 31 miles (50 km) between Maximowka in the east and Krasnokutsk in the west. It had succeeded in blocking the offensive of the Soviet 1st armored army whilst inflicting heavy losses on it. The next day *III.Pz.Korps* counter-attacked along two axes parallel to *Das Reich* in the direction of Bogoduchoff, in order to cut the lines of communication of the Soviet 6th armored corps, and *Totenkopf* counter-attacked in the direction of Murafa in order to isolate the Soviet units which had ventured to the south of Mertschik. The Soviets, however, were the first to attack. At 03h45, twenty-five tanks broke through the *Totenkopf* lines to the east of Alexandrowka. They were pushed back by the *"Tigers"* of *SS-Pz.Rgt.3*. The Soviets were even more threatening on the left flank of the division: the Guards 5th armored corps and an infantry division crossed the Merla between Krasnokutsk and Kolontajew. At 08h45, *III.Pz.Korps* in turn started to attack. The *Panzerkampfgruppe* of *Das Reich* launched an attack in the direction of Bogoduchoff, with the intention of attacking the flank of the Soviet forces facing *Totenkopf*. It was supported by *SS-Rgt."TE"*, which attacked beyond the Suchoj Mertschik. In spite of their numerical superiority, the Soviets were routed.

Although close to exhaustion by the fighting of the previous days, the 1st armored army took advantage of the nights of **August 12** and **13** to attack to the south of the Merla in the direction of Katschalowka. Swamped by weight of numbers, *SS-Pz.Aufkl.-Abt."T"* had to abandon the area. The Soviets had therefore succeeded in reaching the Kolomak – Konstantinowka sector. As a result of the critical situation on the left flank, the attack by *III.Pz.Korps* was re-assessed. At 07h30, however, *SS-Rgt."TE"* attacked in the direction of Nikitowka. *SS-Rgt."T"* followed suit to the north of Mertschik. The SS made rapid progress, inflicting very heavy losses on the Soviets. In contrast, on the left flank the division reconnaissance group, still isolated, had to continue to withdraw in the face of the Guards 52nd and 90th infantry divisions and the 5th Guards armored corps. Further west *4.Panzerarmee* had succeeded in stopping the Soviet offensive before Achtyrka and was now preparing to launch *XXIV.Pz.Korps* on a counter-attack.

On **August 14** the *"Totenkopf"* and *"Eicke"* regiments regrouped around Perwomaiskyj. They launched their attack at 16h30 against the flank of the Soviet units advancing to the south-west of the Merla. They were supported by the *"Tigers"* of *schw.Pz.Abt.503*. Whilst *SS-Pz.Rgt.3* was joined in a fierce tank battle, the two grenadier regiments made rapid progress towards the west. Despite this advance on the flanks of the Guards 5th armored army, the Soviets continued their offensive to the south-west of Wyssokopolje. At 22h10, General Breith ordered *Totenkopf* to attack in the direction of Konstantinowka and then to wheel to the south east in the direction of Kolomak, in order to take the Soviet units facing *SS-Pz.Aufkl.-Abt."T"* from the rear. The situation at the end of the day was somewhat mixed: *III.Pz.Korps* had succeeded in stabilizing its right flank and center, but the Soviet troops were continuing to move forward dangerously on its left flank where they faced no opposition. The day was also marked by the dismissal of General Kempf, whose repeated demands to obtain authorization to evacuate Charkow had ended up irritating Hitler. He was replaced by General Wöhler and *Armee-Abteilung "Kempf"* was renamed *8.Armee*.

On **August 15** at 06h45 *Totenkopf* resumed its attack in the direction of Konstantinowka in order to destroy the enemy forces that had advanced the south of the Merla and the Mertschik. The day's objective, Konstantinowka, fell into the hands of *I./SS-Pz.Rgt.3.* At 11h15. The bulk of *SS-Rgt."T"* then struck out to the north of the town and pushed on to Sloboka, in the direction of the Merla. The division's two grenadier regiments then wheeled south-east to attack the Soviet units in the Kolomak and Surdowka sector in the rear. Soviet resistance collapsed. The SS captured prisoners by the hundred. Thus, by the middle of the afternoon *Totenkopf* had succeeded in encircling elements belonging to four infantry divisions and the 6th armored corps in the Alexejewka - Konstantinowka - Medjanikij-Bidilo sector. The SS seized Alexejewka during the course of the evening whilst *SS-Pi.-Btl."T"* cut to pieces the Soviet units trapped in Wyssokopolje. The danger on the left flank of *III.Pz.Korps* had been temporarily removed, but the 25 mile (40 km) breach separating *4.Panzerarmee* from *8.Armee* had still not been filled.

The attack continued the next day. The sector located to the north of Alexejewka was cleared out around 11h00, with the Soviets leaving 250 dead on the battlefield. Towards midday, *Totenkopf* regrouped to launch an attack to the north, in the direction of the Merla river. In the evening of **August 17**, *Heeresgruppe "Süd"* gave its orders for the next day: *XXIV.Pz.Korps* (*4.Panzerarmee*) was to launch an attack from the Achtyrka sector towards the south east in the direction of Kotelwa in order to establish a link with *III.Pz.Korps* (*8.Armee*) on the Merla. *Totenkopf* was given the mission of crossing the Merla at Ljubowka and Oleinikoff. At 10h30, as planned, *III./"TE"* launched an attack towards the Merla at Ljubowka. It was a bloody failure. Losses were high. Soviet losses, however, were also very heavy: 44 Russian tanks were destroyed by the Totenkopf units on the banks of the Merla. During the night of **August 18** to **19** and in the morning, shock units from the *"Eicke"* and *"Totenkopf"* regiments attempted to cross the Merla again, in the face of the solid defensive network set up by the Soviets. This time a firm bridgehead was established in the middle of the day, after very heavy fighting. On **August 20** at about 14h00 Kolontajew fell into the hands of the SS. SS motocyclists made contact with the grenadiers of *II./"T"* arriving from the East. *Brückenkolonne J842* was then attached to the division and *1.Kp./SS-Pi.-Btl."T"* (*SS-Ostuf.* Barth) started to build an additional bridge. Baum immediately organized the widening of the bridgehead, whilst launching patrols northward. By the end of the afternoon, *3.Kp./SS-Pz.Aufkl.-Abt."T"* had finally established contact with *Kampfgruppe "Graf von Strachwitz"* of the *"Grossdeutschland"* (*XXIV. Pz.Korps, 4.Panzerarmee*) division. From then on the objective of *Heeresgruppe "Süd"* was to reinforce the link between *8.Armee* and *4.Panzerarmee*. On the 21st, *SS-Ostubaf.* Baum was wounded in the shoulder and had to hand over command of his regiment to *SS-Stubaf.* Karl Ullrich. At 09h10, the entry in the *KTB* of *III.Pz.Korps* showed: *"SS- "T" is involved in very fierce fighting with the Guards 4th armored corps, who are attacking along the Kolontajew - Kotelewka line from the west"*. It became desperately urgent for the Germans to reinforce their units to the north of the Merla in order to form a continuous front line. In the morning, attacks by the 1st armored army made the positions of *SS-Pz.Aufkl.-Abt."T"* impossible to hold, and at 11h00 it was forced to withdraw between Parchomowka and Kotelewka, thus severing the link with *Pz.Füs.-Rgt."GD"*. There was also fighting in the right sector of *Totenkopf*: what remained of the Guards 14th armored brigade unsuccessfully attempted to break through the *I./"TE"* lines at Ljubowka. At 16h30, *Brücko J842* finished building a bridge over the Merla and the *Panzerkampfgruppe* of *Totenkopf* could finally be launched towards Parchomowka in order to re-establish the connection with *Grossdeutschland*. The link was made at 19h40. This success was bought at a high price: *I./SS-Pz.Rgt.3 "T"* now comprised only 24 panzers and the loss of life was very high, especially amongst the officers and NCOs. Very often sergeants were in command of companies with corporals in charge of sections. The formidable division which had gone into battle at the assault on Koursk, at the start of July, was now only a shadow of its former self. Despite this catastrophic situation in terms of personnel, *8.Armee* ordered that its sector be extended up to Parchomowka! On the morning of August 23, *15.(Kradsch.)Kp."T"* succeeded in re-establishing links with the *7.Panzerdivision* near Kotelwa. The breach separating the *4.Panzerarmee* and the *8.Armee* had now been firmly closed. At midday the *Totenkopf*, with *7.Panzerdivision* and *Grossdeutschland*, were placed under the command of *XLVII.Pz.Korps* (Lemelsen), which became responsible for the eastern flank of *8.Armee* between the Merla and the Worskla. The counter-attack by *III.Pz.Korps* to the west of Charkow was therefore finished. *Totenkopf* gained particular renown for first of all stopping the offensive of the 1st armored army, then for inflicting extremely heavy losses on the Guards 5th armored army and Guards 6th army. By the end of this fighting it was a well-proven unit.

SS-Brigadeführer Hermann Priess has taken over from Max Simon on 10 April 1943. He was to prove to be the best divisional commander Totenkopf ever had. (Courtesy Martin Månsson)

SS and *Pzkpfw.III Ausf.J* grenadiers somewhere west of Bjelgorod in late August 1943. (NA)

StuG III and grenadiers in a sunflower field. Danger isn't imminent, as the soldiers aren't wearing helmets. (All rights reserved)

Meldung vom ___1.9.___ 1943

Verband: ᛋᛋ Pz.Gren.Div."Totenkopf"

Unterstellungsverhältnis: XXXXVII.Pz.Korps

1. Personelle Lage am Stichtag der Meldung:

a) Personal:

	Soll	Fehl
Offiziere	850	373
Uffz. . .	4157	2273
Mannsch.	15839	5389
Hiwi . . .	1199	720
Insgesamt	22045	8755

c) In der Berichtszeit eingetroffener Ersatz:

	Ersatz	Genesene
Offiziere	–	–
Uffz. und Mannsch.	1645	119

b) Verluste und sonstige Abgänge in der Berichtszeit vom __1.8.__ bis __31.8.__

	tot	verw.	verm.	krank	sonst.
Offiziere	26	92	–	17	–
Uffz. und Mannsch.	627	2823	58	699	1511
Insgesamt	653	2915	58	716	1511

d) Über 1 Jahr nicht beurlaubt:

insgesamt: 2162 Köpfe 16,9 % d. Iststärke

davon:

12–18 Monate	19–24 Monate	über 24 Monate
2116	44	2

Platzkarten im Berichtsmonat zugewiesen: 40

2. Materielle Lage:

	Gepanzerte Fahrzeuge							Kraftfahrzeuge				
	Stu. Gesch.	III	IV	sonst. Pz.Kpfw.	VI	Schb.Pz. Pz.Sp. Art.Pz.B.	Pak SF	Kräder			Pkw	
								Ketten	m.angetr. Bwg.	sonst.	gel.	O
Soll (Zahlen)	35	78	54	22	15	234	10	–	619	746	1063	200
einsatzbereit zahlenm.	15	23	9	29	1	121	4	–	484	407	726	179
in % des Solls	42	30	22	131	6	51	40	–	78	54	68	89
in kurzfristiger Instandsetzung (bis 3 Wochen) zahlenm.	6	21	23	1	9	11	2	–	82	130	78	23
in % des Solls	17	25	42	4	60	4	20	–	13	19	7	11

	noch Kraftfahrzeuge						Waffen			
	Lkw				Ketten-Fahrzeuge		s Pak	Art.-Gesch.	MG. ( )	sonstige Waffen
	Maultiere	gel.	O	Tonnage	Zgkw.	RSO				
Soll (Zahlen)	–	1028	1053	–	278	73	21	54	1688 (595)	
einsatzbereit zahlenm.	258	489	1143	–	220	53	14	48	1334 (415)	
in % des Solls			86	–	79	72	67	89	79 (63)	
in kurzfristiger Instandsetzung (bis 3 Wochen) zahlenm.	23	24	102	–	25	14	3	4	142 (54)	
in % des Solls			8	–	8	19	14	7	8 (8)	

*) Zgkw. mit 1–5 t, **) Zgkw. mit 8–18 t
( ) davon MG. 42

3. Pferdefehlstellen:

State of the division on the 1st of September 1943. It lacks 8755 men compared to its theoretical numbers, and only 9 *Pzkpfw.IV* out of the 54 it should have and a single *Pzkpfw.VI* "*Tiger*" out of 15 are in working order.

The Soviet offensive towards Charkow

The timing of the attack has taken the Germans completely by surprise and they do not even succeed in reoccupying their pre-Citadel positions. In the sector of the offensive, Manstein can only muster 15 divisions, 3 of which are armoured divisions, againt 11 Soviet armies. The reinforcement provided by *III.Pz.Korps* cannot alter the course of events.

Opposite: the first elements of *Totenkopf* to arrive west of Charkow are those of the reconnaissance battalion which is now led by *SS-Stubaf.* Krauth, Lino Masarie having been wounded during the fighting on the Mius. Their first mission is to send out patrols to locate Soviet troops. (NA)

A *StuG.III* negociates rough terrain. (Collection privée S.)

Situation south of the Merla on the 14th of August 1943.

Superb shot of a *StuG.III Ausf.G* assault gun with its crew and a *Panzerschütze* in black uniform. They are all wearing different uniforms. (Private collection.)

1. This motorcyclist is carrying a captured *PPSh 41* submachine gun, a common practice in the German army.(Private collection.)

2. On the afternoon of 8 August, skirmishes with advanced elements of the soviet forces (112th armoured brigade) start on the Mertschik at Alexandrowka. The *Totenkopf* regiment repels an enemy attack and starts to dig in on defensive positions. (NA)

3. The *Wiking* division is withdrawn from the Golaja-Dolina sector and heads towards the fighting in Charkow. Heavy traffic causes delay. (NA)

4. *Totenkopf* speads out the arrival of its units in the Charkow sector. A convoy advances in the open plain. Shown here on the foreground is a one ton *Sd.Kfz.10* semi-tracked vehicle. (NA)

5. Soviet aircraft now rule the skies and the *Flak* unit of the division is working hard to repel the attacks of enemy fighter-bombers. Shown here is a *Flak 37* on a *Sd.Kfz.6* chassis. (NA)

5

A *Luftwaffe Flak-Regiment* west of Charkow brings to a halt a menacing raid on the Donets city by soviet armour with its 88mm guns. An *SS-KB* attached to *Totenkopf* has taken a photograph of an observation post of this regiment which has been set up on a haystack. (NA)

Opposite, right: the men of the division are exhausted by the heavy fighting and take every opportunity to get some sleep and regain some strength.(NA)

Below: after the heavy fighting in Koursk and on the Mius, morale is still very high. The camouflaged overall is a common item among the SS during the summer of 1943. (NA)

On the 11 August, the 1st company of the engineers battalion repels several soviet attacks east of the railways station at Wodjanaja. (NA)

These men are painting kill markings around the gun of their panzer. The division armoured regiment has been quite successful during the fighting on the Mertschik but suffered severe losses. *5.Kp./SS-Pz.Rgt.3* lost its new commander, *SS-Ostuf.* Nerpel. (NA)

Discussion in a command post during a lull in the fighting.
The soldier on the right wears an identification tag. (NA)

The United Kingdom provided tanks to the Soviet Union.
This *Churchill* tank was destroyed by a 75mm or 88mm hit.
(NA)

The Germans lose Charkow

Although *III.Pz.Korps*, with the SS divisions *"Das Reich"*, *"Totenkopf"*, *"Wiking"* and the *Heer 3.Panzerdivision* managed to reestablish a link with *4.Panzerarmee* after a remarkable defensive battle against an enemy far more powerful, both in numbers and in equipment, a defense which led to the near-total destruction of two Soviet armored armies, the situation in the Charkow section was going far less smoothly for the Germans. The large Ukrainian city changed hands on **August 23** for what would be the last time during the war. It then seemed impossible for the Germans to remain on the Charkow-Bjelgorod axis and the loss of Southern Ukraine seemed inevitable, despite the reestablishment of a continuous front between *4.Panzerarmee* and *8.Armee*. On **August 25**, with the Soviets at their heels, *AOK 8* ordered the retreat of *XLVII.Pz.Korps*. It began in the afternoon: the non-essential vehicles were sent south of the Merla by Kolontajew and regrouped in the Otrada - Filenkoff sector. Russian prisoners transported the wounded by stretcher over more than a mile (2 km) through swampland. *XLVII.Pz.Korps* retreated along the Kotelewka–Kotelwa line during the day of **August 26**. In the afternoon they were informed by aerial reconnaissance that the Soviet forces were building up considerably in front of the lines being held by *Totenkopf*. Seventy tanks in the Ljubowka – Kotelwa sector were specifically pointed out. From the early morning of **August 27**, the Soviets attacked the division's positions. Their assault was broken by artillery fire and several tanks were destroyed, but the link with *7.Panzerdivision* was ruptured. Meanwhile, the Soviets were amassing a sizable force on the northern flank of *Heeresgruppe "Süd"* facing *4.Panzerarmee* and *8.Armee* in order to penetrate the German front and reach the Dnieper. Von Manstein's army group, stretched over a distance of 600 miles (980 km), no longer had the means to resist such a thrust. In the *Totenkopf tanks*, only a very few were aware of just how precarious the situation was. Pushed back to the Merla, the division found itself in the center of the Soviet drive. The division was responsible for holding an area far too large for its forces and very few bridges, under enemy fire, were available to cross the river. Its positions were limited to a few isolated strongpoints, a situation which was starting to become routine. It was not uncommon that a single machinegun had to cover up to 300 meters of front. The personnel crisis was so severe that the lightly wounded were obliged to stay on the front line without being treated at the first-aid station. On the 28, *XLVII.Pz.Korps* ordered the breach separating *7.Panzerdivision* from Totenkopf to be closed up. *Totenkopf* was only able to gather five tanks and a handful of scouts. Lacking the necessary resources, the counterattack failed. On the 29, the Soviets attacked once again and managed to break through the German lines near Hill 144,2. Since there were no more reserves available, troops had to be called in from other sectors to close this breach. Some alert units were set up and sent into the fight. The following day, the Soviets tried to take advantage of the *Totenkopf*'s lack of personnel and exploit the opening made in the lines in front of Hill 144,2. They regrouped new forces and attacked at 03h10. Yet, despite their small numbers, the SS man-

aged to hold their positions. The losses were so high that *II./"T"* and *I./"TE"* had to be dissolved and their remaining men sent to the other grenadier battalions. On **September 1**, the Soviets penetrated the lines of *223.ID* and crossed the Merla, spreading out south of Karaikosowka. The transportation units of *Totenkopf* were directly threatened and had to form alert units to establish a line of defense to the north of Konstantinowka. Fighting also took place at the Kolontajew bridgehead where the *SS* grenadiers chose to die where they stood rather than retreat. In the evening, the division announced that it was short of about 9000 men. The situation was catastrophic as this number represented the large majority of the combatants (grenadiers, scouts, sappers, and tank crews). The losses among the noncommissioned officers were particularly severe. These officers would be very difficult to replace. The division urgently needed to be reestablished, but the general situation was such that it to be kept at the front. On **September 2**, at 05h15, the Soviet artillery woke the Germans from their brief sleep. The entire sector of *Totenkopf* was under fire. At 06h45, *SS-Rgt."T"* was attacked by 35 *T-34* tanks. The Soviets attacked wave after wave, pushing them back during the course of violent battles. At noon, aerial reconnaissance showed 45 Soviet tanks on their way to Kotelewka, followed by another 20 or so. These tanks were in addition to the 50 tanks already facing the positions held by *Totenkopf*. *SS-Pz.Rgt.3* was sent in to fight and succeeded in destroying about 40 tanks. But the situation remained precarious, particularly on the *XLVII.Pz.Korps*' left flank, which the Soviets were attacking with gusto. Until about noontime, *SS-Rgt. "T"* and *SS-Pz.Aufkl.-Abt."T"* were engaged in close combat and succeeded in beating back all the Soviet assaults. The bodies of the dead Russian soldiers were piling up in front of the SS positions. At the start of the evening, the division informed *XLVII.Pz.Korps* that 72 Russian tanks had been knocked out and that fourteen attacks had been held off during the previous 24 hours.

On **September 3**, the Soviets managed to break through the front of *7.Panzerdivision* to the south-east of Kotelwa. Elements of the *Totenkopf* were then sent to the breach and put into action against approximately 40 Russian tanks. Ten *T-34*s were destroyed, and they were able to plug the breach by the end of the day. The situation then became very complicated because at that moment, to the south of the Merla and therefore near the rear lines of the division, concentrations of Soviet forces arriving from Kustarewka, lost two days earlier by *223.ID*, were spotted to the west of Turowo. These Russian units were already heading for Slobodka. Since *Totenkopf* had no units in reserve, troops had to be called in from the rear echelons. On **September 6**, General Lemelsen expressed his qualms regarding *8.Armee* regarding the situation south of the Merla. All their hopes lay in a counter-attack by *SS-Pz.Aufkl.-Abt."T"* at Slobodka. But the attack had to be terminated at 11h20 due to heavy losses. The battalion commander, *SS-Ostuf.* Fürter, was seriously wounded and was replaced by *SS-Hstuf.* Berg. It then became impossible to oust the Soviets from their position. Consequently, on **September 9**, *AOK 8* ordered the *Totenkopf* to retreat to the southern bank of the Merla.

Operation: "Scorched Earth"

Totenkopf began to withdraw its forces during the night between 9 - 10 September. During the previous few weeks, *Totenkopf* had faced the successive attacks of eight divisions of infantry, one airborne division, nine armored brigades and two mechanized brigades. Never defeated, it was with a feeling of colossal waste that the men of the division began abandoning the posts they had defended at such a dear price. They left behind them the tombs of hundreds of their comrades killed in action. The high command had also decided to apply the "scorched earth policy"- anything that could be used by the Soviet war machine was to be either transported west or destroyed. Villages and crops were burned down. Men old enough to bear arms were taken away with the German columns, willingly or by force. This was yet another tragedy to befall Ukraine.

On **September 11**, *XLVII.Pz.Korps* announced to *8.Armee* that *"the retreat had gone according to plan."* *Totenkopf* no longer had enough infantry or panzers to resist the Soviet infiltrations. On the left flank, the link between *8.Armee* and *4.Panzerarmee* was in danger of being lost, and *Grossdeutschland*, holding the right flank of *XLVIII.Pz.Korps* (*4.Panzerarmee*), was no longer in a position to stop the southward advance of the Soviets. On **September 13**, *Heeresgruppe "Süd"*, ordered *8.Armee* to pulling back towards the *"Berta I"* line . The next day Manstein commanded Hoth to abandon the link with *8.Armee* and to turn its right flank westward, directing its front on a north-south axis in order to cover Kiev. Consequently the *8.Armee* was forced to speed up its retreat in order to free up enough troops to close the gap that would open up between the two armies.

On **September 15**, *Totenkopf* reorganized its positions during the course of the night and directed its defense towards the North, the East, and the South. The Soviets arrived and began to attack to the north of Otrada, then to the south of Konstantinowka. They were held off each time by the SS. All in all however, these combats were relatively inconsequential, because farther to the north, the loss of Nezhin let loose a wave of panic in the German High-Command. Hitler finally authorized the general retreat towards the Dnieper, while asking *1.Panzerarmee* to reinforce the bridgehead at Saporoshje in order to protect the manganese mines at Nikopol. Hitler's habit of favoring the economic aspects at the expense of tactical necessity would once again prove to be disastrous. Von Manstein, who had hoped to withdraw his troops so as to reinforce the northern flank of his army group, was obliged to send them to Saporoshje, a sector that was tactically of lesser importance. At about 22h50, *Heeresgruppe "Süd"* then gave the order for the general retreat of *8.Armee*. The retreat would take place over the entire front of the army group – i.e. over 430 miles (700 km)! The retreat of *8.Armee* was a highly complicated operation to carry through: its armored corps were currently engaged on its left flank, their mission being to protect the retreat of the rest of the army through Poltawa in the direction of Tscherkassy and Krementschug, and then cover its movements and act as a rear guard.

Totenkopf remained at the front until **September 19**. The following day it evacuated its positions during the course of the night, towards the *"Franziska"* line. In order to cover their retreat, a few units are left behind as a rear guard, remaining engaged on the previous front until the morning. Some units of the division were already crossing over the Worskla. The transportation units were blocked at Poltawa in an immense traffic jam, where thousands of vehicles were jammed in an ocean of refugees and demoralized soldiers. Soviet airplanes were dropping their bombs in the middle of the columns of wagons and cars, and in the crowds of people and animals. Everything was in complete disorder and those witnessing the spectacle were no longer able to believe in the German victory. On September 21 the division retreated to the western bank of the Worskla. As soon as the river was crossed, *I./SS-Pz.Rgt.3 "T"* was sent to Grafenwöhr to be reoutfitted with *Pzkpfw.V "Panther"* tanks, under the command of *SS-Stubaf. Meierdress*.

On **September 22**, *Totenkopf* proceeded with its retreat in accordance with its prescribed orders. At the rear, the transportation units were stuck on the Poltawa–Krementschug *"Rollbahn"*, teeming with retreating infantry divisions. A wave of refugees, stretched out a hundred yards on both sides of the road, along with their pathetic carts and their livestock, followed the divisions. All were trying to reach Dnieper before the Soviets. Rumors were breaking out among the ranks: the Dnieper had been solidly fortified with impregnable bunkers and networks of trenches. It was already being called the *"Ostwall"*, the "East Wall" behind which they hoped to finally be able to defend themselves and rest up. Their disenchantment was to be extremely cruel. At the time, the retreat was taking placing in stages each day, on improvised lines of defense called: "Katrin", "Laura", "Martha" or "Lili Marlene". On **September 26**, *XLVIII.Pz.Korps* left its bridgehead at Krementschug. Its sector was entrusted to *XI.AK*, to which the division now belonged. Although in this sector the retreat was proceeding smoothly, elsewhere the situation was becoming catastrophic for the Germans. In the course of the day, the Woronesch Front established a bridgehead at the bend of the Dnieper under Perejaslaw, and the Steppe Front crossed the river in three locations between Krementschug and Dnjepropetrowsk. During the next few days, it would succeed in connecting all three bridgeheads in order to form a single bridgehead, 9 miles (15 km) deep and 30 miles (50 km) wide. The bridgehead was established exactly midway between the crossing points chosen by the Germans. On **September 27**, *XI.AK* started to occupy its new positions on the southern bank of the Dnieper. The retreat continued steadily, under constant pressure from the Soviet troops. At noon *Totenkopf* started to cross the river. The battle was raging all over the bridgehead. Attacks to the south of Pustowitowo and Pissarschtschina were held off. The *Totenkopf* units moved to the southern bank and regrouped in the Kamenno-Potozkoje and Kriukoff sector, to the south east of Krementschug. On **September 29th**, the Soviets succeeded in opening up several breaches in the *XI.AK*'s defense. In the *Totenkopf* sector, they managed to reach the batteries of *SS-Art.-Rgt."T"*. The artillery units opened fire on the hordes of enemy infantry at point-blank range. The SS grenadiers mounted a counter-attack and pushed back the Soviet troops. The retreat could then continue in the direction of the "von Rundstedt" bridge, over which no more vehicles were to pass. Only a few groups of men were then crossing the bridge. At 11h05, *XI.AK* announced: *"Most of SS-"T" has passed to the southern bank and relieved the units of 282.ID."* At 16h30, the Russian air force bombarded the bridge. A direct hit on a demolition charge blew up half of the structure. A few men and some heavy weaponry were still crossing the river by the rail bridge, and at 19h00, the order was given to blow the bridge. A number of the division's units were left behind on the eastern bank. They crossed the river a few minutes later on inflatable dinghies. At 21h45 *XI.AK* announced to *8.Armee* that *"the Krementschug bridgehead has been evacuated according to plan"*.

The Germans lose the Donets basin

Despite the success achieved by *III.Pz.Korps* and the *Totenkopf* on the Merla, the situation is becoming critical for the Germans in the Charkow sector. *General* Kempf is dismissed for his insistance on being allowed to evacuate the city. His successor, *General* Wöhler comes to the same conclusion two days only after taking charge. Manstein at last gives his consent on 21 August and on 23 August, the big city of the Donets changes hands one last time.

III.Pz.Korps with three *SS* divisions and an armoured division of the *Heer* succeeds in closing the gap west of Charkow and inflicts very heavy losses to two Soviet armies. (NA)

Armoured elements of *Totenkopf* – shown here is a *Sd.Kfz.251 Ausf.C* of *I.(gep.)/SS-Pz.-Gren. Rgt.1 "T"* – begin withdrawing on 26 August. (NA)

The Soviets try to stay in close contact with the retreating Germans by launching forays with strong reconnaissance elements. Their ardour is doused by counter-attacks by the *Totenkopf* which inflict substantial losses. Prisoners are searched in the Kotelewka sector. (NA)

The retreat of the *Totenkopf*: from 10 September, the division abandons its positions on the Merla. Flak guns of *SS-Flak-Abt. "Totenkopf"* – shown here 37mm guns on *Sd.Kfz.6* chassis – move towards the south-west. (NA)

On 20 September, the division reaches the banks of the Worskla, the only natural barrier of importance between the Donets and the Dniepr. There are only a few bridges so all available means are used to cross the river. (NA)

2 and **3.** Rain starts falling from the middle of September and turns roads into mire. Prisoners are enrolled to make them passable but improvised means are required to move heavy vehicles like this lorry. (NA)

1. The retreat to the Dniepr is executed in a staged withdrawal. Intermediary positions are held for a day or two, sometimes for a few hours only. This soldier, his sniper mask rolled over his helmet, has dug in near his 150mm infantry gun. (NA)

3

4. In the late summer greyness, the division is withdrawing across the plains of Ukraine. *Tigers* cover the retreat. (Private collection.)

5. Motocyclists of *11.Kp.* of regiment *"Totenkopf"* or *"Eicke"*. They do not have any energy left to attempt a smile for the photographer. (NA)

4

5

1, 2 and **3.** Grenadiers get some food during the retreat. The sullen faces contrast with the smiles shown by the photographers two years before. (NA)

4. *Marder III Ausf. H* of the anti-tank group cover the retreat by keeping enemy armour at bay. This tank-hunter is a hybrid design, consisting of a 7.5cm *Pak 40* on a Czech *LT-38* tank and 418 were built. (NA)

5. *SS-Feldersatz-Bataillon "Totenkopf"* is the first unit of the division to reach the western side of the Dniepr. Its men are seen here receiving more combat training at Selenoje . (NA

Three batteries of *SS-Flak-Abt. "Totenkopf"* are equipped with 8.8cm guns. This *Flak 36* is apparently being used as a field gun. (NA)

The retreat to the Dniepr and the Krementschug bridgehead is executed alongside units of the *Heer*. A position of *168.ID* in the Reschetilowka area. (NA)

Delaying actions in daytime followed by withdrawal at night have exhausted the men. The soldier on the left finds enough energy to clean his rifle. (NA)

Jammed vehicles in the mist of the Ukrainian autumn in the Krementschug area where the divisions of *XI.AK* have only one bridge to cross the Dniepr. (NA)

The coming of autumn worsens the state of the roads, adding hardship to the German retreat. (Private Collection)

A *StuG.III* of *Totenkopf* (or belonging to *6.Pz.Div.*,since both units share the same tactical marking since the battle of Kursk) crosses the railway bridge over the Dniepr. The bomb on the right is destined to blow up the bridge. (ECPA)

341

Counter-Attack at Kriwoi-Rog

At the beginning of October *Totenkopf* found itself on the west bank of the Dniepr, to the south-west of Krementschug, between Kutshanowka and Uspenko-je. To its left *282.ID,* to its right *106.ID.* There was no question of rest for these men as, contrary to rumors, no line of defense existed along the river. It was therefore necessary to construct new positions whilst sending forces to assist *106.ID* against the Soviet bridgehead which had been established to the west of Koleberda. The division general staff used these few days of relative calm to reorganize certain units: the antitank battalion and the assault gun group were therefore temporarily combined. This new unit was placed under the command of *SS-Stubaf.* Grunert.

On **October 15**, the Steppes Front went on the offensive against the left flank of *1.Panzerarmee* (Mackensen). The central point of the attack was located in the Borodajewka sector towards the south of Mischurin-Rog and at Kommunar. Its objective was Kriwoi-Rog, a major supply center and a vital communications hub for *1.Panzerarmee.* The Soviets advanced deep into German lines east of Annowka towards the south-east, to the rear of *XI.AK.* On the 17th, *Totenkopf* received orders to plug the breach which had opened between *106.ID* (*XI.AK, 8.Armee*) and *6.Panzerdivision* (*LVII.Pz.Korps, 1.Panzerarmee*). *Totenkopf* assembled between Losowatka and Iwanowka. There it came under the command of *XL.Pz.Korps* (Henrici). The situation was becoming worse by the hour, however, and it became impossible to wait for support from *24.Panzerdivision* as von Manstein had hoped. He therefore decided to send *Totenkopf* against the northern flank of the Soviet 18th armored corps, towards the south-east in the direction of Popelnastoje. On **October 20**, *6.Panzerdivision* armored forces and *SPW* came under the command of the division. On **October 22**, *11.Panzerdivision,* reinforced by *gep. Gruppe "Biermeier",* set off from Nowo Starodup. The Soviets were driven from the field and fled to the north-east. The day was also marked by a change of name which affected all *Waffen-SS* units. By order of *SS-FHA* the division was re-named *3.SS-Panzerdivision "Totenkopf". SS-Pz.Gren.Rgt.1 "Totenkopf"* was renamed and became *SS-Pz.Gren.Rgt.5 "Thulé".* In practice the name "Thulé" was never to be used and all documentation relating to the regiment would continue to use the former name (*"Totenkopf"*). *SS-Pz.Gren.Rgt.3 "Theodor Eicke"* was also numbered in accordance with the new sequence for Waffen-*SS* regiments and therefore became *SS-Pz.Gren.Rgt.6 "Theodor Eicke".* All other divisional units gained the number "3" together with the prefix *"Panzer-"* (e.g. *SS-Panzer-Nachrichten-Abteilung 3*).

On **October 24**, *XL.Pz.Korps,* which had finally been joined by *14.* and *24.Panzerdivisionen,* was given the task of destroying the Soviet forces located to the west of the Ingulez. On the 25th the Soviets were at the gates of Kriwoi-Rog. German preparations were therefore hastened. On **October 28**, *XL.Pz.Korps* finally went on the attack. *Totenkopf* came up against the right flank of the Soviet 5th corps. Its armored

group and *III. /"TE"* soon reached Olympiadowka. The elements of three Russian divisions threatening the left flank of the *SS* were pushed back past the Ingulez. The fighting was fierce but in the afternoon the bulk of the Soviet forces, caught in the pincer movement to the south of Nowaja Praga, were finally cut to pieces to the west of the Ingulez: 74 Russian tanks were destroyed and there was very heavy loss of life. On the morning of the 29th, *Totenkopf* continued its attack towards the south, thus barring the way to Soviet forces who were fighting a rearguard action. In order to relieve their units trapped in the *XL.Pz.Korps* noose, the Soviets launched several attacks on the eastern flank of *Totenkopf* in the Federowka sector. The division's right flank was also under pressure from Soviet forces trying to escape from the pocket in the Dubowyj - Olympiadowka sector. All the Soviet assaults were held in check by the *SS* infantry during particularly savage fighting, but consequently a large part of the *XL.Pz.Korps* forces was tied up in a sector which had become of secondary importance. It was therefore impossible for *Totenkopf* to push further south in the direction of Petrowo. On the 30th, *14.Panzerdivision* managed to establish a bridgehead on the east bank of the Ingulez. It was joined there by *24.Panzerdivision* which also established a bridgehead at Ternowatka. This was a remarkable success which closed the door to Kriwoi-Rog to the Soviets. The breach was closed.

Defensive fighting for the bend in the Dniepr

On **November 3**, *Totenkopf* had the task of preventing the Soviets from extending their bridgehead at Petrowo. At 07h30 it reported that it had destroyed fifty T-34s to the east of Petropol. This was a major defensive success, but the first days of November were primarily marked by the departure of numerous officers from the division. *Totenkopf* had to give up some of its staff in order to help reform *16.SS-Panzergrenadier-Division "Reichsführer-SS".* A worse time could not have been chosen, since the shortage of officers due to the heavy losses sustained by the division since the battle of Kursk was becoming critical. Furthermore, it was the most experienced officers who were chosen to serve in the new unit created in Slovenia under the iron hand of Max Simon.

On **November 6**, *76.ID* began to relieve *Totenkopf,* which had to regroup around Losowatka and Geikkowka. *Totenkopf* was therefore able to take advantage of these few days of respite to reorganize. Otto Baum, returning from convalescence, resumed command of the *"Totenkopf"* regiment and Karl Ullrich was given command of the *"Theodor Eicke"* regiment. On November 14, hell broke out once more: the Soviets attacked *76.ID* and the right wing of *384.ID.* The German lines were penetrated. *Totenkopf* was immediately thrown into the breach. The *SS* succeeded in stabilizing the situation. On **November 15**, the division took up position between Ternowatka up to the north-east of Bairak. The Soviets rapidly went on the attack with vast numbers of forces. They were held off with very heavy losses: the division claimed that 71 tanks had been destroyed. This defensive success in the face of attacks by two armored brigades, a mechanized brigade, an assault gun regiment and seven (!) infantry divisions, brought congratulations from von Manstein. During the days that followed the front line was to remain stable, despite the attacks kept up by the Soviets, especially in the Bairak sector.

On **December 5**, the Soviets went on the offensive once more. They wiped out what remained of *384.ID* and broke out into open land, threatening to cut off the railways leading to Kriwoi-Rog. Units from *Totenkopf (SS-KGr. "Seela")* were immediately called on for help. Their counter-attacks slowed down the progress of the Soviet forces but could not halt it. During this time the remainder of *Totenkopf* was engaged between Krassno Konstantinowka and Reje-wa Alexandrowka in a war of static positions.

Fighting in the Kirovograd region

Totenkopf spent the final part of the year quietly in its positions to the east of Gurowka. Although this period was not spent in battle, it was nevertheless spent on the front line, which meant that the division could not rebuild its strength. On December 31, the division consisted of just 413 officers plus 8325 NCOs and other ranks, out of a theoretical strength of 841 officers, 4086 NCOs and 15,478 other ranks. As for the armored units, the division could only muster 5 *Pzkpfw.III*, 6 *Pzkpfw.IV*, 2 *Pzkpfw.VI "Tigers"*, 1 *Bef.Pz.*, 6 *StuG.III* and 4 *Marder II* in working order..

On **January 5, 1944**, the Soviets launched a new large-scale offensive, this time much further to the north, on both sides of Kirovograd. *8.Armee* front broke in many places and there was a real threat that encirclement would be achieved. Faced with this dramatic situation, on **January 6** von Manstein ordered *Kampfgruppe "Laackmann" (II./SS-Pz.Rgt.3 and SS-Pz.Aufkl.-Abt.3)* to counter attack in the direction of Pokrowskoje through which the supply lines for the Soviet forces threatening Kirowograd passed. On **January 7** the attack was launched at 06h00 hours in thick fog. Faced with solid antitank defenses, losses soon became very heavy. At 11h35 hours, *LII.AK* gave the order to halt the attack. On **January 8**, *Totenkopf* received the order to take the Kirowograd sector and regroup around Bobrinez. On **January 16**, the division launched its counter-attack to the north of Owsjanikowka. Up until midday, everything went perfectly for the *SS*. But suddenly everything became more complex. The *SS* were forced to dig in where they were, in order to resist Soviet counter-attacks. On **January 18**, defensive fighting continued in the Bogodarowka sector. The front became quite once again after **January 23**. The Soviets were in fact preparing to encircle *XI.AK* and *XXXII.AK* around Korsun. On **January 25** at 10h00 hours, the Soviets went on the attack against *376.ID*, *282.ID* and *Totenkopf*. They were pushed back once more after very heavy fighting. The situation was becoming more critical on the left flank of *XLVII.Pz.Korps*, however, where the 20th Russian armored corps was moving through open ground and was no longer encountering any resistance. On **January 28** it joined up with the forward units of the 6th armored army at Swenigorodka, encircling six divisions of *8.Armee* and opening up the road from the Bug and Romania. On **January 30**, the fighting in the *Totenkopf* sector become less intense, with the Soviets preferring to concentrate their efforts further north in order to consolidate their stranglehold around Korsun. For more than a month afterwards the Kirowograd sector was to remain relatively calm, with the few attacks carried out by the Soviets not having any significant effect on the shape of the front.

At the beginning of March, the Germans were faced with a disastrous situation. On the 4th, the 1st Ukraine Front broke through the *4.Panzerarmee* line between Schepetowka and Rowno and pressed forward southwards with two armored armies. The next day the 2nd Ukraine Front followed suit and attacked towards the south-west in the direction of Uman and the Bug. An immense encirclement of *1.Panzerarmee* was clearly taking shape. On **March 8**, *Totenkopf* was ordered to regroup around Nowo Ukrainka. Already *Kampfgruppe "Laackmann"* was engaged at Iwanowka supporting *Grossdeutschland*, which was being assailed by nine infantry divisions and three armored brigades. On **March 11**, the first *Totenkopf* convoys of left Nowo Ukrainka for Perwomaisk, a town located on the Bug. On **March 13**, the units which had managed to get to the south of the river headed towards Balta. The next day the division took over responsibility for the western flank of *8 Armee*. Its task was to establish a line of defense, facing northwards along the river Sawranka, between Petschana to the east and Tschetschelnik to the west. It was placed under the command of *VII.AK (Gen.d.Art. Hell)*. The first Soviet units arrived at the Sawranka in the evening of **March 15**, and were immediately engaged in fighting. Their attacks were beaten off by the *"Eicke"* regiment, gaining precious time, since the majority of the division was still to the north of the Bug. The overall situation, however, remained catastrophic for the Germans. There was no longer any organized resistance in the breach that had opened between *1.Panzerarmee* and *8.Armee*. The Soviet forces were able to surge through freely and were already threatening Winnitza. On **March 20** the last convoys of the division arrived at Balta. The next day it drew back to the Ljubomirka - Iwaschkowo line. The Soviets, however, were already to the west of the Dniestr and were threatening Balti, more than 60 kilometers to the west of Balta. The battle raged on, and the *SS*, lacking heavy weaponry support, sustained terrible losses. Every meter of ground had to be fought for, frequently with grenades or bayonets. On the 23rd the Soviets broke through the *Totenkopf* lines. Their superiority in numbers was overwhelming: they attacked with nine infantry divisions and an armored brigade to the north, the north-east and north-west of Balta. *Totenkopf* was quickly cut off at the rear. At 19h00 hours, the SS managed to escape from the pocket by hand-to-hand fighting. Men were able to make it through, but many vehicles became bogged down and had to be abandoned. The division nevertheless was able to re-establish a more or less coherent front to the south of the town after the 27th, but now retreat in good order towards the Dniestr was taking place. On April 2, *Totenkopf* reached Dubossary, a town located on the Dniestr, 50 miles (80 km) to the south-west of Balta. The river was crossed without delay and the division moved slowly across Bessarabia towards Kischinew. On **April 13**, it reached the region to the west of Roman, where it was placed under the command of *LVII.Pz.Korps* (v. Funck).

Fighting in Romania. Reconstitution

The greater part of *Totenkopf* set up camp in the Trifesti - Carligu - Dumesti - Negresti - Secueni sector in mid-April. The rest of the division (*SS-Pz.Rgt.3, SS-StuG.-Abt.3, SS-Flak-Abt.3* and three out of the four groups of the *SS-Pz.Art.-Rgt.3*) were transferred to the east of Bacau to be re-constituted there. On **April 16**, Himmler ordered that *II./"T"* and *I./"E"* at Heidelager were to be re-formed with recruits from *16.SS-Panzergrenadier-Division "RF-SS"*. This division provided 4500 men for *Totenkopf*. On **April 18**, the division received the order to send a tactical intervention group into the Mircesti - Halaucesti sector to support the Romanian 6th ID.

On **May 2**, at 04h15 hours, the Soviet artillery opened fire, first of all in the sector held by *Grossdeutschland,* then between Siret and the Moldau. The Soviets then sent nearly 350 tanks into the battle. Under attack by around sixty tanks, the Romanian forces were scattered. The Soviets broke through in the direction of Targul Frumos. At 16h45 hours, the *Totenkopf* tactical intervention group went on the counter-attack. In the air, the *Luftwaffe* sent 600 aircraft into battle, the largest aerial force since Kursk. The division was involved in fighting for Helestieni for three days followed by a long period of calm,

which the division was to use to its advantage to reconstitute its units.

On **June 20**, *SS-Gruf.* Priess was placed at the disposal of the *SS-FHA.* He was temporarily replaced at the head of the division by *SS-Ostubaf.* Ullrich. In order to come into line with the new *Panzerdivision* type 44 organization, on **July 1** the assault gun group was replaced by an antitank battalion. The same day *SS-Ostubaf.* Eberhardt replaced Baldur Keller as an Chief of staff of the division. During the night of **July 6** to 7 *Totenkopf* received the order to join *Heeresgruppe "Mitte"* as quickly as possible, where the situation was becoming desperate for the Germans.

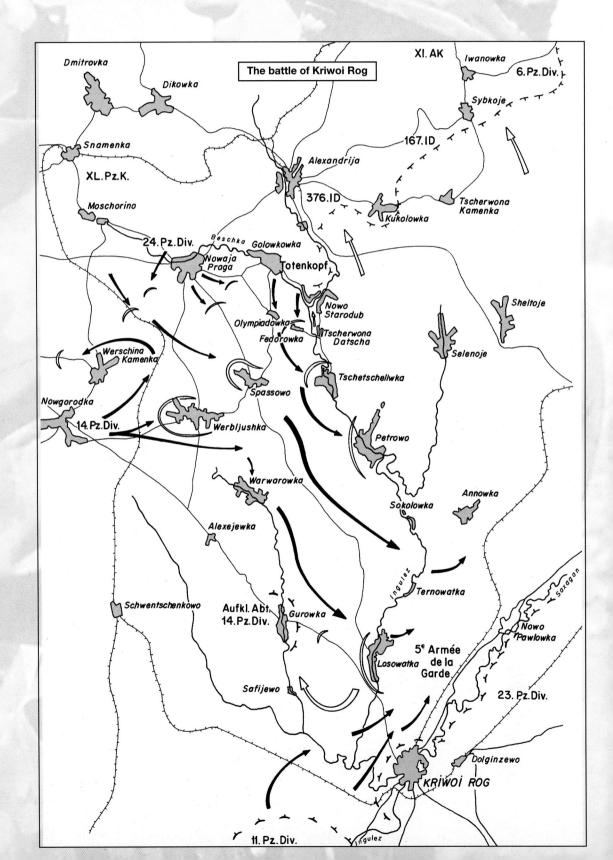

The battle of Kriwoi Rog

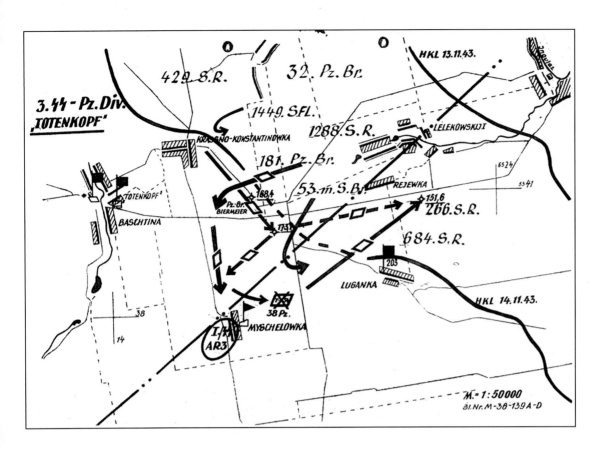

The crew of this heavy loaded *Pzkpfw. III* has stopped along a road to take a short meal. (S.' private collection)

A *T-34/76* and a 122 mm howitzer were destroyed by the *Totenkopf*'s men south of Kirowograd. Despite significant losses, the Red Army is moving forward relentlessly west of the Dniepr. (NA)

345

From the Dniepr to Romania
From October 1943 to June 1944, *Totenkopf* kept retreating, while fighting tough defensive combats, from the banks of the Dniepr to the Romanian region of Jassy. In the course of this long-lasting withdrawal, the division was almost annihilated in the battle of Balta where, though completely surrounded, it finally extricated itself from a trap that may well have been lethal. But this was very costly, especially in equipment.

1. Anti-tank mines ("*Teller-Minen*") are being unloaded from *Sd.Kfz.250* during a counterattack towards Kriwoi-Rog. It's October and the earth is soaked. Only tracked vehicles can move on such ground. (NA)

2. Carrying their mines, these men are going up front. Notice their parkas and big mitts. They must be quite far away from first lines, since they aren't wearing helmets. (NA)

3. A photograph of a grenadier wearing a woollen hat. He was given the Iron Cross 2nd class. (NA)

4. Companions are exchanging cigarettes. They are wearing death's-heads on their collars. A few pictures from this report were used to illustrate articles or books about the *Leibstandarte*. The *SS-KB* who took them was attached to the *Totenkopf*, even though both divisions fought in very remote sectors at that time. (NA)

5. Reinforcements arrive to the front. Most of these young recruits are wearing coats, which is far from convenient for combat. (NA)

A photograph of an *SS-Unterscharführer* (sergeant) wearing Iron Crosses 2nd and 1st class, a bronze wound medal and, oddly enough, a tank assault badge. (NA)

Das Ritterkreuz erhielt:

Aufn.: ⚡-PK.-Kriegsberichter Adendorf

⚡-Obersturmführer Riefkogel

⚡-PK. — Mit unverminderter Wucht drängte das ⚡-Panzerkorps im März 1943 die Sowjets gegen den Donez zurück. In der Nacht gelang es jedoch den Gegnern, an einer Stelle durchzubrechen. Die Feinde erneut zu werfen, war der richtige Auftrag für ⚡-Obersturmführer Riefkogel. Mit zwei Panzern stieß er mitten in den Gegner, erledigte zwei feindliche Panzer und wehrte einen Gegenstoß ab. Einige Stunden später sah ⚡-Obersturmführer Riefkogel den Gegner neu herankommen. Kurz entschlossen überfiel er die Sowjets wie der Blitz, schoß vier T 34 ab und setzte nachdrängender sowjetischer Infanterie so entscheidend zu, daß sie den Kampf aufgab.

Geboren am 7. 1. 1913 in Celle bei Hannover, trat Waldemar Riefkogel 1934 in die Schutzpolizei ein, meldete sich zu Beginn des Westfeldzuges freiwillig zur ⚡-Polizeidivision und wurde für Tapferkeit vor dem Feinde zum Feldwebel und zum Leutnant befördert. Im Osten erwarb er sich das Eiserne Kreuz 1. Kl. Infolge einer Knieverletzung kam er zur Panzerwaffe und übernahm im Juli 1942 nachdem er zur Waffen-⚡ übergestellt war, eine Kompanie in einem ⚡-Panzerregiment. Seine Männer erfüllte ⚡-Obersturmführer Riefkogel mit seinem eigenen draufgängerischen Geist, der sie vorwärts riß und zur höchsten Leistung befähigte.

⚡-Kriegsberichter Richard M. Allesch.

A tank force is organizing itself before combat. On the right, a soldier is cleaning an *Sd.Kfz.250/7* mortar barrel. (NA)

Close-up view of an 81mm mortar (*m.Gr.W.34*)'s crew. Its chief must be the soldier on the left, since he is the only one to be entitled to binoculars. (NA)

Two grenadiers are looking at a Soviet 85mm anti-aircraft gun. Like the Germans, the Red Army commonly uses anti-air-craft heavy pieces for anti-tank purposes. (NA)

An *Sd.Kfz.250* is going through the plain. On such terrain, a vehicle may be seen kilometres away, which makes it an easy target. Speed is thus key to escape enemy fire. (NA)

A Soviet anti-tank position has been destroyed. A 45mm *M1942* gun was shot around the shield. A little more effective than the German 37mm gun, it was produced in large quantities and was used until the end of the war. (NA)

1. The photographs are presented following film order. Logically, the armoured force is shown here coming back from mission. But quite oddly, the Marder II and the *Sd.Kfz.250* are going opposite sides. (NA)

2. Interesting picture of an *Sd.Kfz.250/1* equipped with a *MG42* and a *MG34*. (NA)

3. A soldier is setting the detonator of a *Tellermine 35*. This type of weapon is essential to the German retreating from the whole Eastern Front. (NA)

3

SS-Hauptsturmführer Adolf Pittschellis. He wears the German Cross in gold he won on 23rd October 1942. (NA)

Motorcyclists on a half muddy, half frozen road. Contrary to summer 1941, motorcyclists weren't used for combat, but as couriers. (NA)

February 1944. The *Totenkopf* sector west of Kirowograd has remained relatively calm for almost a month. Men make the most of it by improving comfort of their positions. Notice the leather outfits that don't conform to the regulations. (NA)

Burial of an unidentified *SS-Panzeroffizier* belonging to *7.Kp./SS-Pz.Rgt.3.* The coffin has been placed on top of the tank turret. Of special interest are the three vertical bars, a remnant from Zitadelle, though the *Pzkpfw.IV Ausf.H* has since been whitewashed for winter camouflage. (Courtesy Tim Willemsen)

These photographs have been taken from a personal album belonging to this dashing young officer serving within *SS-Pz.Rgt.3*. His name and his precise unit are unfortunately unknown to the author. Noteworthy are his white *Kombi* and his armband with the inscription *"Totenkopf"*. The tank is a *Pzkpfw.III Ausf.J*. (Courtesy Tim Willemsen)

A very short illustrated report on a light anti-aircraft piece (*2cm-Flak 38*) and its crew. Men are warmly dressed and seem to keep high spirits, maybe because a nice bottle of wine has just been delivered. (NA)

1. March 1944. Calm times were short-lived. Battle is raging again, this time in the sector of Balta, where the division must protect the retreat of *8.Armee*. In this defensive context, the *StuG.III*, whose squat figures are clearly noticeable here, are most useful. (NA)

2. One of the four *Tigers* of the division still in working order in early march. *SS-Pz. Rgt.3's* tanks must grow in number to fill in the numerous breaches in the German lines. (NA)

3. Division transfer from Perwomaisk to Balta takes place on roads turned into oceans of mud by the thaw. This *Gleisketten-Lkw. Opel-Blitz "Maultier"* seems to come off quite all right thanks to its caterpillar tracks. (NA)

4. On the contrary, this *Opel-Blitz* doesn't have caterpillar tracks, and therefore must be tracked to move on such tricky ground. (NA)

This road is under Soviet scrutiny, as this sign shows. (NA)

To prevent or at least reduce this surveillance, these men from a building unit are making do as best they can... (NA)

1. Here is the result. It hardly protects them at all, and this *Schwimmwagen* must above all count on its engine to escape enemy fire. (NA)

2. A *Luftwaffe* unit soldier photographed by a *Totenkopf KB*. He probably belongs to a Flak group. (NA)

3. In mid-March, the division has only a thousand fit grenadiers left. The artillery's role becomes even more important, then. The maintaining of the lines depends mostly on how precise are the data this observer collects. (NA)

1

2

3

4

1. *SS-Ostubaf*. Karl Ullrich during the retreat to Romania. Notice the armband bearing the inscription "*Theodor Eicke*". (S.' private collection)

2. Karl Ullrich with NCOs from his staff during the battle of Balta. (S.' private collection)

3. June 1944. *SS-Gruppenführer* Hermann Pries is saying his farewell to the division. (S.' private collection)

4. The Krass family together after Hugo ? whose head was wounded on the Eastern front when leading *SS-Pz.Gren.Rgt.2 "LSSAH"* ? was awarded the Knight's Cross with Oak Leaves. His brother Boris, sitting on his right, is then the head of *III./SS-Pz.Art.-Rgt.3 "Totenkopf"*. (S.' private collection)

SS-Gruppenführer Hermann Priess leaves the division. His *Adjutant*, *SS-Sturmbannführer* Walther Stadl-bauer, is seated behind him. Notice the death's head painted on the side of the car. This was not a common practice as the divisional insignia was more often placed on the mud-guard or at the back of the car. (Courtesy Martin Månsson)

1. Exercises in cooperation with a Romanian unit. Here are three of their officers, easily recognizable from their very flat cap. (S.' private collection)

2. These soldiers from *16.(Pi.)Kp./SS-Pz.Gren.Rgt.6* "Theodor Eicke" were commissioned to build bases of operations in the sector of Ruginoasa. (Private collection)

A wounded Otto Baum must be evacuated from the front. After his convalescence, he isn't to join the division, but to give several lectures in various *Waffen-SS* schools. The picture shows him with Sepp Dietrich and Max Wünsche next to a *Jagdpanzer IV*. (S.' private collection)

Ritterkreuzträger Bruno Hinz is *SS-Uscha*. Melchior Mödlinger's best men during the latter's wedding in Prague. Mödlinger served within *SS-StuG.-Abt.3*. (S.' private collection)

15

Battle in Poland from July to December 1944

Walter Model rescues the remnants of *Heeresgruppe "Mitte"* from annihilation and succeeds in establishing a new defensive line in Poland. (Rights reserved)

SS-Gruppenführer (on this photograph *SS-Obergruppenführer*) Kurt von Gottberg is in charge of police units in the Grodno sector before the arrival of the *Totenkopf*. (Rights reserved)

Counter-Attack at Grodno

After the collapse of the *Heeresgruppe "Mitte"* in Belarus, Field Marshal Model attempted to reestablish a united front on the Niemen, with the remains of a group of armies that had lost 23 of its 38 divisions. He was counting on using the *Totenkopf* as a mobile reserve behind a front line broken everywhere. On **July 13**, *SS-Obf.* Hellmuth Becker was chosen to lead the division. While waiting for his arrival, the command of the group was shared by *SS-Ostubaf.* Eberhardt and Ullrich.

The Grodno sector was being held by the *Korpsgruppe "von Gottberg"*, supported by the *Korpsgruppe "Weidling"* on its right flank. On its left flank, a gaping breach extended from von Gottberg's troops to the *XXXIX.Pz.Korps*. The *5.Panzerdivision* attempted to seal off the breach as best it could. The next day, the *Totenkopf* was placed under the command of the *4.Armee* and ordered to establish a defensive position to the north-west of Grodno in the Kielbasin – Bakuny sector. The Soviets had already crossed the Niemen and were threatening the Grodno - Sopockinie road. The *Totenkopf* was forced to split its forces on either side of Grodno to help the police units of the *Korpsgruppe "von Gottberg"*. On **July 17**, it tried to intercept the Russian troops, attacking to the south-west, and take control of the Zarzyca bridge, which was the crossing point for the Soviet reinforcements. The *SS* attacked and succeeded in clearing the western bank of the Niemen over a distance of about 8 miles (12 km) to the north-west of Grodno. At nightfall, two Soviet divisions were still to the west of the Niemen, between Grodno and Druskieniki. On **July 18** the division attacked the Soviets to the north, pushing them back behind the Niemen. During this time, however, the Soviets were breaking through the front further to south and had already reached Lipsk. This gave the Soviets the opportunity to take Grodno from behind by attacking through Dabrowa and to surround the entire left flank of the *Korpsgruppe*, including the Totenkopf units to the north-west of Grodno! Eberhardt promptly sent the *I./"T"*. to Grodno. In the evening, the *Totenkopf* announced that the breach separating it from the *XXXIX.Pz.Korps* had been narrowed but not totally sealed off. On **July 19** the division resumed its attacks to the North: Sopockinie fell into its hands, while to the south-west the *I./"T"* succeeded in taking of Lipsk. The threat to the rear of the *Korpsgruppe* was thus temporarily staved off. On **July 20**, there was still a gap 4 miles (6 km) wide separating the *Totenkopf* from the *5.Panzerdivision*. But the Soviets eventually reacted and launched counter-attack after counter-attack. They succeeded in penetrating the *Korpsgruppe's* lines in several places along its left and right flanks. In overall situation of the Germans was very difficult: the Russians had opened up a large breach between the *4.Armee* and the *2.Armee* in the Byalistok sector. On **July 21**, on the *Totenkopf's* northern flank, the Soviets were trying to reduce the Sopockinie salient. They managed to cut off the road leading from Sopockinie to Grodno. Attacked from

all sides, the *SS* had to pull back around a few defensive moles. The situation became critical on **July 23** to the south-west of Grodno in the Sokolka-Kuznica sector where the lines of the *Korpsgruppe "Weidling"* were entrenched. The *Totenkopf*, which was being joined by the last of the units left in Rumania, received the order to retreat to the *"Wiesel Stellung"* - the Popilja sector. On **July 24**, the *SS-KGr. "Eckert"* (*II./"E"*) launched a counter-attack on Sokolka in the gap separating the *4.Armee* from the *2.Armee*. The *SS* crushed all resistance at about 15h00. They then continued their advance southward and succeeded in linking up with the *12.Panzerdivision*. At the same time the majority of the *Totenkopf* pulled back between Karolin and the sector south-west of Lipsk. Another difficult mission would be in store for them in the next few days: the *Heeresgruppe "Mitte"* had in fact decided to place it under the command of the *2.Armee* because the southern wing of the group of armies had been just smashed to pieces by the pounding of the *1st White Russian Front*. The Bug had been crossed and the Brest-Litowsk garrison was cut off. A breach approximately 60 miles (100 km) long now separated the *2.Armee* from the *4.Panzerarmee (He.Gr. "Nordukraine")*. The Soviet troops were now in a position to threaten the Vistule. In order to deal with this disastrous situation, the German High Command decided to build a line of defense directed to the south between Biala, Podlaska, and Siedlce with the remains of the *VIII.AK* and the *XX.AK*, brought together under the *Gruppe "von Roman"*. This group urgently requested the aid of the *Totenkopf*, since the 47th Soviet army was attacking towards Siedlce in an attempt to cut it off from its rear lines.

The battles for Siedlce

On **July 25**, the *IV.SS-Pz.Korps,* arriving from Metz, was given the order to close off the breach separating the *9.Armee* from the *2.Armee.* Not yet operational, its general staff was located at Rembertow, under the command of the *Gruppe "von Roman"*. The first unit of the *Totenkopf* to reach *Siedlce* was the *I./SS-Pz.Rgt.3*. On arrival at Siedlce the battalion received orders to clear the road leading to Miedzyrzec, and at about 20h00 twenty Panthers attacked towards the south-east. They had just passed the embankment of the Siedlce - Mordy railway when they came under heavy anti-tank fire, and had to retreat towards the city, abandoning seven tanks on the terrain. The next day, the *Totenkopf* units began to fall back one after another from the Niemen front, heading towards Sokolow, a town about 25 miles (40 km) to the north of Siedlce. *SS-Obf.* Becker set up his headquarters there and the division was then put under the command of the *Gruppe "von Roman"*. The *III./"T"* was the first grenadier battalion to set up its position around Siedlce. At the same time, farther west, Soviet troops had just cut off the road to Warsaw near Kaluszyn. To the east, the situation was worse: from Brest-Litowsk to Miedzyrzec, the southern flank of the

2.Armee had been overrun. The *XX.AK* could no longer be supplied via the road leading from Sokolow to Losice. The *2.Armee* reported that it was being attacked by two Soviet armies between Miedzyrzec and Siedlce, which were trying to encircle it from the South, and by five armies which were trying to break through its lines to the east. On **July 27**, while the Soviets were crossing the Vistule to south of Pulawy, the *Heeresgruppe "Mitte"* temporarily abandoned its project to plug the gap separating the *9.Armee* from *2.Armee* by sending in the *IV.SS-Pz.Korps*, since the *5.SS-Panzerdivision "Wiking"* was heavily engaged in fighting at Czeremcha and the majority of the *3.SS-Panzerdivision "Totenkopf"* was being kept near Siedlce. Furthermore, the *"Totenkopf"* was stretched out over nearly 95 miles (150 km), its fuel supply lines were not secure, and its staff was still incomplete and non-operational! The *II./"E"* was nevertheless sent to the west of Siedlce to clear the road to Kaluszyn. After progressing about 4 miles (6 km), the SS were stopped in front of Stare-Iganie. Still worse for the Germans, some Soviet units had managed to infiltrate to the north of Siedlce, from where they threatened the arrival of the *Totenkopf* reinforcements! Out of fuel, the *Totenkopf* was immobilized in the Sokolow sector. During the evening of **July 28**, while the *Wiking* and the *Totenkopf* were under the command of the *IV.SS-Pz.Korps,* the units of the *"Hermann Göring"* at Kaluszyn disengaged from their positions, breaking the link with the *Totenkopf*.

On **July 29**, the situation at Siedlce became more and more difficult for the *Totenkopf:* they were fighting hand to hand and the city was engulfed in flames. **July 30** marked a turning point in the situation: the line of defense of the *73.ID* in front of Warsaw finally caved in to the pounding by the Soviet troops. To the south, the 16th armored corps captured Otwock and Wiazowna, which were being defended by the *19.Panzerdivision*, and reached Majdan. The breach made by the Soviet 16th armored corps allowed the 8th armored corps to continue its advance to Okuniew. North-east of Warsaw, the 3rd armored corps attacked westward towards Wolomin. Faced with this situation, the *Totenkopf* convoys arriving from the Grodno sector were forced to stop their transfer to Siedlce at Warsaw. There were a number of tracked units of the *13.(IG)Kp./"T"*, eight assault guns and the vehicles of the *SS-Pz.Jg.-Abt.3*, 10 Pzkpfw.IVs and Tigers from the *6.* and *7.Kp./SS-Pz.Rgt.3*. They would later fight against the Polish insurgents. By the beginning of the afternoon the Soviets had already reached the south of Radzymin. The Soviets therefore relegated Warsaw to a position of secondary importance. In addition to the strategic advantage of Radzymin, it would also be true to state that for the Soviets, arriving on their last legs from an offensive launched on June 22 to the east of the Dnieper, the capture of Warsaw would have created colossal logistics problems. The preparations for the counter-attack by the *IV.SS-Pz.Korps* were sped up and some 26 000 US gallons (100 m3) of fuel were rapidly delivered to the *"Wiking"* division. *SS-Obf.* Nikolaus Heilmann (*Chef Gen.Stab IV.SS-Pz.Korps*) announced to the *2.Armee* that the assault would begin at 16h30. The *Totenkopf* was unable to participate in the offensive: its units had been occupied the entire day in terrible defensive battles near Siedlce. The town, under attack from all sides apart from a narrow corridor to the north-west, was nothing but a pile of smoking ruins. Numerous Soviet tanks had been destroyed, but the division had also lost a sizeable part of its forces. The division had only 78 grenadiers for each 1000 yards of front, while the Soviets disposed of more than 3000! Near 23h00, the *Totenkopf* abandoned its positions

and retreated behind the Liwiec, to the north-west of Siedlce.

The division's fighting near Stanislawow

On **August 1**, while the Polish insurrection was causing unrest in Warsaw, the *Totenkopf* was located on the Liwiec, between Proszew and Krzeslin. Shortly before 21h00, it received orders to go to the Stanislawow sector. Its mission was to cover the rear of the *Wiking* which was attacking, together with the *XXXIX.Pz.Korps*, the 3rd Soviet armored corps near Wolomin. On **August 3**, the *Totenkopf* first set up between Kamionka and Proszero, with its positions turned southward. This new sector to be held appeared even more dangerous than the Siedlce sector: the Soviets were putting pressure on the sector in order to relieve their 3rd and 8th armored corps, engaged in battle to the south of Radzymin and around Okuniew. On attack followed another for two days, inflicting further losses on the already severely weakened units of the *Totenkopf*.

August 5 was marked by the destruction of the 3rd Soviet armored corps in the Wolomin pocket, by the concentric attacks of the *XXXIX.Pz.Korps* and the *Wiking (IV.SS-Pz.Korps)*. The aim of the Germans was now to reestablish a continuous front line north of Okuniew. In the *Totenkopf's* sector the defensive fighting continued, still as costly in men. A sudden calm settled in on the front from **August 6**: the Soviets were in the process of reorganizing themselves outside Warsaw, where the tactical situation had changed since the stinging defeat of the 2nd armored corps. On **August 10**, after a brief lull in the fighting, the Soviets returned to the offensive between Bialystock and Warsaw. From daybreak, Soviet artillery began to pound the positions held by the SS. This barrage preceded a series of infantry and tank attacks. The numeric superiority of the attackers was so great that breaches were opened up in the lines of the *Totenkopf*, which was unable to stave off attacks launched by six infantry divisions! The fiercest battles were fought between Ludwinow and Natolin, where the Soviets launched no fewer than fifteen assaults, each one the strength of a regiment and supported by tanks. In the evening the *Totenkopf* units began to retreat on the *"Schwarze Linie"*, between Oseczyzna and Polazie. The retreat continued the next day towards the *"Grüne Linie"*. On August 12, the *Totenkopf* took control of the sector previously held by the *4.Panzerdivision* between Grzybowka and Ostrowec, on either side of Wolomin, between *73.ID* to the south and the *Wiking* to the north-east.

The battles for Warsaw

On **August 18** at 09h00 the ground began to shake. Hundreds of artillery pieces had just opened fire. The explosions were so close to one another that it was impossible to distinguish one from the next. All the positions and all the quarters were bombarded. Even the oldest members of the division had never before seen such a barrage of fire. At 11h15, eight infantry divisions with tank support attacked the positions of the *IV.SS-Pz.Korps*. Their objective was the Bug. The losses among the SS were appalling. The Soviets moved along the Warsaw-Bialystock railway line to the south-west and reached the Cienka sector at dusk. Attacks and counter-attacks succeeded one another with little significant change to the front. On July 21, the *IV.SS-Pz.Korps* reported that the *Totenkopf* had destroyed 51 Soviet tanks and shot

General der Artillerie Helmut Weidling is the commander of *Korps "Weidling"* on the Niemen front. (NA)

Waldemar Riefkogel, commander of *1.Kp. / SS-Pz.Rgt.3*. (Rights reserved)

Fritz Biermeier, commander of *II./SS-Pz.Rgt.3* during the fighting in Poland. (Rights reserved)

The infamous Oskar Dirlewanger leads a disciplinary unit with a sinister reputation. It will be responsible for looting and massacres during the Warsaw fighting. (Rights reserved)

down 4 Soviet airplanes since **August 18**. On **August 22**, according to information gathered from Russian prisoners, the losses of the 47th and 70th armies were so great that the infantry units of the 2nd armored corps had to be called in to swell their ranks! On **August 25**, after four days of relative calm, the Soviets struck out once again on the offensive. They had the advantage of an enormous numerical superiority: a whole army against each German division! The artillery bombardment commenced at 03h00 and continued until 07h30. The 47th, 70th, and 28th armies then attacked. In the *Totenkopf* sector, the Soviets broke through in the direction of Dobczyn. They were held back and the previous positions were reestablished nearly everywhere. The next day, the Soviets increased the intensity of their attack in the direction of the Bug. At about 10h00, the entire sector from Dobczyn to Wola-Rasztowska was bombarded by the Russian artillery, then swarms of fighter-bombers attacked the advanced positions of the SS. The SS were attacked nineteen separate times by enemy planes during the course of the day! Following these attacks, the infantry and the tanks began to assault the lines. The *Totenkopf* managed to hold all its lines. Ten Soviet tanks were destroyed. To the north, however, the *Wiking* had not been able to hold out against the Russian advance to the north-east of Radzymin. There was no longer any reason for the *Totenkopf* to remain in the Klembow salient. The *IV.SS-Pz.Korps* was therefore authorized to retreat behind the Rzadza. The retreat took place during the course of the afternoon, while the civilian population began to evacuate Radzymin. On the 29th, the Soviets multiplied their attacks to the east and north-east of Radzymin. They stormed the positions of the *I./"T"* between Wiktorow and Dybowa. In the evening, the *IV.SS-Pz.Korps* reported that due to the tremendous losses its infantry had suffered, the front stretching from Dybowa to Zjawisko was being held only by a few strongpoints. The next day, the Soviets succeeded in surrounding Radzymin. The Soviet forces took full control of the city at 18h00. There was no alternative for the *Totenkopf* but to try to reestablish a line of defense south of Radzymin and north-east of Wolomin. On **August 31**, the Soviets continued pushing toward Warsaw by attacking on both sides of the Radzymin–Prague road. The fighting intensified again on **September 1**, when the Soviets resumed the general offensive against the lines held by the *IV.SS-Pz.Korps*. The *Totenkopf* had to hold out against powerful attacks supported by increasing numbers of tanks. The following day, despite considerable losses, the Soviets continued their attacks to the south-east of Radzymin, on a narrower and narrower front, in order to concentrate as many tanks as possible at the point of attack. At 09h45, with thirty tanks supported by countless infantry, the Soviets broke through the *III./"E"* lines between Czarna Duza and Nadma. The *Totenkopf*'s tanks and tank destroyers fought non-stop: the Soviets lost 35 tanks and 15 antitank guns near Nadma, and their advance seemed to be contained. On **September 3**, the Soviets sent several regiments against Czarna Duza and Nadma, where they were driven back, and also against Borki, where the remains of the *I./"E"* were too weak to stave them off. On **September 4**, the Soviets concentrated their efforts against the left wing of the *2.Armee* and reorganized their forces in the sector of the *IV.SS-Pz.Korps*. This delay gave the SS a short break. The *Totenkopf* then took stock of its losses since August 5: 3486 killed, wounded, or missing in action. These losses forced them to evacuate the Wolomin salient during the night of September 6 and set up on the Ossow - Nadma line. *SS-Brigaf.* Becker's greatest concern was the situation of the grenadier regiments: their battalions had been

reduced to a few dozen able-bodied fighters and, at the end of this summer of 1944, no personnel were available to fill the ranks other than a few *Luftwaffe* ground staff, untrained in infantry combat, and some Ukrainians who were originally intended to reinforce the *14.Waffen-Grenadier-Division der SS*! On September 13, the battle was raging once again, this time in the Marki sector, where 25 Russian tanks were destroyed by the *1.Kp./SS-Pz.Rgt.3*. The pressure of the 47th and 70th Soviet armies was so great that the *IV.SS-Pz.Korps* was forced to pull back its positions further westward during the night between September 14 and 15. The *Totenkopf* then held the line going from the north of Hill 96, to the west of Tomaszow, up to north of Aleksandrow. These new positions were solidly built and all the Soviet attacks in the following days failed to break through.

At the beginning of October, the Soviets seemed to be preparing a new large scale offensive. The *IV.SS-Pz.Korps* intelligence services spotted 130 artillery batteries, 16 rocket-launcher batteries, and 71 anti-aircraft batteries set up against the center and the right wing of the army corps positions. In addition, 20 000 men had arrived to reinforce the 14 divisions confronting the German army. During the next few days, the artillery of the *IV.SS-Pz.Korps* bombarded the trenches of the Soviet infantry, the battery positions and command centers that had been spotted. On **October 8**, the division once again lost one of its best officers - *SS-Staf.* Karl Ullrich - who had just been appointed to the head of the *5.SS-Panzerdivision "Wiking"*. He was replaced at the head of the *SS-Pz.Gren.Rgt.6 "TE"* by *SS-Ostubaf.* Franz Kleffner.

On **October 10**, at 09h00, the Soviet artillery opened fire on the *Totenkopf* positions. More than 100 000 shells pulverized on the sector. The Soviet offensive had just begun. Its objective was to establish a bridgehead on the Vistule between Warsaw and Modlin. The fighting was particularly heavy at Michalow-Grabina, where the *II./"E"* was practically annihilated in just a few minutes. The *III./"E"* had to hold out against three Soviet divisions coming from both sides of Rembelszczyzna! To the south of Aleksandrow, however, the *III./"T"* managed to hold off the assaults of the Guards 76th infantry division. The day took a terrible toll on the forces: the ranks of the grenadier companies, already thinned, had melted like snow in the sun. However, the division had destroyed twelve Soviet tanks and inflicted such heavy losses on the attackers that on the following day they were far less aggressive. On August 12, the Soviets returned to the offensive with five divisions in the Rozopole sector and four more in the Josefow sector! The grenadiers succeeded in stopping the Soviet advance after losing a lot of ground. The next day the Soviets continued their offensive under the rain, supported by 230 batteries. Despite their immense statistical and material superiority, they were pushed back everywhere: their head-on and unimaginative assaults were blocked by accurate fire from the *IV.SS-Pz.Korps* and by panzer counter-attacks. In five days of combat, the *IV.SS-Pz.Korps* lost 5000 men. But the Soviet offensive was marking time. With fourteen divisions amassed on a front 9 miles (14 km) wide against two armored SS divisions, the Soviets had been unable to reach the Vistule. When this titanic battle came to an end, the *Totenkopf* were completely worn out. On **October 27**, the AOK 9 ordered the *Totenkopf* to retreat on the "Fuchs-Stellung" (Jablonna - Chotomow - Szybalin). This retreat marked the end of the third battle for Warsaw. From **October 10 to 28**, the *IV.SS-Pz.Korps* claimed the destruction of 138 tanks, and 164 guns and artillery pieces. The Soviets lost between 30 000 and 35 000

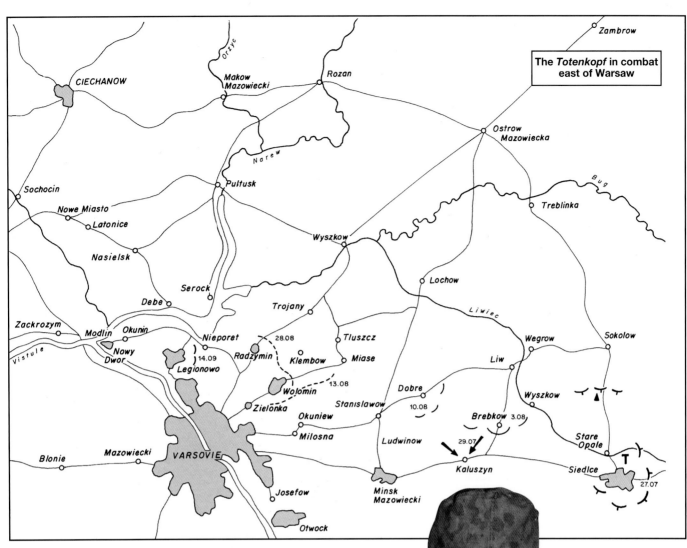

The *Totenkopf* in combat east of Warsaw

men. The *Totenkopf* had lost 6 *Pzkpfw.IVs,* 12 *Pzkpfw.V Panthers* and 9 *StuG.IIIs.* All that remained were 12 *Pzkpfw.IVs,* 8 *Pzkpfw.V Panthers,* 6 *Pzkpfw.VI Tigers,* 14 *StuG.IIsl* and 12 *Jg.Pz.IVs.* The *Totenkopf* did not change position until December 3. From this date on, the division started to be relieved by the *"Wiking"* division and was transferred to the Nasielk - Plonsk - Zichenau sector, to be placed in reserve of the *2.Armee.* A brief overhaul was carried out.

Four pocket jacket model 44 with "pea-pattern" camouflage. (Private collection.)

This is Hermann Buchner's grave as it could be seen just after his burial. His numerous and prestigious medals have been placed under the cross. During the early stages of the war, SS soldiers tended to be buried under the Tyr rune rather than the cross, a Christian symbol. (Courtesy Martin Månsson)

371

SS-Unterscharführer of the division in "pea pattern" M-1944 uniform. He wears the Demjansk badge on his left sleeve. (Private collection.)

1

2

1. The first elements of the *Totenkopf* to reach the border between Bielorussia and Poland are under the command of Erich Eberhardt, shown here while serving as chief of staff of division *"Prinz Eugen"*. (NA)

2. The *Totenkopf* mission is to secure the front line along the Niemen in the Grodno sector. An SS soldier in conversation with a Bielorussian peasant. He wears a camouflaged jacket of a non standard pattern, maybe the work of the divisional tailors. (NA)

3 and **4.** The *Totenkopf* strength has been renewed with very young recruits mostly from *SS-Pz.Gren.Ausb.-u.-Ers.-Btl. 3* based in Warsaw. *SS-IG.Ausb.-u.Ers.-Abt.1* from Breslau contributes with a few dozens soldiers seen here during instruction with an *le.IG18* 75mm infantry gun. (NA)

3

4

The *Totenkopf* is the only SS division to keep its *Tiger* tank company. Those of the *Leibstandarte* and of the *Das Reich* have both been transformed into independant battalions for service in *I.* and *II.SS-Pz.Korps*. The *Tigers* of the *Totenkopf* will demonstrate exceptional longevity since they will be in action until April 1945 whereas production of the *Pzkpfw.VI Ausf.E "Tiger"* had ended in May 1944 ! (NA)

This *Tiger* lies in a ditch after running off the road. This sort of incident was not exceptional because of insufficient training of the drivers and high fatigue levels. (Private collection.)

As the Soviets enjoy near absolute control of the skies over the central front, *Flak* has a particular importance. This 37mm gun is well camouflaged with foliage which is typical of 1944. (NA)

I./SS-Pz.Rgt.3 : instruction and combat

Contrary to what has been written in many books, *Panthers* were delivered to the *Totenkopf* only in January 1944 and *I./SS-PzRgt.3* was not sent to combat until July. Because of slow deliveries, *SS-Pz.Rgt.3* is equipped with *Panther A* as well as G models. 4 tanks were delivered on 13 January 1944, 6 on 3 March 1944 along with 2 *Bergepanther* and 7 in April. In May, 12 *Panther* of the battalion are transferred to another unit. There are only 5 tanks left for instruction. Deliveries are resumed on 8 June (5 tanks) and speed up from the middle of the month (13 tanks on 17 June and 54 on 25 June).

Training on the new tanks. At full speed (roadspeed 46 km/h, offroad 24 km/h), this tank kicks up an awful lot of dust. (Private collection.)

Battalion NCOs. They are all recipients of the iron cross second class and at least three of them wear the iron cross first class. (Private collection.)

1, 2 et **3.** The *Panther* is rightly considered as the best German tank of the second world war since it combined firepower, mobility and protection. The 75mm *KwK 42 L/70* was nearly as efficient as the 88mm gun on the *Tiger I Ausf.E*. Its well-sloped armour was 80mm thick at the glacis and 110mm thick at the mantlet. Wide tracks, an advanced suspension system and its powerful 700 hp *Maybach HL230P 30V-12* engine ensured remarkable mobility. Its main weakness was laying in its unreliable gearbox. It was a redoutable adversary for Allied tanks. The Americans considered that 5 *Sherman* tanks were required to destroy a single *Panther*.

4

3

4. The *Totenkopf* is now confined to a defensive role. Assault guns like the *StuG.III* shown here are extremely useful thanks to their very low profile despite insufficient firepower when facing the new soviet heavy tanks. (NA)

5. Familiar photograph of a *Pzkpfw.IV Ausf.J* of *SS-Pz.Rgt.3* which has never been as yet correctly captioned. From the rest of the photographs in the same sequence, we know that this shot was taken during maintenance at the rear of the front in Poland which explains the cover on the gun muzzle. (NA)

5

1. Karl Ullrich, left, and his *Regiment-Adjutant*, *SS-Hstuf*. Rolf Ditzenbach. (Private collection.)

2. Soviet air force has gained complete supremacy of the skies. This 37mm gun crew has shot down a few of them as shown by the kill markings around the gun tube. (Private collection.)

3. Erwin Meierdress is the commander of the *Panther* battalion of the division. He is a daring leader but lacks tactical nous which has lead to heavy losses. (*Berliner Illustrierte Zeitung*, 17 august 1944 issue)

4. HQ of *IV.SS-Pz.Korps* during a visit by Walter Model. *SS-Ostuf.* Steinecke (first orderly officer of the *Totenkopf*), *SS-Obf.* Becker (commander of the *Totenkopf*), *SS-Gruf.* Gille (commander, *IV.SS-Pz.Korps*) and an unidentified *SS-Stubaf.*. (Private collection)

5. Grenadiers are crammed in this schwere *Einheits-Pkw. Kfz.18*, proof of a lack of motorised vehicles. (*Das schwarze Korps*, 10 August 1944 issue.)

1, 2, 3 and **4.** Until 1943 the *Totenkopf* was the hammer and now it has turned into an anvil. Its grenadiers spend their time preparing new defensive positions. Good spirits are de rigueur in the presence of the *Propaganda-Kompanie* photographer. Narew sector, automn 1944. (NA)

5. A battery of *Wespe* (105mm howitzers on *Pzkpfw.II* chassis) opens fire to stop yet another soviet attack. (NA)

6. *SS-Sturmbannführer* Adolf Pitschellis, shown here at Modlin at the end of 1944, kept a detailed journal of his experience during the war, extracts of which are present in this book. (Private collection.)

Photographs probably taken at the end of November or in early December. These *Panther* tanks were then kept in reserve in the Okunin sector.

1. Two *SS-Unterscharführer* in front of Erwin Meierdress's *Panther* coded "I01". Erwin Meierdress is the battalion commander. They are Georg Kasehage, left and Josef Hirsch. (Private collection.)

2. *SS-Uscha.* Söhrmann in front of "I01". Note the roughly painted camouflage and cross. (Private collection.)

3. "I01" during maintenance in a factory near the mouth of the Bug river, home of the headquarters of the maintenance unit. From left to right : *SS-Oscha.* Beetsch (*Chef I-Staffel I./SS-Pz.Rgt.3*), *SS-Uscha.* Hirsch and one *SS-Oscha.*. (Private collection.)

4. *SS-Uscha.* Söhrmann (*Panzerfunker* of the *Panther* "I01") wears the reversible parka over his black *Panzertruppen* uniform. This type of parka was introduced the preceding autumn.(Private collection.)

1

2

3

4

1. After repairs, « I01 » is driven under shelter to protect it from the attentions of soviet aircraft. (Private collection.)

2. *SS-Uscha.* Söhrmann, radio operator of "I01". (Private collection.)

3. "I01" crew member. He has taken the place of the radio operator who is sitting at the commander's cupola. (Private collection.)

4. "I02", the tank of the battalion *Adjutant, SS-Ostuf.* Richard Strobl. (Private collection.)

5. December 1944 : Hungary bound. The *Panther* are on flat cars, always a delicate situation when in open field. (Private collection.)

4

5

Poland, summer 1944. Interesting picture of the staff of an unidentified battalion from the division. Men are scrutinizing terrain with binoculars. The unit is about to move into action. (MNZS)

SS-Stubaf. Fritz Eckert (*Kdr. II./"Eicke"*) is holding a courier a message. According to Karl Ullrich, his direct superior, Eckert is "conscientious, honest, precise and frank. He's a man of sound morals, slender, tenacious and persevering. He skilfully carries out his functions as battalion commander. He's got good results. A self-confident and beyond reproach officer. Liked by his comrades. Good behaviour when out of service. A good national-socialist who communicates it convincingly." (MNZS)

Trucks are dropping off grenadiers in the gathering zone. Notice the heterogeneous outfits: M43 and M44 tunics, camouflaged overalls, heavy cotton jacket (far left), laced boots, low boots, helmets with or without covers, peak visor cap… (MNZS)

A column leaves to reach its start positions. Men are heavily loaded. Marching like this under the sun and on such a sandy ground is exhausting. (MNZS)

These grenadiers are miming assault for the photographer, judging by the lax behaviour of men in the background. It's a shame, as the situation was both plausible and spectacular! (MNZS)

A young grenadier consults his *Gruppenführer* before the attack. The soldiers bear boots while *Grenadiere*, in this period of the war, are equipped of brodequins. Maybe are they *Pioniere*? (MNZS)

Left: A barn is burning, men are running for shelter. It's summer 1944, and the *Totenkopf* is sent from one spot to another on a front where breaches open on various sectors. (MNZS)

These soldiers are crossing a road on a seemingly deserted village. Given the smoke misting over the landscape in the background, there was combat here. (MNZS)

391

Above: The soldier of the opposite picture has set his *MG-34* on a destroyed *Zis-3* gun. It is probably an awkward reconstitution for the photographer, as the machine gun is pointing at the German lines... More interesting are the men's camouflaged overalls. (MNZS)

Opposite: A machine gun server is preparing a cartridge belt in expectation of the battle to come. The presence of a doll in the back of the vehicle adds an eccentric touch! (MNZS)

Below: A Soviet base of operations has been crushed to silence. These men are passing by abandoned individual holes. Boxes of 76.2 mm shells can be seen on the foreground. (MNZS)

Junction with an unidentified armoured unit from the *Heer*. It might be elements from the *19.Panzerdivision* alongside which the *Totenkopf* fought in the Warsaw area. (MNZS)

Inspection of an abandoned Russian base of operation. It is remarkably camouflaged. The barrel on the left must belong to a 45 mm anti-tank gun. (MNZS)

Orders are received on the radio. It's July, and the outfits received in the springtime are still in good condition. (MNZS)

The crew of a 75 mm infantry gun *(le.IG18)* carefully camouflaged with straw. Notice the M44 outfits very common throughout the division. Grapes don't look so ripe! (MNZS)

1. *SS-Pz.Aufkl.-Abt.3* elements in the Siedlce area. You can make out the death's-head on the side of the *Schwimmwagen*. In the background is a seldom photographed armoured car, type *Sd.Kfz.233*, in service since 1941 and equipped with a 75 mm gun with a bore 24 calibres in length. (Rights reserved)

2. *Panther* tanks of the *I./SS-Pz.Rgt.3* staff moving towards the front. They are passing by an *Sd.Kfz.233* similar to the one shown on previous picture. (MNZS)

3. The man who took these pictures, *SS-PK* Grönert, is now focusing on the *Sd.Kfz.233* type: two of such vehicles are shown here. According to the KAN of a *Panzerdivision* type 1944, three *Sd.Kfz.233* (or ideally three *Sd.Kfz.234/3*) are theoretically granted to the divisional reconnaissance force staff company. (Rights reserved)

3

A heavily armed *Schwimm-wagen* (with *MG-42* and *Panzerfaust*) somewhere in a Polish wheat plain. The diversity of the men's outfits is an abiding feature of the division during summer 1944. (MNZS)

Judging by the type of weapon carried by the soldiers, this infantry column is getting ready to join a base of operations. The picture was taken on the Eastern Front, and the role of the air force isn't as important as in the west, where movements of troops must be carried much more carefully. (MNZS)

The divisional reconnaissance force and its *Schwimmwagen* are working here in cooperation with assault guns from the *SS-Pz.Jg.-Abt.3*. Strangely, one of them is still equipped with *Ostketten*, which are set in case of harsh climate. (MNZS)

This patrol has put its *Schwimmwagen* in the shelter of small locusts to watch the enemy. Notice the ten grenades hanging on the side of the vehicle. (MNZS)

1. *Totenkopf* infantrymen are going through an old forest. It was in a similar environment, in Sopockinie, that the Soviets had positioned many snipers on treetops. This kind of suicide mission had good results in terms of losses inflicted to the Germans… (MNZS)

2. A Sherman tank has been captured by some men from the *Totenkopf* who hastened to try it out. Throughout the war, the Americans and British delivered huge quantities of equipment and supplies to the Soviets. If allied tanks were much criticized by their Russian crews, however, jeeps, GMC trucks, and food were greatly appreciated. (Rights reserved)

3. A *T-34/85* has been destroyed in the sector of Siedlce. Grenadiers are examining it with curiosity, since this type of tank has only appeared lately on the battlefield. According to the writings on the turret, it belonged to a Guards unit. (Berliner Illustrierte Zeitung)

A *Pzkpfw.VI Ausf.E "Tiger"* from the *9.Kp./SS-Pz.Rgt.3* waiting in ambush under a tree, in firing position. On the 1st of July 1944, the division had 9 *Tiger* in working condition. On the 1st of August, there was only a single left, but seven were waiting to get repaired as soon as possible. (MNZS)

October 1944: the *Totenkopf* is engaged in fierce combats in the sector of Modlin. Here, a *Pzkpfw.V "Panther" Ausf.A* is coming across a few grenadiers wearing odd outfits. (VHA)

These soldiers are probably coming back from the front, as they look rather relieved than anxious, but that might be only an impression. Oddly enough, one of them is wearing two belts, while the other has a rough sheepskin jacket. (VHA)

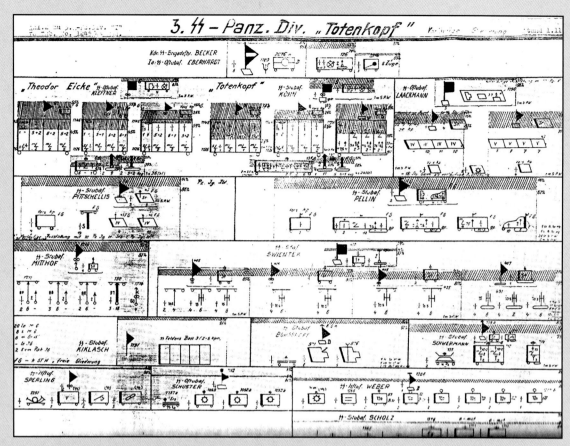

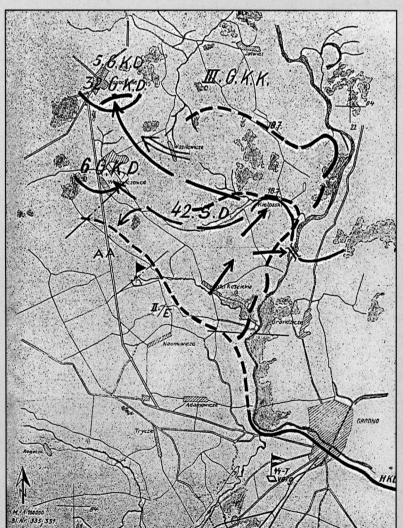

Opposite : fighting in Kielbasin (18 july 1944)
Below : fighting on the Niemen (16 July 1944)

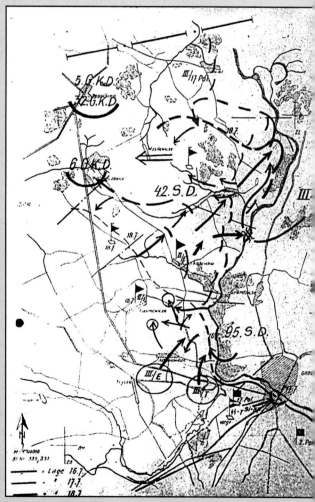

These panzergrenadiers are moving up front, perched on *Pzkpfw.IV* from the division.

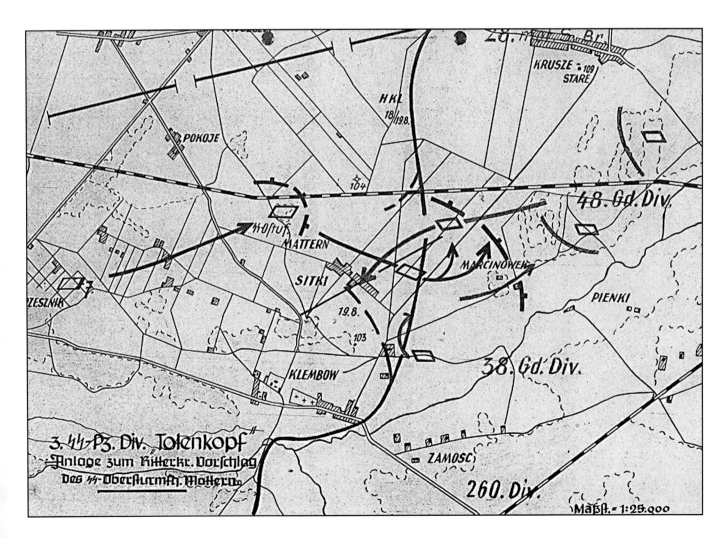

Fighting in Klembow

16

Attempted breakthroughs towards Budapest

Transfer to Hungary

On the **25th of December** 1944, *Totenkopf* and *Wiking* received order to rush to Hungary. For the last two days, the Soviet troops had been surrounding Budapest and its garrison. Hitler decided to transfer *IV.SS-Pz.Korps* there right away, contrary to the opinion of his generals, who were expecting a general offensive of the Soviets in Poland in the next few days. Opinions also differed regarding the place wherefrom the relief operation of Budapest should be launched. The Germans were hesitating between the north ("Konrad") and the south ("Paula") options. The first was ultimately chosen, even though the terrain wasn't favourable to a panzer deployment. The offensive was to start on the 1st of January 1945 at 7.30 pm. Moreover, *III.Pz.Korps* (Breith) was to carry out a diversion attack west of Szekesfehervar. Never had an offensive been launched with so little preparation and in so short a time: when the order to attack was given ? on the 30th of December for the 1st of January ? most units from *IV.SS-Pz.Korps* were still on their way, and some of them hadn't even left Poland! The Germans had to attack with hardly half of their full power, which was already smaller than the Soviets'. On the **28th of December**, the first convoys of *Totenkopf* started to arrive at Komarom. They had brought with them the reconnaissance, the *"Eicke"* regiment, and part of the armoured regiment. These units were at once subordinated to *6.Armee (Armeegruppe "Balck")*. In the evening of December **31st**, the *"Eicke"* regiment went off to fight and relieved a unit from the *"Feldherrnhalle"* division in Szöny. At midnight, artillery from *23.Panzerdivision* opened fire north-east of Berhida, about 80 km south of positions occupied by *Totenkopf*. *Korpsgruppe "Breith" (III.Pz.Korps)* was the one to launch a diversion attack. On the **1st of January 1945**, the arrival of *IV.SS-Pz.Korps* south of the Danube went unnoticed by the Soviets, thanks to a low ceiling preventing reconnaissance flights. The *Totenkopf*'s objective was to seize Dunalmaas, a town built on the Danube's south bank, and then to carry on along the river to link up with the bridgehead *96.ID* was to set further east.

The first two attempts to free Budapest

On the 1st of January, at 7.30 pm sharp, *IV.SS-Pz.Korps* moved into attack between Tavaros and the Danube. Grenadiers from *Totenkopf* quickly reached the south edge of Dunalmaas. The next day at 5 am, divisional artillery opened fire and the armoured regiment came to back up the attack. The city was forcefully defended and the SS progressed slowly as far as the church, before being stopped by intense Soviet fire. Several panzers were lost and the division mourned the death of *SS-Stubaf.* Meierdress, one of its most experienced officers. It was then decided to skirt round the city from south, and to reach the road set along the Danube near Neszmely. Aware that they were being taken from the rear, Soviet troops in Dunalmaas ran away. The city was cleaned up in no time: grenadiers and panzers then

rushed east and managed to make contact with *96.ID* infantrymen in Sütto. At around noon, junction was made with the second bridgehead set on the Danube by *96.ID* in Nyerges Ujfalu. There, the SS destroyed several Russian tanks before moving on towards Bajot. But just as the Germans had dreaded, terrain wasn't fit at all anymore for a tank raid. The icy road which meandered through the mountain was hard to negotiate for panzers. Grenadiers had to fight on their own, but still managed to take Bajot. *Totenkopf* launched into attack again on the night of **January 2nd**: *Gruppe "Eicke"* seized Bajna and captured 14 guns there. But the Soviets started reacting by sending fresh troops to the sector of Bicske. In the afternoon of January 3rd, they counterattacked towards Bajna and Nagysap. There were high losses in both camps and among civilians. On the **4th of January**, *IV.SS-Pz.Korps* carried on its offensive. Each new day made it more difficult for the Germans, as the Soviets were throwing all available forces into the battle. In spite of everything, *Gruppe "Eicke"* managed to break through the anti-tank barrage east of Bajna. On the left flank, *SS-Pz.Aufkl.-Abt.3* took Savisap, after being shot at by the inhabitants, most of them of Czech origin. The Hungarians in the area called this town "little Moscow". In its report, *Totenkopf* stated that the population was "evacuated" afterwards, without more explanations. On the **5th of January**, *Totenkopf* assault groups kept on progressing towards south-east and arrived at Szomor. SS grenadiers then tried to seize the town in a single raid, taking advantage of the morning mist. It only resulted in a deadly fiasco: the road to the village was covered with German casualties, caught out by the defenders' machine gun fire. *SS-Pz.Rgt.3* was called for help. A terrible tank battle started northwest of Szomor, where 45 *T-34* had been spotted. Soviet resistance finally collapsed late in the afternoon, but there were far too many losses for so little terrain won. On the next day, *Totenkopf* resumed its attack southeast towards Zsambek. The heights ahead of the town were spiked with anti-tank guns and buried tanks. This time, in spite of all its efforts, the division couldn't move any further. Soviet resistance gathered momentum as *IV.SS-Pz.Korps* got closer to Budapest. On the 8th, *Totenkopf* settled as defence before Many, Zsambek and Kirva. Operation *"Konrad"* was definitely abandoned. *"Konrad 2"* was to follow in its wake. This time the aim was to attack simultaneously from mounts Pilis with *5.SS-Panzerdivision "Wiking"*, *711.ID* and *96.ID*, and from the sector Mor - Varpalota with *III.Pz.Korps*. *"Konrad 2"* was launched as early as on the 9th of January, and ended with yet another failure.

"Konrad 3"

On the **13th of January**, *IV.SS-Pz.Korps* received order to reach the sector north-east of Veszprem. This time the operation aimed at trying to release Budapest by attacking south of Szekesfehervar, and then moving up towards the Hungarian capital east of Lake Velencze. In fact, it truly was the south option (operation *"Paula"*), which had been rejected on the

Army corps general Wöhler is the leader of army group "south" in Hungary. Although undeniably a skilled tactician, he cannot turn the tide of events. (Rights reserved)

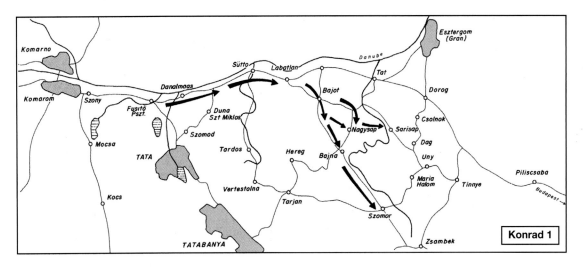

Konrad 1

Boris Kraas, artillery gunner turned tank hunter. He is the brother of Hugo Kraas, who was then the commander of *12.SS-Panzerdivision "Hitlerjugend"*. (J. Charita collect.)

28th of December by the German staff, only to come back later under the name of *"Konrad 3"*. *IV.SS-Pz.Korps* moved into attack on the **18th of January** at 4.30 am, between Lake Balaton and Csor. On the right flank, *Kampfgruppe "Eckert"* managed to break through the Soviet lines and to reach canal Sarviz, 17 kilometres away from its start positions, south of Tacz. *Kampfgruppe "Kraas"* crossed canal Sarviz on the railway bridge north-east of Szabadbattyan. It allowed it to take from the rear the Soviet troops fighting north-east of Tacz and to inflict very heavy losses on them. On the left flank, *Kampfgruppe "Kleffner"* took Jenö after violent street fights and, north of the town, *III./"TE"* managed to go on as far as Falubattyan. On the **20th of January**, *Kampfgruppe "Eckert"* resumed its advance before meeting with a

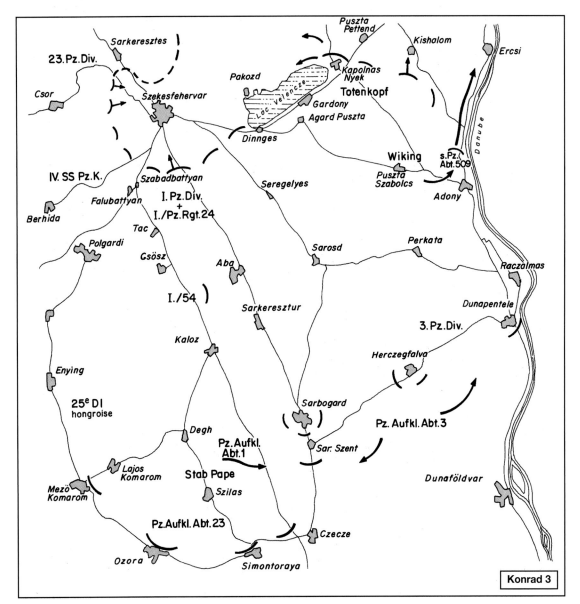

Konrad 3

405

Strange vehicle: it seems an 2.8cm anti-tank gun has been mounted on a *Sd.Kfz. 250/9*, normally equipped with a 2cm gun. The anti-tank version of this semi-tracked vehicle is the *Sd.Kfz. 250/11*. The soldier on the right is wearing a hood. (NA)

Adolf Pittschellis is another who will find his death on the Hungarian front. Hungary will be the grave of the division. (Rights reserved)

strong resistance before Seregelyes. The Soviets let the grenadiers come very close to their position and then opened fire at point-blank range on the assailants, who were caught up in deep snow. The *Totenkopf* armoured force couldn't help them, as it was itself stuck in swamps south-west of the town. At about noon, *Kampfgruppe "Eckert"* tried again to seize Seregelyes, this time from the south, while the reconnaissance battalion and Boris Krass' anti-tank battalion attacked north of the town. Soviet resistance was smashed at about 3.40 pm. *Kampfgruppe "Eckert"* then chased after the Soviets elements fleeing north-east. Meanwhile, the *Totenkopf* armored force (*SS-Kampfgruppe "Pittschellis"*) reached Dinnyes and rushed along the south bank of Lake Velencze towards Gardony. There, it only met with feeble resistance. On the **21st**, *SS-Pz.Aufkl.-Abt.3* succeeded in reaching the sector of Vali. But German hopes were short-lived. As a matter of fact, the 5th Guards cavalry corps had settled down in the meantime on the heights north of the river: all the attempts at setting a bridgehead were crushed with awful losses for the assailants. On the **22nd of January**, *SS-Pz.Aufkl.-Abt.3* and *s.Pz.Abt.509* tried again to cross the Vali, this time in the sector of Kishalom. But the Soviets were now launching new forces into battle, and the German offensive marked time. On the 24th, *IV.SS-Pz.Korps* tried once more to cross the Vali, beyond which the Soviets had set a solid defensive network stretching over deep. Kishalom and Nagyhalom were seized but faced with the Soviet 2nd Guards mechanised corps and 5th cavalry corps, further advance now seemed impossible. The attack resumed on the night of the 25th. Fierce resistance from the 4th Guards army made progress difficult. Several panzers were thus the victims of the anti-tank front set around Pettend. However, a breach was opened in the opposing defence system. Although it had broken deeply into the Russian lines, *Totenkopf* had to bury itself on acquired positions to protect itself against rough enemy counterattacks. This "thimble" stuck towards Val along the Vali's south bank proved itself particularly difficult to defend. Indeed, there were only 3 tanks and 3 assault guns left in working order and the division had to face an entire Soviet armoured corps. The next day, the Soviets launched a powerful counterattack against the *Armeegruppe "Balck"*'s south flank between canal Sarviz and the Danube. More than a hundred tanks rushed against the *IV.SS-Pz.Korps'* north flank

between Vereb and Val. The German front was falling apart. The situation became so critical that *Heeresgruppe "Süd"* ordered the end of "Konrad 3". In late afternoon, *Totenkopf* announced the destruction of 110 Soviet tanks between Lake Velencze and the Vali. But losses were also considerable among its own ranks. In the evening, it received order to withdraw to the line Baracska - Pettend - Kapolnas Nyek. This withdrawal meant the end of hope for the Budapest garrison, which was now abandoned to its fate.

January 1945. *SS-Ostuf.* Seehaus (Chef of *SS-Div.-Begleit-Kp.3*) and an officer from the *Heer*. (Private Collection)

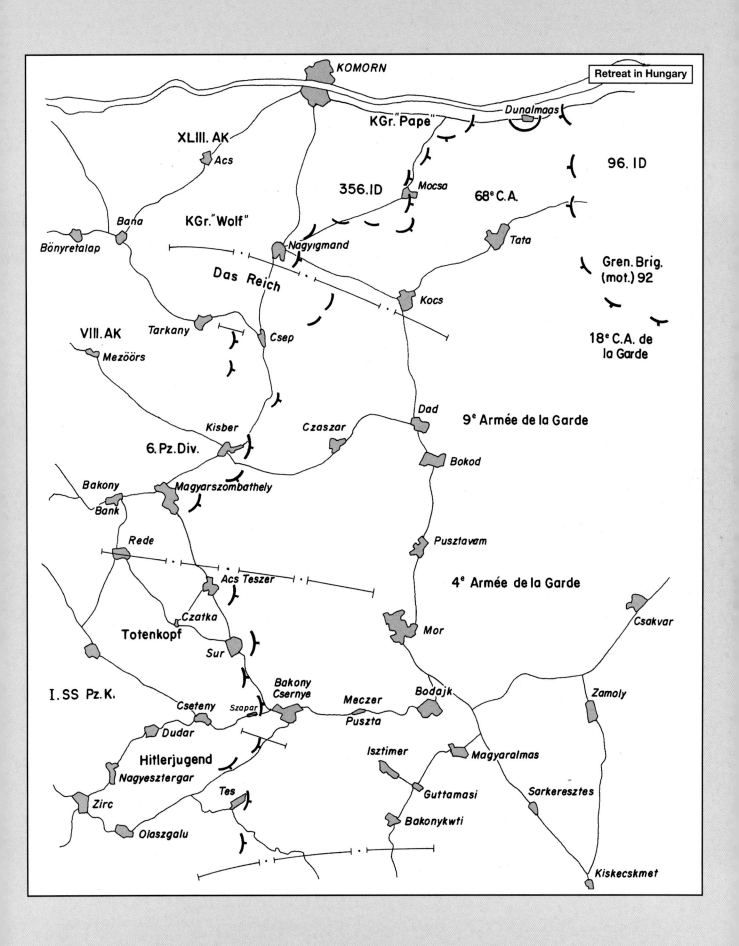

KOMORN

XLIII. AK

Acs

KGr."Pape"

Dunalmaas

96. ID

356. ID

Mocsa

68ᵉ C.A.

Bana

KGr."Wolf"

Tata

Bönyretalap

Nagyigmand

Gren. Brig.
(mot.) 92

Das Reich

Kocs

VIII. AK

Tarkany

Csep

18ᵉ C.A. de
la Garde

Mezöörs

Kisber

Czaszar

Dad

9ᵉ Armée de la Garde

6. Pz. Div.

Bokod

Bakony

Magyarszombathely

Bank

Rede

Pusztavam

Acs Teszer

4ᵉ Armée de la Garde

Czatka

Csakvar

Totenkopf

Sur

Mor

I. SS Pz. K.

Bakony
Csernye

Meczer

Bodajk

Zamoly

Cseteny

Szapar

Puszta

Dudar

Hitlerjugend

Isztimer

Magyaralmas

Nagyesztergar

Tes

Sarkeresztes

Zirc

Guttamasi

Olaszgalu

Bakonykwti

Kiskecskmet

Retreat in Hungary

<table><tr><td>17</td><td></td></tr></table>

The last battles

General der Panzertruppen Hermann Balck had a particularly strained relationship with the chiefs of the SS divisions under his command. (All rights reserved)

Retreat towards Szekesfehervar

On the **28th of January**, after breaking deep into the front between the Sarviz canal and the Danube, the Soviets moved up north in large numbers, thus threatening the *IV.SS-Pz.Korps*' rear. They tried to repel the Germans far away from the Danube by focusing most of their efforts on the sector of Vali. On the **31st**, the Russians directed their efforts on Szekesfehervar and drove *356.ID* from the field. Aware of this new danger looming over its whole army, *Armeegruppe "Balck"* decided right away to engage in this critical sector a *Kampfgruppe* from *Totenkopf*, reinforced by *s.Pz.Abt.509*, *Werfer-Brigade 17* and the battalion from *Volksartillerie-Korps 403* still fighting within the *IV.SS-Pz.Korps*. It is worth noting that from the 1st to the 31st of January, *Totenkopf* had 813 men killed, 3300 injured and 237 missing. Throughout the same period, it reported the destruction or capture of 387 tanks, 792 guns and 832 various vehicles.

In the evening of February 1st, regiment "*Eicke*" was already fighting north of Szekesfehervar. It managed to repel several Russian attacks thanks to the efficient backup of twenty "*Panther*" tanks from *I./Pz.Rgt.24*. But the situation took a turn for the worse during the following afternoon: the Soviets managed to cut the road Szekesfehervar - Seregelyes. A counterattack was launched on the **3rd of February**, but the Soviets were hanging on strong to terrain, and the *Totenkopf*'s south flank showed worrying weaknesses. The next day, *SS-Brigaf.* Becker decided to send *Kampfgruppe "Kleffner"* towards the road to Mor, to attack on the flank the Soviet troops defending the road to Zamoly. A terrible battle started: the Soviets lost 38 tanks, 50 anti-tank guns and 40 trucks. But in the evening, *IV.SS-Pz.Korps*, which thought itself victorious, had to give up *s.Pz.Abt.509*, *SS-Regiment "Ney"*, *I./Pz.Rgt.24* and *1.Panzerdivision* to *III.Pz.Korps* after a Soviet breakthrough south of Lake Velencze! Thus it had to put itself on the defensive the next day. Besides, there were such losses that the dead and injured had to be replaced by untrained men. Consequently, *III./"T"* was given to *SS-Hstuf.* Korsemann, a former police general degraded for cowardice when facing the enemy, who only had a tiny experience on the front. Fortunately for *Totenkopf*, it was enjoying a period of relative calm in its sector of the front. By the **13th of February**, its strength was: 294 officers, 2492 NCOs and 8984 privates. On the **19th of February**, *SS-Stubaf.* Kühn took command of the "*Totenkopf*" regiment. It had just been reinforced with new recruits from the *Luftwaffe* and the *Kriegsmarine*. A handful of survivors from "*Florian Geyer*" and "*Maria Theresia*" cavalry regiments also joined its ranks. On the **6th of March**, *6.Panzerarmee* (*He.Gr. "Süd"*) and *2.Panzerarmee* (*OB "Südost"*) moved into offensive (operation "*Frühlingserwachen*") unequalled resources on the Eastern front since the battle of Kursk. However, at *IV.SS-Pz.Korps* headquarters, optimists were few and far between: they had to give up the main part of their artillery to support the operation, while the Soviets had more than 120 batteries between

Szekesfehervar and Zamoly! On the **11th of March**, while *Frühlingserwachen* was sinking – both literally and metaphorically – the division had 16 *Pzkpfw.IV*, 8 *Pzkpfw.V "Panther"*, 7 *Pzkpfw.VI "Tiger"*, 5 *Jg.Pz.IV* and 17 *StuG.III*, which made a total of 53 tanks in working order. Tank hunters and assault guns were still gathered within *SS-Pz.Jg.-Abt.3*, which was strangely entrusted to *SS-Stubaf.* Ludwig Zeitz, an officer from "*Kama*" division, who had no experience of armour whatsœver. During the following days, *IV.SS-Pz.Korps* units reported large gatherings of Soviet troops before their lines. Aware of the danger looming over the *6.Panzerarmee*'s rear, *Armeegruppe "Balck"*'s staff planned to send reinforcements to *IV.SS-Pz.Korps*, but these weren't to reach the sector of Zamoly before four days, even though the Soviet offensive was expected for the morrow!

Defeat in Hungary

On the **16th of March**, as *IV.SS-Pz.Korps* had feared, the Soviets launched their big counteroffensive north of Lake Velencze. The centre of gravity of the attack was somewhere between the 8th Hungarian corps and *Totenkopf*. On these thirty kilometres of front, the 9th Guards army and the 4th Guards army lined up respectively 180 and 170 guns and rocket launchers per kilometre. Within. *IV.SS-Pz.Korps*, losses were appalling. *SS-Ostubaf.* Franz Kleffner was killed inside his *SPW*, shot at full blast by a shell. Thanks to the involvement of all heavy weapons, artillery and tanks, the Soviet assault was more or less contained in the afternoon. But on the left, as the Germans had feared, Hungarian troops scattered. *II./"T"* found itself outflanked from all sides. Its commander, *SS-Hstuf.* Bachmann, was killed. The battalion, except for its 5th company, was hacked to pieces. The next day, the Soviets resumed their offensive between Szekesfehervar and the south of mounts Vertes. Everywhere, breaches opened that *Totenkopf* couldn't possibly seal anymore. Söred and Magyaralmas were lost. German High Command reacted at last in the evening by ordering *I.SS-Pz.Korps* to counterattack towards Zamoly. This order put an end to *Frühlingserwachen*. On the **18th of March**, the Soviets managed to break the contact between *Wiking* and *Totenkopf* north-west of Szekesfehervar. German resistance was starting to weaken, and losses were disastrous. *SS-Flak-Abt.3* lost its commander, *SS-Stubaf.* Mitthof, killed in Guttamasi. The anti-tank battalion was annihilated and all its officers, except *SS-Stubaf.* Zeitz, were killed or shot themselves in the brain to avoid falling alive into Russian hands. On the **19th of March**, between Szekesfehervar and the Vertes mountains, the Germans and the Hungarians were inexorably repelled westwards. The 6th Guards armoured army moved into offensive with its 425 tanks and assault guns against the *Totenkopf*'s positions! Its mission was to enlarge the breach between Berhida and Veszprem, and to annihilate, alongside the 26th and 27th armies, the German forces that were still south of Lakes Balaton and Velencze. For the *Totenkopf*'s men, the clash was hellish. Some of the division's units were lost with all hands in the battle. In no time did the Soviets occupy the positions that had been planned for the *I.SS-Pz.Korps*' counterattack, whose success was thus compromised before its very start! On the **20th of March**, battle reached its climax. Launching quantities of tanks and countless infantry against the *Heeresgruppe* Süd's south and north flanks, the Soviets tried to cut it off from its rear. The next day, *Totenkopf* was subordinated to *I.SS-Pz.Korps*, that was now fighting between Varpalota, in the south, and Sur, in the north. Soon before midday, Varpalota finally fell into Soviet hands. Men from *Totenkopf* and *Leibstandarte* tried to set a new defensive line a bit further south, against the attacks of three fusilier divisions. Further north, the situation was even trickier for the Germans: there was a large breach between *I.* and *II.SS-Pz.Korps* wherefrom some Soviet motorised units were rushing in. Between Sur and Kisber, only a few elements from *Totenkopf* and *SS-Rgt. "Ney"* were putting up a genuine resistance. On the **23rd of March**, Soviet troops broke effortlessly through the lines of *I.SS-Pz.Korps*, whose divisions all fought for their lives. Veszprem fell. The *Totenkopf*'s survivors withdrew to the forest of Bakony, towards Papa. It seemed then that *SS-Brigaf.* Becker's staff had most difficulty to run its units, that had been scattered by the Soviet offensive and were now retreating without any contact with one another. There were no such things as regiments of battalions anymore: they were all reduced to some mere *Kampfgruppen*. The division had virtually ceased to exist as an organised unit. With the seizing of Szekesfehervar and Veszprem, the Soviets ended the first phase of their offensive towards Vienna. In the evening of **March 25th**, *6.Panzerarmee* decided to withdraw along canal Marczal and behind the river Raba, an affluent of the Danube, because the breach separating it from *6.Armee* could not be sealed. *Totenkopf* settled there the next day as well as it could. In the afternoon of the **27th**, the Soviets tried repeatedly to cross the Raba between Vag and the bridgehead in Marczaltö, but were repelled each time by the *Totenkopf*'s men. These few defensive achievements were only delaying an inescapable fate. On the *I.SS-Pz.Korps*' right flank, the Soviets managed to cross the river with powerful motorised armoured units. On the 28th, the Soviets threatened the *Totenkopf*'s rear from their bridgehead in Morichida. *I.SS-Pz.Korps* ordered right away desertion of the *"Susannen-Stellung"* and withdrawal beyond the sector of Rabnitz - Repcze. On the **29th of March**, Soviet troops crossed the Rabnitz, passed Klostermarienberg and rushed towards Oberpullendorf, thus reaching the *Reichsschutzstellung*, a fortified line stretching along the Austrian border. They were now at the Viennese basin's gates! On the **30th of March**, *Totenkopf* was assailed west of Csapod by forty tanks or so. There was no other choice but to withdraw westwards.

The last battles in Austria

On the **31st of March**, breach driving *6.Armee* and *6.(SS-)Panzerarmee* apart was now stretching from Rechnitz to Mattersburg, that is to say for more than fifty kilometres. The bulk of *Totenkopf* withdrew on the *Reichsschutzstellung*, between Holling and Grosszinkendorf. *SS-Brigaf.* Becker undertook right away to refit *SS-Pz.Rgt.3*: 1st battalion, which had not a single officer left, was dissolved and its men transferred to the 2nd battalion. *SS-Stubaf.* Anton Berlin then took the head of what was left of the regiment. In late morning, the 1st Guards mechanised corps moved into attack behind a firestorm, and broke through the division's lines in Holling. But Soviet tanks must then pause momentarily to wait for the infantry from the 20th Guards fusilier corps. This hitch allowed *Totenkopf* to withdraw in proper order to the western bank of the Neusiedler-See and to Sopron. At 8.20 pm, the *6.SS-Panzerarmee*'s 1st staff officer announced to *Heeresgruppe "Süd"* that *Totenkopf* was assailed by sixty Soviet tanks or so. The next day, the Soviets crossed the Reich's border. A few elements from *Totenkopf* were still fighting to slow down Soviet progress while some isolated groups were withdrawing towards mounts Leitha. On the **2nd of April**, what was left of the division (25% of its theoretical strength) was joined to *II.SS-Pz.Korps* in the sector of Eisenstadt. Its survivors tried in vain to set a boundary line between Donnerskirchen and Gramatneusiedl. It was quickly shattered by the Soviet troops' assaults. These were now only fifty kilometres or so away from Vienna. Wiener Neustadt fell almost without fighting. On the other hand, the Austrian capital would be defended, as claimed on the radio Gauleiter von Schirach, the Reich Defence Commissioner. Public notices summoning women and children to leave the city were put up walls. Cavalry general von Bünau was entrusted the defence of the Habsburgs' city. As for the Soviets, they spread the word that the Red Army was not fighting against the Austrian people but against German occupying forces. And a group of Viennese resistance fighters promised the armed uprising of the population against the Germans…

On the **4th of April**, the 3rd Ukrainian Front took Baden and thus got itself an ideal base of operations to surround Vienna from south and west. In the sector of Margarethen am Moos, elements from *SS-Pz.Gren.Rgt.5 "T"* succeeded in setting up a counterattack and taking Rauchenwarth back for a few hours. They also repelled some Russian tanks backed up by women soldiers before Götzendorf, thus winning a short break for the rest of the division, which withdrew in late afternoon towards river Fischa. On the 6th of April, the 3rd Ukrainian Front launched its final assault on Vienna. Starting at 7.30 am, a massive artillery pounding fell on German defenders. The 20th Guards fusilier corps broke through the *Totenkopf*'s lines in Schwechat, thereby cutting the road to Vienna for the division's *Kampfgruppen* facing the 46th Soviet army. These had to make their way along the Danube towards the Prater. Some groups remained isolated on the river's southern bank, where they were to be quickly annihilated. The 5th Guards airborne division drove *Kampfgruppe "Kühn"* from the field level with central cemetery and reached the Simmering-Hauptstrasse at around noon. Attacked by twelve tanks, Max Kühn's men destroyed ten with their *Panzerfaust*. The pleas of the injured who were asking the Viennese for help or shelter went unanswered. Those who were thirsty weren't given as much as a glass of water either: the Austrians' enthusiasm for Greater Germany and its soldiers now belonged to the past. On the following days, battles carried on relentlessly in Vienna. In a report, *Heeresgruppe "Süd"* informed *OKH* that *"defensive battles are made even more difficult because of the Viennese population's significant support of the enemy. Civilians and some people wearing German uniforms are taking part in the battle, especially on the front's rear. Supplying in some sectors is thus jeopardized."* Attacks succeeded one another, making all the *Totenkopf*'s *Kampfgruppen* give in. These mostly fought without any contact with each other, just holding blocks of houses or isolated districts. Front wasn't continuous anymore. The Soviets used this opportunity to send tanks through breaches towards the city centre, forcing the Ger-

This *T-34/85* has been destroyed by a *Totenkopf Panzerknacker*. This shot has been taken by *SS-KB* Grönert during "Konrad 3". (Heimdal)

mans to counterattack in small groups, which only brought about more losses. *Totenkopf* was driven back northwards. On the **10th of April**, Vienna defenders were slowly repelled towards the Danube canal. *Totenkopf* set a new defensive line north of the Stadionbrücke to the Augartenbrücke. On the **12th of April**, the Soviets tried to crush the *II.SS-Pz.Korps'* units between the Danube canal and the river itself. Their vanguards were three hundred meters south of the Reichsbrücke. In the 2nd district, Russian troops managed to cross the canal and appeared unexpectedly behind the *SS* rear. Both sides fought for every house. Several Soviet tanks were destroyed with *Panzerfaust* but it was now useless. Outflanked from all sides, the *Totenkopf*'s *Kampfgruppen* were compelled to retreat. Once General Rendulic had agreed, the *6.SS-Panzerarmee*'s staff ordered that as many troops as possible should move to the Danube's north bank. *Totenkopf* escaped by the Reichsbrücke. North of the Danube, the situation wasn't better for the Germans. The 46th Soviet army had launched a raging offensive and taken Essling, at the expense of *Totenkopf* and *37.SS-Kavallerie-Division "Lützow"*. The battle of Vienna ended on the afternoon of **April 13th**. On the **15th**, the *Totenkopf*'s withdrawal along the Danube's banks was carried out, but cost them astounding losses. The Soviet shot on sight on the division's slow-moving columns, plunging it into a state of panic. Even the oldest soldiers had never seen such disaster. Vehicles and corpses lined the road in a macabre way. Those who managed to get across Soviet firewall gathered between Leobendorf and Stockerau.

On the **19th of April**, *Totenkopf* was put in charge of the sector going from Stockerau to Krems along the Danube's north bank. Front was very quiet. The main difficulty the division was confronted with was resupplying, which was carried out every other day because of petrol shortage.

On the **1st of May**, men heard about Hitler's death. There were still many Nazis within *Totenkopf*. The mood turned to despair. But discipline remained rigorous. Vehicles and weapons were still maintained, while officers set up drill again… On the **4th of May**, the division received order to form a defensive front on the west, facing the *XIIth US Corps*. *SS-Pz.Aufkl.-Abt.3* and *SS-Rgt. "T"* were thus engaged along the Danube, from Grein to Freistadt. On the **5th of May**, a *Kampfgruppe* from *III./ "TE"* gathered on Zell's marketplace. White flags had already been hoisted on windows for the imminent arrival of American troops. The SS opened fire on these signs of surrender. The atmosphere was heavy. At about noon, the first tanks from the *11th US Armored Division* were announced before the town coming from Pregarten. The *SS* then deployed themselves on either side of the church. Tanks reached the cemetery, where the first battle between the *Totenkopf* and the Americans began. An *SS* was killed. After one and a half hour, *Kampfgruppe* received order to disengage towards Pierbach and Königswiesen. On the **6th of May**, *Heeresgruppe "Süd"* (Rendulic) ordered its units not to resist the American troops anymore. As for *Totenkopf*, elements were still moving from the eastern to the western front, but contrary to instructions, the *SS* kept fighting against the Americans.

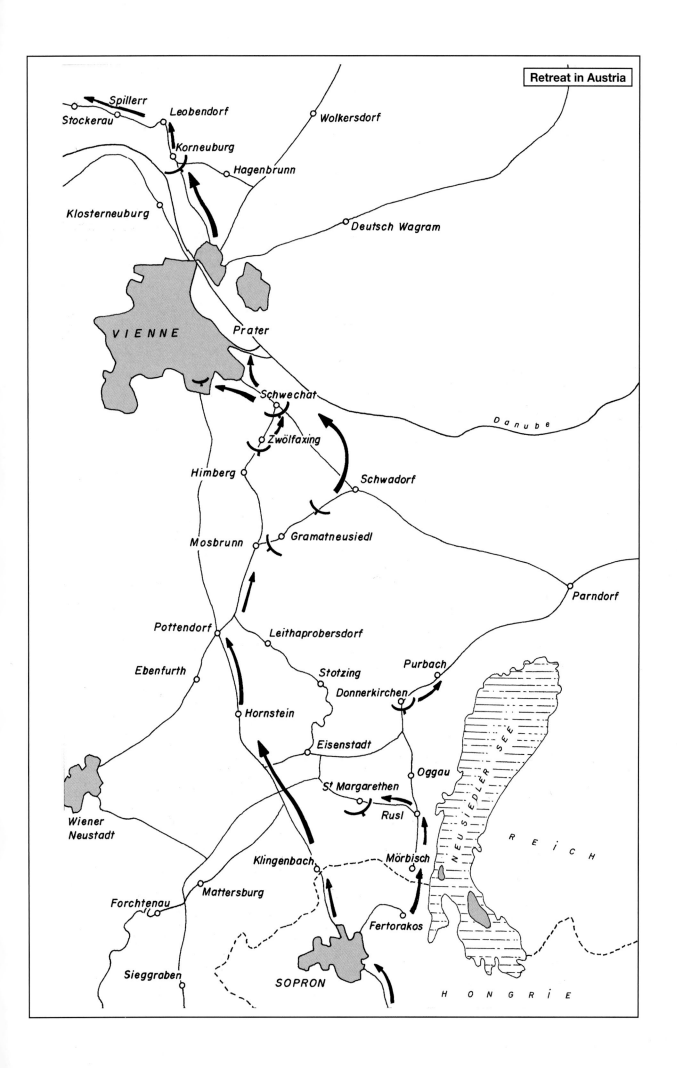

Retreat in Austria

The surrender

On the **7th of May**, at 2.41 am, *General* Jodl signed in Reims a draft agreement for the *Wehrmacht* surrender. It was to take effect from the 8th of May at 11 pm. From that very moment, the units were to remain where they were. During the day, *General* Rendulic went to the *3rd US Army3rd US Army*'s headquarters and got them to accept his troops' surrender, even though they had kept fighting relentlessly on the Eastern Front. At about 3 pm, one of the ministers of the new German government, Graf Schwerin von Krosigk, announced the surrender on the radio. The men's spirits couldn't have been lower. The only thing they could do now was to avoid falling into Soviet hands. Hellmuth Becker ordered the troops' immediate departure towards the Enns, which marked the demarcation line. On the **8th of May**, the bulk of the division arrived before the demarcation line at midnight exactly. The American orderlies refused to let them in! Soon enough, thousands of vehicles gathered along the road to Pregarten. Driven by despair and the obsessive fear of falling into Soviet hands, the SS forced the barricade but were stopped a few kilometres away by some tanks blocking the way. They were disarmed and packed in a valley where thousands of other soldiers from all sections soon joined them. Between 80 and 90% of *Totenkopf* had managed to cross the demarcation line. On the 14th of May, after being separated from the women who accompanied them, SS and *Wehrmacht* soldiers started marching in groups of five hundred, surrounded by tanks from the *11th US Armored Division.* From the start, American officers let them know that any man trying to escape would be shot down. The march quickly turned into a nightmare. Exhausted by the pace set by tanks and by the lack of food from previous days, many soldiers let themselves fall by the side of the road and were killed on the spot by American guards. Men reached Pregarten, where the population flung at them: *"The Russians are waiting for you!"* Indeed, three kilometres east of the city, a Soviet political officer, escorted by tanks driven by women soldiers, was roaring in a loudspeaker: *"None of you will ever go back!"* Most soldiers from the division were transported by boat to Odessa, where they were scattered among numerous prison camps. Some of them were only released in 1955. Others, less fortunate, never came back.

General der Kavallerie von Bünau run the Vienna garrison in April 1945.
(Rights reserved)

1. *5.SS-Panzerdivision "Wiking"* is fighting alongside *Totenkopf* during the battle of Szekesfehervar. Exhausted, its grenadiers have something to eat next to their shelters. (Guglielmi Collection)

2. A trench dug in the Hungarian plain. Notice how the men are still quite well-equipped for this time of the war. (Guglielmi Collection)

3. Franz Kleffner with members of his staff. At this period of the war, it may be wondered why he looks in such good mood! (Museum of Modern History in Ljubljana)

4. An infantry column from a *Heer* unit is going off to war somewhere in a district of Vienna devastated by artillery fire. (Guglielmi Collection)

1. A 20 mm anti-aircraft defence gun unlimbered close to the Lake Velencze's banks, in the crepuscular light of Hungarian winter. (NA)

2. Grenadiers in a trench flown over by Soviet planes. They are wearing the reversible winter outfit model 1943. Notice the hoods, worn over or under helmets. (Rights reserved)

3. Watching of enemy positions in the Puszta. (Guglielmi Collection)

4. A *Schwimmwagen* stuck in the mud in the Puszta. (Rights reserved)

Panzer IV of the *7./SS-Pz.Rgt.3* at the end of the year on 1944 in Hungary.

Return of patrol, during the first in the days of 1945 in Hungary. A wounded man is waiting his evacuation in the sled.

415

These two last photos give evidence of the division's employment in Hungary during the last month of the war. (See previous chapter).

SS-Infanterie-Regiment 9 « Thule⁽¹⁾ »

Textes/texts :
Charles Trang
Photos :
Martin Månsson

Naissance de l'unité

Le *SS-Sonder-Bataillon « Reitz »* est constitué le 24 juin 1940 à la caserne SS de Stralsund à partir du *III./SS-Totenkopf-Standarte 5*, de recrues nées en 1921 et 1922 et de cadres issus du *III./SS-Totenkopf-Rekruten-Standarte*. En outre, une section de canons d'infanterie est cédée par le régiment « *Germania* » et une section antichar par la *Leibstandarte SS « Adolf Hitler »* et la *SS-Verfügungsdivision*. Le 28 juin, le bataillon est rebaptisé *verstärktes SS-Totenkopf-Bataillon « Norwegen »*. Il comprend alors 13 officiers, 62 sous-officiers et 871 hommes de troupe (total : 946). De Stralsund, il est transféré à Stettin d'où il embarque pour la Norvège. Arrivé à Oslo, il rejoint Kirkenes, ville située sur le cercle polaire. Il est alors rebaptisé *SS-Totenkopf-Bataillon « Kirkenes »*. Il a pour mission d'assurer la protection du secteur Jacobselven - Tana. Le 23 août, il est décidé de former un deuxième bataillon et, avec le premier, de constituer ainsi un régiment. La nouvelle unité voit donc le jour le 1er septembre 1940 à Posen-Treskau. Elle est commandée par le SS-Sturmbannführer Herms*. Son personnel est essentiellement issu de la *12.SS-Totenkopf-Standarte*, du *SS-Ersatz-Bataillon « Der Führer »* (alors basé à Graz-Wetzelsdorf) et du *SS-Regiment « Germania »*. A la fin du mois de septembre, le bataillon est à son tour transféré en Norvège. Les deux unités doivent assurer la garde des fjords de Tana et Varanger.

Le 15 octobre, une section de DCA légère, cédée par la *SS-Fla-MG-Ers.-Kp. « Arolsen »* (SS-Ostuf. Fend), vient les renforcer. En outre, une batterie d'obusiers est mise sur pied à Berlin-Lichterfelde par le *SS-Ustuf.* Nickmann* à partir du *SS-Art.-Ers.Rgt.* afin d'augmenter leur puissance de feu. Le 15 novembre, l'état-major de la *9.SS-Totenkopf-Standarte* est dissous. Sa section de transmissions est cédée à la *SS-Totenkopf-Standarte « Kirkenes »* que dirige le *SS-Ostubaf.* Ernst Deutsch*. Celle-ci sera plus tard rebaptisée *SS-Totenkopf-Standarte 9 « Kirkenes »*.

Le 1er février 1941, un troisième bataillon est formé sous la conduite du *SS-Stubaf.* Klein*. Une semaine plus tard, le régiment change une nouvelle fois de dénomination et devient la *9.SS-Standarte* avant d'être rebaptisée *SS-Infanterie-Regiment 9 (mot.)* le mois suivant.

Après avoir été rattaché au *SS-Kampfgruppe « Nord »*, le régiment est subordonné à partir du 1er mai 1941 à la *702.Infanterie-Division*. Au cours du mois de juin, il reçoit une compagnie du génie (*SS-Ustuf.* Eichhorn*). En revanche, il doit céder sa 12e compagnie au *SS-IR 6*, ce dernier ayant perdu quatre-vingts hommes de sa 6e compagnie lors du naufrage du vaisseau « *Blenheim* ». Le 6 juin, une nouvelle 12e compagnie doit donc être formée à Stettin à partir de la *SS-Wach-Kompanie « Obersalzberg »*. Son chef est le *SS-Hstuf.* Keidel*. Le 15 juin, le régiment est subordonné à l'*AOK « Norwegen »*. Une semaine plus tard, alors que les forces de l'Axe envahissent l'URSS, il demeure le long de la côte norvégienne à Vardsö (*III./SS-IR 9*), Vardö (*II./SS-IR 9*) et Kirkenes (*I./SS-IR*

The birth of the unit

The SS-Sonder-Bataillon "Reitz" was formed on 24 June 1940 in the SS barracks at Stralsund with recruits born in 1921 and 1922 and officers coming from III./SS-Totenkopf-Rekruten-Standarte. An additional infantry gun section was provided by the "Germania" regiment and an anti-tank section by Leibstandarte SS "Adolf Hitler" and SS-Verfügungsdivision. On 28 June, the battalion was renamed verstärktes SS-Totenkopf-Bataillon "Norwegen". It had a strength of 13 officers, 62 non-commissioned officers and 871 soldiers (a total of 946 men). From Stralsund, it was transferred to Stettin, from where it embarked for Norway. Upon its arrival at Oslo, it moved to Kirkenes, a town situated within the Arctic Circle. Then it was renamed SS-Totenkopf-Bataillon "Kirkenes". Its mission was to cover the Jacobselven - Tana sector. On 23 August, the decision was taken to raise a second battalion and a regiment was formed combining the two battalions. This new unit was formed on 1 September in Posen-Treskau. It was commanded by SS-Sturmbannführer Herms and its personnel essentially came from 12.SS-Totenkopf-Standarte, SS-Ersatz-Bataillon "Der Führer" (based at Graz-Wetzelsdorf at the time) and SS-Regiment "Germania". At the end of September, the battalion was in turn transferred to Norway. The two units had to guard the Tana and Varanger fjords.

On 15 October, a section of light AA guns, issued from SS-Fla-MG-Ers.-Kp. "Arolsen" (SS-Ostuf. Fend), came as reinforcement. In addition, a battery of howitzers was mobilised at Berlin-Lichterfelde by SS-Ustuf. Nickmann from SS-Art.-Ers.Rgt., in order to increase their fire power. On 15 November, the headquarters of 9.SS-Totenkopf-Standarte was dissolved. Its transmissions section was given to SS-Totenkopf-Standarte "Kirkenes" which was commanded by SS-Ostubaf. Ernst Deutsch. It was later renamed SS-Totenkopf-Standarte 9 "Kirkenes".

On 1 February, a third battalion was created under the supervision of SS-Stubaf. Klein. One week later, the regiment changed its name once again and became 9.SS-Standarte before being renamed SS-Infanterie-Regiment 9 (mot.) the following month.

After having been attached to SS-Kampfgruppe "Nord", on 1 May it was subordinated to 702.Infanterie-Division. During the month of June, it received a company of engineers (SS-Ustuf. Eichhorn). In exchange, it had to give up its 12th company to SS-IR 6, as the latter had lost eighty men from its 6th company when the vessel "Blenheim" was shipwrecked. On 6 June, a new 12th company then had to be formed at Stettin from SS-Wach-Kompanie "Obersalzberg", which was commanded by SS-Hstuf. Keidel. On 15 June, the regiment was placed under AOK "Norwegen". One week later, when the Axis Forces invaded the Soviet Union, it occupied the length of the Norwegian coast to Vardsö (III./SS-IR 9), Vardö (II./SS-IR 9) and Kirkenes (I./SS-IR 9). At the time, it was 3,071 men strong and subordinated to Gebirgs-Korps "Norwegen" commanded by General Dietl. On 29 June, the latter took offensive action in the direction of Murmansk. SS-IR 9 was not engaged until the third week of August. On 26 August, it was attached to 2.Gebirgs-Division. Its first battalion (I./SS-IR 9, SS-Stubaf. Deisenhofer) came to rein-

NB. : les astéristiques (*) renvoient aux notes biographiques concernant les officiers publiées, dans *Totenkopf* pp 490 à 500, paru aux éditons Heimdal en 2006.

I

9). Il est alors fort de 3 071 hommes et dépend du *Gebirgs-Korps « Norwegen »* du général Dietl. Le 29 juin, ce dernier passe à l'offensive en direction de Mourmansk. Le *SS-IR 9* n'est engagé qu'à partir de la troisième semaine d'août. Le 26, il est rattaché à la *2.Gebirgs-Division*. Son premier bataillon (*I./SS-IR 9*, *SS-Stubaf.* Deisenhofer) vient renforcer le *SS-IR 7*. Il passe la Kairala et parvient jusqu'aux rives de la Nurmitunturi. Il se bat durement deux jours plus tard dans la vallée d'Ahkioja. Le 30, il s'attaque aux positions soviétiques situées à l'ouest d'Alakurtti, les force et atteint Tuntsajok. Ces succès sont payés au prix fort : le bataillon déplore 52 tués et 52 blessés. A l'issue de ces combats, le *I./SS-IR 9* est placé en réserve du *XXXVI.AK* dans le secteur de Luostari. Le 5 septembre, le reste du régiment reçoit la mission suivante : élargir la tête de pont à l'est de la Liza. L'attaque est lancée le 8. Malgré son enthousiasme, le *II./SS-IR 9* du *SS-Stubaf.* Herms subit de très lourdes pertes devant les positions solidement aménagées par les Soviétiques au niveau de la cote 129. Le *III./SS-IR 9* du *SS-Stubaf.* Dusenschön parvient à s'emparer de la cote 173,7. Une contre-attaque russe repousse le *II./SS-IR 9* tandis que le *III./SS-IR 9* se fait également bousculer à l'est de Lopatkina. Son chef est blessé. Tout le flanc gauche de la *2.Gebirgs-Division* se trouve ainsi menacé. Les chasseurs alpins contre-attaquent alors avec le *I./Geb. Jg.Rgt.137* et les Russes sont finalement tenus en respect. Le 9 septembre, le *Gruppe « Deutsch »* se rassemble derrière la cote 173,7. Le *II./SS-IR 9* est relevé par le *Pi.-Btl.82*. Les jours suivants, la *2.Gebirgs-Division* continue à attaquer, mais sans résultat probant. Le 16, le *I./SS-IR 9* est rattaché à la *3.Gebirgs-Division* et relève le *III./IR 388* (*Gruppe « Ledebur »*) de part et d'autre de la Liza jusqu'au lac Wiljärvi. Le 19, le *Gebirgs-Korps « Norwegen »* est définitivement bloqué sur la route de Mourmansk et doit se mettre sur la défensive. Du 20 au 23, le *I./SS-IR 9* participe à une opération de nettoyage à l'est de la Liza sur les arrières du *Geb.Jg.Rgt.138*. Le 24, il se retire sur la rive occidentale entre le lac Nosh-Jarvi et la cote 77,4. Quelques jours plus tard, il rejoint le reste du régiment dans le secteur de Petsamojokki. Le 14 octobre, le *SS-IR 9* est directement subordonné à l'*AOK « Norwegen »* et reçoit l'ordre de gagner la région de Rovaniemi afin de soutenir le 3ᵉ corps finlandais à l'est de Kiestinki. Le 28, la *SS-Batterie « Nickmann »* devient la 3ᵉ batterie du régiment d'artillerie de la *SS-Division « Nord »*. Le *SS-IR 9 (mot.)* vient se regrouper au sud de la voie ferrée Kiestinki - Louhi. Il passe à l'attaque le 1ᵉʳ novembre par un froid épouvantable. Deux lignes de défense soviétiques sont bousculées avant que la progression ne soit bloquée : les SS ne peuvent atteindre les lacs Yelovoje et Werschnejeosero. Le régiment reste engagé de part et d'autre de la rivière Gankachvaara jusqu'au 18 novembre. Il est ensuite transféré dans le secteur de Taivalkoski et Pudasjärvi. Ses armes et son matériel sont cédés à la *SS-Division « Nord »*. Le *III./SS-IR 9*, qui ne compte plus que 202 hommes valides, et la *Pi.-Kp./SS-IR 9* lui sont rattachés. La *leichte Infanterie-Kolonne* est intégrée aux *Nachschubdienste/SS-Division « Nord »* tandis que le reste du régiment se rassemble à Helsinki. De là, il rejoint Tallinn. Ses pertes subies sur le front de Finlande s'élèvent à 359 tués, 233 blessés et 106 disparus. De Tallinn, il gagne Narwa.

Le 20 décembre, il est rattaché au *Heeresgruppe « Nord »* et placé en réserve de la *18.Armee*. Afin de regonfler les effectifs des compagnies, le *II./SS-IR 9* est dissous et ses éléments sont dispersés au sein des autres unités régimentaires. Ainsi, à la veille de Noël, le *SS-IR 9 (mot.) « Thule »* possède la structure suivante :

force *SS-IR 7*. It crossed the Kairala river and reached the shores of the Nurmitunturi river. Two days later, it fought hard in the Ahkioja Valley. On 30 August, it attacked the Soviet positions to the west of Alakurtti, pushing them back and reaching Tuntsajok. A very high price was paid for this progress: The battalion lost 52 dead and 52 wounded. As a result of the fighting, *I./SS-IR 9* was placed in reserve behind the *XXXVI.AK* lines in the Luostari sector. On 5 September, the rest of the regiment received the following mission: To enlarge the bridgehead to the east of the Liza river. The attack was launched three days later. Despite its enthusiasm, *II./SS-IR 9* commanded by *SS-Stubaf.* Herms suffered heavy losses confronting the positions firmly established by the Soviets on hill 129. *III./SS-IR 9* commanded by *SS-Stubaf.* Dusenschön took hill 173.7. A Russian counter-attack pushed *II./SS-IR 9* back, while *III./SS-IR 9* was also driven back to the east of Lopatkina and its commander was wounded. Hence the entire left flank of *2.Gebirgs-Division* was threatened. Then the Gebirgsjäger counter-attacked with the support of *le.I./Geb.Jg.Rgt.137* and the Russians were finally kept at bay. On 9 September, Gruppe "Deutsch" assembled behind hill 173.7. *II./SS-IR 9* was relieved by *Pi.-Btl.82*. In the days that followed, *2.Gebirgs-Division* continued to attack, but without convincing results. On 16 September, *I./SS-IR 9* was attached to *3.Gebirgsjäger-Division* and it relieved *III./IR 388* (Gruppe "Ledebur") on both sides of the Liza river up to Lake Wiljärvi. On 19 September, Gebirgs-Korps "Norwegen" was permanently blocked on the road to Murmansk and had to build defensive positions. Between 20 and 23 September, *I./SS-IR 9* participated in a mop up operation to the east of the Liza river in the rear of *Geb.Jg.Rgt.138*. On 24 September, it retreated to the western shore between Lake Nosh-Jarvi and hill 77.4. Several days later, it rejoined the rest of the regiment in the Petsamojokki sector. On 14 October, *SS-IR 9* was directly subordinated to AOK "Norwegen" and received orders to take control of the Rovaniemi region in order to support the 3rd Finnish Corps to the east of Kiestinki. On 28 September, SS-Batterie "Nickmann" became the 3rd battery of the artillery regiment of SS-Division "Nord". *SS-IR 9 (mot.)* regrouped south of the Kiestinki - Louhi railway. It moved to attack on 1 November in terrible cold weather. Two Soviet lines of defence were destroyed before their progression was stopped: The SS were unable to reach the lakes of Yelovoje and Werschnejeosero. The regiment remained stationed on both sides of the Gankachvaara river until 18 November. It was later transferred to the Taivalkoski and Pudasjärvi sectors. Its weapons and material were given to SS-Division "Nord". *III./SS-IR 9*, which consisted in no more than 202 men who were still fit for service, and *Pi.-Kp./SS-IR 9* were attached to it. Its leichte Infanterie-Kolonne was aggregated to Nachschubdienste/SS-Division "Nord" while the rest of the regiment assembled in Helsinki. From there, it moved to Tallinn. The losses suffered by the regiment on the Finnish front totalled 359 dead, 233 wounded and 106 missing. From Tallinn, it reached Narwa. On 20 December, it was subordinated to Heeresgruppe "Nord" and placed in reserve of 18.Armee. In order to boost the companies' forces, *II./SS-IR 9* was dissolved and its men were divided among the other units of the regiment. Hence on Christmas Eve, *SS-IR 9 (mot.)* "Thulé" had the following structure:

- Stab, Stabs-Kp.
- I.Btl. (SS-Hauptsturmführer Kiklasch)
- III.Btl. (SS-Hauptsturmführer Spanka)
- 13.(IG)Kp. (SS-Obersturmführer Förster*)
- 14.(Pz.Jg.)Kp. (SS-Hauptsturmführer Schulz)
- 15.(Pi.)Kp. (SS-Obersturmführer Kinzler)

Its fighting forces comprised 24 officers, 65 non-commissioned officers and 448 soldiers, for a total of 537 men.

- Stab, Stabs-Kp.
- I.Btl. (SS-Hauptsturmführer Kiklasch)
- III.Btl. (SS-Hauptsturmführer Spanka)
- 13.(IG)Kp. (SS-Obersturmführer Förster*)
- 14.(Pz.Jg.)Kp. (SS-Hauptsturmführer Schulz)
- 15.(Pi.)Kp. (SS-Obersturmführer Kinzler)

Ses effectifs combattants sont de 24 officiers, 65 sous-officiers et 448 hommes de troupe, soit un total de 537.

Après une brève période passée à Narwa, le régiment est envoyé à Kingisepp puis c'est à pied qu'il rejoint Menewscha, ville située à l'embouchure de la Tigoda. Le 14 janvier 1942, il est subordonné au *I.AK* et rattaché à la *291.Infanterie-Division* du *Generalleutnant* Herzog. Le 26 février, le *SS-Obf.* Lothar Debes remplace le *SS-Ostubaf.* Ernst Deutsch à la tête du régiment. Celui-ci résiste à tous les assauts soviétiques lors des furieux combats de l'hiver et du printemps sur le front du Wolchow. Le 7 juillet 1942, ses survivants sont enfin relevés et embarquent à Tschudowo en direction de Paderborn. Deux semaines plus tard, le *SS-IR 9 « Thule »* est intégré à la *SS-Panzergrenadier-Division « Totenkopf »* et devient le *SS-Kradschützen-Regiment « Thule »*.

Commandeurs du régiment

01.09.40- ? : *SS-Sturmbannführer* Herms
? - 25.02.42 : *SS-Obersturmbannführer* Deutsch
26.02.42-21.07.42 : *SS-Oberführer* Debes

Croix allemande en or

28.02.42 : *SS-Hauptsturmführer* Spanka
(Fhr. III./SS-IR 9 « Thule »)

After a brief period spent in Narwa, the regiment was sent to Kingisepp and travelled on foot to Menewscha, a town located at the mouth of the Tigoda river. On 14 January 1942, it was subordinated to I.AK and attached to 291.Infanterie-Division commanded by Generalleutnant Herzog. On 26 February, SS-Obf. Lothar Debes replaced SS-Ostubaf. Ernst Deutsch at the head of the regiment. The latter resisted to every Soviet attack during the furious combats which took place during the winter and spring months on the Wolchow front. On 7 July 1942, its survivors were relieved and embarked in Tschudowo towards Paderborn. Two weeks later, SS-IR 9 "Thule" was integrated into SS-Panzergrenadier-Division "Totenkopf" and became SS-Kradschützen-Regiment "Thule".

Regiment commanders

01/09/40- ?: SS-Sturmbannführer Herms
? – 25/02/42: SS-Oberstumbannführer Deutsch
26/02/42-21/07/42: SS-Oberführer Debes

German gold cross

28/02/42: SS-Hauptsturmführer Spanka
(Fhr. III./SS-IR 9 "Thule")

---

(1) Le navigateur grec Pythéas donne le nom de «Thulé» à une île atteinte au III° siècle av. J.-C. qu'il présente comme la dernière île de l'actuel archipel britannique. Il s'agissait soit de l'Islande, peut-être des îles Féroé, du Groenland ou soit encore du nord de la Norvège (Hålogaland). Pythéas indique (d'après Strabon, Géographie, I, 4) avoir atteint Thulé après six jours de navigation depuis les îles Shetland. Il décrit Thulé, à des latitudes proches du cercle polaire, comme une île habitée où l'on pratique « la culture du blé et l'élevage des abeilles ». Les nuits d'été ne dureraient que deux à trois heures. Après une journée de navigation vers le nord, il prétend avoir atteint les premières glaces de la banquise. Le nom de Thulé figure notamment dans l'Enéide du poète romain Virgile, et il est généralement admis que Ultima Thulé des anciens Grecs désignait les terres les plus au nord et tout particulièrement la Scandinavie. Ptolémée le situe au 63° N de latitude dans son ouvrage Géographie. Au moyen âge, Ultima Thule est parfois utilisé comme nom latin pour le Groenland lorsque Thule désigne l'Islande.

Une société de recherches ethnographiques Thule est née au début du XX° siècle, à l'origine un groupe d'études ethnologiques s'intéressant tout spécialement à l'Antiquité germanique. Partant du postulat que l'Ultima Thulé des anciens Grecs désignait les terres les plus au nord et tout particulièrement la Scandinavie, certains membres de ce groupe pensaient que Thulé était ce qui subsistait de Hyperborée des Grecs (litt. « au-delà de Borée », Borée désignant la divinité incarnée par le vent du nord), un continent disparu, et que celui-ci était le berceau de la race aryenne. La guerre de 1914-18 dispersa ses collaborateurs dont un grand nombre furent tués. La paix revenue, le groupe se reforma, devenant la Thule-Gesellschaft (Société Thulé ou l'Ordre de Thulé) créée par le baron Rudolf von Sebottendorff le 17 août 1918. Elle prit une nouvelle orientation sous l'influence de l'écrivain et professeur d'histoire Paul Rohrbach, qui a publié de nombreux ouvrages relatifs à l'Asie et au pangermanisme. Un autre membre influant fut Dietrich Eckart, lequel y introduisit Alfred Rosenberg (le « philosophe » officiel du nazisme). Jusque-là le groupe Thulé n'était qu'une sorte d'académie dilettante, légèrement snob (selon W. Gerson, Le nazisme société secrète, N.O.E., 1969). Diffusée à Munich, l'idéologie de cette société prônait l'antisémitisme (selon Werner Gerson, op.cit.), l'antirépublicanisme, le paganisme et le racisme. Son symbole, la croix de Wotan (autre nom d'Odin, Wotan ou Wodan en langue germanique), n'est pas sans rappeler la croix gammée.

Avec la croissance du NSDAP, le déclin de la société Thulé a lieu lors du décret de 1937, qui interdisait toutes les loges franc-maçonnes et toutes les organisations apparentées aux loges. Quant à Sebottendorff, il se serait suicidé en se jetant dans le Bosphore en 1945.

(1) In the 3rd century BC, Greek navigator Pytheas reached an island he thought was the last island of today's British Isles, and named it "Thule". Truly, it was either Iceland, the Faroe Islands, Greenland, or maybe some island north of Norway (Hålogaland). Pytheas stated (according to Strabo, Geography, I, 4) that having sailed from the Shetland Islands, he had reached Thule after six days of navigation. He described Thule – which was situated at latitudes close to the polar circle – as an inhabited island, where people "grow wheat and keep bees". According to him, summer nights only lasted two or three hours there. He claimed that, after sailing north for a day only, he reached the realm of the ice floe. Thule's name appears notably in Roman poet Virgil's Aeneid, and it is generally admitted that the ancient Greeks' "Ultima Thule" designated the northernmost lands, and especially Scandinavia. In his Geography, Ptolemy located the spot at latitude 63°north. In the Middle Ages, "Ultima Thule" was sometimes used as the Latin name for Greenland, "Thule" being Iceland.

A society for ethnographic research named Thule was created at the dawn of the 20th century; it was originally a study group specialized in ethnology, and especially in Germanic Antiquity. Basing their judgement on the postulate that the ancient Greeks' Ultima Thule stood for the northernmost lands, and Scandinavia in particular, some members of the group thought that Thule was what was left of the Greeks' Hyperborea (literally, "beyond Boreas", Boreas being the god of the north wind), a vanished continent, and that it was the cradle of the Aryan race. The First World War had the members go their separate ways, and many were killed. When peace came back, the group formed up again and became the Thule-Gesellschaft (the Thule Society or the Order of Thule), created by Baron Rudolf von Sebottendorff on the 17th of August 1918. It took a new direction under the influence of writer and history professor Paul Rohrbach, who published many books on Asia and Pan-Germanism. Another influential member was Dietrich Eckart, who introduced Alfred Rosenberg (the official "philosopher" of Nazism) to the group. Until then, the Thule group had only been some kind of dilettante and slightly snobbish academy (so argues W. Gerson, Le nazisme société secrète, N.O.E., 1969). Spread in Munich, the society's ideology advocated anti-Semitism (according to Werner Gerson, op.cit.), anti-republicanism, paganism and racism. Its symbol, the Wotan cross (the other name of Odin, Wotan or Wodan in German), is quite evocative of the swastika.

The progress of the NSDAP saw the decline of the Thule society, which culminated in 1937, when a decree forbade freemason lodges and any organisation akin to lodges. As for Sebottendorff, he presumably committed suicide in 1945 by throwing himself into the Bosporus.

Portrait de l'auteur de cet album photographique, datant de 1940. Notre homme est alors *SS-Sturm-mann* et sert au sein de la *SS-Totenkopf-Division*. Celui-ci a gardé son vieil uniforme qu'il portait avant-guerre lorsqu'il faisait partie de la *3.SS-Totenkopf-Standarte « Thüringen »*, comme le montre le chiffre « 3 » visible sur sa patte d'épaule gauche.

This portrait of the photograph album's author, has been taken in 1940. At that time, our man was SS-Sturmann and served in SS-Totenkopf-Division. He had retained the old uniform he wore before the war, when he belonged to 3.SS-Totenkopf-Standarte "Thüringen", as shown by the number "3" which can be seen on his left shoulder patch.

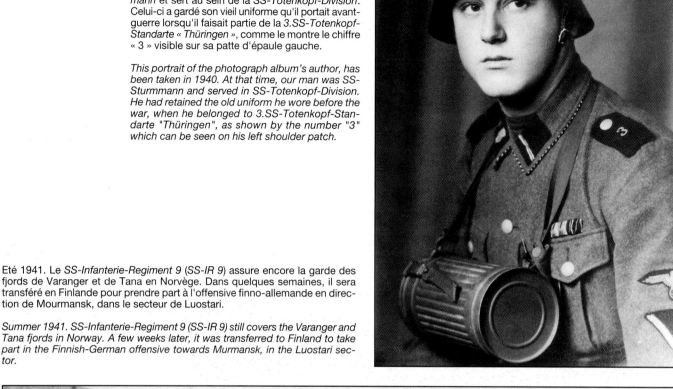

Eté 1941. Le *SS-Infanterie-Regiment 9 (SS-IR 9)* assure encore la garde des fjords de Varanger et de Tana en Norvège. Dans quelques semaines, il sera transféré en Finlande pour prendre part à l'offensive finno-allemande en direction de Mourmansk, dans le secteur de Luostari.

Summer 1941. SS-Infanterie-Regiment 9 (SS-IR 9) still covers the Varanger and Tana fjords in Norway. A few weeks later, it was transferred to Finland to take part in the Finnish-German offensive towards Murmansk, in the Luostari sector.

Exercice en Norvège. L'auteur de l'album est le passager avant droit, portant un brassard blanc. La voiture est un *Kübelwagen Adler Typ 3*. Celle-ci est équipée d'un moteur 6 cylindres en ligne de 2,916 litres développant 60 chevaux à 3 300 tours par minute. C'est un 4x2 capable d'atteindre 80 km/h sur route et possédant une autonomie de 500 km (consommation de 17 litres aux 100 km sur route). L'insigne régimentaire, un bateau viking, est visible sur le garde-boue avant droit.

Exercise in Norway. The author is the passenger on the right seat, wearing a white armband. The car is a Kübelwagen Adler Typ 3. It was equipped with a 2.916 litre in-line 6 cylinder engine, yielding 60 horsepower and 3300 rpm. It was a 4x2 vehicle, capable of reaching 80 km/hr on the road, with a range of 500 km (consumption of 17 litres per 100 km on the road). The regiment symbol, a longship, is visible on the front right fender.

Le régiment a maintenant été transféré en Finlande, sur le front de la Liza, où il combat sous la direction de la *2.Gebirgs-Division*. Notre homme chevauche un side-car *DKW NZ 350*, aisément reconnaissable à son écusson placé sur le côté du réservoir. Cette moto possède un moteur de 346 centimètres cubes développant 11 chevaux à 4 000 tours par minute. Cela suffit à lui assurer une vitesse maximale de 100 km/h. On remarquera les insignes régimentaires et tactiques. Notre homme appartient à la batterie d'artillerie motorisée du régiment.

The regiment has now been transferred to Finland, on the Liza front, where it fought under the command of 2.Gebirgs-Division. Our man is straddling a DKW NZ 350 sidecar, easily recognisable from the badge on the side of the tank. This motorcycle had a 346 cc engine yielding 11 horsepower at 4,000 rpm, which was sufficient to provide it with a maximum velocity of 100 km/hr. Note the regiment and tactical insignia. Our man belonged to the regiment's motorised artillery battery.

Marche vers le front. La plupart des hommes ont revêtu une blouse camouflée, à l'exception de celui qui remonte la colonne motorisée. Ce cliché permet d'apercevoir l'armement dont est pourvue l'unité : il s'agit d'un canon d'infanterie de 7,5 cm *(le.IG18)*. La voiture visible au centre de la photographie est un *Kübelwagen Adler Typ 3*.

March towards the front. The majority of the men are wearing camouflaged smocks, except for the man walking along the motorised column. The plate facilitates the identification of the weaponry with which the regiment was provided: It is a 7.5 cm (le.IG18) infantry gun. The car visible in the centre of the photograph is a Kübelwagen Adler Typ 3.

Une belle photographie montrant notre homme sur un chemin de rondins, quelque part sur le front de la Liza. Il a maintenant été promu *SS-Rottenführer* et il est équipé d'une *MP40*.

This beautiful photograph is showing our man on a log track, somewhere on the Liza front. He has been promoted to SS-Rottenführer and is equipped with a MP40.

L'utilisation des voies ferrées permet d'acheminer hommes et matériels vers le front dans de bonnes conditions. Visiblement, cette ligne devait servir au transport de minerais, abondants dans cette région. Le petit convoi dépasse la position d'artillerie du régiment et on peut ici apprécier l'abondance des munitions qui ont été tirées.

The use of railways eased the transportation of men and materials to the front in good conditions. This line was clearly built to transport minerals, which were abundant in the region. The small convoy is going past the position of the regiment's artillery and the abundance of ammunition that had been fired can be seen.

Très intéressante photo d'un homme du *SS-IR 9*. Celui-ci porte, comme un grand nombre de ses camarades, la tête de mort héritée des *SS-Toten-kopfverbände*. On remarquera les chaussures qui sont en dotation au sein des unités de *Gebirgsjäger*, ce que n'est pas le *SS-IR 9*. A l'arrière, les panneaux indiquent que les bâtiments abritent le secrétariat et les 1re et 2e sections de la compagnie portant le numéro de code postal 04018. Cette compagnie est donc la *13.(IG)Kp./SS-IR 9*.

Interesting photo of a man from the SS-IR 9. Like a great number of his comrades, he is wearing the death's head inherited from the SS-Toten-kopfverbände. Note the shoes, usually allocated to Gebirgsjäger units, which SS-IR 9 was not. In the background, the boards indicate that the buildings shelter the 2nd and 3rd sections of the company, bearing the postcode 04018. Hence this company is the 13.(IG)Kp./SS-IR 9.

En passant sur la rive orientale de la Liza, les hommes du régiment découvrent un paysage de toundra bien particulier dont la traversée se fait au prix d'énormes efforts. Ce camion *Ford G917T*, un 4x2 possédant un moteur V8 de 3,6 litres développant 90 chevaux à 3 800 tours par minute, ne possède pas les capacités suffisantes pour avancer seul dans un tel bourbier.

By crossing over to the eastern shore of the Liza river, the men of the regiment discovered a quite peculiar tundra landscape, which was crossed with great effort. The Ford G917T van, a 4x2 with a 3.6 litre V8 engine yielding 90 horsepower at 3800 rpm, was unable to advance unaided through such a quagmire.

Deux motocyclistes posent pour le photographe devant les locaux aperçus sur la précédente photo. Les tâches de boue montrent que leurs manteaux de caoutchouc sont des plus utiles. L'homme de gauche porte une carabine *K98 k* en bandoulière. Celle-ci aura été l'arme produite en plus grand nombre par l'Allemagne au cours de la guerre : environ 15 millions d'exemplaires !

Two motorcyclists are posing for the photograph in front of the premises appearing in the previous photo. The mud stains show that their waterproof coats were the most useful ones. The man on the left is carrying a K98 k rifle across his shoulder. It is the weapon which has been produced in greatest numbers by Germany during the course of the war with about 15 million units!

Arrivée du courrier. C'est toujours un moment très attendu au sein de la troupe. Il est vrai que les hommes qui ont appartenu au *SS-Bataillon « Reitz »*, noyau du régiment, ne sont pas partis en permission depuis plus d'un an.

The post arrives. This was always a long-awaited moment among the troops. The men who had served in SS-Bataillon "Reitz", who formed the core of the regiment, had not taken a leave for more than a year.

Aperçu du terrain très particulier sur lequel le régiment se bat dans le secteur de la Liza. Cette toundra n'est traversée que par de très rares routes qui se transforment en bourbiers à l'automne et au printemps. Seuls des véhicules comme ce tracteur soviétique capturé, peuvent s'y mouvoir grâce à leurs larges chenilles.

This picture shows the very particular terrain of the Liza sector on which the regiment has to fight. This tundra is only crossed by rare roads which become quagmires in spring and autumn. Only vehicles like this captured Soviet tractor were able to manoeuvre there, thanks to their large tracks.

Le tracteur tire ici un canon d'infanterie *le.IG18* de la *13.(IG)Kp./SS-IR 9*. On peut ici apprécier la difficulté de ce terrain. Dans ces conditions, même ce tracteur a de la peine à gravir cette pente à la fois boueuse et rocailleuse. Les servants du canon doivent l'aider en poussant l'attelage.

Here, the tractor is towing a le.IG18 infantry gun of 13.(IG)Kp./SS-IR 9. The difficulty of the terrain can be appreciated here. Under these conditions, even the tractor experienced difficulty climbing the muddy and rocky slope. The men of the gun crew were forced to help by pushing the equipment.

Convoi de la *13.Kp./SS-IR 9*. Ce *Kübelwagen Adler Typ 3* s'est mis en conformation hivernale avec capote fermée. Il s'agit du 15ᵉ véhicule de la compagnie. Celui-ci est immatriculé « 97606 ». Les numéros allant de 97001 à 99999 sont alors attribués aux unités qui dépendaient du *Befehlshaber der Waffen-SS in Norwegen*.

Convoy of 13.Kp./SS-IR 9. This Kübelwagen Adler Typ 3 is in winter conformation with the hood closed. It is the 15th vehicle of the company, with the registration number "97606". The numbers from 97001 to 99999 were assigned to the units attached to the Befehlshaber der Waffen-SS in Norwegen.

Un cimetière du régiment dans le secteur de la Liza. Dès la mi-septembre 1941, après un mois d'engagement, le *III./SS-IR 9* ne comptait déjà plus que 150 combattants valides.

A regiment graveyard in the Liza sector. From mid-September 1941, after one month of service, III./SS-IR 9 had only 150 men fit for service left.

Un canon d'infanterie de 7,5 cm *(le.IG18)* en batterie. Il est protégé des éclats par quelques rondins. Le dégel a transformé la position en véritable cloaque. On imagine aisément quelles conditions infernales ont dû supporter les combattants sur le front russe !

A 7.5cm (le.IG18) infantry gun in battery. It was protected with a few logs. The thaw had turned its position into an authentic cesspit. One can easily imagine the infernal conditions that the fighters must have had to endure on the Russian front!

Ravitaillement des troupes et de la population civile. Le camion de droite appartient à la *SS-Division « Nord »* dont l'insigne tactique est parfaitement visible. Ceci signifie que la photo a ici été prise par un membre du *III./SS-IR 9 (SS-Hstuf.* Spanka) qui a combattu à partir du 2 décembre 1941 pendant quelques jours avec cette division.

Supplies are brought to the troops and the civilian population. The lorry on the right belongs to SS-Division "Nord" whose tactical insignia is clearly visible. This means that this photo has been taken by a member of III./SS-IR 9 (SS-Hstuf. Spanka) which fought with this division for several days from 2 December 1941.

Visite du *Generaloberst* Dietl. Celui-ci profite de l'occasion pour féliciter des hommes à qui vient d'être attribuée la Croix de fer de deuxième classe. Contrairement au *SS-Kampfgruppe « Nord »*, le *SS-IR 9* n'a pas connu de baptême du feu catastrophique sur le front de Finlande. Il a cependant subi de lourdes pertes au sud de la Liza.

Visit from Generaloberst Dietl. He takes advantage of the occasion to congratulate several men of the regiment who have just been decorated with the iron cross, 2nd class. Unlike SS-Kampfgruppe "Nord", SS-IR 9 has not experienced a catastrophic baptism of fire on the Finnish front. Nevertheless, it has suffered heavy losses south of the Liza river.

Cet officier non identifié décore de la Croix de fer de 2ᵉ classe des hommes de son unité. Il s'agit peut-être du *Regiments-Adjutant*, le *SS-Ostuf.* Rudolf Wehrhahn, un ancien de la *14.Kp./ « Deutschland »* qui sera tué le 25 mars 1942 alors qu'il dirigeait la *5.Kp./SS-IR 9.*

This unidentified officer decorates men of his unit with the iron cross, 2nd class. He is perhaps the Regiments-Adjutant, SS-Ostuf. Rudolf Wehrhahn, a veteran from 14.Kp./"Deutschland", who will be killed on 25 March 1942 while in command of 5.Kp./SS-IR 9.

Ci-dessus : Groupe de soldats du *SS-IR 9* lors d'une halte au cours d'un transfert. On remarquera les tenues, guère adaptées au froid qui règne dans le Grand Nord. On notera que la plupart portent encore au col la tête de mort, indiquant ainsi qu'ils servaient auparavant au sein de *SS-Totenkopf-Standarten* ou de la *SS-Totenkopf-Division*.

Above: Group of soldiers from SS-IR 9 during a pause over the course of a transfer. One can notice that their clothing is hardly adapted to the cold which is reigning in the Great North. Note that most of them are still wearing the death's head on their collars, indicating that they have previously served in SS-Totenkopf-Standarten or SS-Totenkopf-Division.

Ci-dessous : Colonne de voitures s'apprêtant à se mettre en marche. Il s'agit de *Kübelwagen Adler Typ 3 Gd*, un véhicule construit entre 1939 et 1940. Le véhicule de tête ne possède pas la roue de secours latérale, contrairement à ceux qui le suivent. Cette voiture lourde peut tracter des canons légers, type *Pak 36* de 3,7 cm ou *le.IG18* de 7,5 cm, comme c'est ici le cas.

Below: Column of cars preparing to start their march. These vehicles are Kübelwagen Adler Typ 3 Gd, built between 1939 and 1940. The leading car does not have the emergency wheel on his side, as the one behind does. This heavy vehicle can tow light guns, like the 3.7 cm Pak 36 and the 7.5 cm le.IG18, as is the case here.

8 décembre 1941 : le *SS-IR 9* doit en principe rentrer en Allemagne. Les combats livrés en Carélie lui auront coûté 359 tués, 233 blessés et 106 disparus sur un effectif initial de 3 071 hommes. Il est assez rare de voir que le nombre de tués excède celui des blessés. Est-ce dû à l'insuffisance des services médicaux régimentaires ou aux conditions dantesques de l'hiver polaire ?

8 December 1941: In principle, SS-IR 9 has to return to Germany. The fighting carried out in Karelia has cost them 359 dead, 233 wounded and 106 missing from a force of 3,071 men. It is quite rare to observe that the number of dead exceedes the number of wounded. Is this due to the inadequacy of regiment medical services and the Dantesque conditions of the polar winter?

Hiver 1941 – 1942. Un convoi du *SS-IR 9* traverse une ville finlandaise (Helsinki ?) ayant subi un bombardement soviétique, à en juger par les maisons détruites que l'on peut apercevoir sur la droite. Sans doute s'agit-il de traces de la guerre russo-finlandaise de 1940.

Winter 1941-1942. A convoy from SS-IR 9 in a Finnish town (Helsinki?) that has suffered a Soviet bombing, judging by the destroyed houses that can be seen on the right. Undoubtedly, these are traces of the Russian-Finnish War of 1940.

Mauvaise nouvelle : en raison de la situation catastrophique du *Heeresgruppe Nord*, le régiment ne rentre plus en Allemagne mais doit débarquer à Tallinn pour gagner, via Narwa et Kingisepp, l'embouchure de la Tigoda où il sera subordonné au *I.AK*. Au moment d'embarquer en bateau, les hommes ont été débarrassés de leurs armes et de leurs paquetages.

Bad news: Due to the catastrophic situation of Heeresgruppe Nord, the regiment will not be sent back to Germany, but has to disembark at Tallinn to reach the mouth of the Tigoda river via Narwa and Kingisepp, where it has to be subordinated to I.AK. Just before boarding the ship, the men are relieved of their weapons and packs.

Le commandant du *SS-IR 9* est le *SS-Ostubaf.* Ernst Deutsch, un SS des premières heures (SS-Nr.6116) qui a servi dès juillet 1933 au sein de la *Leibstandarte*. En août 1936, il a été nommé à la tête du *SS-Bataillon « Nürnberg »* puis, en novembre 1939, du *I./SS-Totenkopf-Rekruten-Standarte*. En mai 1940, il est muté au *II./SS-IR 7* ; le 19 août suivant, il dirige le *I./SS-Rgt.« Kirkenes »*. Le 10 février 1941, il est promu commandant du *SS-IR 9*. Réputé honnête et possédant le sens de l'honneur, il est toutefois susceptible et sujet à des sautes d'humeur. Des crises nerveuses rejaillissant sur la sûreté de son commandement amèneront son limogeage de la *9.SS-Panzerdivision « Hohenstaufen »* en janvier 1944.

The commander of SS-IR 9 was SS-Ostubaf. Ernst Deutsch, an SS officer of the early days (SS N°. 6116), who had served in Leibstandarte since July 1933. In August 1936, he was named in charge of SS-Bataillon "Nürnberg" and then in November 1939 of I./SS-Totenkopf-Rekruten-Standarte. In May 1940, he was transferred to II./SS-IR 7 and on the 19th of the following August, he was placed in command of I./SS-Rgt. "Kirkenes". On 10 February 1941, he was promoted at the head of SS-IR 9. Though he had the reputation to be honest and to possess a real sense of honour, he was nevertheless touchy and subject to mood swings. These nervous attacks affected the reliability of his command, resulting in his dismissal from 9.SS-Panzerdivision "Hohenstaufen" in January 1944.

Un *Kfz.15 Horch* en route vers le front de la Tigoda en direction de Menewscha. Son immatriculation n'est malheureusement pas visible.

A Kfz.15 Horch en route towards the Tigoda front, in the direction of Menewscha. Unfortunately, its registration plate is not visible.

Tempête de neige. Sur le front de Leningrad, les conditions hivernales éprouvent les hommes et les véhicules. Les fourgons hippomobiles s'y meuvent plus rapidement que les motos, comme le prouve ce cliché pris dans le secteur de Menewscha.

Snow storm. On the Leningrad front, the winter conditions tested both men and vehicles. Horse-drawn wagons were able to move faster than motorcycles, as demonstrated by this photograph which has been taken in the Menewscha sector.

Embouteillage sur le front de la Tigoda. On voit ici un *le.IG18* tracté par une voiture lourde dont les roues sont équipées de chaînes. Le canon lui-même a en partie été protégé des intempéries par une couverture. A noter l'insigne régimentaire, visible sur le garde-boue arrière droit de la voiture.

Traffic jam on the Tigoda front. Here, a le.IG18 can be seen being towed by a heavy car with chained wheels. The cannon itself had been partially protected from the bad weather by a cover. Note the regiment insignia which is visible on the rear right-hand fender of the vehicle.

Des chars *Pzkpfw.III Ausf.H* apparte-
nant vraisemblablement au *Pz.Rgt.29
(12.Panzerdivision)* viennent soutenir
le *SS-IR 9 (mot.)* sur le front de la Tigoda.

*Pzkpfw.III Ausf.H tanks, probably
belonging to Pz.Rgt.29 (12.Panzerdi-
vision), are providing back up to SS-
IR 9 (mot.) on the Tigoda front.*

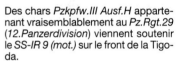

L'auteur de l'album s'essaye au *MG-
34*. Celle-ci est montée sur un trépied
antiaérien et possède le viseur adap-
té. La mitrailleuse *MG-34* a été produite par plusieurs sociétés au cours
de la guerre : Berlin-Suhler Waffen und
Fahrzeugwerke, Gustloff Werke,
Maget, Mauser Werke, Steyr Daimler
Puch et Waffenfabrik Brünn (Brno).
Cette dernière usine, construite en
Moravie (Tchécoslovaquie), allait
continuer sa production bien après
1945.

*The author tries out a MG-34. The
weapon is mounted on an anti-aircraft
tripod and has adapted sights. The
MG-34 machinegun was manufactured by several companies over the
course of the war: Berlin-Suhler Waffen und Fahrzeugwerke, Gustloff
Werke, Maget, Mauser Werke, Steyr
Daimler Puch and Waffenfabrik Brünn
(Brno). The latter factory, built in Mora-
via (Czechoslovakia), was to continue
its production until well after 1945.*

Evacuation de blessés par traîneau. En l'absence de routes carrossables et en raison de l'enneigement important, ce mode de transport est rapidement privilégié par l'armée allemande. Dans ces conditions hivernales extrêmes, la démotorisation de la Wehrmacht s'impose.

Evacuating the wounded by sleigh. In the absence of roads suitable for motor vehicles due to the significant snow coverage, this mode of transport was quickly favoured by the German Army. In extreme winter conditions, the Wehrmacht was unable to make use of its motorised vehicles

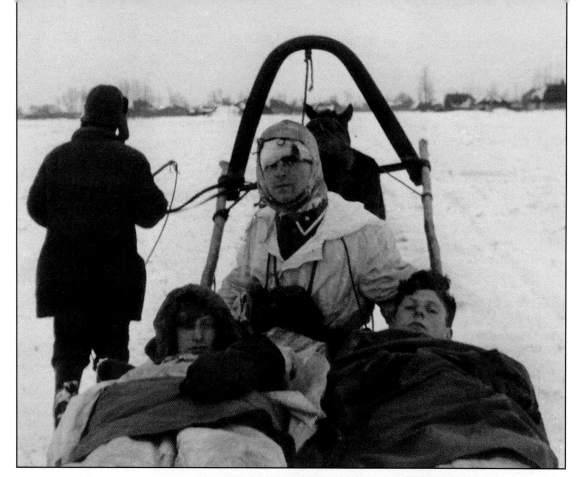

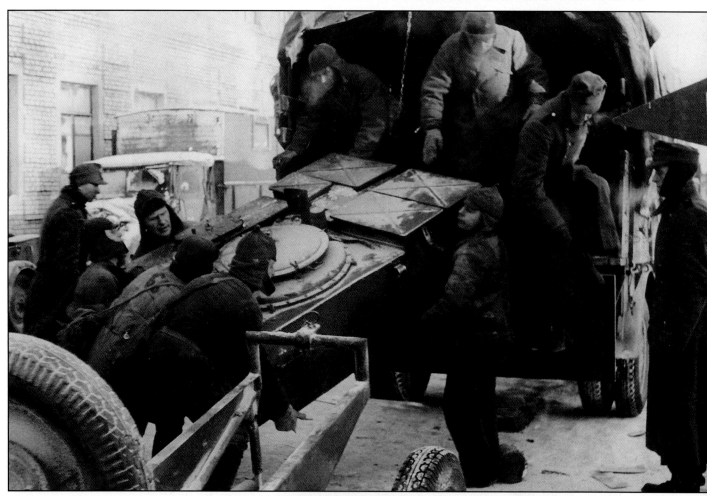

Déchargement d'une « roulante » par des prisonniers russes (*Hiwis* ?) devant améliorer l'ordinaire des soldats du régiment. Sur la droite, on peut voir un fanion de la *12.Panzerdivision*.

Unloading a mobile field kitchen by Russian prisoners (Hiwis ?) in order to improve the quality of life of the regiment's soldiers. The 12.Panzerdivision pennant can be seen to the right.

Printemps 1942, le terrible hiver 1941 appartient désormais au passé. Un autre fléau a fait son apparition avec le retour de températures plus clémentes : ce sont les mouches et les moustiques qui pullulent dans la région marécageuse du Wolchow. Des moustiquaires sont ainsi distribuées aux hommes pour les protéger.

Spring 1942; the terrible winter of 1941 was then a matter of the past. Another curse appeared with the return of milder temperatures: Flies and mosquitoes which proliferated in the marshy region of Wolchow. Hence mosquito nets were distributed among the men to protect them.

Repos à proximité d'une voie ferrée. Les hommes prennent le soleil. L'un d'eux a récupéré un casque soviétique qu'une balle a traversé. Un trophée macabre ? Il est à noter que les vieux uniformes avec les têtes de mort au col ont maintenant été remplacés.

Taking a break near an embankment. The men enjoy the sunshine. One of them has recovered a Soviet cap that has been penetrated by a bullet. A macabre trophy? Note that the old uniforms with the death's head on the collars have then been replaced.

Superbe photographie montrant des hommes du régiment avec un civil russe chez lequel ils sont logés.
A superb photograph showing men from the regiment with a Russian civilian who provided them with accommodation.

Construction d'une peti-
te passerelle au-dessus
de cette rigole. L'en-
semble est assez rudi-
mentaire mais ne doit
pas servir au passage de
véhicules.

*Construction of a small
footbridge over a chan-
nel. It is quite rudimen-
tary and cannot be used
by vehicles.*

Un *SS-Unterscharführer* et un *SS-Rottenführer* posent pour le photographe. Le deuxième vient tout juste d'être décoré du *Kriegsverdienstkreuz II.Klasse* (Croix de mérite de guerre de 2ᵉ classe). Cette décoration récompense les soldats œuvrant au sein des unités de soutien logistique.

An SS-Unterscharführer and an SS-Rottenführer are posing for the photograph. The second has just been decorated with the Kriegsverdienstkreuz II.Klasse (war merit cross 2nd class). This medal was awarded to the soldiers serving in logistic support units.

Servants d'un canon d'infanterie de 7,5 cm. Le chef de pièce est un *SS-Hauptscharführer*; celui-ci tient un bâton avec un chiffon accroché à son extrémité. Quelle en est l'utilité ?

7.5cm infantry gun crew. The main element is an SS-Hauptscharführer; he is holding a staff with a cloth attached to its end. What could it be used for?

Le secteur du Wolchow est si horrible avec ses forêts marécageuses, ses mouches, ses moustiques, son climat pénible et son manque de routes qu'il a été vulgairement baptisé par les soldats allemands « *Le trou du c.. du monde* », comme l'indique ce panneau.

The Wolchow sector was horrible, with its swampy forests, flies, tiresome climate and lack of roads. Hence, it was named the "The a...hole of the world" by the German soldiers, as indicated on this board.

Un bunker a été construit en rondins et recouvert d'une épaisse couche de terre. A son entrée, on peut lire sur le panneau « *Au vétéran de la Mer de Glace* » tandis que l'insigne régimentaire a été peint sur son linteau. A n'en pas douter, le *SS-Untersturmführer* se trouvant au centre de la photographie en est un, à en juger par ses décorations (Croix de fer de 2ᵉ et de 1ᵉ classes, médaille des blessés, insigne d'assaut de l'infanterie en argent).

A bunker has been built from logs and covered with a thick layer of earth. At the entrance, one can read "To the ice sea veteran", while the regiment's insignia has been painted on the lintel. There is no doubt that the SS-Untersturmführer who is standing in the centre of the picture, is one of them, judging by his decorations (iron crosses, 2nd and 1st class, wounded badge in silver, and infantry assault badge in silver).

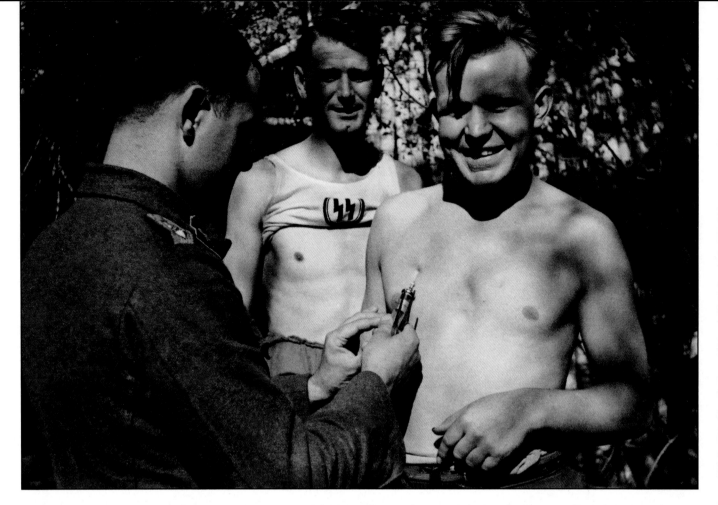

Vaccination pour ces soldats du *SS-IR 9 « Thule »*. Le régiment a été rebaptisé au cours du printemps afin d'honorer sa performance au combat. Lors de son départ de Russie, le général von Both, commandant du *I.AK*, a écrit à son sujet : « *Venant de Finlande en janvier, le* SS-Inf.Rgt.9 *a été subordonné au I.Armeekorps et engagé auprès de la 291.ID sur la Tigoda. Là, par un froid glacial et dans une neige profonde, il a colmaté plusieurs brèches ennemies et s'est emparé d'un camp soviétique lors d'un combat acharné. Quelques semaines plus tard, le régiment a dû être envoyé vers un autre point chaud du corps d'armée, en direction de Mal. Opotschiwalowo pour être engagé aux côtés de la 215.ID. Il s'y est opposé à une nouvelle tentative de percée des Russes. Une brèche ouverte dans un secteur voisin a été également colmatée et le régiment a anéanti l'ennemi qui s'y était engouffré ainsi que deux états-majors de régiments.* »

Vaccination time for the soldiers of SS-IR 9 "Thule". The regiment has been renamed in spring to honour its performance in combat. During its departure from Russia, General von Both, commander of I.AK, wrote on the subject: "Coming from Finland in January, SS-Inf.Rgt.9 was subordinated to I.Armeekorps and stationed in the vicinity of 291.ID on the Tigoda river. There, under freezing cold conditions and deep snow, several breeches in the sector were consolidated and a Soviet camp was captured after a bitter fight. Several weeks later, the regiment was sent to another hot spot in the army corps sector near of Mal. Opotschiwalowo, and engaged with 215.ID. It opposed a new breakthrough attempt by the Russians. An gap in the neighbouring sector had equally been blocked and the regiment annihilated the enemy which had run through as well as two regiments' headquarters".

Un abri, servant sans doute de bar, a été construit dans la forêt, quelque part dans le secteur du Wolchow. On notera les croix gammées et le « *Heil Hitler* » décorant l'ensemble. Les SS étaient des soldats politiques avant que leurs associations ne le renient après la guerre.

A shelter, undoubtedly serving as a bar, was built in a forest somewhere in the Wolchow sector. Note the swastikas and the "Heil Hitler" decorating the place. The SS were political soldiers but after the war, their veterans' associations denied it strongly.

Avant de quitter le front, les hommes du régiment doivent passer par le centre d'épouillage de la *215.ID* (dont l'écusson a été peint sur le panneau) à Tschudowo. Ils vont également pouvoir y prendre un bain, un luxe qu'ils ne pouvaient se permettre en première ligne.

Before leaving the front, the regiment's men have to pass through the delousing centre of 215.ID (whose divisional sign has been painted on the board) in Tschudowo. They can also take a bath, a luxury that they were unable to indulge themselves in on the frontline.

Le ballot pour le départ. La bonne humeur est de mise. Nous sommes en juillet 1942 et le régiment quitte enfin le front de l'Est pour la France où ses survivants doivent constituer le noyau du *schnellen Regiments der SS-Totenkopf-Division* (SS-FHA, Org.Tgb.Nr. 4099/42 geh. v.10.7.1942).

Packing for departure. High spirits were the order of the day. It was July 1942 and the regiment finally left the eastern front for France where the survivors were to form the nucleus of schnellen Regiments der SS-Totenkopf-Division (SS-FHA, Org.Tgb.Nr. 4099/42 geh. v.10.7.1942).

Embarquement des hommes et des véhicules en gare de Tschudowo. Ce camion *Ford G917T* a souffert de son engagement sur le front. Le *SS-Obersturmführer* doit être le chef de la *13.Kp./SS-IR 9*. A noter la toile de tente du *Heer* qui recouvre le capot moteur.

Loading men and vehicles at the Tschudowo station. This Ford G917T has suffered as a result of being stationed at the front. The SS-Obersturmführer must be the commander of 13.Kp./SS-IR 9. Note the Heer tent canvas which is covering the engine bonnet.

Voyage en wagons de marchandises. Que cela ne tienne ! Les hommes sont trop heureux de quitter le front.

Voyage in goods wagons. That one won't hold out! The men were extremely happy to leave the front.

Ci-dessous : Impressionnante vue de la cour principale de la caserne d'Angoulême où se constitue le nouveau régiment (*SS-schnelles Regiment « Thule »*). On aperçoit une grande variété de véhicules. Au premier plan, on voit des tracteurs légers d'une tonne (Sdkfz.10) avec des canons anti-chars *Pak 38* qui leur sont attelés.

Below: *Impressive view of the main court in the Angoulême barracks, where the new regiment (SS-schnelles Regiment "Thule") was formed. The great variety of vehicles can be appreciated. In the foreground, one-ton light tractors can be seen (Sdkfz.10) with Pak 38 anti-tank cannons coupled to them.*

Ci-dessus : Gros plan sur un *SdKfz.10* tractant un canon d'infanterie de 7,5 cm *le.IG18* dans un village des Charentes. Le nouveau régiment ne comprend pas de compagnie de canons d'infanterie mais ses 4e et 8e compagnies, dites « lourdes », ont chacune une section équipée de deux *le.IG18*.

Above: Large view of a SdKfz.10 towing an le.IG18 7.5 cm infantry gun in a village of the Charentes region. The new regiment had no infantry gun companies, but its so-called "heavy" 4th and 8th companies each had a section equipped with two le.IG18.

Ci-dessous : Le plein est fait : on notera que le goulot du réservoir se trouve au milieu de l'habitacle du véhicule !

Below: The tank is full: Note the tank opening in the middle of the vehicle's cabin!

Les servants d'un canon d'infanterie posent pour le photographe devant leur tracteur *SdKfz.10* lors d'une pause repas. A cette période, les unités de la *SS-Panzergrenadier-Division « Totenkopf »* se plaignent de l'insuffisance du ravitaillement.

Infantry gun crew posing for the photograph in front of its SdKfz.10 tractor, while taking a break. During this period, the units of SS-Panzergrenadier-Division "Totenkopf" complained about a lack of food.

Le régiment participe à l'occupation de la Zone Libre en novembre 1942. Ce *SS-Rottenführer* n'a pas pu résister à l'envie de se faire photographier au pied d'un palmier, arbre que les Allemands n'ont pas l'habitude de rencontrer chez eux.

The regiment participated in the occupation of the Free Zone in November 1942. This SS-Rottenführer was unable to resist the temptation of being photographed beneath a palm tree, a tree that the Germans were not accustomed to seeing at home.

Ci-dessus : L'instruction est reprise à la base car le régiment accueille de nombreuses nouvelles recrues. C'est une véritable corvée pour les vétérans qui doivent pourtant s'y plier. Marche dans la campagne charentaise dirigée par le chef de la *8.Kp./ « Thule »*, le *SS-Hstuf.* Horst Steppuhn.

Above: Training was resumed from the beginning, as the regiment had received numerous new recruits. This was really tiresome for the veterans who had to endure it. A march in the Charente countryside directed by the chief of 8.Kp./"Thule", SS-Hstuf. Horst Steppuhn.

Ci-contre : Exercice de tir à la carabine *K98 k*. Vers la fin de la guerre, les modèles assemblés seront dépourvus de la baguette de nettoyage.

Opposite: Shooting practice with a K98 k. rifle. Towards the end of the war, the assembled models lacked their cleaning rods.

Instruction au tir au *MG-34*. Apparemment, le régiment n'a pas encore reçu les nouveaux *MG-42*.

Shooting practice with a MG-34. Apparently, the regiment had not yet received the new MG-42.

Groupe de soldats du régiment, quelque part sur la côte atlantique. Celui de gauche porte sa tenue de treillis sous son manteau.

A group of soldiers from the regiment, somewhere along the Atlantic coast. The one on the left is wearing his drill trousers underneath his greatcoat.

Relève de la garde devant une maison abritant l'un des PC du régiment (sans doute le PC du régiment ou de l'un des deux bataillons). Nous sommes en novembre ou en décembre 1942 et les hommes ont revêtu leurs manteaux.

Relieving the guard in front of a house sheltering one of the regiment's HQ (undoubtedly the HQ of the regiment of one of the two battalions). It was November or December 1942 and the men were wearing their greatcoats.

Exercice sur le canon d'infanterie *le.IG18*. Les hommes ont mis leurs masques à gaz afin de s'entraîner à faire face à toutes les situations, même à l'improbable attaque aux gaz de combat. On notera les tenues de treillis revêtues lors de l'entraînement. Ceci permet d'économiser les uniformes.

Training with a le.IG18 infantry gun. The men have put on their gas masks in order to train confronting all the situations, even the unlikely event of a gas attack during combat. Note the drill clothing used for training. This allowed them to spare their uniforms.

Départ vers le front de l'Est. Nous sommes donc en janvier 1943. Notre homme a été promu *SS-Unterscharführer*. On le voit ici en compagnie d'autres sous-officiers du régiment. Une habitante d'Angoulême, sans doute leur logeuse, est venue leur dire au revoir sur le quai de la gare.

Leaving for the Eastern Front, January 1943. Our man has been promoted to SS-Unterscharführer. He is seen here in the company of some of the regiment's other non-commissioned officers. One of the residents of Angoulême, undoubtedly their landlady, has come to the station platform to bid them farewell.

Opposite page

Au-dessus : Arrivée en Ukraine. La température y est glaciale. Le capotage de ce *Steyr Typ 1500 A/1* est devenu indispensable. Cette voiture lourde, pesant 4 160 kg à pleine charge, est mue par un moteur V8 de 3,517 litres développant 85 chevaux à 3 000 tours par minute. Elle atteint la vitesse de 90 km/h sur route et de 45 km/h en tout terrain. Il s'agit en effet d'un 4x4 dont la production s'est échelonnée entre 1941 et 1944.

Above: *Arriving in Ukraine. The temperature there was icy. The cabin of the Steyr Typ 1500 A/1 had become indispensable. This heavy vehicle, weighing 4.160 kg when full, was moved by a 3.517 litre engine yielding 85 horsepower and 3,000 rpm. It reached a velocity of 90 km/hr on the road and 45 km/hr off-road. This 4x4 was produced between 1941 and 1944.*

Ci-contre : Printemps 1943. Sous-officiers du régiment posant devant un camion de leur unité. On notera l'absence de bande de bras et les casquettes camouflées.

Opposite: *Spring 1943. Non-commissioned officers from the regiment are posing in front of one of their unit's trucks. Note the absence of armbands and their camouflaged caps.*

Maintenance sur un canon *le.IG18*. Nous sommes en plein été 1943. Ce sont des mois au cours desquels la division *« Totenkopf »* va réellement jouer un rôle de pompier sur le front, tout d'abord en attaquant en pointe du *II.SS-Pz.Korps* à Koursk, puis en intervenant sur le Mius, puis à l'ouest de Charkow et enfin en couvrant la retraite vers la tête de pont de Krementschug.

Maintenance work on a le.IG18 gun, mid-summer 1943. During these months, the "Totenkopf" division actually fulfilled the role of firemen all along the front, first with II.SS-Pz.Korps attacking at Koursk, then intervening in the Mius sector, then to the west of Charkow and finally covering the retreat towards the bridgehead at Krementschug.

A partir de 1943, l'album de notre homme se fait beaucoup plus erratique, les pellicules photo se faisant plus rares pour les non professionnels. On l'aperçoit ici sur la gauche de la tranchée en compagnie de quelques uns de ses camarades. A noter la *Panzerfaust* posée sur le parapet. A priori, ce cliché doit dater du printemps 1944. A ce moment-là, le *SS-Kradschützen-Regiment « Thule »* n'existe plus, car il a été dissous quelques semaines après les combats de Charkow au cours du printemps précédent.

From 1943 onwards, our man's photo album became a lot more erratic, the photographic films were taken more rarely by non-professionals. He can be made out here on the left side of a trench accompanied by several of his comrades. Note the Panzerfaust placed on the parapet. In principle, this plate was taken in spring 1944. At that time, SS-Kradschützen-Regiment "Thule" was no more, as it had been dissolved several weeks after the fighting at Charkow in April 1943.

Trois des quatre hommes aperçus sur la photographie précédente se retrouvent ici dans une localité. D'après les habits portés par les villageois, il est possible de situer l'action en Roumanie, et d'après la végétation, au plus tard au mois d'avril. L'homme au centre est équipé d'une *Panzerfaust 60*, arme antichar à courte portée (60 m), propulsant une roquette à charge creuse. Celle-ci possède une vitesse initiale de 45 mètres par seconde grâce à une charge propulsive de 140 grammes. Le poids total de l'arme est de 6 kg. On remarquera les grenades à manche *StiGr.43* reconnaissables à leur bouchon allumeur *BZE* monté au sommet du corps.

Three of the four men appearing in the previous photograph are in the village together. Judging by the clothing worn by the villagers, the action can be situated in Romania and from the vegetation, in the month of April at the latest. The man in the centre is equipped with a Panzerfaust 60, a short-range anti-tank weapon (60 metres), launching a hollow charge rocket. This has an initial velocity of 45 metres per second, thanks to a 140 gram propulsion change. The weapon weighs a total of 6 kg. Note the StiGr.43 stick hand grenades recognisable by their BZE ignition caps mounted at the top of the main body.

Belle photographie montrant notre homme en manteau de caoutchouc et en compagnie d'un autre *SS-Unterscharführer*. Tous deux sont armés d'une *MP40*.

Beautiful photograph showing our man in a waterproof coat in the company of another SS-Unterscharführer. They are both armed with MP40s.

Exceptionnelle photographie prise depuis une tranchée et montrant un *T-34* détruit devant les positions de la division. L'adjectif « exceptionnelle » a été employé car il était en principe interdit que les soldats prennent des photographies sur le front. Cette tâche était du domaine réservé des *PK*.

This is an exceptional photograph taken from a trench showing a destroyed T-34 in front of the division's positions. The adjective "exceptional" is used because orders had been given to forbid individual soldiers to take photographs on the frontline. The task was reserved to the PK.

Un *SS-Sturmmann* essaie de mesurer la profondeur de ce cratère provoqué par l'explosion d'une bombe (l'hypothèse la plus vraisemblable) ou d'un obus de très fort calibre.

An SS-Sturmmann trying to measure the depth of a crater produced by a bomb explosion (the most likely hypothesis) or a large calibre shell.

A partir du mois de mai 1944, la division « *Totenkopf* » est reconstituée sur les arrières du front, en Roumanie. On doit ici se trouver dans un mess de sous-officiers. On remarquera le blason porté sur l'épaule gauche (*Demjanskschild*) par ce vétéran de la poche de Demjansk.

From May 1944, the "Totenkopf" division was refitted behind the front in Romania. This must have been the non-commissioned officers' mess. Note the shield on the left shoulder (Demjanskschild) of this veteran of the Demjansk sector.

De nombreux exercices sont effectués au cours de ce printemps 1944 car il faut intégrer de nombreuses nouvelles recrues mais aussi l'évolution des techniques de combat.

Numerous exercises are carried out in spring 1944, because of the need to integrate the large number of new recruits and also due to the progression of combat techniques.

Ci-contre : Un peu de repos pour ces vétérans du front de l'Est. Tous sont au moins décorés de la Croix de fer de 2ᵉ classe. On notera les bandes de bras de la *Totenkopf*.

Opposite: *A short break for these Eastern Front veterans. They are all decorated at least with iron crosses 2nd class. Note the Totenkopf armbands.*

Ci-dessous : Sieste inopinée pour cet opérateur radio. Son abri a été constitué d'une toile de tente de la *Waffen-SS* combinée à une du *Heer*, ce qui explique les différents motifs de camouflage.

Below: *Unexpected snooze for this radio operator. His shelter had been built from a Waffen-SS tent canvas combined with Heer canvas, which explains the different camouflage patterns.*

Ci-dessus : rassemblement d'une compagnie. A voir l'air interrogatif des soldats du rang et les visages pleins de confiance des sous-officiers, on peut deviner qu'il s'agit peut-être d'une cérémonie destinée à accueillir de nouvelles recrues.

Above: A company assembly. From the interrogative air among the ranking soldiers and the non-commissioned officers' faces full of confidence, one could deduce that the ceremony was dedicated to receiving new recruits.

Nouvel exercice sur le terrain, cette fois-ci en présence d'officiers roumains, reconnaissables à leurs casquettes en forme de poêle à frire. On remarquera l'éventail des tenues portées.

A new terrain exercise, this time in the presence of Romanian officers, identifiable from their frying-pan shaped caps. Note the range of different clothing worn.

Ci-dessus : Autre photographie montrant le même exercice. Il n'y a pas deux hommes habillés de façon identique ! Même les officiers roumains portent chacun des tenues différentes.

Above: Another photograph showing the same exercise. There are no two men dressed in the same manner! Even the Romanian officers are all wearing different clothing.

Ci-dessous : Fin de l'exercice. Les commentaires sont utiles pour faire progresser l'instruction. L'officier en charge de l'exercice doit être celui qui est vêtu d'une blouse camouflée d'une coupe très inhabituelle. Sans doute l'œuvre d'un tailleur de la division.

Below: End of the exercise. The comments were useful for the progression of the training. The officer in charge of the exercise must be the one who is wearing a camouflaged shirt with a very unusual cut, undoubtedly the work of one the division's tailors.

Ci-dessus : Fin juin 1944. Le *SS-Gruppenführer* Hermann Priess fait ses adieux à la *Totenkopf* et notre photographe amateur était là pour immortaliser l'instant. Les officiers se trouvant derrière lui n'ont malheureusement pas pu être identifiés.

Above: *End of June 1944. SS-Gruppenführer Hermann Priess says his goodbyes to Totenkopf and our amateur photographer was there to immortalise the moment. Unfortunately, we have not been able to identify the officers standing behind him.*

Encore un exercice avant de repartir sur le front. Il semble qu'il s'agisse ici d'un simple *Drill*.

Yet another exercise before leaving for the front. It appears to be a simple Drill.

Soldats dè la *Totenkopf*. Ceux-ci sont tous des vétérans. Ces derniers évitaient généralement de se lier avec des nouvelles recrues : en effet, les premiers à tomber au combat étaient le plus souvent les plus novices. Il fallait par conséquent les fuir pour ne pas avoir à pleurer ensuite leur mort, moyen assez efficace pour ne pas sombrer sur le plan moral et psychologique.

Totenkopf soldiers. All of them are veterans. They generally kept clear of the new recruits: Actually, the first to fall in combat were mainly the most novice solders. Consequently, they were avoided to prevent having to mourn their death, a quite effective strategy for avoiding morale and psychological decline.

Hiver 1944 – 1945. Nous nous trouvons sur les arrières du front en Pologne. De nouvelles recrues sont accueillies et sont envoyées une dernière fois à l'exercice. Il s'agit également de la dernière photo de l'album. Nous ne connaissons malheureusement pas le sort de son propriétaire d'alors.

Winter 1944-1945, behind the front in Poland. The new recruits have been assembled and sent on a final exercise. This is also the last photo of the album. Unfortunately, we do not know the fate of the owner from this point onwards.

Conclusion

Some close links with the Nazi concentration camps system

During the Nuremberg trial, Paul Hausser denied any connection between the *Waffen-SS* and the Nazi death camps. Yet documents from the German archives are unequivocal on this subject: hundreds of officers served alternatively in both organizations, and thousands of shifts in staff were carried out throughout the war. For the matter at hand, the question of whether there was a connection between the camps administration and the division doesn't even arise: from the very beginning, a third of the *Totenkopf* was made up of recruits from SS formations with death's-heads – hence the division's name –, the core of its managerial staff came from the *SS-Totenkopf-Verbände*'s disciplinary body, and its commandant was Theodor Eicke himself, the man who had till then been entrusted with the task of organizing and managing camps' administration. It is worth noting that, with a single exception, Eicke transferred all the officers from the disciplinary body to the *Totenkopf*, and that some of them were associated with other criminal organizations or themselves committed atrocities after leaving the division. The reader will find in appendix 4 of this book a table stating the names of all the division's officers who served in these camps before and during the war. It calls for several comments. First, it doesn't claim to be exhaustive, as it was impossible for the author to consult all the service records of each SS officer who had served in the division. The figure given here is slightly different from French MacLean's estimation in his book *"The Camp Men"*. It reaches almost 200 (MacLean has 159). However, these few differences notwithstanding, both studies reach the same conclusion: no other SS division counted in its ranks as many officers who had served in camps as the *Totenkopf*. Besides, staff transfers between the division and the camps took place continually. As a result, as of spring 1941, an office was set in Dachau to deal with all administrative questions specific to the *SS-Totenkopf-Division*. Furthermore, the *SS-Totenkopf-Standarten*, established for the camps' guard after the division was set up, repeatedly sent some staff to the *Totenkopf*, as well as to other *Waffen-SS* units, to make up for losses on front. Camp staff with particular skills (doctors, mechanics, radio operators, cooks, etc.) were also transferred to the *Totenkopf* when necessary. However, transfers the other way about happened mostly for disciplinary reasons. Unfortunately, it isn't possible to ascertain the exact number of soldiers transferred to the division and the other way around, since most originals are now missing. Thus, the division's close connections with the concentration camp system, as well as the hateful indoctrination preached by the Nazi political officials, and the methods used by Theodor Eicke to mould his men, were certainly at the root of the atrocities related in this book.

A fearsome war machine

Facts show that at first, the *Totenkopf* didn't make much impression on the battlefield. With a third of its strength made out of concentration camps guards, a third of old reservists and a third of young inexperienced recruits, all of them trained by officers who were more used to act as torturers than to lead men to war, the division hadn't really won fame during the French campaign in May and June 1940. Shaken up by their excessive losses due to their lack of experience and their foolhardiness, Theodor Eicke's men committed many acts of violence. Not any other division in the German army surpassed then on this matter. True, the *SS-Verfügungs*-Division, the Leibstandarte *SS "Adolf Hitler"* or even some units from the *Heer* also perpetrated massacres, but only the *Totenkopf* was responsible for such systematic crimes throughout France. After the campaign, the noticeable injection of young blood into the staff, the experience won on front, and the resulting drilling carried out for eleven months radically transformed the behaviour of the division when fighting. And it was on the extremely hostile conditions of war on the Eastern Front that the *Totenkopf* proved to be one of the best divisions in the *Waffen-SS*, if not in the whole German army. Reading the various chapters of this book is enough to realize how the *Totenkopf* fought throughout the war with unmatched fanaticism and abnegation. The battle of Demjansk might be the best example here. Besides, thanks to its own qualities – self-sacrifice, outstanding resistance, esprit de corps – the division was much more efficient in defence than in attack. Indeed, its lack of expertise regarding armoured weapons really handicapped its units during offensive operations. It must be said in its defence that it was only given very little time to become acquainted with panzers and how particular their use was. The *Totenkopf* staff's lack of experience in this field also prevented it from making the most of some situations and turning them into victories. True, these major faults reduced its output, but not to too large an extent, since it is no overstatement to claim that the division was the most feared in all the German army, because of the terrible brutality it showed in all its interventions. Having learnt to know it at their expense, the Soviets took the habit of attacking units next to it rather than the division itself whenever possible. The fanaticism soldiers showed somewhat explains the very high amount of losses the division was inflicted all through the war. It should be reminded though that it was almost always engaged in the toughest sectors of the front, where battle was most intense. The officers' inexperience was also at the root of pointless losses, especially during the French campaign in spring 1940. Thereafter, this defect was very much fixed, and although the *Totenkopf* couldn't get great tacticians, it counted in its ranks exceptional men leaders, most of them from formations bearing the death's-head, or at least inflexibly national-socialists. These officers and NCOs displayed so many qualities in combat that it eventually dented the *Totenkopf*, which had to give many of them away for the setting up of other *Waffen-SS* units. The fact that it was able to maintain such a level of performance in warfare in spite of the true drain of first rate officers proved it had a singular capacity to generate men leaders of exceptional calibre.

The *Totenkopf* wasn't a division like others: its origins, its links with concentration camps, the personality of its first commandant, the terrible brutality of its men in action and its peerless fanaticism clearly differentiated it from other units in the *Wehrmacht* or even in the *Waffen-SS*. In that regard, despite the wonders its soldiers made on the Eastern Front, it remained what was worse in the Nazi regime.

Structur of command

Postes et unités	Automne 1939 – Hiver. 1941	Printemps 1941 – Automne 1942
Divisions-Kommandeur	SS-Gruf. Eicke	SS-Gruf. Eicke, SS-Staf. Kleinheisterkamp SS-Brigaf. Keppler, SS-Obf. Simon
Ia	SS-Staf. Freiherr von Montigny SS-Ostubaf. Geisler (m.d.F.b) SS-Brigaf. Knoblauch, SS-Stubaf. Lammerding	SS-Stubaf. Lammerding, SS-Stubaf. Rudolf Schneider
Ib	SS-Ostubaf. Geisler, SS-Hstuf. Rudolf Schneider	SS-Stubaf. Rudolf Schneider
Ic	SS-Hstuf. Franke-Gricksch, SS-Hstuf. Bunsen	SS-Hstuf. Bunsen, SS-Hstuf. Häussler, SS-Hstuf. Karl-Heinz Conrad
IIa	SS-Hstuf. Hoppe, SS-Hstuf. Stadlbauer	SS-Hstuf. Stadlbauer
IIb	SS-Hstuf. Berger, SS-Hstuf. Schöffel	SS-Hstuf. Schöffel
III	SS-Stubaf. Leo Ernst, SS-Hstuf. Thumm	SS-Stubaf. Thumm, SS-Ostuf. Ziak, SS-Stubaf. Dr Barth
IVa	SS-Ostubaf. Kaindl	SS-Ostubaf. Kaindl, SS-Hstuf. Ulmer
IVb	SS-Staf. Dr Genzken, SS-Staf. Dr Rothardt, SS-Brigaf. Dr Grawitz	SS-Staf. Dr Hock
IVc		SS-Ostuf. Dr Maahsen
V	SS-Hstuf. Friedrich Schuster	SS-Hstuf. Friedrich Schuster
01	SS-Hstuf. Siegfried-Max Schultz, SS-Hstuf. Küchle, SS-Ostuf. Dr Karl-Heinz Conrad	SS-Ostuf. Dr Karl-Heinz Conrad, SS-Hstuf. Kopp, SS-Hstuf. Witte
02	SS-Ostuf. Wachsmann, SS-Ostuf. Woith	SS-Ostuf. Stürzbecher
03	SS-Ostuf. Benner, SS-Ostuf. Reder, SS-Ostuf. Ballasejus, SS-Ostuf. Friedrich	SS-Ostuf. Friedrich, SS-Ostuf. Schön, SS-Ustuf. Klinter
04	SS-Ostuf. Kopp	SS-Ostuf. Kopp
Kdt. Stabsquartier	SS-Hstuf. Hartjenstein, SS-Hstuf. Bartelt	SS-Ostuf. Schmidt
Kartenstelle		SS-Ostuf. Egelhaaf
WaMun	SS-Ostuf. Karl Weiss	SS-Ostuf. Heinrich, SS-Ostuf. Töffling
Div.-Sich.-Kp.		SS-Hstuf. Heinrich Bock
FG-Trupp	SS-Ostuf. Seitz	SS-Ostuf. Seitz, SS-Ostuf. Stadler
z.b.V	SS-Stubaf. Jansen, SS-Stubaf. Fuhrländer	
SS-T.IR 1	SS-Staf. Simon	SS-Staf. Simon, SS-Ostubaf. Becker (m.d.F.b)
Adjutant SS-T.IR 1	SS-Hstuf. Stolley, SS-Hstuf. Grässler	SS-Hstuf. Grässler, SS-Ostuf. Zielke
Ord.Offz. SS-T.IR 1	SS-Ostuf. Collani, SS-Ostuf. Molt, SS-Ustuf. Gessner, SS-Ostuf. Martin Weidlich	SS-Ostuf. Martin Weidlich, SS-Ostuf. Kirschstein, SS-Ustuf. Fritz Weidlich, SS-Ustuf. Löger
Nachr.-Offz. SS-T.IR 1	SS-Ustuf. Rumohr, SS-Ostuf. Erwin Schumacher, SS-Ustuf. Bäume, SS-Ustuf. Werner Schumacher	SS-Ostuf. Bäume, SS-Ustuf. Schwarzkopf, SS-Ostuf. Weimer, SS-Ustuf. Weissenbacher
IVa SS-T.IR 1	SS-Hstuf. Küster, SS-Hstuf. Walter Hoffmann	SS-Hstuf. Hagen, SS-Hstuf. Schmid, SS-Hstuf. Richard Wagner, SS-Hstuf. Burger
IVb SS-T.IR 1	SS-Stubaf. Dr Wohlrab	SS-Stubaf. Dr Wohlrab, SS-Stubaf. Dr Walter Pfitzner, SS-Hstuf. Dr Hermann Eckert
IVd SS-T.IR 1		SS-Hstuf. Dr Bewarder
TFK SS-T.IR 1	SS-Hstuf. Wahl	SS-Hstuf. Wahl
TFW SS-T.IR 1	SS-Ustuf. Huber	
I./SS-T.IR 1	SS-Stubaf. Hellmuth Becker	SS-Ostubaf. Hellmuth Becker, SS-Hstuf. Blumenthal, SS-Hstuf. Zollhöfer
Adjutant I./SS-T.IR 1		SS-Ostuf. Berg, SS-Ostuf. Strecker SS-Ostuf. Werner Frank, SS-Ostuf. Stürzbecher, SS-St.OJ Endemacher
Ord.Offz. I./SS-T.IR 1	SS-Ustuf. Rosenfelder, SS-Ustuf. Sachse	SS-Ustuf. Blössl, SS-St.OJ Werdendach, SS-Ustuf. Giras, SS-Ustuf. Nusser
IVa I./SS-T.IR 1	SS-Hstuf. Drube, SS-Ostuf. Brehm	SS-Hstuf. Brehm, SS-Ostuf. Richard Wagner
IVb I./SS-T.IR 1	SS-Ostuf. Dr Weyand	SS-Hstuf. Dr Wihan, SS-Ostuf. Dr Puhr
TFK I./SS-T.IR 1	SS-Hstuf. Wiesinger	
1.Kp./SS-T.IR 1	SS-Hstuf. Wimmer, SS-Hstuf. Kurtz	SS-Ostuf. Baer, SS-Hstuf. Bunsen, SS-Ostuf. Schrep, SS-Hstuf. Hans Meyer, SS-Ostuf. Zluhan
2.Kp./SS-T.IR 1	SS-Hstuf. Lönholdt, SS-Ostuf. Eduard Weber	SS-Ostuf. Alexander Herrmann, SS-Ostuf. Rupprecht Quidde, SS-Hstuf. Stöter, SS-Ostuf. Ditzenbach, SS-Ostuf. Kaddatz, SS-Ustuf. Martz, SS-Ostuf. Eduard Weber, SS-Ostuf. Rosenow
3.Kp./SS-T.IR 1	SS-Hstuf. Schubach	SS-Ostuf. Amberg, SS-Ostuf. Fust, SS-Ostuf. Herchet, SS-Ostuf. Goroncy, SS-Ostuf. Patzak, SS-Hstuf. Josef Maier, SS-Hstuf. Schiweck
4.Kp./SS-T.IR 1	SS-Ostuf. Kron	SS-Hstuf. Cornelius, SS-Ostuf. Gölles, SS-Ostuf. Matz
II./SS-T.IR 1	SS-Stubaf. Deisenhofer, SS-Hstuf. Lönholdt, SS-Hstuf. Wilhelm Schulze	SS-Hstuf. Wilhelm Schulze, SS-Ostuf. Uhl, SS-Stubaf. Deisenhofer, SS-Hstuf. Krauth, SS-Hstuf. Fritz Eckert
Adjutant II./SS-T.IR 1	SS-Ostuf. Stadlbauer, SS-Ostuf. Biermeier	SS-Ostuf. Biermeier, SS-Ostuf. Werner Frank
Ord.Offz. II./SS-T.IR 1	SS-Ostuf. Biermeier, SS-Ostuf. Schassberger	SS-Ostuf. Schassberger, SS-Ostuf. Leistner, SS-Ostuf. Herchet, SS-Ustuf. Weiler
IVa II./SS-T.IR 1	SS-Ostuf. Burger	SS-Ustuf. Backe, SS-Ostuf. Gustav Schumacher
IVb II./SS-T.IR 1	SS-Hstuf. Dr Schlegel, SS-Ostuf. Dr Lichem	SS-Hstuf. Dr Hermann Eckert, SS-Ustuf. Dr August Hagemaier
IVd II./SS-T.IR 1		SS-Ustuf. Wettwer
TFW II./SS-T.IR 1		SS-Ustuf. Müller
TFK II II./SS-T.IR 1		SS-Hstuf. Uhl
5.Kp./SS-T.IR 1	SS-Ostuf. Häussler	SS-Hstuf. Häussler, SS-Ostuf. Fredrich, SS-Ostuf. Klinter, SS-Ostuf. Buchner, SS-Hstuf. Ehlert, SS-Ostuf.

		Kabel
6.Kp./SS-T.IR 1	SS-Ostuf. Ahlemann, SS-Ostuf. Robert-Adolf Frank, SS-Ostuf. Dr Bernhard Frank	SS-Hstuf. Bernhard Frank, SS-Hstuf. Bunsen, SS-Ostuf. Paul Krauss, SS-Hstuf. Sayle
7.Kp./SS-T.IR 1	SS-Hstuf. Hurter, SS-Ostuf. Kuntze	SS-Ostuf. Kuntze, SS-Hstuf. Prem, SS-Hstuf. Weidig, SS-Hstuf. Nitsch
8.Kp./SS-T.IR 1	SS-Hstuf. von Hoym	SS-Hstuf. Kron, SS-Ostuf. Christoph, SS-Ostuf. Fritz Eckert
III./SS-T.IR 1	SS-Stubaf. Bestmann	SS-Hstuf. Kurtz, SS-Hstuf. Witte, SS-Hstuf. Schubach, SS-Hstuf. Hans Meyer, SS-Hstuf. Arnim Grunert
Adjutant III./SS-T.IR 1	SS-Ostuf. Weber Eduard	SS-Ustuf. Burckhardt, SS-Ostuf. Weidlich
Ord.Offz. III./SS-T.IR 1	SS-Ustuf. Buchner, SS-Ustuf. Ditzenbach	SS-Ostuf. Leistner, SS-Ustuf. Stienen, SS-Ustuf. Schutzbach
IVa III./SS-T.IR 1	SS-Ustuf. Heinz Schuster	SS-Ostuf. Geng, SS-Ustuf. Heinz Schuster
IVb III./SS-T.IR 1	SS-Ostuf. Dr Krieglstein	SS-Ostuf. Dr Klimsza
IVd III./SS-T.IR 1	SS-Ustuf. Dr Vonberg	
TFK III./SS-T.IR 1	SS-Ustuf. Wahrmann	
9.Kp./SS-T.IR 1	SS-Hstuf. Schellong, SS-Ostuf. Rosenbusch, SS-Ostuf. Josef Maier, SS-Hstuf. Grünewälder	SS-Hstuf. Prem, SS-Hstuf. Kurt Mayr, SS-Ostuf. Buchner, SS-Hstuf. Ehlert
10.Kp./SS-T.IR 1	SS-Hstuf. Küchle	SS-Hstuf. Hans Meyer, SS-Ostuf. Richard Baumann, SS-Ostuf. Ditzenbach, SS-Ostuf. Wedenig, SS-Ustuf. Ohlmeier, SS-Ostuf. Trauner
11.Kp./SS-T.IR 1	SS-Hstuf. Krauth	SS-Ostuf. Reder, SS-Ostuf. Josef "Pepi" Maier, SS-Ustuf. Herbstleb, SS-Ostuf. Trauner, SS-Ostuf. Kaireit, SS-Hstuf. Kriz
12.Kp./SS-T.IR 1	SS-Hstuf. Kron, SS-Hstuf. Klein, SS-Hstuf. Riedel	SS-Hstuf. Riedel, SS-Hstuf. Hesselmann, SS-Ostuf. Noak, SS-Ostuf. Zielke
13.(IG)Kp./SS-T.IR 1	SS-Hstuf. Paul Schulz	SS-Ostuf. Bonnet, SS-Hstuf. Korff
14.(Pz.Abw.)Kp./SS-T.IR 1	SS-Hstuf. Bochmann, SS-Ostuf. Reder, SS-Ostuf. Mooslechner	SS-Ostuf. Zippel, SS-Ustuf. Bachmann, SS-Ostuf. Klingelhöfer, SS-Ostuf. Jaensch, SS-Hstuf. Zippel
15.(Kradsch.)Kp./SS-T.IR 1	-	SS-Hstuf. Krauth, SS-Ostuf. Hans Stange, SS-Ostuf. Koppenwallner, SS-Hstuf. Riede, SS-Hstuf. Stürzbecher
16.(Pi.)Kp./SS-T.IR 1	-	SS-Ostuf. Iser, SS-Ostuf. Konrad Lang, SS-Hstuf. Blank, SS-St.OJ Überbacher
le.Inf.Kol. SS-T.IR 1	SS-Stubaf. Hauck	
SS-T.IR 2	SS-Staf. Nostitz, SS-Staf. Bertling, SS-Staf. Herrmann	SS-Staf. Karl Herrmann
Adjutant SS-T.IR 2	SS-Ostuf. Reum, SS-Ostuf. Reder, SS-Hstuf. Grässler, SS-Ostuf. Berlin, SS-Ostuf. Stürzbecher, SS-Hstuf. Peiper	SS-Ostuf. Zielke
Ord.Offz. SS-T.IR 2	SS-Ustuf. Haarberg, SS-Ustuf. Berg	SS-Ustuf. Berg
Nachr.Offz. SS-T.IR 2	SS-Ostuf. Wegener, SS-Ostuf. Hüttig	SS-Ustuf. Braunolte
IVa SS-T.IR 2	SS-Ustuf. Kittstein	
IVb SS-T.IR 2	SS-Stubaf. Dr Ehrsam	
TFW/SS-T.IR 2	SS-Ostuf. Amerongen	
z.b.V (8.40-10.40)	SS-Hstuf. Collani	
Stabs-Kp./SS-T.IR 2	SS-Hstuf. Unger	
I./SS-T.IR 2	SS-Stubaf. Fortenbacher	SS-Stubaf. Fortenbacher
Ord.Offz. I./SS-T.IR 2	SS-Ostuf. Robert Frank	SS-Ustuf. Heinz Müller (SS-Nr. 351 228)
IVa I./SS-T.IR 2	SS-Ostuf. Layer	
IVb I./SS-T.IR 2	SS-Ostuf. Dr Stelling	SS-Hstuf. Dr Hintermeyer
TFK I./SS-T.IR 2	SS-Ostuf. Schüle	
1.Kp./SS-T.IR 2	SS-Ostuf. Josef Maier, SS-Hstuf. Kaltofen, SS-Ostuf. Marienfeldt	SS-Ostuf. Kaddatz, SS-Ostuf. Lorenz
2.Kp./SS-T.IR 2	SS-Hstuf. Stöter	SS-Hstuf. Stöter
3.Kp./SS-T.IR 2	SS-Hstuf. Knöchlein, SS-Ostuf. Reder	SS-Ostuf. Löw
4.Kp./SS-T.IR 2	SS-Hstuf. Schroedel, SS-Ostuf. Kaddatz	SS-Ostuf. Füll
II./SS-T.IR 2	SS-Hstuf. Karl Kummer, SS-Hstuf. Dallinger, SS-Stubaf. Lippert, SS-Stubaf. Jakob Kommer	SS-Stubaf. Kommer
IVa II./SS-T.IR 2	SS-Ostuf. Neubauer	
IVb II./SS-T.IR 2	SS-Hstuf. Dr Franz Sturm, SS-Ostuf. Dr Witteler	
5.Kp./SS-T.IR 2	SS-Hstuf. Heinrich Albrecht, SS-Hstuf. Knöchlein	
6.Kp./SS-T.IR 2	SS-Hstuf. Dallinger	SS-Hstuf. Dallinger, SS-Ostuf. Kurt Herrmann
7.Kp./SS-T.IR 2	SS-Ostuf. Spanka, SS-Ostuf. Wedenig	SS-Ostuf. Wedenig
8.Kp./SS-T.IR 2	SS-Hstuf. Blumenthal	SS-Hstuf. Zech
III./SS-T.IR 2	SS-Hstuf. Schulze, SS-Stubaf. Schleifenbaum, SS-Hstuf. Blumenthal	SS-Hstuf. Blumenthal
Ord.Offz. III./SS-T.IR 2	SS-Ustuf. Boldt	SS-Ustuf. Gierass
IVa III./SS-T.IR 2	SS-Ostuf. Zeber, SS-Ustuf. Liepelt	
IVb III./SS-T.IR 2	SS-Hstuf. Dr Zwirner	
9.Kp./SS-T.IR 2	SS-Ostuf. Holzapfel, SS-Hstuf. Zollhöfer	
10.Kp./SS-T.IR 2	SS-Hstuf. Schneider, SS-Hstuf. Wawrzik, SS-Hstuf. Lönholdt	SS-Ostuf. Gruner, SS-Ostuf. Marz
11.Kp./SS-T.IR 2	SS-Hstuf. Sander, SS-Hstuf. Willy Schulz	SS-Ostuf. Christoph
12.Kp./SS-T.IR 2	SS-Hstuf. Plorin	SS-Ostuf. Gölles
13.(IG)Kp./SS-T.IR 2	SS-Hstuf. Kleffner	SS-Hstuf. Kleffner
14.(Pz.Abw.)Kp./SS-T.IR 2	SS-Ostuf. Prinz, SS-Ostuf. Karl-Heinz Friderici, SS-Hstuf. Grässler, SS-Hstuf. Hartrampf	SS-Hstuf. Heinrich Bock
15.(Kradsch.)Kp./SS-T.IR 2	-	SS-Ostuf. Unseld
le.Inf.Kol. SS-T.IR 2	SS-Ostuf. Marienfeldt	

SS-T.IR 3	SS-Staf. Götze, SS-Obf. Erbprinz zu Waldeck und Pyrmont, SS-Staf. Kleinheisterkamp	SS-Staf. Kleinheisterkamp, SS-Staf. Karl Herrmann, SS-Ostubaf. Becker (m.d.F.b)
Adjutant SS-T.IR 3	SS-Hstuf. Sparmann	SS-Ostuf. Reinecke, SS-Ostuf. Pauly, SS-Hstuf. Stieglitz
Ord.Offz. SS-T.IR 3	SS-Ustuf. Baumann, SS-Ostuf. Valtin	SS-Ostuf. Unseld, SS-Ostuf. Eduard Weber, SS-Ostuf. Lenz
Zahnarzt SS-T.IR 3		SS-Ustuf. Bewarder
Nachr.Offz. SS-T.IR 3		SS-Ustuf. Meitzel
IVa SS-T.IR 3	SS-Hstuf. Sulzbach	SS-Ostuf. Erb, SS-Hstuf. Hagen, SS-Hstuf. Wetzel
IVb SS-T.IR 3	SS-Ostuf. Dr Knapp, SS-Hstuf. Dr Kamholz	SS-Hstuf. Dr Wertschützky, SS-Hstuf. Dr Kamolz
IVd SS-T.IR 3	SS-Ustuf. Dr Rathcke	
Nachr.-Offz. SS-T.IR 3	SS-Ostuf. Schröter, SS-Ostuf. Stieglitz	SS-Hstuf. Arnim Grunert
TFK SS-T.IR 3	SS-Ostuf. Heinz	
TFW SS-T.IR 3	SS-Ustuf. Josef Pfister	SS-Ostuf. Josef Pfister
I./SS-T.IR 3	SS-Stubaf. Bellwidt, SS-Ostubaf. Reitz	SS-Stubaf. Petersen, SS-Hstuf. Launer, SS-Hstuf. Hartjenstein, SS-Hstuf. Hoppe, SS-Hstuf. Knöchlein
Adjutant I./SS-T.IR 3		SS-Ostuf. Willi Baumann, SS-Ustuf. Herrmann
Ord.Offz. I./SS-T.IR 3	SS-Ustuf. Sachse, SS-Ustuf. Willi Baumann	
IVa I./SS-T.IR 3	SS-Ostuf. Walter Bahnsen	SS-Ustuf. Gustav Schumacher, SS-Ostuf. Kirsamer, SS-Ostuf. Wienbeck
IVb I./SS-T.IR 3	SS-Hstuf. Dr Weyand	SS-Hstuf. Dr Weyand, SS-Ostuf. Dr Delitz
Zahnarzt I./SS-T.IR 3		SS-Ostuf. Dr Schmitt
TFK I./SS-T.IR 3		SS-Ostuf. Körner
1.Kp./SS-T.IR 3	SS-Hstuf. Thier	SS-Hstuf. Thier, SS-Ostuf. Sellmann, SS-Hstuf. Schiweck
2.Kp./SS-T.IR 3	SS-Hstuf. Breddemeier, SS-Hstuf. Launer	SS-Hstuf. Störter, SS-Ostuf. Gerhard Krüger
3.Kp./SS-T.IR 3	SS-Hstuf. Georg Braun	SS-Hstuf. Georg Braun, SS-Ostuf. Pfannmüller, SS-Hstuf. Ceconi, SS-Ostuf. Schiweck, SS-Ostuf. Singer, SS-Ostuf. Sellmann, SS-Ustuf. Glimm, SS-Ustuf. Karthaus, SS-Ostuf. Wilfried Richter
4.Kp./SS-T.IR 3	SS-Hstuf. Besch, SS-Hstuf. Baier	SS-Hstuf. Hoppe, SS-Ostuf. Heinz Pfitzner, SS-Hstuf. Zorn, SS-Ostuf. Kurt Herrmann
II./SS-T.IR 3	SS-Stubaf. Petersen	SS-Hstuf. Ruppmann, SS-Hstuf. Thier, SS-Hstuf. Lönholdt, SS-Ostuf. Radünz, SS-Hstuf. Witte, SS-Hstuf. Launer, SS-Stubaf. Carstens, SS-Hstuf. Kühn
Adjutant II./SS-T.IR 3		SS-Ostuf. Radünz, SS-Ustuf. Theodor Rademacher, SS-Ostuf. Heinz Müller (SS-Nr. 307171)
Ord.-Offz. II./SS-T.IR 3	SS-Ostuf. Bauer	SS-Ustuf. Heinz Müller (351228), SS-Ustuf. Pollner
IVa II./SS-T.IR 3	SS-Ostuf. Kirsamer	SS-Hstuf. Kirsamer
IVb II./SS-T.IR 3	SS-Ostuf. Dr Helmrich	SS-Hstuf. Dr Hub, SS-Hstuf. Dr Stelling, SS-Hstuf. Dr Ehrsam, SS-Ostuf. Dr Aldabert Kaufmann, SS-Hstuf. Gerhard Peters
TFK II./SS-T.IR 3		SS-Hscha. Balzer, SS-Ostuf. Dümmer
5.Kp./SS-T.IR 3	SS-Hstuf. Heinke, SS-Hstuf. Lietz, SS-Ostuf. Brinkmann	SS-Hstuf. Brinkmann, SS-Ostuf. Gnabs, SS-Ustuf. Graunke, SS-Ustuf. Barnikel, SS-Ostuf. Kersten, SS-Ostuf. Heitner
6.Kp./SS-T.IR 3	SS-Ostuf. Hoffmeyer, SS-Hstuf. Kimmel, SS-Ostuf. Töpperwien	SS-Ostuf. Töpperwien, SS-Ostuf. Töffling
7.Kp./SS-T.IR 3	SS-Hstuf. Hans Meyer, SS-Ostuf. Gradl	SS-Ostuf. Hilgenstock, SS-Ostuf. Grosche, SS-Ostuf. Kersten
8.Kp./SS-T.IR 3	SS-Hstuf. Wittl	SS-Hstuf. Wittl, SS-Hstuf. Launer, SS-Ostuf. Schrader, SS-Hstuf. Fricke, SS-Ostuf. Ueberlacker
III./SS-T.IR 3	Major d. Schupo. Schulze, SS-Stubaf. Dusenschön, SS-Hstuf. Baum	SS-Stubaf. Baum, SS-Hstuf. Prechtl, SS-Hstuf. Gigerl, Hauptmann von Pahlen
Adjutant III./SS-T.IR 3		SS-Ostuf. Möller, SS-Ustuf. Grütte
Ord.Offz. III./SS-T.IR 3	SS-Ostuf. Pauly	SS-Ostuf. Stroop, SS-Ustuf. Fiehn
Zahnarzt III./SS-TIR 3		SS-Ustuf. Firmenich
IVa III./SS-T.IR 3		SS-Ostuf. Wetzel
TFK III./SS-T.IR 3		SS-Ostuf. Reif
9.Kp./SS-T.IR 3	SS-Hstuf. Urbanitz	SS-Ostuf. Kunkel, SS-Hstuf. Prechtl, SS-Ostuf. Weigert, SS-Ustuf. Redlich
10.Kp./SS-T.IR 3	SS-Hstuf. Wolfram Schneider	SS-Hstuf. Wolfram Schneider, SS-Hstuf. Gwosdz, SS-Ustuf. Rudolf Fischer, SS-Hstuf. Möller, SS-Ostuf. Heynig
11.Kp./SS-T.IR 3	SS-Hstuf. Laackmann	SS-Hstuf. Rädecke, SS-Ostuf. Pellin, SS-Ostuf. Schassberger, SS-Ostuf. Endress
12.Kp./SS-T.IR 3	SS-Hstuf. Dusenschön, SS-Ostuf. Anlauft, SS-Ostuf. Zielske, SS-Hstuf. Ruppmann	SS-Hstuf. Schroedel, SS-Ostuf. Vogel, SS-Ostuf. Hans Jung, SS-Ostuf. Reif, SS-Ustuf. Erwin Schulz, SS-Ostuf. Anlauft
13.(IG)Kp./SS-T.IR 3	SS-Ostuf. Kühn	SS-Hstuf. Kühn, SS-Ostuf. Karl-Heinz Lorenz
14.(Pz.Abw.)Kp./SS-T.IR 3	SS-Ostuf. Steinert, SS-Hstuf. Walter Pfeiffer, SS-Ostuf. Berlin, SS-Hstuf. Hartrampf	SS-Hstuf. Hartrampf, SS-Ostuf. Ernst Wagner
15.(Kradsch.)Kp./SS-T.IR 3	-	SS-Hstuf. Hohenester, SS-Hstuf. Hardieck, SS-Ustuf. Hansen, SS-Ostuf. Unseld, SS-Ostuf. Scharke, SS-Hstuf. Singer
16.(Pi.)Kp./SS-T.IR 3	-	SS-Ustuf. Schwermann
le.Inf.Kol. SS-T.IR 3		SS-Hstuf. Eberhard
SS-T.Art.-Rgt.	SS-Staf. Allihn, SS-Ostubaf. Priess	SS-Staf. Priess
Adjutant SS-T.Art.-Rgt.	SS-Ostuf. Burböck	SS-Hstuf. Thiele, SS-Ostuf. Guckenberger
Ord.Offz. SS-T.Art.-Rgt.		SS-Ustuf. Sürenhagen, SS-Ostuf. Fritz Albrecht, SS-

		Ustuf. Nitz
IVa SS-T.Art.-Rgt.		SS-Hstuf. Paulsen
IVb SS-T.Art.-Rgt.	SS-Stubaf. Dr Edwin Jung	SS-Hstuf. Dr Schlegel
Zahnarzt SS-T.Art.-Rgt.		SS-Ostuf. Dr Ernst Müller
TFK SS-T.Art.-Rgt.	SS-Ostuf. Heinz Funke, SS-Ostuf. Mühfellner	SS-Ostuf. Mühfellner, SS-Ustuf. Sorge
TFW SS-T.Art.-Rgt.		SS-Ostuf. Prosinski
Nachr.-Offz. SS-T.Art.-Rgt.	SS-Ostuf. Walter Schmidt, SS-Ostuf. Messerle	SS-Hstuf. Max Grunert, SS-Hstuf. Hüttig
Mess-Bttr./SS-T.Art.-Rgt.	SS-Ostuf. Zientarski, SS-Ostuf. Brodersen	SS-Hstuf. Brodersen, SS-Ostuf. Hutt
I./SS-T.Art.-Rgt.	SS-Stubaf. Brasack	SS-Hstuf. Martin Stange, SS-Hstuf. Haas
Adjutant I./SS-T.Art.-Rgt.	SS-Ustuf. Meierdress	SS-Ostuf. von Liebe, SS-Ostuf. Dost, SS-Ostuf. Dauselt
Ord.Offz. I./SS-T.Art.-Rgt.		SS-Ostuf. Orth
IVa I./SS-T.Art.-Rgt.	SS-Ostuf. Friedrich Knorr	SS-Ustuf. Heckmann
IVb I./SS-T.Art.-Rgt.		SS-Ostuf. Dr Förster
Nachr.Offz. I./SS-T.Art.-Rgt.	SS-Ustuf. Messerle, SS-Ustuf. Konrath	SS-Ostuf. Kurt Ehlers
TFW I./SS-T.Art.-Rgt.	SS-Ostuf. Hornung	
1.Bttr./SS-T.Art.-Rgt.	SS-Ostuf. Pittschellis	SS-Ostuf. Pittschellis, SS-Ostuf. Heyse, SS-Ostuf. Naujok, SS-Ostuf. Quitmeyer
2.Bttr./SS-T.Art.-Rgt.	SS-Ostuf. Brohl, SS-Ostuf. Richberg, SS-Hstuf. Joachim Richter, SS-Ostuf. Westmann	SS-Hstuf. Jantsch, SS-Ostuf. Wiese, SS-Ostuf. Heyse, SS-Hstuf. Hans Walter
3.Bttr./SS-T.Art.-Rgt.	SS-Hstuf. Girmann, SS-Ostuf. Haas	SS-Ostuf. Haas, SS-Ostuf. Gerth, SS-Hstuf. Jantsch
II./SS-T.Art.-Rgt.	SS-Stubaf. Priess, SS-Hstuf. Martin Stange	SS-Stubaf. Brasack, SS-Stubaf. Swientek, SS-Hstuf. Pittschellis, SS-Ostuf. Günther Neumann
Adjutant II./SS-T.Art.-Rgt.	SS-Ostuf. Pittschellis, SS-Ostuf. von Liebe	SS-Ostuf. Heyse
Ord.Offz. II./SS-T.Art.-Rgt.	SS-Ostuf. Des Coudres	
IVa II./SS-T.Art.-Rgt.		SS-Ostuf. Killisch
IVb II./SS-T.Art.-Rgt.	SS-Ostuf. Dr Förster	SS-Hstuf. Dr Förster
Nachr.-Offz. II./SS-T.Art.-Rgt.	SS-Ustuf. Dehmel, SS-Ostuf. Runde	SS-Ustuf. Steinle
TFK II./SS-T.Art.-Rgt.	SS-Ustuf. Gloe	SS-Ustuf. Gloe
4.Bttr./SS-T.Art.-Rgt.		SS-Ostuf. Günther Neumann
5.Bttr./SS-T.Art.-Rgt.	SS-Ostuf. Kausch	SS-Ostuf. Stimmfeld, SS-Ustuf. Ulrich Fischer, SS-Ostuf. Rickert, SS-Hstuf. Franz Jakob
6.Bttr./SS-T.Art.-Rgt.	SS-Hstuf. von Freyberg	SS-Hstuf. von Freyberg, SS-Ostuf. Rauch
III./SS-T.Art.-Rgt.	SS-Stubaf. Sander	SS-Hstuf. Thiele, SS-Hstuf. Pittschellis, SS-Stubaf. Moder
Adjutant III./SS-T.Art.-Rgt.		SS-Ustuf. Finger, SS-Ostuf. von Liebe
Ord.Offz. III./SS-T.Art.-Rgt.		SS-Ustuf. Töpfer
IVa III./SS-T.Art.-Rgt.	SS-Ustuf. Boxheimer	SS-Ostuf. Franz-Josef Weber
IVb III./SS-T.Art.-Rgt.	SS-Ustuf. Dr Regner	
Nachr.-Offz. III./SS-T.Art.-Rgt.	SS-Ostuf. Günther Neumann	SS-Ustuf. Hassel
TFK III./SS-T.Art.-Rgt.		SS-Hstuf. Götz
TFW III./SS-T.Art.-Rgt.	SS-Ustuf. Kühner	SS-Ustuf. Rassmann
7.Bttr./SS-T.Art.-Rgt.	SS-Hstuf. Martin Stange	SS-Hstuf. Richberg, SS-Hstuf. Martin Stange, SS-Hstuf. Pittschellis, SS-Ostuf. Kraas, SS-Ostuf. Gerth
8.Bttr./SS-T.Art.-Rgt.	SS-Hstuf. Boysen, SS-Hstuf. Stoll	SS-Hstuf. Stoll, SS-Ostuf. Runde
9.Bttr./SS-T.Art.-Rgt.	SS-Hstuf. Franz Jakob	SS-Hstuf. Franz Jakob, SS-Hstuf. Schützenhofer, SS-Ostuf. Kraas
IV.SS-T.Art.-Rgt.	SS-Stubaf. Dr Jur. Katz, SS-Ostubaf. Brasack (m.d.F.b), SS-Stubaf. Dr Jur. Katz	SS-Stubaf. Sander, SS-Hstuf. Swientek, SS-Hstuf. Messerle, SS-Stubaf. Sander
Adjutant	SS-Ostuf. Messerle, SS-Ostuf. Dr Conrad, SS-Ostuf. Mösinger, SS-Ostuf. Kraas	SS-Ostuf. Kraas, SS-Ustuf. Heinzelmann, SS-Ustuf. Adam
Nachr.-Offz. IV./SS-Art.-Rgt.	SS-Ustuf. Mogel, SS-Ostuf. Messerle, SS-Ostuf. Konrath	SS-Ostuf. Konrath, SS-Ustuf. Thyarks
Art.-Verbindungskommando	SS-Ustuf. Kahlhammer, SS-Ustuf. Hölzgen, SS-Ustuf. Kraas, SS-Ustuf. Heinzelmann	SS-Ustuf. Heinzelmann, SS-Ustuf. Hasselbach, SS-Ustuf. Perl
IVa IV./SS-T.Art.-Rgt.	SS-Ustuf. Liese, SS-Ustuf. Wilken	SS-Ostuf. Guckes, SS-Ustuf. Jordt
IVb IV./SS-T.Art.-Rgt.	SS-Ostuf. Dr Busse	SS-Hstuf. Dr Busse, SS-Hstuf. Dr Schlögel
IVd IV./SS-T.Art.-Rgt.	SS-Ostuf. Dr Hasselbach	SS-Ostuf. Dr Müller
TFK IV./SS-T.Art.-Rgt.	SS-Hstuf. Herbert Peschke	SS-Ostuf. Winners, SS-Ustuf. Komorowski
TFW IV./SS-T.Art.-Rgt.	SS-Ustuf. Prosinski	SS-Ostuf. Prosinski, SS-Ustuf. Hesse
Stabs-Bttr. IV./SS-T.Art.-Rgt.	SS-Ustuf. Mogel, SS-Ostuf. Messerle, SS-Ostuf. Mösinger	SS-Ustuf. Heinzelmann, SS-Ostuf. Adam, SS-Ustuf. Thyarks, SS-Ostuf. de Groot
10.Bttr./SS-T.Art.-Rgt.	SS-Ostuf. Einspänner, SS-Ostuf. Hagemeier	SS-Hstuf. Wilhelm Hagemeier, SS-Ostuf. Förster, SS-Ostuf. de Groot, SS-Ostuf. Konrath
11.Bttr./SS-T.Art.-Rgt.	SS-Ostuf. Westmann, SS-Hstuf. Eggert	SS-Ostuf. Mösinger, SS-Ostuf. Weisse, SS-Ostuf. Kreibich
12.Bttr./SS-T.Art.-Rgt.	SS-Ostuf. Schützenhofer, SS-Hstuf. Girmann	SS-Hstuf. Girmann, SS-Ostuf. Messerle, SS-Ustuf. Holst, SS-Ostuf. Konrath, SS-Hstuf. Messerle
SS-T.Aufkl.-Abt.	SS-Stubaf. Hierthes, SS-Hstuf. Grünewälder, SS-Stubaf. Bestmann	SS-Stubaf. Bestmann, SS-Hstuf. Knaack, SS-Stubaf. Deisenhofer, SS-Stubaf. Kurtz
Adjutant SS-T.Aufkl.-Abt.	SS-Hstuf. Kemmetmüller, SS-Hstuf. Collani, SS-Ostuf. Otto Borchert	SS-Ostuf. Dege, SS-Ostuf. Oberlies
Ord.Offz. SS-T.Aufkl.-Abt.	SS-Ustuf. Eichelsbacher, SS-Ustuf. Dege	
IVa SS-T.Aufkl.-Abt.	SS-Ostuf. Kurt Kaufmann	SS-Hstuf. Schlesinger, SS-Ostuf. Pink
IVb SS-T.Aufkl.-Abt.	SS-Hstuf. Bender	SS-Hstuf. Dr Kuhn
IVd SS-T.Aufkl.-Abt.	SS-Ostuf. Dr Tracksdorf	
Nachr.-Offz. SS-T.Aufkl.-Abt.	SS-Hstuf. Krüger	SS-Ostuf. Fritzsche, SS-Ustuf. Weimer
TFK SS-T.Aufkl.-Abt.	SS-Ustuf. Richard Walther	SS-Ostuf. von Mühlen, SS-Ostuf. Fenneberg
1.Kp./SS-T.Aufkl.-Abt.	SS-Hstuf. Hermann Brandt, SS-Ostuf. Saalbach	SS-Ostuf. Spitt, SS-Ostuf. Zieger, SS-Hstuf. Schiwek, SS-

		Ostuf. Masarie
2.Kp./SS-T.Aufkl.-Abt.	SS-Ostuf. Hardieck, SS-Ostuf. Beeck, SS-Ostuf. Hans Neumann	SS-Ostuf. Beeck, SS-Hstuf. Elmar Gabriel, SS-Ostuf. Dege, SS-Ostuf. Detlef Bartels, SS-Hstuf. Waller
3.Kp./SS-T.Aufkl.-Abt.	SS-Ostuf. Hardieck, SS-Ustuf. Rohde	SS-Hstuf. Knaack, SS-Ostuf. Hans Neumann, SS-Ostuf. Notdurft
4.Kp./SS-T.Aufkl.-Abt.	-	SS-Hstuf. Rehder, SS-Ostuf. Sieck
SS-T.Pi.-Btl.	SS-Stubaf. Lammerding, SS-Hstuf. Ullrich	SS-Hstuf. Erich Becker, SS-Stubaf. Ullrich
Adjutant SS-T.Pi.-Btl.	SS-Ostuf. Pedersen, SS-Ustuf. Friedrich	SS-Ostuf. Wolff, SS-Ostuf. Paetznik, SS-Ustuf. Barth
IVa SS-T.Pi.-Btl.	SS-Ustuf. Rahm, SS-Ostuf. Karl Brandt	SS-Ostuf. Karl Brandt, SS-Hstuf. Loos
IVb SS-T.Pi.-Btl.	SS-Ostuf. Overhoff	SS-Hstuf. Reich, SS-Ostuf. Overhoff, SS-Ostuf. Scholz
Zahnarzt SS-T.Pi.-Btl.		SS-Ostuf. Dr Kunz
TFK SS-T.Pi.-Btl.	SS-Ostuf. Besch	SS-Hstuf. Besch
1.Kp./SS-T.Pi.-Btl.	SS-Hstuf. Wawrzik, SS-Hstuf. Erich Becker , SS-Ostuf. Müller	SS-Hstuf. Peiper, SS-Ostuf. Otto Friedrich, SS-Ostuf. Siegfried Müller
2.Kp./SS-T.Pi.-Btl.	SS-Ostuf. Lotz, SS-Hstuf. Erich Becker	SS-Ostuf. Monich, SS-Ostuf. Lotz, SS-Ostuf. Philipp Krauss, SS-Ostuf. Neuhof
3.Kp./SS-T.Pi.-Btl.	SS-Ostuf. Seela	SS-Hstuf. Seela, SS-Ostuf. Kaysers, SS-Ostuf. Petschat, SS-Ostuf. Wiese, SS-Hstuf. Seela
4.Kp./SS-T.Pi.-Btl.	SS-Hstuf. von Bödungen, SS-Ostuf. Knaack	
Brücko	SS-Ostuf. Besch, SS-Ustuf. Hermann Otto	SS-Ostuf. Muth
le.Pi.Kol.	SS-Ustuf. Kaysers	
SS-T.Nachr.-Abt.	SS-Stubaf. Sansoni	SS-Hstuf. Schumacher Erwin
Adjutant SS-T.Nachr.-Abt.	SS-Ostuf. Schröter	SS-Ostuf. Boggrefe
IVa SS-T.Nachr.-Abt.	SS-Ostuf. Siegfried Conrad	
IVb SS-T.Nachr.-Abt.		SS-Hstuf. Dr Max Peters
TFK SS-T.Nachr.-Abt.	SS-Ustuf. Laubenheimer	
TFN SS-T.Nachr.-Abt.	SS-Ustuf. Beneder	SS-Ostuf. Henning
1.(Fe)Kp./SS-T.Nachr.-Abt.	SS-Ostuf. Kunkel, SS-Ustuf. Günther	SS-Hstuf. Mattiat, SS-Hstuf. Werner Schumacher, SS-Hstuf. Boggrefe
2.(Fu)Kp./SS-T.Nachr.-Abt.	SS-Hstuf. Erwin Schumacher	SS-Ostuf. Höhne, SS-Ostuf. Rumohr
le.Nachr.Kol.	SS-Ostuf. Bäume	
SS-T.Pz.Abw.Abt.	SS-Stubaf. Leiner, SS-Stubaf. Frimmersdorf	SS-Stubaf. Frimmersdorf, SS-Hstuf. Bochmann
Adjutant SS-T.Pz.Abw.-Abt.	SS-Ustuf. Zipp	SS-Ustuf. Zipp
Ord.Offz. SS-T.Pz.Abw.-Abt.	SS-Ustuf. Eigler	SS-Ustuf. Burnester
Nachr.Offz. SS-T.Pz.Abw.-Abt		SS-Ostuf. Grams
IVa SS-T.Pz.Abw.-Abt.	SS-Ostuf. Andresen, SS-Ostuf. Borsum	SS-Hstuf. Borsum, SS-Ostuf. Mader
IVb SS-T.Pz.Abw.-Abt.	SS-Hstuf. Dr Mühlich, SS-Ostuf. Dr Klimsza	SS-Ostuf. Dr Kohbrock
IVd SS-T.Pz.Abw.-Abt.		SS-Ustuf. Metz
TFK SS-T.Pz.Abw.-Abt.	SS-Ustuf. Theile	SS-Ustuf. Kriems (?)
TFW SS-T.Pz.Abw.-Abt.	SS-Ustuf. Funke	SS-Ustuf. Funke
1.Kp./SS-T.Pz.Abw.-Abt.	SS-Hstuf. Hartrampf, SS-Ostuf. Vogel	SS-Ostuf. Vogel, SS-Hstuf. Kanth, SS-Hstuf. Beyerlein
2.Kp./SS-T.Pz.Abw.-Abt.	SS-Ostuf. Bildstein, SS-Hstuf. Bochmann	SS-Hstuf. Bochmann, SS-Ostuf. Pfarre, SS-Ustuf. Theile
3.Kp./SS-T.Pz.Abw.-Abt.	SS-Hstuf. Eichler, SS-Ostuf. Eigler	SS-Ostuf. Eigler, SS-Hstuf. Eichler, SS-Ostuf. Flohr
SS-T.Flak-Abt.	-	SS-Hstuf. Kron
Adjutant		SS-Ustuf. Hauk, SS-Ostuf. Sturm
Ord.Offz. SS-T.Flak		SS-Ustuf. Sturm
IVa SS-T.Flak-Abt.		SS-Hstuf. Burger, SS-Ustuf. Werner
IVb SS-T.Flak-Abt.		SS-Ostuf. Dr Knapp
Nachr.-Offz. SS-T.Flak-Abt.		SS-Ostuf. Rühmer
TFK SS-T.Flak-Abt.	-	SS-Ostuf. Mutz, SS-Hstuf. Wagner
1.Bttr./SS-T.Flak-Abt.		SS-Hstuf. Knöchlein
2.Bttr./SS-T.Flak-Abt.		SS-Hstuf. Grässler, SS-Ostuf. Erhard Lehmann
3.Bttr./SS-T.Flak-Abt.		SS-Ostuf. Hohmüller, SS-Ostuf. Wisheu
Fahr-Kol./SS-T.Flak-Abt.		SS-Ustuf. Gehrke
SS-T.Felders.-Btl.	-	SS-Stubaf. Kommer
SS-T.Nachschubdienste	SS-Staf. Tschimpke, SS-Hstuf. Hartjenstein	SS-Hstuf. Hartjenstein, SS-Hstuf. Scheungraber
Adjutant Nachsch.Dienste		SS-Ustuf. Fischbach, SS-Ustuf. Sturm
IVa Nachsch.Dienste	SS-Ostuf. Loos	SS-Ostuf. Traeger
IVb Nachsch.Dienste	SS-Ostuf. Dr Thumstadter	
TFK Nachsch.Dienste	SS-Ostuf. Stolze	SS-Ostuf. Stolze, SS-Ostuf. Rasokat
1.kl.Kol.	SS-Ostuf. Pohlen, SS-Ostuf. Fent	
2.kl.Kol.	SS-Ustuf. Hauk	
3.kl.Kol.	SS-Ustuf. Rasokat	SS-Ostuf. Rasokat
4.kl.Kol.	SS-Hscha Köhler	
5.kl.Kol.	SS-Ostuf. Jens Friederici	SS-Ostuf. Pistotnik
6.kl.Kol.	SS-Ustuf. Pistotnik	SS-Ostuf. Renken
7.kl.Kol.	SS-Ustuf. Renken	
8.kl.Kol.	SS-Ostuf. Hein	
9.kl.Kol.	SS-Hscha Krahl	
10.gr.Kol.	SS-Ostuf. Masarie	
11.gr.Kol.	SS-Ustuf. Lindner	
12.gr.Kol.	SS-Ostuf. Steinmetz	
Nachschub-Kp.	SS-Hstuf. Hasselbroek	
SS-T.Verwaltungsdienste	SS-Ostubaf. Kaindl	SS-Ostubaf. Kaindl, SS-Hstuf. Ulmer
Verpfl.Amt		SS-Ustuf. Maahsen, SS-Ustuf. Röschmann
Bäckerei-Kp.	SS-Hstuf. Grünewald	SS-Hstuf. Enders
Schlächterei-Kp.		SS-Hstuf. Hans Weber

SS-T.Sanitätsdienste	SS-Staf. Dr Genzken, SS-Staf. Dr Rothardt, SS-Brigaf. Dr Grawitz	SS-Staf. Dr Hock
Adjutant SS-T.San.Dienste	SS-Ostuf. Ding	SS-Hstuf. Dedreux
IVa SS-T.Sanitätsdienste		SS-Ostuf. Blachian
1.Sani.-Kp.	SS-Stubaf. Dr Fehrensen	SS-Stubaf. Dr Richard Schulze
2.Sani.-Kp.	SS-Hstuf. Dr Schmick, SS-Hstuf. Dr Helmut Wolf	SS-Stubaf. Dr Karl Becker
Feldlazarett	SS-Ostubaf. Dr Schlosser	
SS-T.Ski-Kp.	-	SS-Hstuf. Schassberger,
SS-T.StuG.-Bttr.	-	SS-Hstuf. Laackmann, SS-Ostuf. Meierdress
SS-T.Kradsch.-Btl.	-	SS-Ostubaf. Becker
Adjutant SS-T.Kradsch.-Btl.	-	SS-Ustuf. Heine, SS-Ostuf. Hinderer, SS-Ostuf. Endress
Ord.Offz. SS-T.Kradsch.-Btl.	-	SS-Ostuf. Fröhlich, SS-Ostuf. Endress
Nachr.Offz. SS-T.Kradsch.-Btl.	-	SS-Ostuf. Fricke
IVa SS-T.Kradsch.-Btl.	-	SS-Hstuf. Layer
IVb SS-T.Kradsch.-Btl.	-	SS-Hstuf. Dr Wohlfahrt
IVd SS-T.Kradsch.-Btl.	-	SS-Ustuf. Wohlfahrt
Verpfl.Offz./SS-Kradsch.-Btl.	-	SS-Ostuf. Gideon
1.Kp./SS-T.Kradsch.-Btl.	-	SS-Hstuf. Krauth, SS-Hstuf. Eichert
2.Kp./SS-T.Kradsch.-Btl.	-	SS-Hstuf. Hohenester
3.Kp./SS-T.Kradsch.-Btl.	-	SS-Hstuf. Löw, SS-Ostuf. Säumenicht
4.Kp./SS-T.Kradsch.-Btl.	-	SS-Hstuf. Zech
5.Kp./SS-T.Kradsch.-Btl.	-	SS-Hstuf. Kleffner

Postes et unités	Novembre 1942 – Avril 1944
Divisions-Kommandeur	SS-Ogruf. Eicke, SS-Brigaf. Simon, SS-Brigaf. Priess, SS-Ostubaf. Ullrich (m.d.F.b)
Ia	SS-Stubaf. Rudolf Schneider, SS-Stubaf. Keller
Ib	SS-Hstuf. Stürzbecher, SS-Stubaf. Steinbeck, SS-Hstuf. Weidlich
Ic	SS-Ostuf. Klinter, SS-Ostuf. Willer
IIa	SS-Stubaf. Stadlbauer, SS-Hstuf. Schöffel, SS-Stubaf. Schmorell
III	SS-Stubaf. Seifert
IVa & Kdr SS-T.Wi.-Btl.	SS-Hstuf. Friedrich Knorr, SS-Stubaf. Hennicke
IVb & Kdr SS-T.San.-Abt.	SS-Staf. Dr Hock, SS-Ostubaf. Dr Ehrsam
V & Kdr SS-T.Inst.-Abt.	SS-Stubaf. Friedrich Schuster
VI	SS-Stubaf. Fuhrländer, SS-Hstuf. Ciesla
01	SS-Hstuf. Otto Friedrich (SS-Nr. 351207), SS-Ostuf. Hammer, SS-Hstuf. Hufenbach
02	SS-Hstuf. Albohn
03	SS-Ostuf. Willer, SS-Ustuf. Rentsch
04	SS-Ustuf. Schwarzbach
Div.Sicherungs-Kp.	SS-Ostuf. Ehlers, SS-Ostuf. Seehaus
FG-Kp.	SS-Hstuf. Buchegger
SS-Pz.Rgt.3	SS-Stubaf. Leiner, SS-Stubaf. Kunstmann, SS-Stubaf. Bochmann, SS-Stubaf. Laackmann
Adjutant SS-Pz.Rgt.3	SS-Ostuf. Rinner, SS-Hstuf. Dunkmann, SS-Hstuf. Kanth, SS-Hstuf. Wildförster, SS-Ostuf. Prihoda
Ord.Offz. SS-Pz.Rgt.3	SS-Ostuf. Max Lippert (?)
IVa SS-Pz.Rgt.3	SS-Hstuf. Lang, SS-Hstuf. Sperling
IVb SS-Pz.Rgt.3	SS-Hstuf. Dr Mühlich
TFK SS-Pz.Rgt.3	SS-Ustuf. Kademann, SS-Ostuf. Skorzeny, SS-Hstuf. Richard Walther, SS-Ostuf. Feller, SS-Ostuf. Greisinger, SS-Hstuf. Liersch
TFW SS-Pz.Rgt.3	SS-Ostuf. Werner Funke, SS-Ostuf. Richard Müller
Nachr.-Offz. SS-Pz.Rgt.3	SS-Hstuf. Grams, SS-Hstuf. Richard Günther, SS-Ustuf. Lux
Stabs-Kp./SS-Pz.Rgt.3	SS-Hstuf. Hans Fischer, SS-Hstuf. Krapf, SS-Ostuf. Lummitsch, SS-Ustuf. Kriescher
I./SS-Pz.Rgt.3	SS-Hstuf. Meierdress, SS-Hstuf. Säumenicht, SS-Ostuf. Grams
Adjutant I./SS-Pz.Rgt.3	SS-Ostuf. Heckl
Ord.Offz. I./SS-Pz.Rgt.3	SS-Hstuf. Dr Krogh-Christoffersen , SS-Ustuf. Borkmann
IVa I./SS-Pz.Rgt.3	SS-Ustuf. Bruno Wolf
IVb I./SS-Pz.Rgt.3	SS-Hstuf. Dr Mühlich, SS-Hstuf. Dr Krogh-Christoffersen, SS-Ostuf. Dr Reithmeyer
Nachr.-Offz. I./SS-Pz.Rgt.3	SS-Ustuf. Körse
TFK I I./SS-Pz.Rgt.3	SS-Ostuf. Eisele, SS-Ostuf. Klemme
Stabs-Kp. I./SS-Pz.Rgt.3	SS-Ostuf. Otto Friedrich (SS-Nr. 6888)
1.Kp./SS-Pz.Rgt.3	SS-Ostuf. Mooslechner, SS-Ustuf. Quarenski, SS-Ostuf. Lummitsch, SS-Ostuf. Siebenlist, SS-Ostuf. Riefkogel, SS-Ustuf. Rennenkampf
2.Kp./SS-Pz.Rgt.3	SS-Ostuf. Kanth, SS-Ostuf. Flohr, SS-Ostuf. Burgschulte
3.Kp./SS-Pz.Rgt.3	SS-Hstuf. Martin Gross, SS-Ostuf. Nerpel, SS-Ostuf. Altermiller
4.(schw.)Kp./SS-Pz.Rgt.3	SS-Hstuf. Kanth, SS-Hstuf. Mooslechner, SS-Ostuf. Schröder, SS-Ostuf. Richter
9.(schw.)Kp./SS-Pz.Rgt.3 (à partir de mai 1943)	SS-Hstuf. Wilfried Richter, SS-Ustuf. Köhler, SS-Ustuf. Schüssler, SS-Ustuf. Quade, SS-Ostuf. von Kleist, SS-Ostuf. Baetke
II./SS-Pz.Rgt.3	SS-Hstuf. Kunstmann, SS-Stubaf. Bochmann, SS-Hstuf. Biermeier, SS-Ostuf. Mattern
IVa II./SS-Pz.Rgt.3	SS-Ostuf. Ising
IVb II./SS-Pz.Rgt.3	SS-Ostuf. Dr Schorsten, SS-Ostuf. Dr Albert Schmidbauer
Adjutant II./SS-Pz.Rgt.3	SS-Ustuf. Mölleken, SS-Ostuf. Pfahl (?)
Ord.Offz. II./SS-Pz.Rgt.3	SS-Ustuf. Palm
Nachr.-Offz. II./SS-Pz.Rgt.3	SS-Ustuf. Niebius, SS-Ostuf. Trgecjok
Stabs-Kp. II./SS-Pz.Rgt.3	SS-Ostuf. Schröder, SS-Ostuf. Stichnoth
5.Kp./SS-Pz.Rgt.3	SS-Ostuf. Riefkogel, SS-Hstuf. Flohr, SS-Ostuf. Nerpel, SS-Ostuf. Schwieger, SS-Hstuf. Neithardt
6.Kp./SS-Pz.Rgt.3	SS-Ostuf. Wenke, SS-Ostuf. Biermeier, SS-Ostuf. Westphal
7.Kp./SS-Pz.Rgt.3	SS-Hstuf. W. Richter, SS-Hstuf. Otto Friedrich (SS-Nr. 6888), SS-Ostuf. Behr, SS-Ostuf. Heddicke, SS-Ostuf. Faux, SS-Ostuf. Mattern
Pz.Wk.-Kp./SS-Pz.Rgt.3	SS-Ostuf. Theile

Pz.Pi.-Kp./SS-Pz.Rgt.3	SS-Hstuf. Siegfried Müller, SS-Ostuf. Kinzler, SS-Ustuf. Dähnert
SS-Schtz.Rgt. "Thulé"	SS-Ostubaf. Lammerding
IVa SS-Schtz.Rgt. "Thulé"	SS-Ostuf. Bricks
IVb SS-Schtz.Rgt. "Thulé"	SS-Hstuf. Dr Tippmann
TFK SS-Schtz.Rgt. "Thulé"	SS-Hstuf. Uhl, SS-Hstuf. Richard Walther
TFW SS-Schtz.Rgt. "Thulé"	SS-Ustuf. Biberger
I./"Thulé"	SS-Stubaf. Kleffner, SS-Hstuf. Häussler
Adjutant I./"Thulé"	SS-Ostuf. Endress, SS-Ustuf. Schasche, SS-Ustuf. Furchtlehner
Nachr.Offz. I./"Thulé"	SS-Ustuf. Schönherr
IVa I./"Thulé"	SS-Ostuf. Ohde
IVb I./"Thulé"	SS-Ostuf. Dr Kohbrock
TFW I./"Thulé"	SS-Ustuf. Loritz
1.Kp./"Thulé"	SS-Ostuf. Vogt, SS-Ostuf. Hammer
2.Kp./"Thulé"	SS-Hstuf. Eichert
3.Kp./"Thulé"	SS-Hstuf. Zech, SS-Hstuf. Schoor
4.Kp./"Thulé"	SS-Hstuf. Waller, SS-Ustuf. Saalfrank
II./ "Thulé"	SS-Stubaf. Bochmann, SS-Hstuf. Deege, SS-Hstuf. Zech
Adjutant II./"Thulé"	SS-Ostuf. Thie (?)
Ord.Offz. II./"Thulé"	SS-Ustuf. Palm
Nachr.Offz. II./"Thulé"	SS-Ustuf. Hans Schulze
TFW II./"Thulé"	SS-Ustuf. Hammerich
5.Kp./"Thulé"	SS-Hstuf. Säumenicht
6.Kp./"Thulé"	SS-Ostuf. Deege
7.Kp./"Thulé"	SS-Hstuf. Arnold, SS-Hstuf. Säumenicht
8.Kp./"Thulé"	SS-Hstuf. Steppuhn
SS-T.Pz.Gren.Rgt.1	SS-Obf. Simon, SS-Ostubaf. Baum, SS-Stubaf. Ullrich, SS-Ostubaf. Baum
Adjutant SS-T.Pz.Gren.Rgt.1	SS-Ostuf. Weidlich, SS-Hstuf. Kaddatz, SS-Ustuf. Düsterwald, SS-Ustuf. Dareb
Ord.Offz. SS-T.Pz.Gren.Rgt.1	SS-Ustuf. Brunst (à partir de nov. 1943)
IVa SS-T.Pz.Gren.Rgt.1	SS-Hstuf. Rudolf Wagner
IVb SS-T.Pz.Gren.Rgt.1	SS-Stubaf. Dr Hintermeyer
Nachr.-Offz. SS-T.Pz.Gren.Rgt.1	SS-Ostuf. Fricke, SS-Ustuf. Pfeiffer, SS-Ustuf. Obst
TFK SS-T.Pz.Gren.Rgt.1	SS-Hstuf. Wahl, SS-Hstuf. Uhl
TFW SS-T.Pz.Gren.Rgt.1	SS-Hstuf. Zwerger
Stabs-Kp./SS-T.Pz.Gren.Rgt.1	SS-Ostuf. Rauert
I./SS-T.Pz.Gren.Rgt.1	SS-Ostubaf. Baum, SS-Hstuf. Reder, SS-Ostubaf. Rudolf Schneider, SS-Hstuf. Rosenow, SS-Hstuf. Fritz Eckert
Adjutant I./SS-T.Pz.Gren.Rgt.1	SS-Ustuf. Paukner, SS-Ustuf. Düsterwald, SS-Ustuf. Pach
Ord.Offz. I./SS-T.Pz.Gren.Rgt.1	SS-Ustuf. Kolasius
IVb I./SS-T.Pz.Gren.Rgt.1	SS-Ostuf. Dr Lindner, SS-Ostuf. Dr Bastian
TFK I./SS-T.Pz.Gren.Rgt.1	SS-Ustuf. Wurm
TFW I./SS-T.Pz.Gren.Rgt.1	SS-Ustuf. Glaser
1.Kp./SS-T.Pz.Gren.Rgt.1	SS-Ostuf. Otto Fischer, SS-Ostuf. Weiler, SS-Hstuf. Zluhan, SS-Ustuf. Brunst, SS-Ostuf. Spaargaren, SS-Hstuf. Fritz Eckert, SS-Ostuf. Beybel, SS-Ostuf. Kinast
2.Kp./SS-T.Pz.Gren.Rgt.1	SS-Hstuf. Rosenow, SS-Ostuf. Kurt Herrmann, SS-Ostuf. Rautell
3.Kp./SS-T.Pz.Gren.Rgt.1	SS-Hstuf. Reder, SS-Ostuf. Matz, SS-Ostuf. Burkhardt, SS-Ostuf. Friedrich Stange, SS-Ostuf. Herbstleb, SS-Ostuf. Meck, SS-Ostuf. Herchet, SS-Ustuf. Warth
4.Kp./SS-T.Pz.Gren.Rgt.1	SS-Ostuf. Saalfrank, SS-Hstuf. Berg, SS-Hstuf. Friedrich Stange
II./SS-T.Pz.Gren.Rgt.1	SS-Hstuf. Wilhelm Schulze, SS-Hstuf. Fritz Eckert, SS-Stubaf. Häussler, SS-Hstuf. Stienen
Adjutant II./SS-T.Pz.Gren.Rgt.1	SS-Ostuf. Leistner
Ord.Offz. II./SS-T.Pz.Gren.Rgt.1	SS-Ustuf. Brunst
IVa II./SS-T.Pz.Gren.Rgt.1	SS-Ustuf. Strohbach, SS-Ustuf. Eckstein
IVb II./SS-T.Pz.Gren.Rgt.1	SS-Ostuf. Dr Felser, SS-Ostuf. Dr Peter Jakob
IVd II./SS-T.Pz.Gren.Rgt.1	SS-Hstuf. Wettwer
TFK II./SS-Pz.Gren.Rgt.1	SS-Ustuf. Maier, SS-Ustuf. Benzberg, SS-Ostuf. Haugg
5.Kp./SS-T.Pz.Gren.Rgt.1	SS-Ostuf. Ambrosius, SS-Hstuf. Weisse, SS-Hstuf. Jens Friederici, SS-Hstuf. Kalle, SS-Hscha Obermeier
6.Kp./SS-T.Pz.Gren.Rgt.1	SS-Ostuf. Blössl, SS-Ustuf. Schütze
7.Kp./SS-T.Pz.Gren.Rgt.1	SS-Hstuf. Glaub, SS-Ostuf. Stienen
8.Kp./SS-T.Pz.Gren.Rgt.1	SS-Hstuf. Filleböck
III./SS-T.Pz.Gren.Rgt.1	SS-Stubaf. Schubach, SS-Stubaf. Ullrich, SS-Stubaf. Schubach, SS-Hstuf. Zielke, SS-Hstuf. Jaensch
Adjutant III./SS-T.Pz.Gren.Rgt.1	SS-Ustuf. Wiedemann, SS-Ostuf. Ahamer, SS-Ostuf. Brunst
Ord.Offz. III./SS-T.Pz.Gren.Rgt.1	SS-Ostuf. Wallner
IVa III./SS-T.Pz.Gren.Rgt.1	SS-Ostuf. Fritz Hartmann
IVb III./SS-T.Pz.Gren.Rgt.1	SS-Hstuf. Dr Kleinknecht
9.Kp./SS-T.Pz.Gren.Rgt.1	SS-Hstuf. Kaddatz, SS-Ostuf. Karthaus, SS-Hstuf. Stienen, SS-Ostuf. Lehnhardt
10.Kp./SS-T.Pz.Gren.Rgt.1	SS-Hstuf. Hans Meyer, SS-Ostuf. Berghammer, SS-Ostuf. Kollmer, SS-Ustuf. Jensen, SS-Hstuf. Enzner, SS-Ostuf. Rautell, SS-Ostuf. Dettweiler
11.Kp./SS-T.Pz.Gren.Rgt.1	SS-Ostuf. Bäuerle, SS-Ostuf. Bachmann, SS-Ustuf. Kell, SS-Hstuf. Hofer
12.Kp./SS-T.Pz.Gren.Rgt.1	SS-Hstuf. Zielke, SS-Hstuf. Jaensch, SS-Ostuf. Laasch, SS-Ostuf. Brunst, SS-Hstuf. Hausdorf
13.(IG)Kp./SS-T.Pz.Gren.Rgt.1	SS-Ostuf. Fürleger, SS-Ostuf. Budischek
14.(Flak)Kp./SS-T.Pz.Gren.Rgt.1	SS-Hstuf. Streibl, SS-Ostuf. Schütz, SS-Hstuf. Jaensch
15.(Aufkl.)Kp./SS-T.Pz.Gren.Rgt.1	SS-Hstuf. Stürzbecher, SS-Ostuf. Auer, SS-Hstuf. Hans Meyer, SS-Ostuf. Kallwitz
16.(Pi.)Kp./SS-T.Pz.Gren.Rgt.1	SS-Hstuf. Kopp, SS-Ustuf. Bergmann
SS-T.Pz.Gren.Rgt.3	SS-Staf. Hellmuth Becker, SS-Stubaf. Launer, SS-Ostubaf. Ullrich
Adjutant SS-T.Pz.Gren.Rgt.3	SS-Hstuf. Ditzenbach
Ord.Offz. SS-T.Pz.Gren.Rgt.3	SS-Ostuf. Büngeler, SS-Ostuf. Kallert
Nachr.Offz. SS-T.Pz.Gren.Rgt.3	SS-Ostuf. Rabius, SS-Ustuf. Rave
IVa SS-T.Pz.Gren.Rgt.3	SS-Hstuf. Wedell, SS-Hstuf. Vahle
IVb SS-T.Pz.Gren.Rgt.3	SS-Stubaf. Dr Hub
IVd SS-T.Pz.Gren.Rgt.3	SS-Hstuf. Dr Firmenich
TFK SS-T.Pz.Gren.Rgt.3	SS-Hstuf. Paul Günther

TFW SS-T.Pz.Gren.Rgt.3	SS-Hstuf. Josef Pfister, SS-Ostuf. Glaser
Stabs-Kp. SS-T.Pz.Gren.Rgt.3	SS-Hstuf. Hoffmeyer, SS-Hstuf. Dümmer
I./SS-T.Pz.Gren.Rgt.3	SS-Stubaf. Knöchlein, SS-Hstuf. Pellin
IVa I./SS-T.Pz.Gren.Rgt.3	SS-Ustuf. Dennersmann, SS-Ustuf. Petermann
IVb I./SS-T.Pz.Gren.Rgt.3	SS-Hstuf. Dr Butzal
1.Kp./SS-T.Pz.Gren.Rgt.3	SS-Ostuf. Schmölzing, SS-Ostuf. Trautmann
2.Kp./SS-T.Pz.Gren.Rgt.3	SS-Ostuf. Johann Bartels
3.Kp./SS-T.Pz.Gren.Rgt.3	SS-Ostuf. Glimm, SS-Ostuf. Kamphenkel, SS-Ostuf. Bockhorn
4.Kp./SS-T.Pz.Gren.Rgt.3	SS-Hstuf. Kaddatz
II./SS-T.Pz.Gren.Rgt.3	SS-Stubaf. Launer, SS-Hstuf. Wolfram Schneider, SS-Hstuf. Pellin, SS-Stubaf. Launer
Adjutant II./SS-T.Pz.Gr.Rgt.3	SS-Ostuf. Berghofen, SS-Ustuf. Sakewitz, SS-Ostuf. Berghofen, SS-Ostuf. Kopetz
Ord.Offz. II./SS-T.Pz.Gren.Rgt.3	SS-Ustuf. John
IVa II./SS-T.Pz.Gren.Rgt.3	SS-Hstuf. Kirsamer, SS-Ustuf. Dennersmann
IVb II./SS-T.Pz.Gren.Rgt.3	SS-Ostuf. Dr Wirth, SS-Ostuf. Dr Kanzlivius
5.Kp./SS-T.Pz.Gren.Rgt.3	SS-Ostuf. Kohl, SS-Ostuf. Clausen, SS-Ostuf. Kröner, SS-Ostuf. Kaptur, SS-Ostuf. Kräutler, SS-Ostuf. Pisarik, SS-Ostuf. Effner
6.Kp./SS-T.Pz.Gren.Rgt.3	SS-Ostuf. Hehn, SS-Hstuf. Kaptur, SS-Ustuf. Misling, SS-Ustuf. Panczyk
7.Kp./SS-T.Pz.Gren.Rgt.3	SS-Hstuf. Renoldi, SS-Ustuf. Kurt Herrmann, SS-Hstuf. Penninger
8.Kp./SS-T.Pz.Gren.Rgt.3	SS-Hstuf. Milius, SS-Ostuf. John
III./SS-T.Pz.Gren.Rgt.3	SS-Stubaf. Kühn, SS-Hstuf. Kaddatz, SS-Hstuf. Pellin
Adjutant III./SS-T.Pz.Gren.Rgt.3	SS-Ustuf. Flemming, SS-Ostuf. Heinz Müller (SS-Nr. 351228), SS-Ustuf. Fahrenbach
Ord.Offz. III./SS-T.Pz.Gren.Rgt.3	SS-Ustuf. Krücke, SS-Ostuf. Schade
IVa III./SS-T.Pz.Gren.Rgt.3	SS-Ustuf. Hamm
IVb III./SS-T.Pz.Gren.Rgt.3	SS-Hstuf. Dr Weissleder, SS-Ustuf. Dr Bullerschen
9.Kp./SS-T.Pz.Gren.Rgt.3	SS-Hstuf. Hans Otto, SS-Ustuf. Petersen, S-Ostuf. Ernst Müller, SS-Ostuf. Bollhardt,
10.Kp./SS-T.Pz.Gren.Rgt.3	SS-Ostuf. Frommhagen, SS-Ostuf. Gärtner, SS-Ustuf. Misling, SS-Hstuf. Endress, SS-Hstuf. Truls, SS-Ostuf. Nebelung
11.Kp./SS-T.Pz.Gren.Rgt.3	SS-Hstuf. Kimmel, SS-Ostuf. Brüderle, SS-Ostuf. Kolonko, SS-Ustuf. Franke
12.Kp./SS-T.Pz.Gren.Rgt.3	SS-Hstuf. Wolfram Schneider, SS-Ostuf. Heinz Müller, SS-Hscha Fehlhaber, SS-Ostuf. Fiehn, SS-Hstuf. Schneeberger
13.(IG)Kp./SS-T.Pz.Gren.Rgt.3	SS-Ostuf. Bockhorn, SS-Ostuf. Greger, SS-Ostuf. Mainz, SS-Hstuf. Endress
14.(Flak)Kp./SS-T.Pz.Gren.Rgt.3	SS-Ostuf. Harnisch, SS-Ostuf. Mainz, SS-Ustuf. Erdmann, SS-Ustuf. Wolfgang Knorr, SS-Ostuf. Rudolf Sturm, SS-Ostuf. Heinlein, SS-Ostuf. Wolfgang Knorr
15.(Aufkl.)Kp./SS-T.Pz.Gren.Rgt.3	SS-Hstuf. Stieglitz, SS-Ustuf. Schmitz
16.(Pi.)Kp./SS-T.Pz.Gren.Rgt.3	SS-Ostuf. Schwermann, SS-Ustuf. Becker-Zumbusch, SS-Ostuf. Donner, SS-St.OJ Nickelsen
SS-T.Art.-Rgt.	SS-Staf. Priess, SS-Stubaf. Swientek
Adjutant SS-T.Art.-Rgt.	SS-Hstuf. von Liebe
Ord.Offz. SS-T.Art.-Rgt.	SS-Ostuf. Bischoff
Nachr.Offz. SS-T.Art.-Rgt.	SS-Ostuf. Stiller, SS-Ustuf. Fritz Schmidt, SS-Ostuf. Schönherr
IVa SS-T.Art.-Rgt.	SS-Hstuf. Franz-Josef Weber
IVb SS-T.Art.-Rgt.	SS-Stubaf. Dr Witteler, SS-Hstuf. Dr Helmrich
Beob.-Bttr./SS-T.Art.-Rgt.	SS-Ustuf. Vitovec, SS-Hstuf. Läpke, SS-Ostuf. Dorando
I./SS-T.Art.-Rgt.	SS-Stubaf. Martin Stange, SS-Hstuf. Schützenhofer, SS-Hstuf. Franz Jakob
Ord.Offz. I./SS-T.Art.-Rgt.	SS-Ustuf. Eisenhut
TFK I./SS-T.Art.-Rgt.	SS-Ustuf. Placke
1.Bttr./SS-T.Art.-Rgt.	SS-Ostuf. Heyse
2.Bttr./SS-T.Art.-Rgt.	SS-Ostuf. Fritz Albrecht, SS-Hstuf. Dost, SS-Ostuf. Riedle
3.Bttr./SS-T.Art.-Rgt.	SS-Ostuf. Huth, SS-Hstuf. von Liebe, SS-Ostuf. Kober
II./SS-T.Art.-Rgt.	SS-Stubaf. Swientek, SS-Hstuf. Günther Neumann, SS-Hstuf. Lorenz Schmidbauer
Adjutant II./SS-T.Art.-Rgt.	SS-Ostuf. Kauth
Nachr.-Offz. II./SS-T.Art.-Rgt.	SS-Oscha. Holtz
IVb II./SS-T.Art.-Rgt.	SS-Hstuf. Dr Helmrich, SS-Hstuf. Dr Hub
4.Bttr./SS-T.Art.-Rgt.	SS-Hstuf. Lorenz Schmidbauer, SS-Ostuf. Straatmann
5.Bttr./SS-T.Art.-Rgt.	SS-Ostuf. Günther Neumann, SS-Ostuf. Bronke (?)
6.Bttr./SS-T.Art.-Rgt.	SS-Ostuf. Krocza, SS-Hstuf. Perl
III./SS-T.Art.-Rgt.	SS-Hstuf. Pittschellis, SS-Hstuf. Schützenhofer, SS-Hstuf. Kraas, SS-Hstuf. Wilhelm Hagemeier, SS-Hstuf. von Liebe, SS-Hstuf. Günther Neumann
IVb III./SS-T.Art.-Rgt.	SS-Hstuf. Dr Höller
Nachr.-Offz. IV./SS-T.Art.-Rgt.	SS-Ustuf. Kurt Fischer
TFK III./SS-T.Art.-Rgt.	SS-Ustuf. Mörke, SS-Hstuf. Herbert Peschke
7.Bttr./SS-T.Art.-Rgt.	SS-Ostuf. Schönefeldt, SS-Hstuf. Lorenz Schmidbauer, SS-Hstuf. Gerth
8.Bttr./SS-T.Art.-Rgt.	SS-Ostuf. Fettkötter, SS-Ostuf. Dauselt, SS-Hstuf. Guckenberger, SS-Hstuf. Kraas, SS-Ustuf. Jäger, SS-Hstuf. Dauselt
9.Bttr./SS-T.Art.-Rgt.	SS-Ostuf. Alois Becker, SS-Hstuf. Förster
IV./SS-T.Art.-Rgt.	SS-Stubaf. Sander, SS-Stubaf. Swientek, SS-Hstuf. Messerle
Adjutant IV./SS-T.Art.-Rgt.	SS-Ostuf. Jördens, SS-Hstuf. Franz Adam, SS-Ostuf. Töpfer
Art.-Verbindungskommando	SS-Ostuf. Straatmann, SS-Ustuf. Eglseer
Nachr.Offz. IV./SS-T.Art.-Rgt.	SS-Ustuf. Thyarks, SS-Ustuf. Hill, SS-Ustuf. Manthey
IVa IV./SS-T.Art.-Rgt.	SS-Ustuf. Guckes, SS-Ustuf. Jordt, SS-Ustuf. Hassel
IVb IV./SS-T.Art.-Rgt.	SS-Hstuf. Dr Witteler
TFK IV./SS-T.Art.-Rgt.	SS-Ustuf. Goes, SS-Ustuf. Metzinger
TFW IV./SS-T.Art.-Rgt.	SS-Ustuf. Kurzmann
Stabs-Bttr. IV./SS-T.Art.-Rgt.	SS-Ustuf. Thyarks
10.Bttr./SS-T.Art.-Rgt.	SS-Ostuf. Förster, SS-Ostuf. Kober, SS-Ostuf. Töpfer
11.Bttr./SS-T.Art.-Rgt.	SS-Ostuf. Kreibich, SS-Ustuf. Reichardt, SS-Ostuf. Kurt Hartmann
12.Bttr./SS-T.Art.-Rgt.	SS-Ostuf. Konrath, SS-Hstuf. Messerle, SS-Ostuf. Walter Becker
SS-T.Aufkl.-Abt.	SS-Hstuf. Masarie, SS-Stubaf. Kron, SS-Hstuf. Masarie, SS-Hstuf. Lönholdt, SS-Stubaf. Krauth, SS-Ostuf. Fürter, SS-Hstuf. Berg, SS-Hstuf. Säumenicht, SS-Stubaf. Masarie
Nachr.Offz. SS-T.Aufkl.-Abt.	SS-Ustuf. Geiger
IVa SS-T.Aufkl.-Abt.	SS-Ustuf. Helmut Albrecht
IVb SS-T.Aufkl.-Abt.	SS-Hstuf. Dr Jibasek

TFK SS-T.Aufkl.-Abt.	SS-Ostuf. von Mühlen
Stabs-Kp./SS-T.Aufkl.-Abt.	SS-Ostuf. Kolig
1.Kp./SS-T.Aufkl.-Abt.	SS-Hstuf. Jens Friederici, SS-Ostuf. Ziegler, SS-Ostuf. Kinast, SS-Ostuf. Fürter, SS-Ostuf. Kabel, SS-Ostuf. Wiethüchter
2.Kp./SS-T.Aufkl.-Abt.	SS-Hstuf. Dege, SS-Hstuf. Säumenicht, SS-Hstuf. Rohde
3.Kp./SS-T.Aufkl.-Abt.	SS-Hstuf. Eichert, SS-Ustuf. Jung, SS-Hstuf. Steppuhn, SS-Hstuf. Krauth, SS-Ostuf. Hans Schneider, SS-Ostuf. Kabel
4.Kp./SS-T.Aufkl.-Abt.	SS-Ostuf. Tiroch, SS-Hstuf. Dege, SS-Ustuf. Knab
5.(s)Kp./SS-T.Aufkl.-Abt.	SS-Hstuf. Wollner, SS-Hstuf. von Fehrenteil
SS-T.Pi.-Btl.	SS-Stubaf. Seela
Adjutant SS-T.Pi.-Btl.	SS-Ustuf. Schüssler
IVa SS-T.Pi.-Btl.	SS-Hstuf. Giessler, SS-Hstuf. Karl Schmitt, SS-Ustuf. Helmut Albrecht
IVb/SS-T.Pi.-Btl.	SS-Hstuf. Dr Berlinger
Zahnarzt SS-T.Pi.-Btl.	SS-Hstuf. Dr Meimeth
TFK SS-T.Pi.-Btl.	SS-Ustuf. Schilling, SS-Ustuf. Dunkel, SS-Ustuf. Benzberg
Stabs-Kp./SS-T.Pi.-Btl.	SS-Ustuf. Bergmann
1.Kp./SS-T.Pi.-Btl.	SS-Ustuf. Dähnert, SS-Ostuf. Bachtler, SS-Ostuf. Barth, SS-Hstuf. Paetznik, SS-Ustuf. Schüssler, SS-Ostuf. Hoffmann
2.Kp./SS-T.Pi.-Btl.	SS-Hstuf. Neuhof, SS-Ustuf. Hansen, SS-Ustuf. Rehbein, SS-Ostuf. Heinkelein, SS-Ustuf. Ostermayer
3.Kp./SS-T.Pi.-Btl.	SS-Ostuf. Barth, SS-Ostuf. Erich Neumann (SS-Nr. 204324), SS-Ustuf. Dähnert
SS-T.Nachr.-Abt.	SS-Stubaf. Erwin Schumacher, SS-Stubaf. Rumohr, SS-Hstuf. Boggrefe
Adjutant SS-T.Nachr.-Abt.	SS-Ustuf. Steinecke
IVa SS-T.Nachr.-Abt.	SS-Ustuf. Eckstein, SS-Ustuf. Guckes
IVb SS-T.Nachr.-Abt.	SS-Stubaf. Dr Peters, SS-Hstuf. Dr Fink
IVd SS-T.Nachr.-Abt.	SS-Ostuf. Falk
TFN SS-T.Nachr.-Abt.	SS-Hstuf. Towara
1.(Fe)Kp./SS-T.Nachr.-Abt.	SS-Ostuf. Lindmaier, SS-Ostuf. Beinlich
2.(Fu)Kp./SS-T.Nachr.-Abt.	SS-Ostuf. Barton
Leichte Nachrichten Kolonne	SS-Ostuf. Otto Ernst
SS-T.StuG.-Abt.	SS-Stubaf. Laackmann, SS-Hstuf. Korff, SS-Hstuf. Dehmel, SS-Stubaf. Arnim Grunert, SS-Hstuf. Pittschellis
Adjutant SS-T.StuG.-Abt.	SS-Ostuf. Rautell, SS-Ustuf. Halfbrod, SS-Ostuf. Heidler, SS-Ostuf. Albert Müller
Ord.Offz. SS-T.StuG.-Abt.	SS-Ostuf. Jensen
IVa SS-T.StuG.-Abt.	SS-Ostuf. Hintz
Stabs-Bttr./SS-T.StuG.-Abt.	SS-Hstuf. Bock
1.Bttr./SS-T.StuG.-Abt.	SS-Hstuf. Dehmel, SS-Ostuf. Heitner, SS-Ostuf. Lubich von Milovan, SS-Ostuf. Albert Müller
2.Bttr./SS-T.StuG.-Abt.	SS-Hstuf. Hans Walter, SS-Ustuf. Halfbrod, SS-Ostuf. Hensiek
3.Bttr./SS-T.StuG.-Abt.	SS-Hstuf. Linde, SS-Ostuf. Heitner, SS-Ostuf. Lubich, SS-Ostuf. Aderhold
Wk.-Zug/SS-T.StuG.-Abt.	SS-Hstuf. Liersch
SS-T.Pz.Jg.-Abt.	SS-Stubaf. Arnim Grunert
Adjutant SS-T.Pz.Jg.-Abt.	SS-Hstuf. Konrad Scholz (?)
IVa SS-T.Pz.Jg.-Abt.	SS-Hstuf. Seidel, SS-Ostuf. Seinsch
Nachr.-Offz. SS-T.Pz.Jg.-Abt.	SS-Ustuf. Lux
1.Kp./SS-T.Pz.Jg.-Abt.	SS-Hstuf. Zipp, SS-Ostuf. Aderhold
2.Kp./SS-T.Pz.Jg.-Abt.	SS-Ostuf. Hensiek, SS-Ustuf. Jendges
3.Kp./SS-T.Pz.Jg.-Abt.	SS-Hstuf. Karl-Heinz Friderici
SS-T.Flak-Abt.	SS-Stubaf. Kron, SS-Stubaf. Fuhrländer, SS-Hstuf. Rudolf Sturm
Adjutant SS-T.Flak-Abt.	SS-Ostuf. Sturm, SS-Ostuf. Grützmacher
Nachr.-Offz. SS-T.Flak-Abt.	SS-Ustuf. Niebius, SS-Ostuf. Heinz Pfeiffer
Stabs-Bttr./SS-T.Flak-Abt.	SS-Ostuf. Jumpertz, SS-Hstuf. Paul Günther, SS-Ostuf. Gerlach
1.Bttr./SS-T.Flak-Abt.	SS-Hstuf. Hauk
2.Bttr./SS-T.Flak-Abt.	SS-Hstuf. Mitthof, SS-Ostuf. Bielheim, SS-Hstuf. Mitthof
3.Bttr./SS-T.Flak-Abt.	SS-Hstuf. Heinrich Schäfer, SS-Hstuf. Erhard Lehmann
SS-T.Feldersatz-Btl.	SS-Hstuf. Kiklash
Adjutant SS-T.FEB	SS-Ustuf. Wendler
1.Kp./SS-T.FEB	SS-Ostuf. Erich Neumann (SS-Nr. 341976)
2.Kp./SS-T.FEB	SS-Ostuf. Moniulski
4.Kp./SS-T.FEB	SS-Ostuf. Klieforth
5.Kp./SS-T.FEB	SS-Hstuf. Atzrodt
SS-T.Nachschubdienste	SS-Stubaf. Scheungraber
TFW SS-T.Nachsch.Dienste	SS-Ostuf. Behrens
Wk.-Kp. SS-T.Nachsch.Dienste	SS-Ostuf. Hammerich
2.Kol./SS-T.Nachsch.Dienste	SS-Ostuf. Schödel
4.Kol./SS-T.Nachsch.Dienste	SS-Ostuf. Köhler, SS-Ustuf. Hinkel
SS-T.Wi.-Btl.	SS-Hstuf. Friedrich Knorr, SS-Stubaf. Hennicke
Adjutant SS-T.Wi.-Btl.	SS-Ustuf. Lindner
Bäckerei-Kp./SS-T.Wi.-Btl.	SS-Ustuf. Kucharczyk, SS-Hstuf. Enders
Schlächterei-Kp./SS-T.Wi.-Btl.	SS-Hstuf. Hans Weber
Verpfl.Amt	SS-Stubaf. Hennicke, SS-Ustuf. Wenzlitschke, SS-Ostuf. Wolf
Feldkasse	SS-Ostuf. Nees
SS-T.Inst.-Abt.	SS-Stubaf. Friedrich Schuster
1.Wk.-Kp.	SS-Hstuf. Hohenester
2.Wk.-Kp.	SS-Hstuf. Konrad Wagner
3.Wk.-Kp.	SS-Hstuf. Fenneberg
Ersatzteilstaffel	SS-Ostuf. Kupelmeier

Postes et unités	Mai 1944 – Mai 1945
Divisions-Kommandeur	SS-Brigaf. Priess, SS-Ostubaf. Ullrich (m.d.F.b), SS-Obf. Becker
Ia	SS-Stubaf. Keller, SS-Ostubaf. Eberhardt

Ib	SS-Hstuf. Weidlich
Ic	SS-Ostuf. Willer
IIa	SS-Stubaf. Schmorell, SS-Hstuf. Rudolf Sturm
IIb	SS-St.Ob.J. Abel
III	SS-Hstuf. Theodor Junge, SS-Stubaf. Hansen, SS-Stubaf. Willi Schneider
IVa & SS-Wi.-Btl.3	SS-Stubaf. Hennicke, SS-Hstuf. Sperling*
IVb & SS-San.-Abt.3	SS-Ostubaf. Dr Ehrsam, SS-Stubaf. Dr Scholz
IVd	SS-Stubaf. Dr Schoor
V	SS-Stubaf. Friedrich Schuster, SS-Hstuf. Dümmer
VI	SS-Hstuf. Zellmann, SS-Hstuf. Blössl
WuG	SS-Stubaf. Reinhardt
01	SS-Hstuf. Hufenbach, SS-Hstuf. Schröder-Vontin*, SS-Hstuf. Baumann, SS-Hstuf. Steinecke
02	SS-Ostuf. Furchtlehner, SS-Ostuf. Dowideit, SS-Hstuf. Zellmann
03	SS-Ostuf. Harnisch
04	SS-Ostuf. Buske
05	SS-Ustuf. Zingel
Kdt Stabsquartier	SS-Ostuf. Reupert
Div.-Sich.-Kp.	SS-Ostuf. Seehaus, SS-Ustuf. Obereder (?), SS-Ustuf. Zornow
KB-Zug	SS-Hstuf. Akermann
SS-Pz.Rgt.3	SS-Stubaf. Laackmann, SS-Stubaf. Kraas, SS-Stubaf. Pittschellis, SS-Stubaf. Hans Meyer, SS-Ostubaf. Adam, SS-Stubaf. Berlin
Adjutant SS-Pz.Rgt.3	SS-Ostuf. Oeynhausen
Ord.Offz. SS-Pz.Rgt.3	?
Nachr.Offz. SS-Pz.Rgt.3	SS-Ustuf. Uellendahl
IVa SS-Pz.Rgt.3	SS-Hstuf. Bricks
IVb SS-Pz.Rgt.3	SS-Hstuf. Dr Schorsten, SS-Hstuf. Dr Schauermann
TFK SS-Pz.Rgt.3	SS-Ostuf. Feller, SS-Hstuf. Liersch, SS-Hstuf. Klemme
TFW SS-Pz.Rgt.3	SS-Hstuf. Kühner
Stabs-Kp./SS-Pz.Rgt.3	SS-Hstuf. Grams, SS-Hstuf. Hans Fischer, SS-Ustuf. Kriescher, SS-Hstuf. Wildförster, SS-Ostuf. Nadel
I./SS-Pz.Rgt.3	SS-Stubaf. Meierdress, SS-Ostuf. Hans Ernst, SS-Hstuf. Martin
Adjutant I./SS-Pz.Rgt.3	SS-Ostuf. Strobl
Ord.Offz. I./SS-Pz.Rgt.3	SS-Ustuf. Stege, SS-Ustuf. Steinegger, SS-Ustuf. Donnert, SS-Ostuf. Engelbrecht
Nachr.Offz. I./SS-Pz.Rgt.3	SS-Ostuf. Quilitz
IVa I./SS-Pz.Rgt.3	SS-Ostuf. Spieker
IVb I./SS-Pz.Rgt.3	SS-Ustuf. Dr Abt.
TFK I./SS-Pz.Rgt.3	SS-Hstuf. Klemme, SS-Ustuf. Reitwiessner
TFW I./SS-Pz.Rgt.3	SS-Ostuf. Kühner
Stabs-Kp. I./SS-Pz.Rgt.3	SS-Ostuf. Nadel
1.Kp./SS-Pz.Rgt.3	SS-Hstuf. Riefkogel, SS-Hstuf. Leibl, SS-Ostuf. Schramm, SS-Ostuf. Herbatschek, SS-Hstuf. Franz Balzer, SS-Ostuf. Neff
2.Kp./SS-Pz.Rgt.3	SS-Hstuf. Geiling, SS-Ostuf. Heise, SS-Ostuf. von Kögel, SS-Ostuf. Strobl
3.Kp./SS-Pz.Rgt.3	SS-Hstuf. Zech, SS-Ostuf. Herbatschek
4.Kp./SS-Pz.Rgt.3	SS-Ostuf. Lummitsch, SS-Ostuf. Retzdorf, SS-Ostuf. von Kleist, SS-Ostuf. Lummitsch
Vers.-Kp. I./SS-Pz.Rgt.3	SS-Ustuf. Kaden, SS-Oscha. Wunsch
II./SS-Pz.Rgt.3	SS-Stubaf. Biermeier, SS-Hstuf. Lübbelt, SS-Hstuf. Lubich, SS-Hstuf. Leibl
Adjutant II./SS-Pz.Rgt.3	SS-Ostuf. Mölleken
Ord.Offz. II./SS-Pz.Rgt.3	SS-Ustuf. Metzler, SS-Ustuf. Effmann
IVa II./SS-Pz.Rgt.3	?
IVb II./SS-Pz.Rgt.3	?
TFK II./SS-Pz.Rgt.3	SS-Ostuf. Jurda
Stabs-Kp. II./SS-Pz.Rgt.3	SS-Hstuf. Thunig
5.Kp./SS-Pz.Rgt.3	SS-Ostuf. Prihoda, SS-Ostuf. Wenke, SS-Oscha. Marx, SS-Oscha. Peist, SS-Ustuf. Tautkus, SS-Ostuf. Prihoda, SS-Ostuf. Walter Schneider, SS-Ostuf. Wenke
6.Kp./SS-Pz.Rgt.3	SS-Ostuf. Walter Schneider, SS-Hstuf. Schweimer, SS-Ostuf. Hugo (?) Fischer
7.Kp./SS-Pz.Rgt.3	SS-Ostuf. Mattern, SS-Ustuf. Harry Vogel, SS-Ostuf. Faux, SS-Ostuf. Hans Ernst, SS-Ostuf. Mattern
8.Kp./SS-Pz.Rgt.3	SS-Ostuf. Wilhelm Rademacher
Vers.-Kp. II./SS-Pz.Rgt.3	SS-Ostuf. Arndt, SS-Ostuf. Krutzenbichler
9.(Tiger)Kp./SS-Pz.Rgt.3	SS-Ostuf. Baetke, SS-Ostuf. Neidhardt, SS-Hstuf. Fischer, SS-Ostuf. Neidhardt, SS-Hstuf. Ther, SS-Ostuf. Neff, SS-Ustuf. Nagy, SS-Ostuf. Schieffler, SS-Ostuf. Wenke
Pi.-Kp./SS-Pz.Rgt.3	SS-Ustuf. Mink
Kfz.Vers.-Kp./SS-Pz.Rgt.3	SS-Hstuf. Geiling
Pz.Wk.-Kp./SS-Pz.-Rgt.3	SS-Hstuf. Theile
SS-Pz.Gren.Rgt.5 "Totenkopf"	SS-Ostubaf. Baum, SS-Stubaf. Eckert, SS-Stubaf. Kühn, SS-Stubaf. Häussler, SS-Stubaf. Eckert, SS-Stubaf. Kühn
Adjutant SS-Pz.Gren.Rgt.5	SS-Hstuf. Kugler, SS-Ostuf. Basan
Ord.Offz. SS-Pz.Gren.Rgt.5	SS-Ustuf. Alfred Scholz, SS-Ustuf. Konrad, SS-Ustuf. Seebeck
IVa SS-Pz.Gren.Rgt.5	SS-Ostuf. Back, SS-Ostuf. Guckes
IVb SS-Pz.Gren.Rgt.5	SS-Hstuf. Dr Peter Jakob
Nachr.-Offz. SS-Pz.Gren.Rgt.5	SS-Ustuf. Degenkolb, SS-Ustuf. Dehn
TFW SS-Pz.Gren.Rgt.5	SS-Hstuf. Wilden
Stabs-Kp./SS-Pz.Gren.Rgt.5	SS-Hstuf. Zielke, SS-Ostuf. Guckes, SS-Ustuf. Karl Gabriel, SS-Ostuf. Sentker
I./SS-Pz.Gren.Rgt.5	SS-Hstuf. Fritz Eckert, SS-Hstuf. Berg, SS-Hstuf. Stienen, SS-Hstuf. Lubich
Adjutant I./SS-Pz.Gren.Rgt.5	SS-Ostuf. Eilhauer, SS-Ustuf. Jänichen, SS-Ustuf. Flemming, SS-Ustuf. Basta, SS-Ustuf. Flemming
Ord.Offz. I./SS-Pz.Gren.Rgt.5	SS-Ustuf. Farle
IVa I./SS-Pz.Gren.Rgt.5	SS-Ustuf. Manchen
IVb I./SS-Pz.Gren.Rgt.5	?
1.Kp./SS-Pz.Gren.Rgt.5	SS-Hstuf. Bucher, SS-Hstuf. Breckling, SS-Ostuf. Schomaker
2.Kp./SS-Pz.Gren.Rgt.5	SS-Ustuf. Jänichen, SS-Ostuf. Schönberger, SS-St.OJ Rolfs
3.Kp./SS-Pz.Gren.Rgt.5	SS-Hstuf. Ludwig Pfister, SS-Ustuf. Mäckelmann, SS-Ustuf. Ordemann

4.Kp./SS-Pz.Gren.Rgt.5	SS-Ostuf. Glaser, SS-Hstuf. Hildebrandt, SS-Ustuf. Reger
II./SS-Pz.Gren.Rgt.5	SS-Hstuf. Stienen, SS-Hstuf. Fromme, SS-Hstuf. Steppuhn, SS-Ostuf. Brunst, SS-Hstuf. Bachmann, SS-Ostuf. Seifert
Adjutant II./SS-Pz.Gren.Rgt.5	SS-Ostuf. Seifert, SS-Ustuf. Herbert Wahl (?)
Ord.Offz. II./SS-Pz.Gren.Rgt.5	SS-Ustuf. Gann, SS-Ustuf. Spitzmüller
IVa II./SS-Pz.Gren.Rgt.5	SS-Ostuf. Eckstein
IVb II./SS-Pz.Gren.Rgt.5	SS-Ostuf. Dr Lindner
TFK II./SS-Pz.Gren.Rgt.5	SS-Ostuf. Haugg, SS-Ustuf. Benzberg
Stabs-Kp. II./SS-Pz.Gren.Rgt.5	SS-Ustuf. Karl Gabriel
5.Kp./SS-Pz.Gren.Rgt.5	SS-Hstuf. Kalle, SS-Ostuf. Petri, SS-Ostuf. Hecher, SS-Ustuf. Gann, SS-Ostuf. Näher, SS-Ustuf. Renold, SS-Ustuf. Lüdke
6.Kp./SS-Pz.Gren.Rgt.5	SS-Ostuf. Näher, SS-Ostuf. Picus, SS-Hstuf. Wegener, SS-Ustuf. Trattner
7.Kp./SS-Pz.Gren.Rgt.5	SS-Ustuf. Dams (?), SS-Ustuf. Kossligk (?)
8.Kp./SS-Pz.Gren.Rgt.5	SS-Ostuf. Zingler, SS-Hstuf. Filleböck, SS-Ustuf. Obermeier
III./SS-Pz.Gren.Rgt.5	SS-Hstuf. Zielke, SS-Hstuf. Buchner, SS-Hstuf. Bachmann, SS-Hstuf. Stienen, SS-Ostuf. Brunst, SS-Hstuf. Ewald Ehlers, SS-Ostuf. Wolfgang Knorr, SS- Ustuf. Seebeck, SS-Hstuf. Stienen, SS-Stubaf. Kiklasch, SS-Hstuf. Kugler, SS-Ostuf. Basan, SS-Hstuf. Korsemann, SS-Ostuf. Brunst, SS-Hstuf. Kurt Herrmann, SS-Hstuf. Leo Ernst
Adjutant III./SS-Pz.Gren.Rgt.5	SS-Ustuf. Otto Becker
Ord.Offz. III./SS-Pz.Gren.Rgt.5	SS-St.OJ Zwahl, SS-Ustuf. Zährl, SS-Ustuf. Seebeck, SS-Stuscha. Halupa
IVa III./SS-Pz.Gren.Rgt.5	SS-Ostuf. Hartmann
IVb III./SS-Pz.Gren.Rgt.5	?
9.Kp./SS-Pz.Gren.Rgt.5	SS-Hstuf. Stienen, SS-Ostuf. Lehnhardt, SS-Ustuf. Koch, SS-Ustuf. Friedrich Fischer, SS-Ustuf. Zwahl
10.Kp./SS-Pz.Gren.Rgt.5	SS-Ostuf. Gürtner, SS-Ostuf. Görner, SS-Ostuf. Dettweiler, SS-Ostuf. Idler, SS-Ustuf. Grützbach, SS-Ustuf. Macha
11.Kp./SS-Pz.Gren.Rgt.5	SS-Ustuf. Obermeier, SS-Ustuf. Zwahl, SS-Ustuf. Pach (?), SS-Ustuf. Macha
12.Kp./SS-Pz.Gren.Rgt.5	SS-Hstuf. Walter Frank, SS-Ustuf. Mayer, SS-Ustuf. Brunst, SS-Ustuf. Düsel
13.(IG)Kp./SS-Pz.Gren.Rgt.5	SS-Ostuf. Arnhorst, SS-Ustuf. Stammnitz
14.(Fla)Kp./SS-Pz.Gren.Rgt.5	SS-Ostuf. Friedrich Mayr, SS-Ostuf. Wolfgang Knorr
15.(Aufkl.)Kp./SS-Pz.Gren.Rgt.5	SS-Ostuf. Wollschläger
16.(Pi.)Kp./SS-Pz.Gren.Rgt.5	SS-Ustuf. Bergmann
SS-Pz.Gren.Rgt.6 "Theodor Eicke"	SS-Ostubaf. Ullrich, SS-Ostubaf. Kleffner, SS-Ostubaf. Breimaier
Adjutant SS-Pz.Gren.Rgt.6	SS-Hstuf. Endress, SS-Ostuf. Wendler, SS-Ostuf. Strobl
Ord.Offz. SS-Pz.Gren.Rgt.6	SS-Ostuf. Hatz, SS-Ustuf. Galler, SS-Ustuf. Franz Konrad
Nachr.Offz. SS-Pz.Gren.Rgt.6	SS-Ustuf. Rave, SS-Ostuf. Raab, SS-St.OJ Degenkolb
IVa SS-Pz.Gren.Rgt.6	SS-Ostuf. Petermann
IVb SS-Pz.Gren.Rgt.6	
IVd SS-Pz.Gren.Rgt.6	SS-Hstuf. Dr Arens
TFK SS-Pz.Gren.Rgt.6	SS-Ostuf. Gerhard Balzer, SS-Ustuf. Drefahl
TFW SS-Pz.Gren.Rgt.6	SS-Ostuf. Josef Pfister
Stabs-Kp. SS-Pz.Gren.Rgt.6	SS-Hstuf. Dümmer, SS-Ustuf. Knapp
I./SS-Pz.Gren.Rgt.6	SS-Hstuf. Pellin, SS-Hstuf. Frommhagen, SS-Hstuf. Stienen, SS-Hstuf. Frommhagen
Adjutant I./SS-Pz.Gren.Rgt.6	SS-Ustuf. Sobotka
Ord.Offz. I./SS-Pz.Gren.Rgt.6	SS-Ostuf. Haupt, SS-Ustuf. Meister
IVa I./SS-Pz.Gren.Rgt.6	SS-Ostuf. Bechler
IVb I./SS-Pz.Gren.Rgt.6	SS-Hstuf. Dr Babor, SS-Ostuf. Dr Heinz Bahnsen
TFK I./SS-Pz.Gren.Rgt.6	SS-Ostuf. Pietsch
1.Kp./SS-Pz.Gren.Rgt.6	SS-Hstuf. Fromme (?), SS-Hstuf. Gustav Schneider, SS-Ustuf. Wölfler, SS-Ostuf. Willi Borchert
2.Kp./SS-Pz.Gren.Rgt.6	SS-Ostuf. Jann, SS-Ustuf. Waldmann, SS-Ostuf. Hering
3.Kp./SS-Pz.Gren.Rgt.6	SS-Ostuf. Hauber, SS-Ostuf. Heisterkamp, SS-Ustuf. Köhler
4.Kp./SS-Pz.Gren.Rgt.6	SS-Ostuf. Bartholomä (?), SS-Ustuf. Brenner
II./SS-Pz.Gren.Rgt.6	SS-Stubaf. Launer, SS-Hstuf. Schneeberger, SS-Hstuf. Fromme, SS-Hstuf. Fritz Eckert, SS-Hstuf. Silberleitner, SS-Hstuf. Endress
Adjutant II./SS-Pz.Gren.Rgt.6	SS-Ustuf. Alois Richter, SS-Ustuf. Galler
Ord.Offz. II./SS-Pz.Gren.Rgt.6	SS-Ustuf. Galler, SS-Ustuf. Saueresig
IVa II./SS-Pz.Gren.Rgt.6	SS-Ustuf. Kuhn
IVb II./SS-Pz.Gren.Rgt.6	SS-Hstuf. Dr Kanzlivius
TFW II./SS-Pz.Gren.Rgt.6	SS-Ostuf. Prighan
Stabs-Kp. II./SS-Pz.Gren.Rgt.6	SS-Ustuf. Tuma
5.Kp./SS-Pz.Gren.Rgt.6	SS-Hstuf. Bock, SS-Ustuf. Weiser, SS-Ustuf. Georg Otto
6.Kp./SS-Pz.Gren.Rgt.6	SS-Ostuf. Baron
7.Kp./SS-Pz.Gren.Rgt.6	SS-Hstuf. Penninger, SS-Ustuf. Joachim
8.Kp./SS-Pz.Gren.Rgt.6	SS-Ustuf. Söllig, SS-Hstuf. Silberleitner, SS-Ustuf. Hatz
III./SS-Pz.Gren.Rgt.6	SS-Hstuf. Kaddatz, SS-Hstuf. Pellin, SS-Stubaf. Kühn, SS-Hstuf. Ditzenbach, SS-Hstuf. Heinz Müller, SS-Hstuf. Heinrich Bock
Adjutant III./SS-Pz.Gren.Rgt.6	SS-Ustuf. Fahrenbach, SS-Ostuf. Löschnig, SS-Ustuf. Fehlhaber, SS-Oscha. Schade
Ord.Offz. III./SS-Pz.Gren.Rgt.6	SS-Ustuf. Friesenbüchler, SS-Ustuf. Franke
IVa III./SS-Pz.Gren.Rgt.6	?
IVb III./SS-Pz.Gren.Rgt.6	SS-Hstuf. Dr Göttsche, SS-Stubaf. Dr Klimsza
9.Kp./SS-Pz.Gren.Rgt.6	SS-Ostuf. Nebelung, SS-Ustuf. Löschnig, SS-Ostuf. Deeg, SS-Ostuf. Bollhaupt, SS-Ustuf. Häger, SS-Uscha. Lith
10.Kp./SS-Pz.Gren.Rgt.6	SS-Hstuf. Leo Ernst, SS-Ostuf. Nebelung, SS-Ustuf. Illmeier, SS-Hstuf. Reese, SS-Ustuf. Ploetz, SS-Ostuf. Bendfeld, SS-Hstuf. Fiehn
11.Kp./SS-Pz.Gren.Rgt.6	SS-Hstuf. Hofer, SS-Ustuf. Franke, SS-Ostuf. Hillbrecht
12.Kp./SS-Pz.Gren.Rgt.6	SS-Ostuf. Deeg, SS-Hstuf. Heinz Müller, SS-Ustuf. Fehlhaber
13.(IG)Kp./SS-Pz.Gren.Rgt.6	SS-Hstuf. Walter Becker, SS-Hstuf. Endress, SS-Hstuf. Ditzenbach, SS-Ostuf. Söllig
14.(Fla)Kp./SS-Pz.Gren.Rgt.6	SS-Hstuf. Gehrke, SS-Hstuf. Heinlein, SS-Ostuf. Wolfgang Knorr, SS-Ustuf. Lindenberg
15.(Aufkl.)Kp./SS-Pz.Gren.Rgt.6	SS-Hstuf. Pellin, SS-Ustuf. Sommer
16.(Pi.)Kp./SS-Pz.Gren.Rgt.6	SS-Ostuf. Becker-Zumbusch, SS-Ustuf. Nickelsen, SS-Ostuf. Donner, SS-Ustuf. Winkler

SS-Pz.Art.-Rgt.3	SS-Staf. Swientek
Adjutant SS-Pz.Art.-Rgt.3	SS-Hstuf. Baltruweit
Ord.Offz. SS-Pz.Art.-Rgt.3	SS-Ostuf. Bischoff
Nachr.Offz. SS-Pz.Art.-Rgt.3	SS-Ustuf. Seibert, SS-Ustuf. Schweichler
IVa SS-Pz.Art.-Rgt.3	SS-Hstuf. Schlemmer
IVb SS-Pz.Art.-Rgt.3	SS-Stubaf. Dr Helmrich
TFK SS-Pz.Art.-Rgt.3	SS-Hstuf. Willy Frank (?)
TFW SS-Pz.Art.-Rgt.3	SS-Ostuf. Hesse
WaMun SS-Pz.Art.-Rgt.3	SS-Hstuf. Böhme
Stabs-Bttr./SS-Pz.Art.-Rgt.3	SS-Hstuf. Kurzmann, SS-Ustuf. Pomarius
I./SS-Pz.Art.-Rgt.3	SS-Stubaf. Franz Jakob, SS-Hstuf. Kraas, SS-Stubaf. Lorenz Schmidbauer, SS-Hstuf. Grund
Adjutant I./SS-Pz.Art.-Rgt.3	SS-Ustuf. Aeckersberg
Nachr.Offz. I./SS-Pz.Art.-Rgt.3	SS-Ustuf. Zehetner
IVa I./SS-Pz.Art.-Rgt.3	SS-Ustuf. Zimmermann
Stabs-Bttr. I./SS-Pz.Art.-Rgt.3	SS-Ustuf. Romanus
1.Bttr./SS-Pz.Art.-Rgt.3	SS-Ostuf. Kühl, SS-Ustuf. Engelbrecher (?)
2.Bttr./SS-Pz.Art.-Rgt.3	SS-Ostuf. Töpfer, SS-Ustuf. Thyarks
3.Bttr./SS-Pz.Art.-Rgt.3	SS-Ostuf. Kober
II./SS-Pz.Art.-Rgt.3	SS-Hstuf. Lorenz Schmidbauer, SS-Stubaf. Günther Neumann, SS-Stubaf. Lorenz Schmidbauer, SS-Hstuf. von Liebe, SS-Hstuf. Jahnhorst
Ord.Offz. II./SS-Pz.Art.-Rgt.3	SS-Ostuf. Winner
IVb/IV.SS-Pz.Art.-Rgt.3	SS-Ostuf. Dr Mogel
4.Bttr./SS-Pz.Art.-Rgt.3	SS-Ostuf. Kauth
5.Bttr./SS-Pz.Art.-Rgt.3	SS-Ostuf. Bronke, SS-Ustuf. Peitler
III./SS-Pz.Art.-Rgt.3	SS-Hstuf. Günther Neumann, SS-Hstuf. von Liebe, SS-Hstuf. Dost, SS-Hstuf. Nix
Adjutant III./SS-Pz.Art.-Rgt.3	SS-Ustuf. Jacoby, SS-Ustuf. Hühne
IVa III./SS-Pz.Art.-Rgt.3	SS-Ustuf. Manfred Lange
IVb III./SS-Pz.Art.-Rgt.3	SS-Hstuf. Dr Höller
TFW III./SS-Pz.Art.-Rgt.3	SS-Hstuf. Kühner
6.Bttr./SS-Pz.Art.-Rgt.3	SS-Ostuf. Mundt, SS-Ostuf. Speck
7.Bttr./SS-Pz.Art.-Rgt.3	SS-Hstuf. Gerth, SS-Ostuf. Pysarczuk
IV./SS-Pz.Art.-Rgt.3	SS-Hstuf. Messerle, SS-Hstuf. Grund, SS-Stubaf. Messerle, SS-Ostuf. Reichardt, SS-Hstuf. Dost
Adjutant IV./SS-Pz.Art.-Rgt.3	SS-Ostuf. Stiehler
Ord.Offz. IV./SS-Pz.Art.-Rgt.3	SS-Ostuf. Dorschner (?)
Art.-Verbindungskdo IV./SS-Pz.Art.-Rgt.3	SS-Ustuf. Socher, SS-Ustuf. Mundt
IVa IV./SS-Pz.Art.-Rgt.3	SS-Ustuf. Jordt, SS-Ustuf. Hassel, SS-Ustuf. Schütz
IVb IV./SS-Pz.Art.-Rgt.3	SS-Ostuf. Dr Müller
TFK IV./SS-Pz.Art.-Rgt.3	SS-Ostuf. Goes, SS-Ustuf. Metzinger
TFW IV./SS-Pz.Art.-Rgt.3	SS-Ustuf. Schönberg
8.Bttr./SS-Pz.Art.-Rgt.3	SS-Ostuf. Töpfer, SS-Hstuf. Grund, SS-Ostuf. Dauselt, SS-Hstuf. Grund, SS-Ustuf. Zillmer, SS-Ostuf. Riedle
9.Bttr./SS-Pz.Art.-Rgt.3	SS-Ostuf. Reichardt
10.Bttr./SS-Pz.Art.-Rgt.3	SS-Hstuf. Holtheuer, SS-Ostuf. Karl, SS-Ostuf. de Groot, SS-Hstuf. Töpfer, SS-Ustuf. Schaad
SS-Pz.Aufkl.-Abt.3	SS-Stubaf. Masarie, SS-Hstuf. Zech, SS-Hstuf. Keidel, SS-Stubaf. Pellin, SS-Hstuf. Frommhagen, SS-Stubaf. Pellin, SS-Hstuf. Berg, SS-Hstuf. Kurt Herrmann, SS-Ostuf. Geiger
Adjutant SS-Pz.Aufkl.-Abt.3	SS-Ostuf. Wegmann
Ord.Offz. SS-Pz.Aufkl.-Abt.3	SS-Utsuf. Haselbacher, SS-Ostuf. Hesselbarth, SS-Ustuf. Buck
IVa SS-Pz.Aufkl.-Abt.3	SS-Ostuf. Knab
IVb SS-Pz.Aufkl.-Abt.3	SS-Hstuf. Dr Wilhelm Schmidt (?)
Stabs-Kp./SS-Pz.Aufkl.-Abt.3	SS-Ostuf. Heine, SS-Ustuf. Wieland
1.Kp./SS-Pz.Aufkl.-Abt.3	SS-Ostuf. Wiethüchter, SS-Ostuf. Ploner, SS-Ostuf. Schwarzbach
2.Kp./SS-Pz.Aufkl.-Abt.3	SS-Ostuf. Ehler, SS-Ostuf. Geiger, SS-Ostuf. Furchtlehner, SS-Ostuf. Rabitsch, SS-Ostuf. Oberlies, SS-Ustuf. Ellissen
3.Kp./SS-Pz.Aufkl.-Abt.3	SS-Ostuf. Schascha, SS-Ostuf. Conrad Peschke, SS-Ustuf. Karl Schneider, SS-Ustuf. Erdmann (?)
4.Kp./SS-Pz.Aufkl.-Abt.3	SS-Hstuf. Fischer, SS-Hstuf. Kliefoth
SS-Pz.Pi.-Btl.3	SS-Stubaf. Seela, SS-Hstuf. Benz, SS-Hstuf. Schwermann
Adjutant SS-Pz.Pi.-Btl.3	SS-Ostuf. Becker-Zumbusch
Ord.Offz. SS-Pz.Pi.-Btl.3	SS-Ustuf. Göller
IVa SS-Pz.Pi.-Btl.3	SS-Ostuf. Randi (?)
IVb SS-Pz.Pi.-Btl.3	SS-Hstuf. Dr Berlinger
TFK SS-Pz.Pi.-Btl.3	SS-Ustuf. Benzberg
Stabs-Kp./SS-Pz.Pi.-Btl.3	SS-Ustuf. Bergmann, SS-Ustuf. Ostermayer
1.Kp./SS-Pz.Pi.-Btl.3	SS-Hstuf. Barth, SS-Ostuf. Hoffmann, SS-Ustuf. Ellissen
2.Kp./SS-Pz.Pi.-Btl.3	SS-Ustuf. Ostermayer, SS-Ustuf. Göller, SS-Ustuf. Märzinger, SS-Ustuf. Mink
3.Kp./SS-Pz.Pi.-Btl.3	SS-Ostuf. Dähnert, SS-Ostuf. Erich Neumann (SS-Nr. 204324), SS-Hstuf. Vogt
SS-Pz.Nachr.-Abt.3	SS-Hstuf. Borggrefe, SS-Stubaf. Rumohr, SS-Hstuf. Höhne
Adjutant SS-Pz.Nachr.-Abt.3	SS-Ostuf. Rothe, SS-Ustuf. Fahrenbach
IVa SS-Pz.Nachr.-Abt.3	SS-Ustuf. Henne, SS-Ustuf. Wiederhold
IVb SS-Pz.Nachr.-Abt.3	SS-Hstuf. Dr Fink
TFK SS-Pz.Nachr.-Abt.3	SS-Hscha. Schreier
TFN SS-Pz.Nachr.-Abt.3	SS-Ustuf. Storch, SS-Ustuf. Bodler, SS-Ustuf. Kühne
1.Kp./SS-Pz.Nachr.-Abt.3	SS-Hstuf. Beinlich, SS-Ostuf. Basan, SS-Ostuf. Pollmann, SS-Ustuf. Tok (?)
2.Kp./SS-Pz.Nachr.-Abt.3	SS-Hstuf. Barton, SS-Ostuf. Höhne, SS-Ostuf. Eder
Leichte Nachrichten Kolonne	SS-Ostuf. Otto Ernst
SS-Pz.Jg.-Abt.3	SS-Hstuf. Pittschellis, SS-Stubaf. Krass, SS-Ostuf. Kolbe, SS-Stubaf. Zeitz, SS-Ostuf. Halfbrod
Adjutant SS-Pz.Jg.-Abt.3	SS-Ostuf. Kolbe
Ord.Offz. SS-Pz.Jg.-Abt.3	SS-Ostuf. Buck, SS-Ostuf. Sima, SS-Ustuf. Gengenheimer
Nachr.-Offz. SS-Pz.Jg.-Abt.3	SS-Ustuf. Goudschaal
IVb SS-Pz.Jg.-Abt.3	SS-Ostuf. Dr Seinsch

TFK SS-Pz.Jg.-Abt.3	SS-Ustuf. Bitterlich, SS-Hstuf. Liersch
Stabs-Kp./SS-Pz.Jg.-Abt.3	SS-Ostuf. Albert Müller, SS-Ustuf. Malm
1.Kp./SS-Pz.Jg.-Abt.3	SS-Ostuf. Aderhold, SS-Ostuf. Sima, SS-Hstuf. Paul Kunze, SS-Uscha. Pfister
2.Kp./SS-Pz.Jg.-Abt.3	SS-Hstuf. Friedrich Walter, SS-Ostuf. Heinrich, SS-Ostuf. Jesch, SS-Ostuf. Liersch, SS-Ostuf. Albert Müller, SS-Ostuf. Grünewald, SS-Ustuf. Eltz von Rübenach
3.Kp./SS-Pz.Jg.-Abt.3	SS-Ostuf. Lubich, SS-Ostuf. Linde, SS-Ostuf. Heinzmann, SS-Ostuf. Grünewald, SS-Ostuf. Jöst, SS-Ostuf. Lubich, SS-Ostuf. Wandrey
Vers.-Kp./SS-Pz.Jg.-Abt.3	SS-Ustuf. Knöss
SS-Flak-Abt.3	SS-Hstuf. Rudolf Sturm, SS-Hstuf. Mitthof, SS-Hstuf. Löschnigg, SS-Hstuf. Erhard Lehmann
Adjutant SS-Flak-Abt.3	SS-Ustuf. Lindenberg, SS-Ostuf. Fries
Nachr.Offz. SS-Flak-Abt.3	SS-Ostuf. Heinz Pfeiffer
IVb SS-Flak-Abt.3	SS-Stubaf. Dr Klimsza
TFK/SS-Flak-Abt.3	SS-Ostuf. Aniwanter
Stabs-Bttr./SS-Flak-Abt.3	SS-Ostuf. Mösslacher
1.Bttr./SS-Flak-Abt.3	SS-Hstuf. Darms, SS-Hauck
2.Bttr./SS-Flak-Abt.3	SS-Ostuf. Böhle, SS-Hstuf. Mohr
3.Bttr./SS-Flak-Abt.3	SS-Ostuf. Börner, SS-Ostuf. Lenkert
4.Bttr./SS-Flak-Abt.3	SS-Hstuf. Erhard Lehmann, SS-Ostuf. Fries
SS-Felders.-Btl.3	SS-Hstuf. Kiklasch, SS-Stubaf. Kühn, SS-Stubaf. Kiklasch, SS-Hstuf. Hans Eckert, SS-Hstuf. Atzrodt
IVb SS-FEB 3	SS-Stubaf. Dr Fink
TFW SS-FEB 3	SS-Ostuf. Loritz
SS-Wi.-Btl.3	SS-Stubaf. Hennicke, SS-Hstuf. Sperling
Adjutant SS-Wi.-Btl.3	SS-Hstuf. Hillbrecht, SS-Ostuf. Walter Kunze
SS-FPA 3	Feldpostmeister Schnaubelt, SS-Ostuf. Blendinger, SS-Ostuf. Thiel, SS-Ostuf. Bubenheim
Verpfl.Amt	SS-Ostuf. Lindner, SS-Ostuf. Wolf, SS-Ostuf. Westholt
Bäckerei-Kp.	SS-Hstuf. Enders
Schlächterei-Kp.	SS-Hstuf. Rieken
Verwaltungs-Kp.	SS-Ostuf. Westholt
SS-Dinafü 3	SS-Hstuf. Scheungraber, SS-Hstuf. Hans Weber, SS-Stubaf. Scheungraber
IVa Div.Nachsch.Tr.	SS-Ostuf. Bischoff
IVb Div.Nachsch.Tr.	SS-Stubaf. Dr Renner
Kfz.Offz. Div.Nachsch.Tr.	SS-Hstuf. Kuppelmaier
WaMun Div.Nachsch.Tr.	SS-Ostuf. Böhme
Nachsch.-Kp.	SS-Hstuf. Köhler
Wk.-Kp./Div.Nachsch.Tr.	SS-Ostuf. Hammerich
4.Nachsch.Kol.	SS-Ostuf. Karthaus
6.Nachsch.Kol.	SS-Hstuf. Poth
SS-Pz.Inst.-Abt.3	SS-Stubaf. Friedrich Schuster, SS-Hstuf. Dümmer
IVa/SS-Pz.Inst.-Abt.3	SS-Ostuf. Altjohann, SS-Ustuf. Jilek
SS-San.-Abt.3	SS-Ostubaf. Dr Ehrsam, SS-Stubaf. Dr Scholz
1.SS-San.-Kp.3	SS-Stubaf. Dr Scholz, SS-Stubaf. Dr Friedrich Schumacher
2.SS-San.-Kp.3	SS-Stubaf. Dr Polzer
SS-Feldlazarett 3	SS-Stubaf. Dr Stutz, SS-Stubaf. Dr Schwarz

Table of ranks

Heer	Waffen-SS	British Army	US Army
General Feldmarschall		Field-Marshal (5 stars)	
Generaloberst	SS-Oberstgruppenführer und Generaloberst der Waffen-SS	General (4 stars)	General of the Army (5 stars)
General der Infanterie, der Panzertruppen, der Polizei, der Flieger, etc.	SS-Obergruppenführer und General der Waffen-SS	General (4 stars)	General (4 stars)
Generalleutnant	SS-Gruppenführer und Generalleutnant der Waffen-SS	Lieutenant-General (3 stars)	Lieutenant-General (3 stars)
Generalmajor	SS-Brigadeführer und Generalmajor der Waffen-SS	Major-General (2 stars)	Major-General (2 stars)
(without equivalence)	SS-Oberführer	Brigadier (1 star)	Brigadier (1 star)
Oberst	SS-Standartenführer	Colonel	Colonel
Oberstleutnant	SS-Obersturmbannführer	Lieutenant-Colonel	Lieutenant-Colonel
Major	SS-Sturmbannführer	Major	Major
Hauptmann/ Rittmeister	SS-Hauptsturmführer	Captain	Captain
Oberleutnant	SS-Obersturmführer	Lieutenant	First Lieutenant
Leutnant	SS-Untersturmführer	Second Lieutenant	Second Lieutenant
Stabsfeldwebel/ Stabswachtmeister	SS-Sturmcharführer	Regimental Sergent Major	Warrant Officer
Oberfeldwebel/ Oberwachtmeister	SS-Hauptscharführer	Staff Sergeant	Master Sergeant
Feldwebel/ Wachtmeister	SS-Oberscharführer	Sergeant	Technical Sergeant
Unterfeldwebel/ Unterwachtmeister	SS-Scharführer	Lance Sergeant	Staff Sergeant
Unteroffizier	SS-Unterscharführer	Corporal	Sergeant
Obergefreiter	SS-Rottenführer	Lance Corporal	Corporal
Gefreiter	SS-Sturmmann		
Oberschütze (ditto as below)	SS-Obergrenadier, etc.		Private First Class
Schütze, Grenadier, Pionier, etc.	SS-Schütze, etc.	Private	Private

Achevé d'imprimer en avril 2008
sur les presses de
Corelio Printings, Bruxelles
pour le compte des Editions Heimdal